STAR TREK

ARCHIVES 6

Best of
Alternate Universes

IDW Publishing
San Diego

Collection cover by *The Sharp Bros.*
Collection Edits by *Justin Eisinger*
Collection Design by *Tom B. Long*

ISBN: 978-1-60010-522-7
12 11 10 9   1 2 3 4

IDW Publishing is:
Operations:
Ted Adams, Chief Executive Officer
Greg Goldstein, Chief Operating Officer
Matthew Ruzicka, CPA, Chief Financial Officer
Alan Payne, VP of Sales
Lorelei Bunjes, Dir. of Digital Services
AnnaMaria White, Marketing & PR Manager
Marci Hubbard, Executive Assistant
Alonzo Simon, Shipping Manager
Angela Loggins, Staff Accountant

Editorial:
Chris Ryall, Publisher/Editor-in-Chief
Scott Dunbier, Editor, Special Projects
Andy Schmidt, Senior Editor
Justin Eisinger, Editor
Kris Oprisko, Editor/Foreign Lic.
Denton J. Tipton, Editor
Tom Waltz, Editor
Mariah Huehner, Associate Editor
Carlos Guzman, Editorial Assistant

Design:
Robbie Robbins, EVP/Sr. Graphic Artist
Neil Uyetake, Art Director
Chris Mowry, Graphic Artist
Amauri Osorio, Graphic Artist
Gilberto Lazcano, Production Assistant

WWW.IDWPUBLISHING.COM

Special Thanks to Risa Kessler and John Van Citters of CBS Consumer Products for their invaluable assistance.

STAR TREK ARCHIVES, VOLUME 6: BEST OF ALTERNATE UNIVERSES

Featuring:
Star Trek: The Mirror Universe Saga

Written by *Mike W. Barr*
Art by *Tom Sutton &*
Ricardo Villagran
Lettering by *John Costanza,*
Janice Chiang, & Carrie Spiegle
Colors by *Julianna Ferriter*

Star Trek created by
Gene Roddenberry

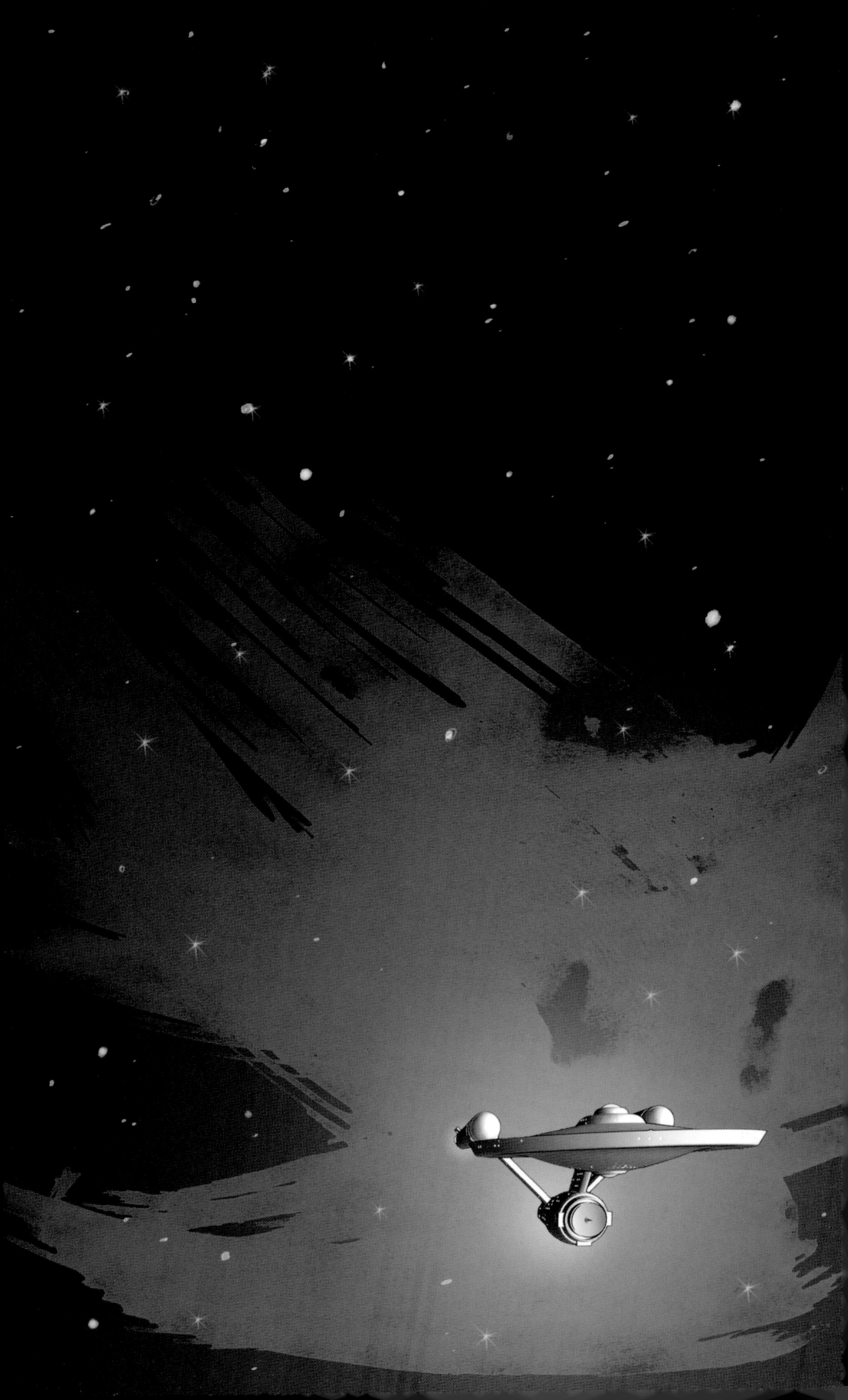

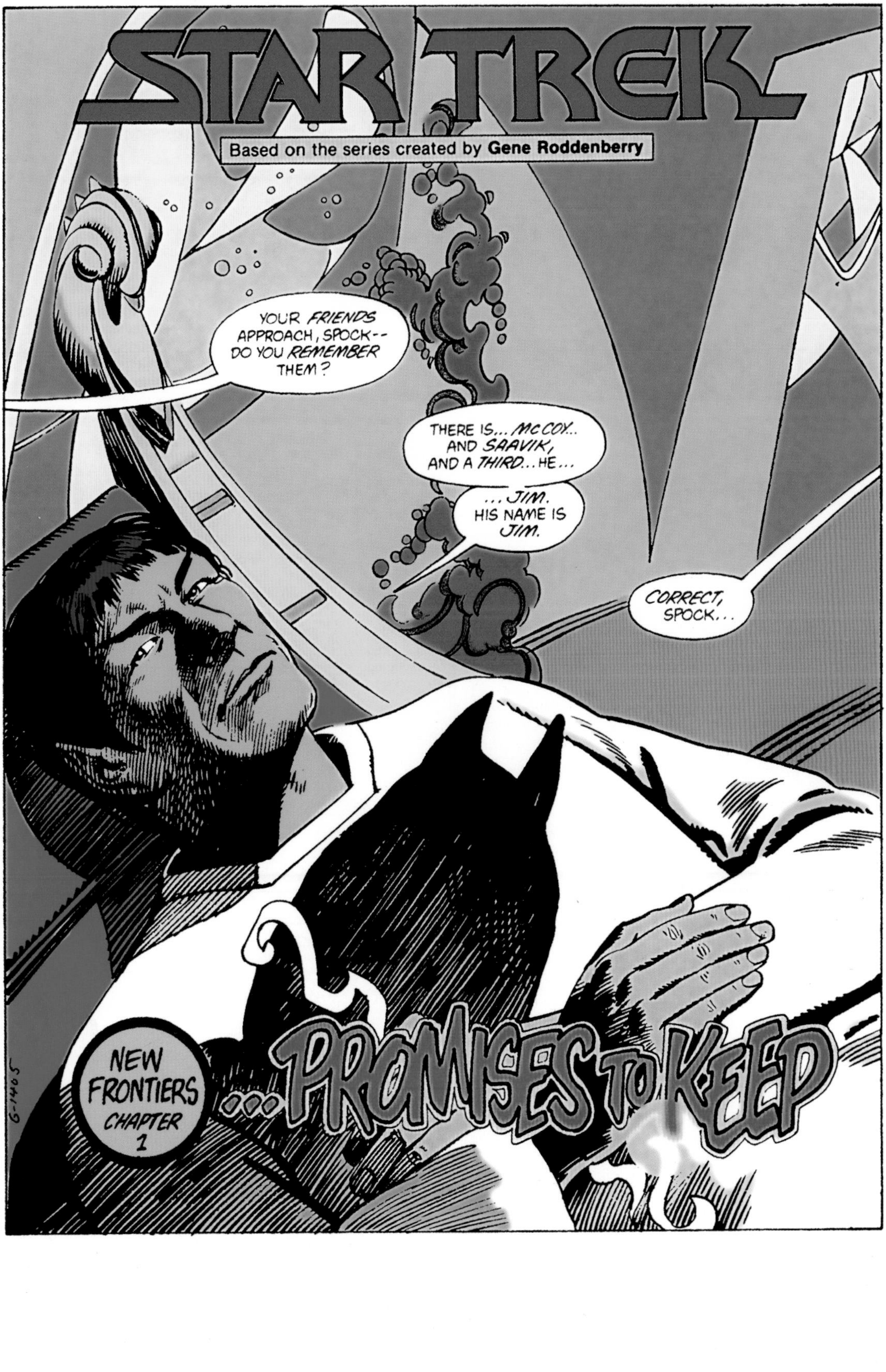
STAR TREK
Based on the series created by Gene Roddenberry
YOUR FRIENDS APPROACH, SPOCK-- DO YOU REMEMBER THEM?
THERE IS... MCCOY.. AND SAAVIK, AND A THIRD... HE...
...JIM. HIS NAME IS JIM.
CORRECT, SPOCK...
NEW FRONTIERS CHAPTER 1
...PROMISES TO KEEP

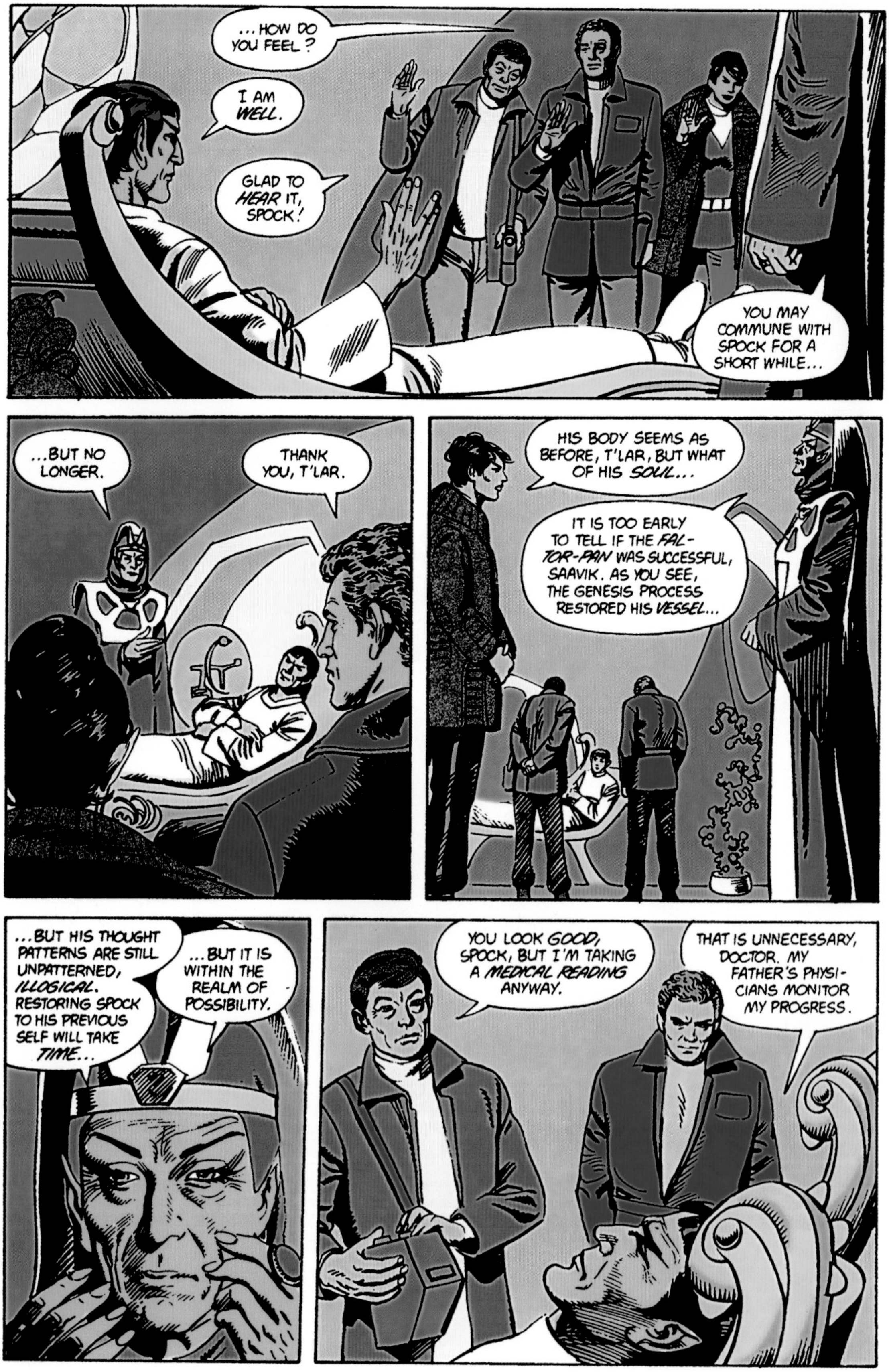
...HOW DO YOU FEEL?
I AM WELL.
GLAD TO HEAR IT, SPOCK!
YOU MAY COMMUNE WITH SPOCK FOR A SHORT WHILE...
...BUT NO LONGER.
THANK YOU, T'LAR.
HIS BODY SEEMS AS BEFORE, T'LAR, BUT WHAT OF HIS SOUL...
IT IS TOO EARLY TO TELL IF THE FAL-TOR-PAN WAS SUCCESSFUL, SAAVIK. AS YOU SEE, THE GENESIS PROCESS RESTORED HIS VESSEL...
...BUT HIS THOUGHT PATTERNS ARE STILL UNPATTERNED, ILLOGICAL. RESTORING SPOCK TO HIS PREVIOUS SELF WILL TAKE TIME...
...BUT IT IS WITHIN THE REALM OF POSSIBILITY.
YOU LOOK GOOD, SPOCK, BUT I'M TAKING A MEDICAL READING ANYWAY.
THAT IS UNNECESSARY, DOCTOR. MY FATHER'S PHYSICIANS MONITOR MY PROGRESS.

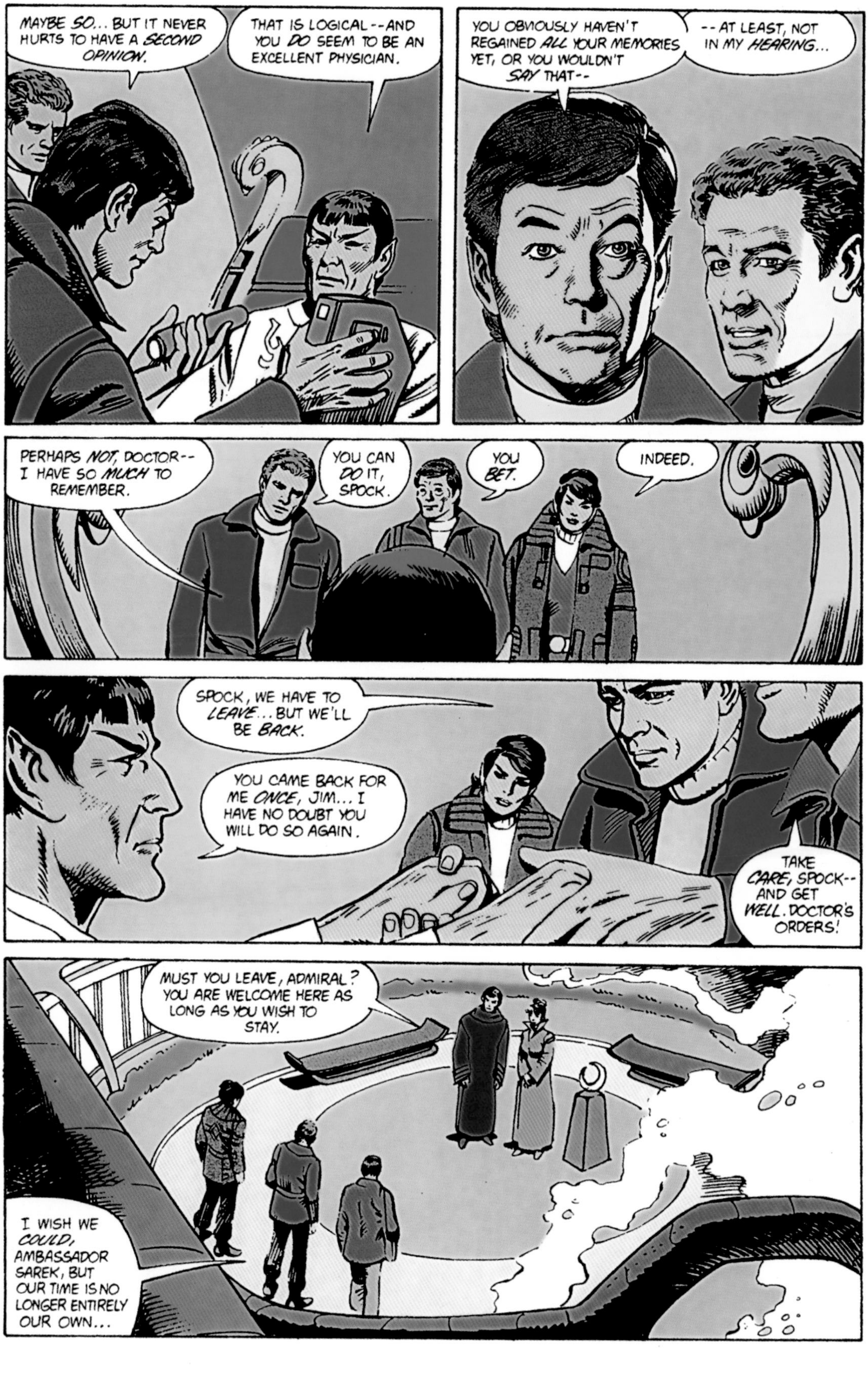
MAYBE SO... BUT IT NEVER HURTS TO HAVE A SECOND OPINION.
THAT IS LOGICAL--AND YOU DO SEEM TO BE AN EXCELLENT PHYSICIAN.
YOU OBVIOUSLY HAVEN'T REGAINED ALL YOUR MEMORIES YET, OR YOU WOULDN'T SAY THAT--
--AT LEAST, NOT IN MY HEARING...
PERHAPS NOT, DOCTOR--I HAVE SO MUCH TO REMEMBER.
YOU CAN DO IT, SPOCK.
YOU BET.
INDEED.
SPOCK, WE HAVE TO LEAVE... BUT WE'LL BE BACK.
YOU CAME BACK FOR ME ONCE, JIM... I HAVE NO DOUBT YOU WILL DO SO AGAIN.
TAKE CARE, SPOCK--AND GET WELL. DOCTOR'S ORDERS!
MUST YOU LEAVE, ADMIRAL? YOU ARE WELCOME HERE AS LONG AS YOU WISH TO STAY.
I WISH WE COULD, AMBASSADOR SAREK, BUT OUR TIME IS NO LONGER ENTIRELY OUR OWN...

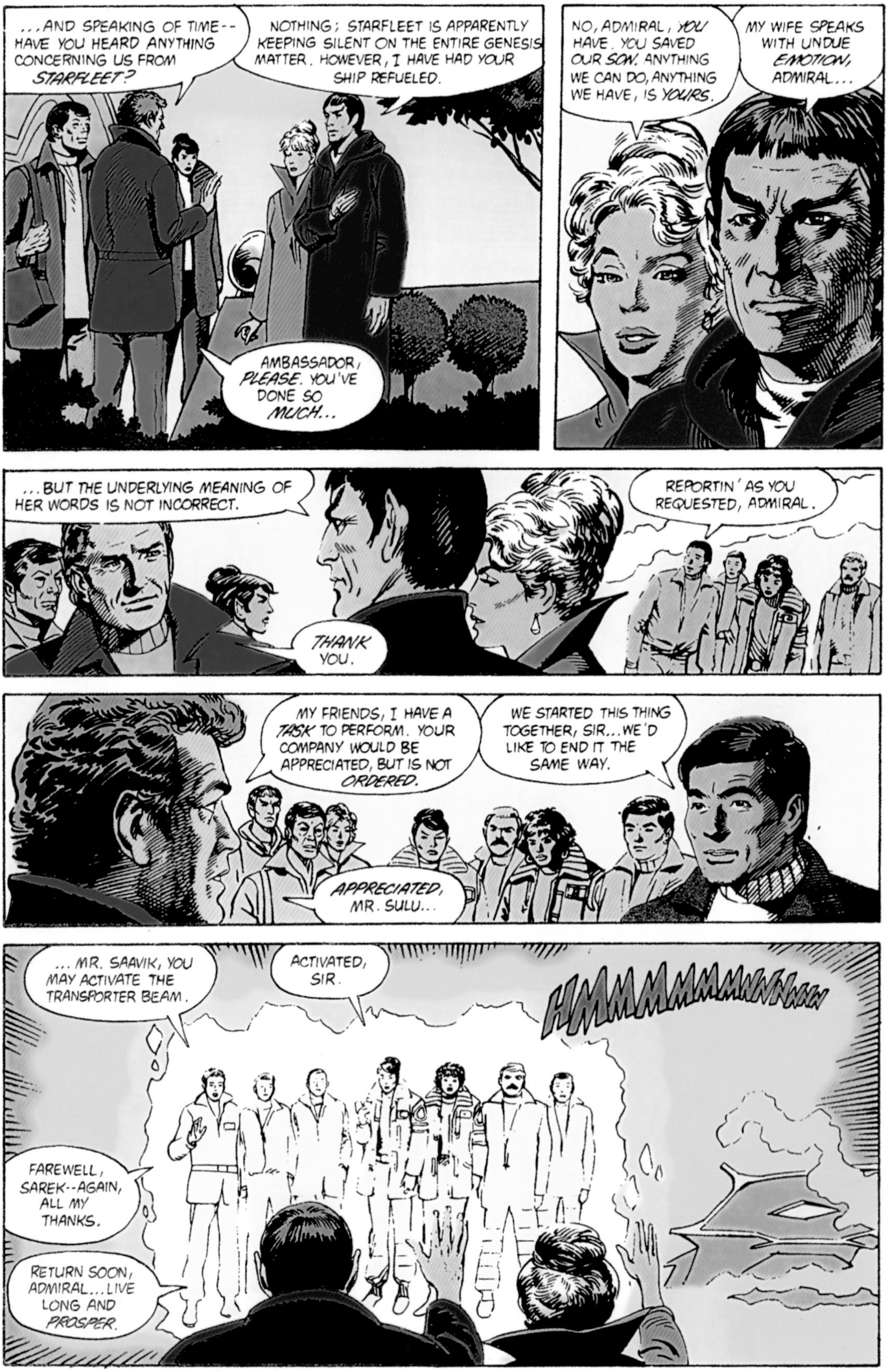
...AND SPEAKING OF TIME--HAVE YOU HEARD ANYTHING CONCERNING US FROM STARFLEET?
NOTHING; STARFLEET IS APPARENTLY KEEPING SILENT ON THE ENTIRE GENESIS MATTER. HOWEVER, I HAVE HAD YOUR SHIP REFUELED.
AMBASSADOR, PLEASE. YOU'VE DONE SO MUCH...
NO, ADMIRAL, YOU HAVE. YOU SAVED OUR SON. ANYTHING WE CAN DO, ANYTHING WE HAVE, IS YOURS.
MY WIFE SPEAKS WITH UNDUE EMOTION, ADMIRAL...
...BUT THE UNDERLYING MEANING OF HER WORDS IS NOT INCORRECT.
THANK YOU.
REPORTIN' AS YOU REQUESTED, ADMIRAL.
MY FRIENDS, I HAVE A TASK TO PERFORM. YOUR COMPANY WOULD BE APPRECIATED, BUT IS NOT ORDERED.
WE STARTED THIS THING TOGETHER, SIR...WE'D LIKE TO END IT THE SAME WAY.
APPRECIATED, MR. SULU...
...MR. SAAVIK, YOU MAY ACTIVATE THE TRANSPORTER BEAM.
ACTIVATED, SIR.
HMMMMMMMNNNNN
FAREWELL, SAREK--AGAIN, ALL MY THANKS.
RETURN SOON, ADMIRAL...LIVE LONG AND PROSPER.

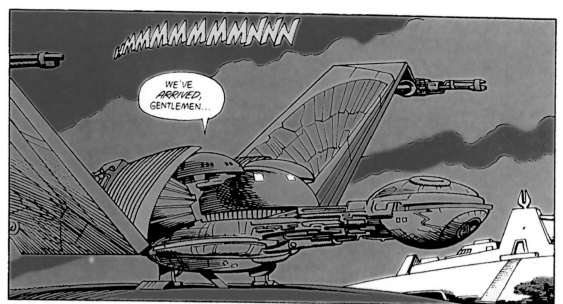

HMMMMMMMNNN

WE'VE *ARRIVED,* GENTLEMEN...

...LET'S GET THIS SHOW ON THE ROAD. STATIONS, EVERYONE.

LIEUTENANT, I'LL BE NEEDIN' YOUR HELP WITH THESE BLASTED KLINGON *WARP ENGINES!*

ACKNOWLEDGED, MR. SCOTT.

HERE'S WHERE WE FIND OUT WHAT YOU'RE ALL MADE OF! ANYONE CAN *LAND* A SHIP...

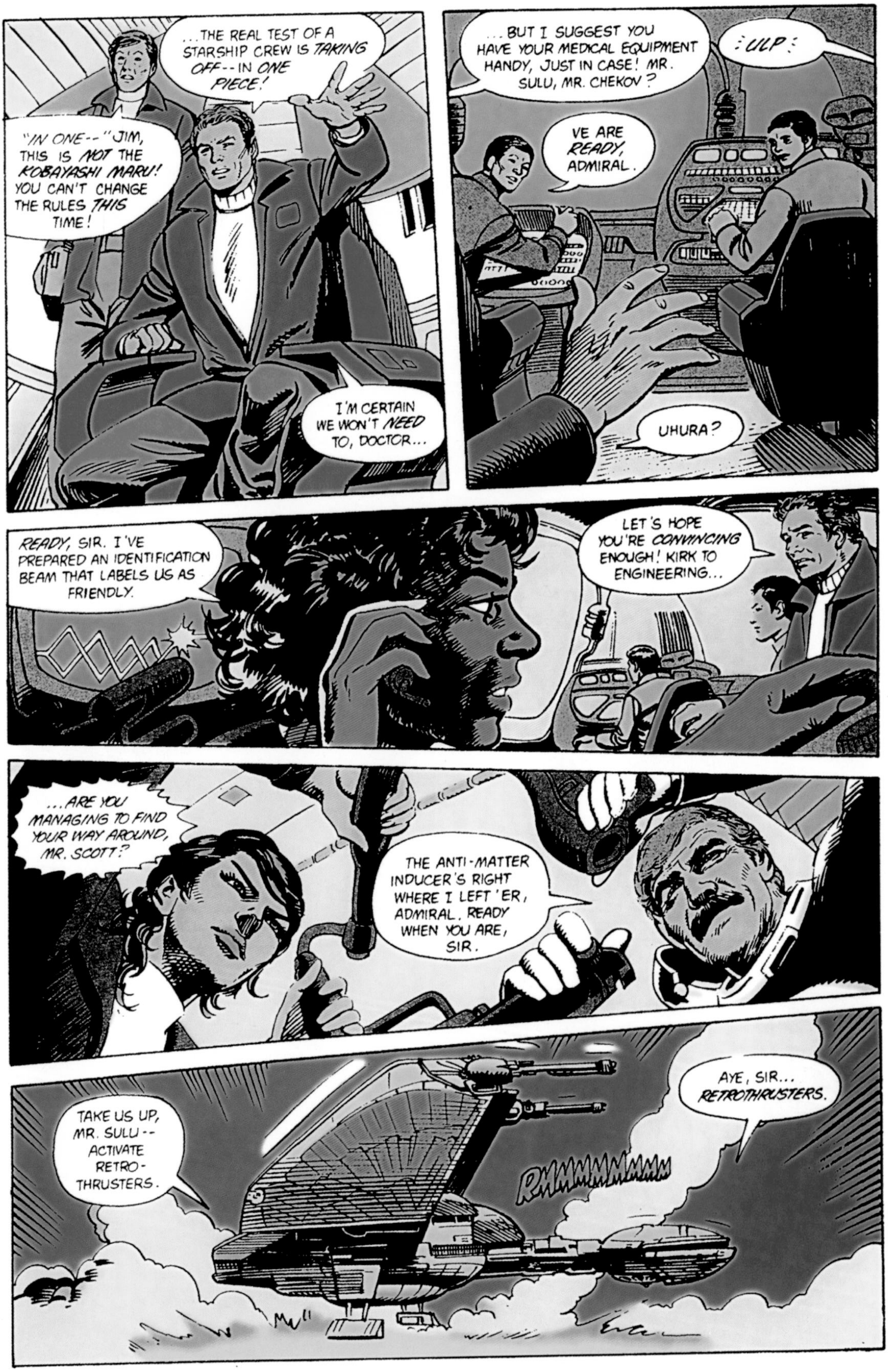
...THE REAL TEST OF A STARSHIP CREW IS TAKING OFF--IN ONE PIECE!
"IN ONE--" JIM, THIS IS NOT THE KOBAYASHI MARU! YOU CAN'T CHANGE THE RULES THIS TIME!
I'M CERTAIN WE WON'T NEED TO, DOCTOR...
...BUT I SUGGEST YOU HAVE YOUR MEDICAL EQUIPMENT HANDY, JUST IN CASE! MR. SULU, MR. CHEKOV?
ULP
VE ARE READY, ADMIRAL.
UHURA?
READY, SIR. I'VE PREPARED AN IDENTIFICATION BEAM THAT LABELS US AS FRIENDLY.
LET'S HOPE YOU'RE CONVINCING ENOUGH! KIRK TO ENGINEERING...
...ARE YOU MANAGING TO FIND YOUR WAY AROUND, MR. SCOTT?
THE ANTI-MATTER INDUCER'S RIGHT WHERE I LEFT 'ER, ADMIRAL. READY WHEN YOU ARE, SIR.
TAKE US UP, MR. SULU-- ACTIVATE RETRO-THRUSTERS.
AYE, SIR... RETROTHRUSTERS.
RMMMMMMMMM

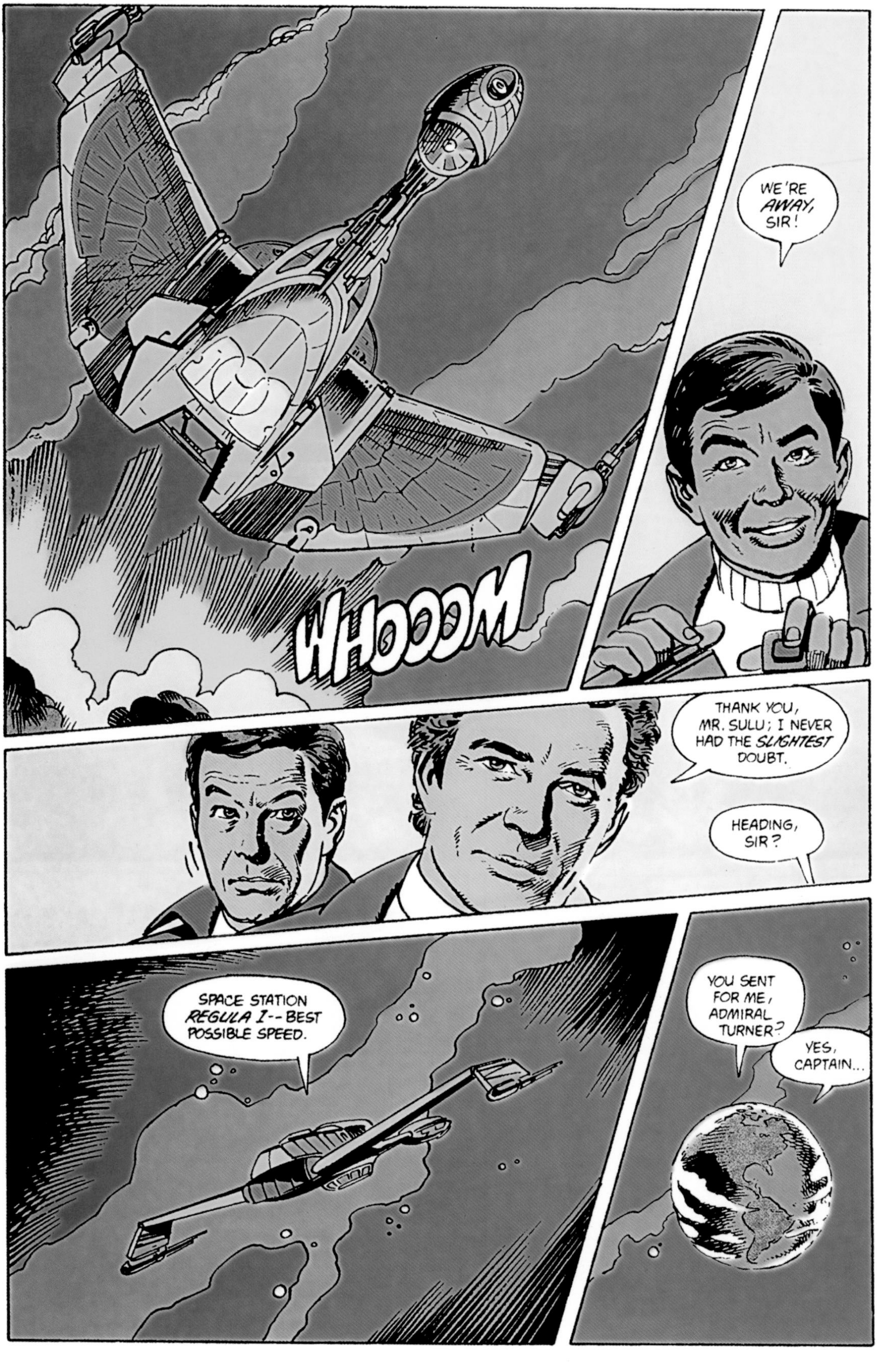
WHOOOOM
WE'RE AWAY, SIR!
THANK YOU, MR. SULU; I NEVER HAD THE SLIGHTEST DOUBT.
HEADING, SIR?
SPACE STATION REGULA I--BEST POSSIBLE SPEED.
YOU SENT FOR ME, ADMIRAL TURNER?
YES, CAPTAIN...

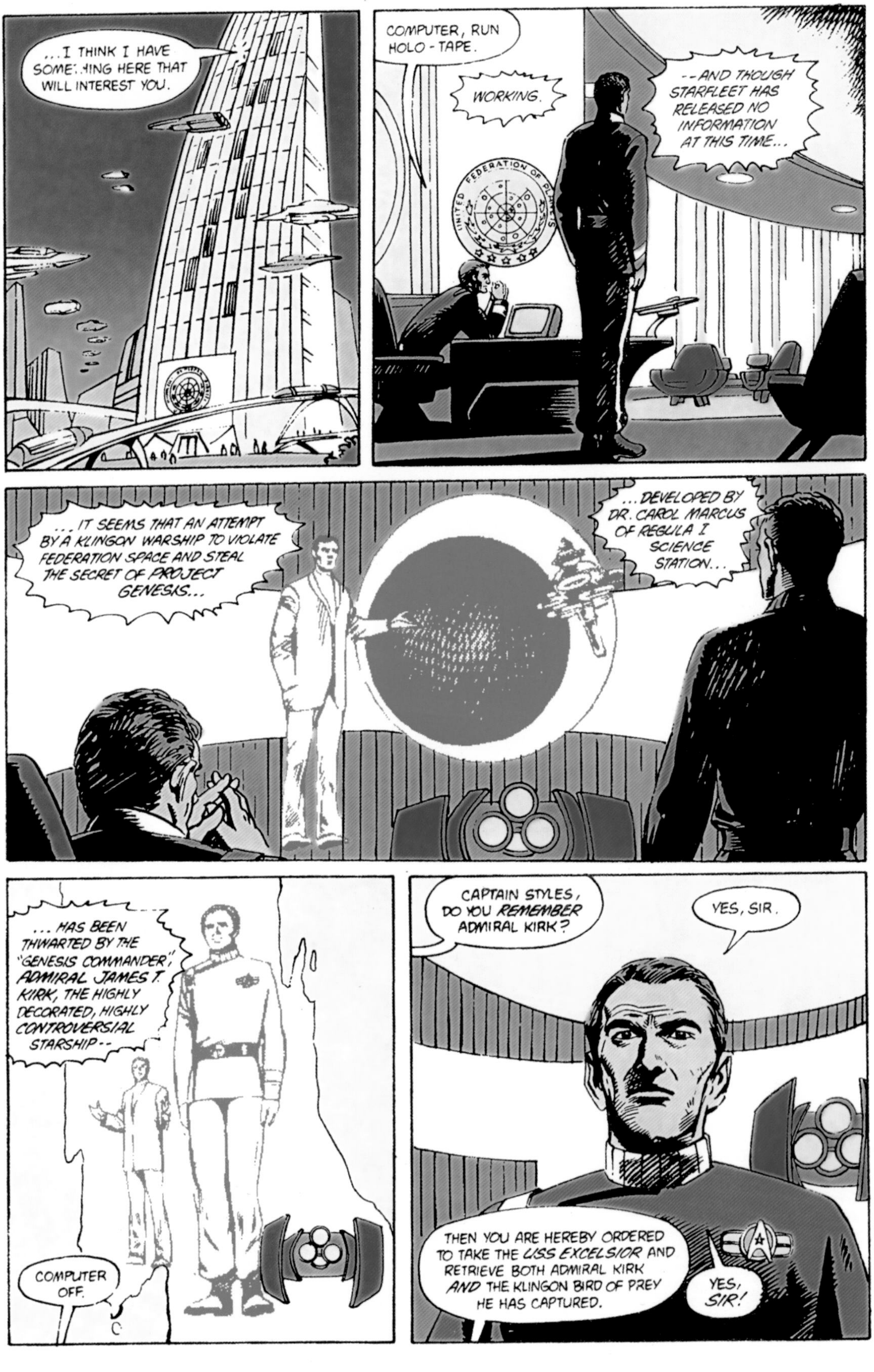
...I THINK I HAVE SOMETHING HERE THAT WILL INTEREST YOU.
COMPUTER, RUN HOLO-TAPE.
WORKING.
--AND THOUGH STARFLEET HAS RELEASED NO INFORMATION AT THIS TIME...
UNITED FEDERATION OF PLANETS
...IT SEEMS THAT AN ATTEMPT BY A KLINGON WARSHIP TO VIOLATE FEDERATION SPACE AND STEAL THE SECRET OF PROJECT GENESIS...
...DEVELOPED BY DR. CAROL MARCUS OF REGULA I SCIENCE STATION...
...HAS BEEN THWARTED BY THE "GENESIS COMMANDER", ADMIRAL JAMES T. KIRK, THE HIGHLY DECORATED, HIGHLY CONTROVERSIAL STARSHIP--
COMPUTER OFF.
CAPTAIN STYLES, DO YOU REMEMBER ADMIRAL KIRK?
YES, SIR.
THEN YOU ARE HEREBY ORDERED TO TAKE THE USS EXCELSIOR AND RETRIEVE BOTH ADMIRAL KIRK AND THE KLINGON BIRD OF PREY HE HAS CAPTURED.
YES, SIR!

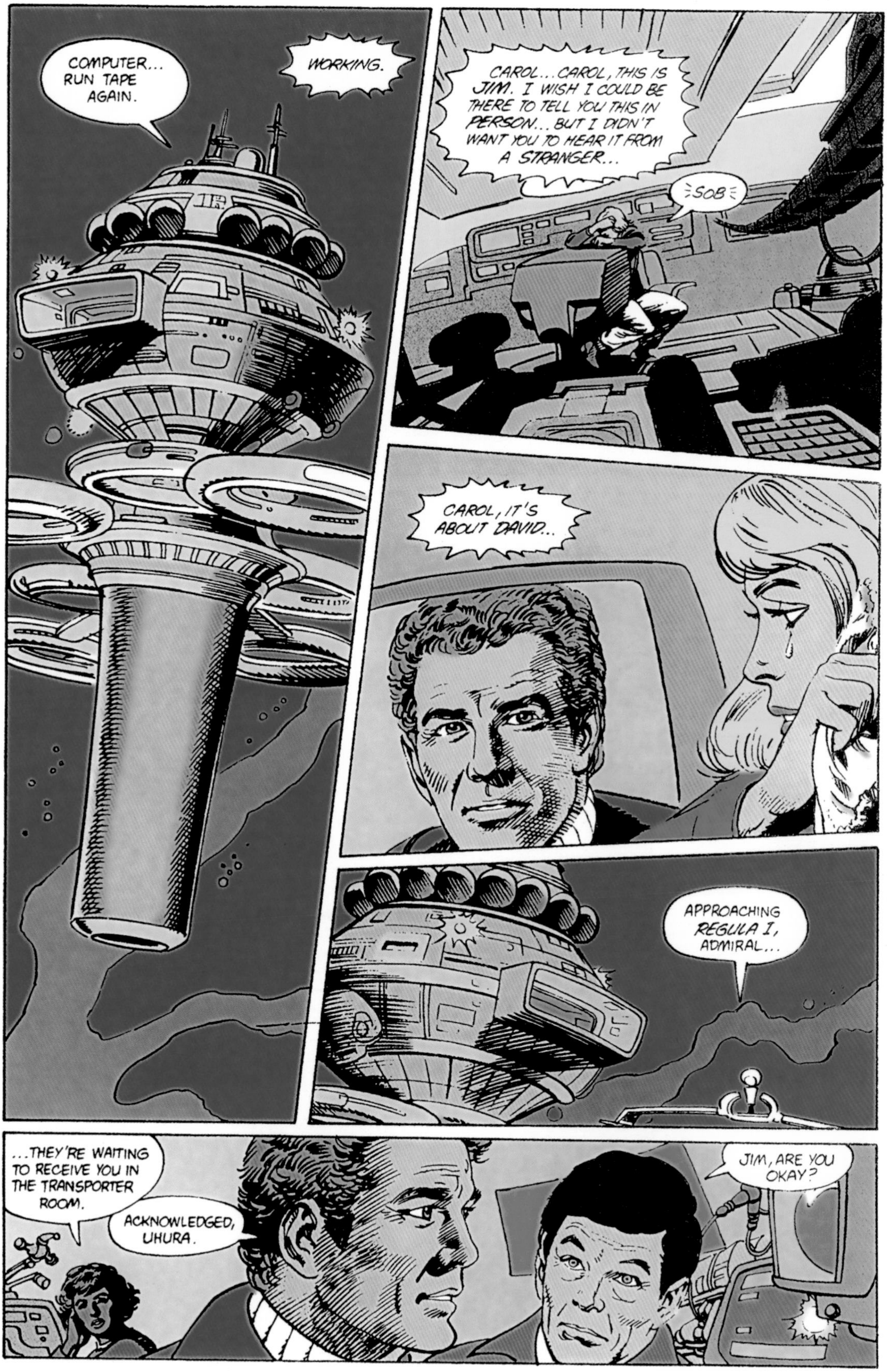
COMPUTER... RUN TAPE AGAIN.
WORKING.
CAROL... CAROL, THIS IS JIM. I WISH I COULD BE THERE TO TELL YOU THIS IN PERSON... BUT I DIDN'T WANT YOU TO HEAR IT FROM A STRANGER...
SOB
CAROL, IT'S ABOUT DAVID...
APPROACHING REGULA I, ADMIRAL...
...THEY'RE WAITING TO RECEIVE YOU IN THE TRANSPORTER ROOM.
ACKNOWLEDGED, UHURA.
JIM, ARE YOU OKAY?

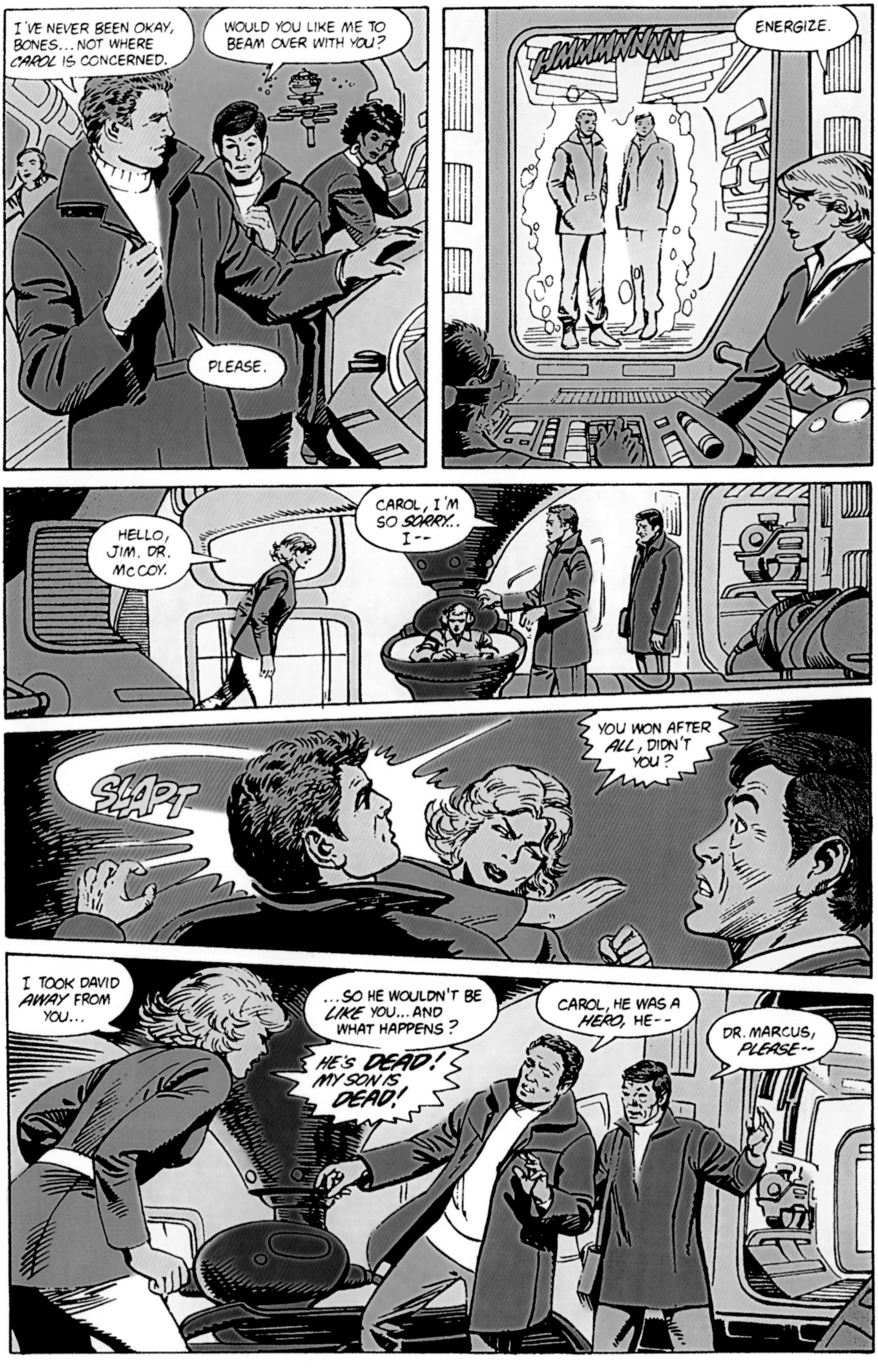
I'VE NEVER BEEN OKAY, BONES... NOT WHERE CAROL IS CONCERNED.
WOULD YOU LIKE ME TO BEAM OVER WITH YOU?
PLEASE.
HMMMNNNN
ENERGIZE.
HELLO, JIM. DR. McCOY.
CAROL, I'M SO SORRY... I--
SLAPT
YOU WON AFTER ALL, DIDN'T YOU?
I TOOK DAVID AWAY FROM YOU...
...SO HE WOULDN'T BE LIKE YOU... AND WHAT HAPPENS?
HE'S DEAD! MY SON IS DEAD!
CAROL, HE WAS A HERO, HE--
DR. MARCUS, PLEASE--

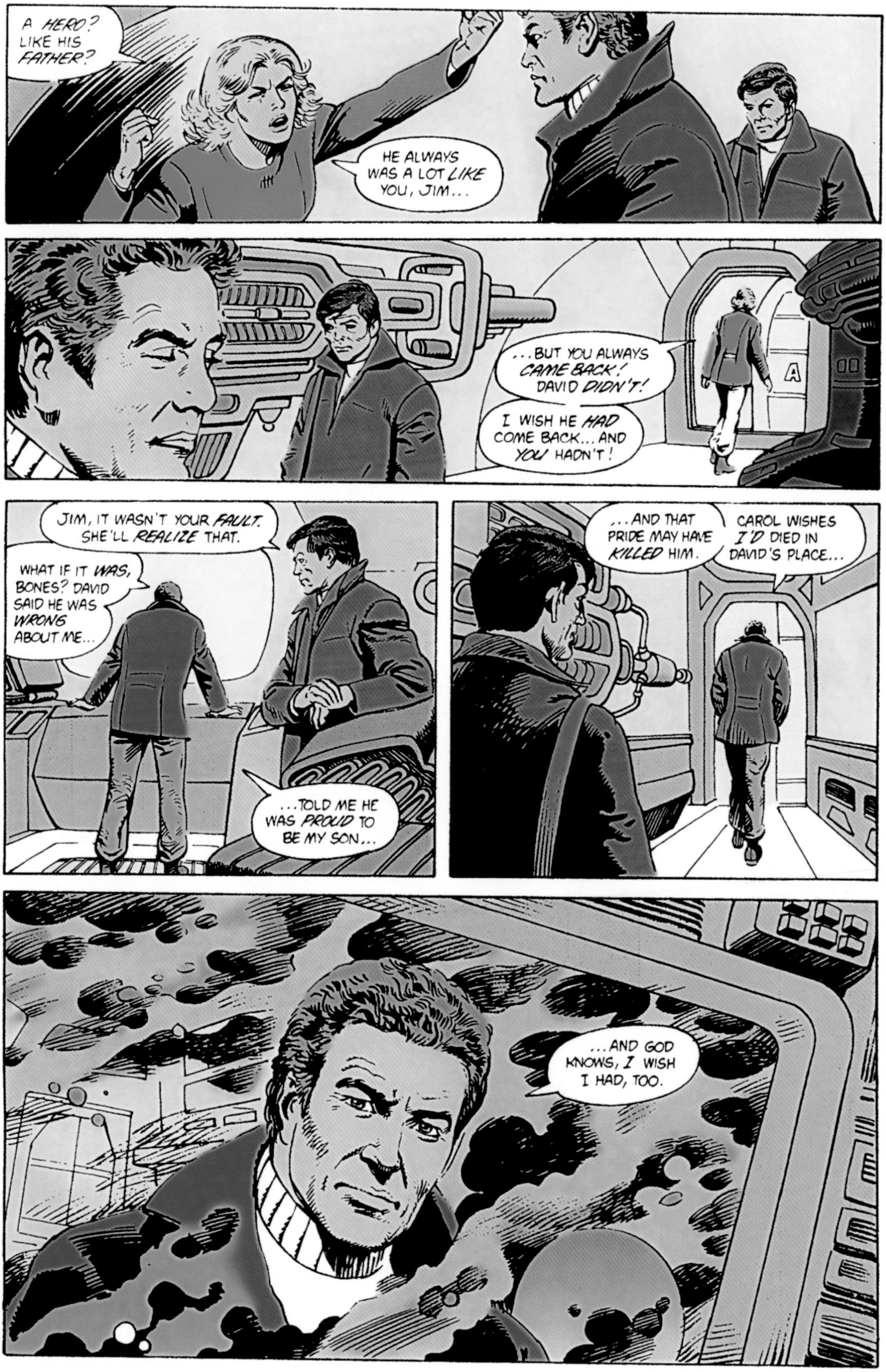
A HERO? LIKE HIS FATHER?
HE ALWAYS WAS A LOT LIKE YOU, JIM...
...BUT YOU ALWAYS CAME BACK! DAVID DIDN'T!
I WISH HE HAD COME BACK... AND YOU HADN'T!
JIM, IT WASN'T YOUR FAULT. SHE'LL REALIZE THAT.
WHAT IF IT WAS, BONES? DAVID SAID HE WAS WRONG ABOUT ME...
...TOLD ME HE WAS PROUD TO BE MY SON...
...AND THAT PRIDE MAY HAVE KILLED HIM.
CAROL WISHES I'D DIED IN DAVID'S PLACE...
...AND GOD KNOWS, I WISH I HAD, TOO.

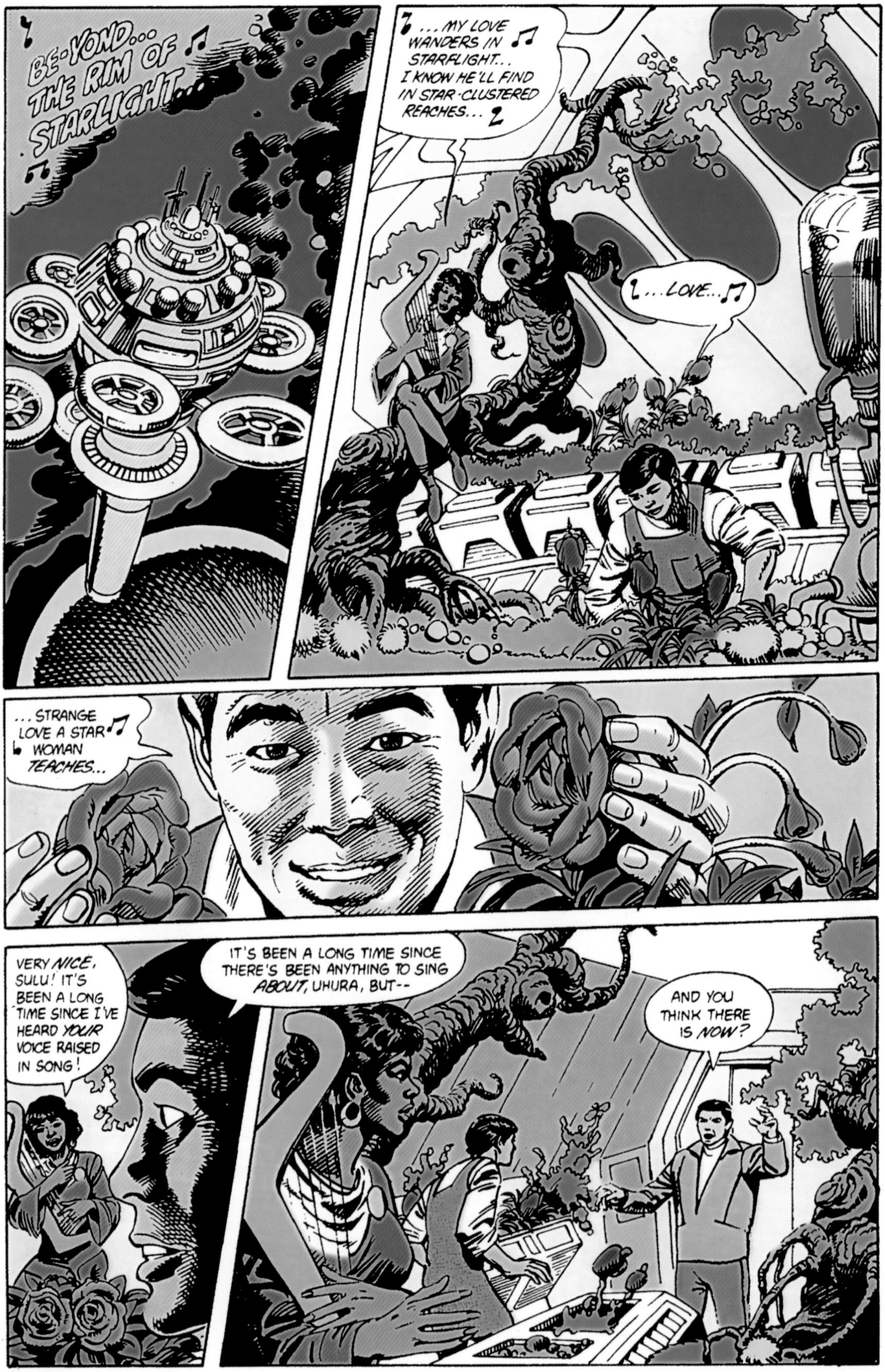
BE-YOND... THE RIM OF STARLIGHT...
... MY LOVE WANDERS IN STARFLIGHT... I KNOW HE'LL FIND IN STAR-CLUSTERED REACHES...
... LOVE...
... STRANGE LOVE A STAR WOMAN TEACHES...
VERY NICE, SULU! IT'S BEEN A LONG TIME SINCE I'VE HEARD YOUR VOICE RAISED IN SONG!
IT'S BEEN A LONG TIME SINCE THERE'S BEEN ANYTHING TO SING ABOUT, UHURA, BUT--
AND YOU THINK THERE IS NOW?

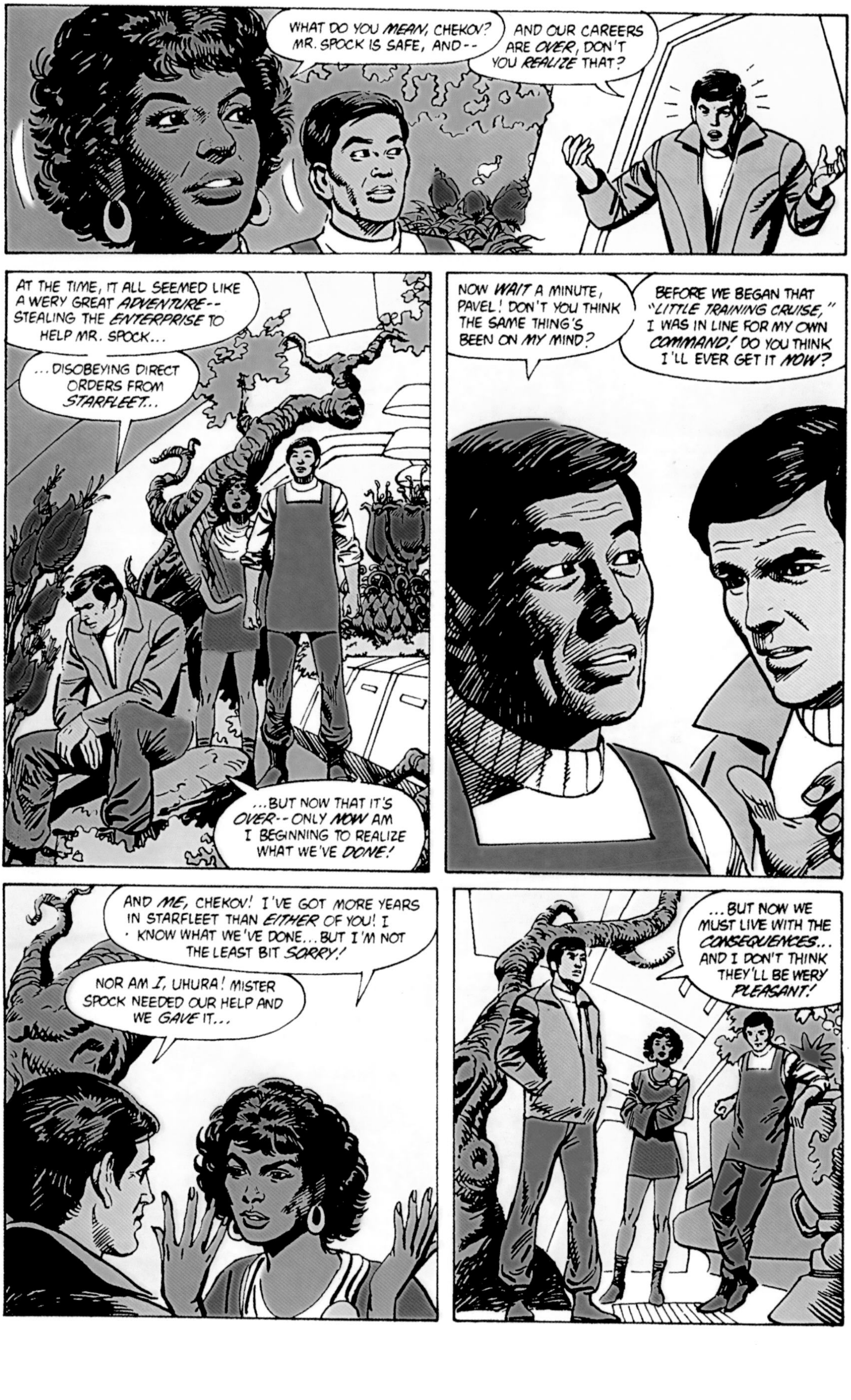
WHAT DO YOU MEAN, CHEKOV? MR. SPOCK IS SAFE, AND--
AND OUR CAREERS ARE OVER, DON'T YOU REALIZE THAT?
AT THE TIME, IT ALL SEEMED LIKE A WERY GREAT ADVENTURE-- STEALING THE ENTERPRISE TO HELP MR. SPOCK...
...DISOBEYING DIRECT ORDERS FROM STARFLEET...
...BUT NOW THAT IT'S OVER--ONLY NOW AM I BEGINNING TO REALIZE WHAT WE'VE DONE!
NOW WAIT A MINUTE, PAVEL! DON'T YOU THINK THE SAME THING'S BEEN ON MY MIND?
BEFORE WE BEGAN THAT "LITTLE TRAINING CRUISE," I WAS IN LINE FOR MY OWN COMMAND! DO YOU THINK I'LL EVER GET IT NOW?
AND ME, CHEKOV! I'VE GOT MORE YEARS IN STARFLEET THAN EITHER OF YOU! I KNOW WHAT WE'VE DONE...BUT I'M NOT THE LEAST BIT SORRY!
NOR AM I, UHURA! MISTER SPOCK NEEDED OUR HELP AND WE GAVE IT...
...BUT NOW WE MUST LIVE WITH THE CONSEQUENCES... AND I DON'T THINK THEY'LL BE WERY PLEASANT!

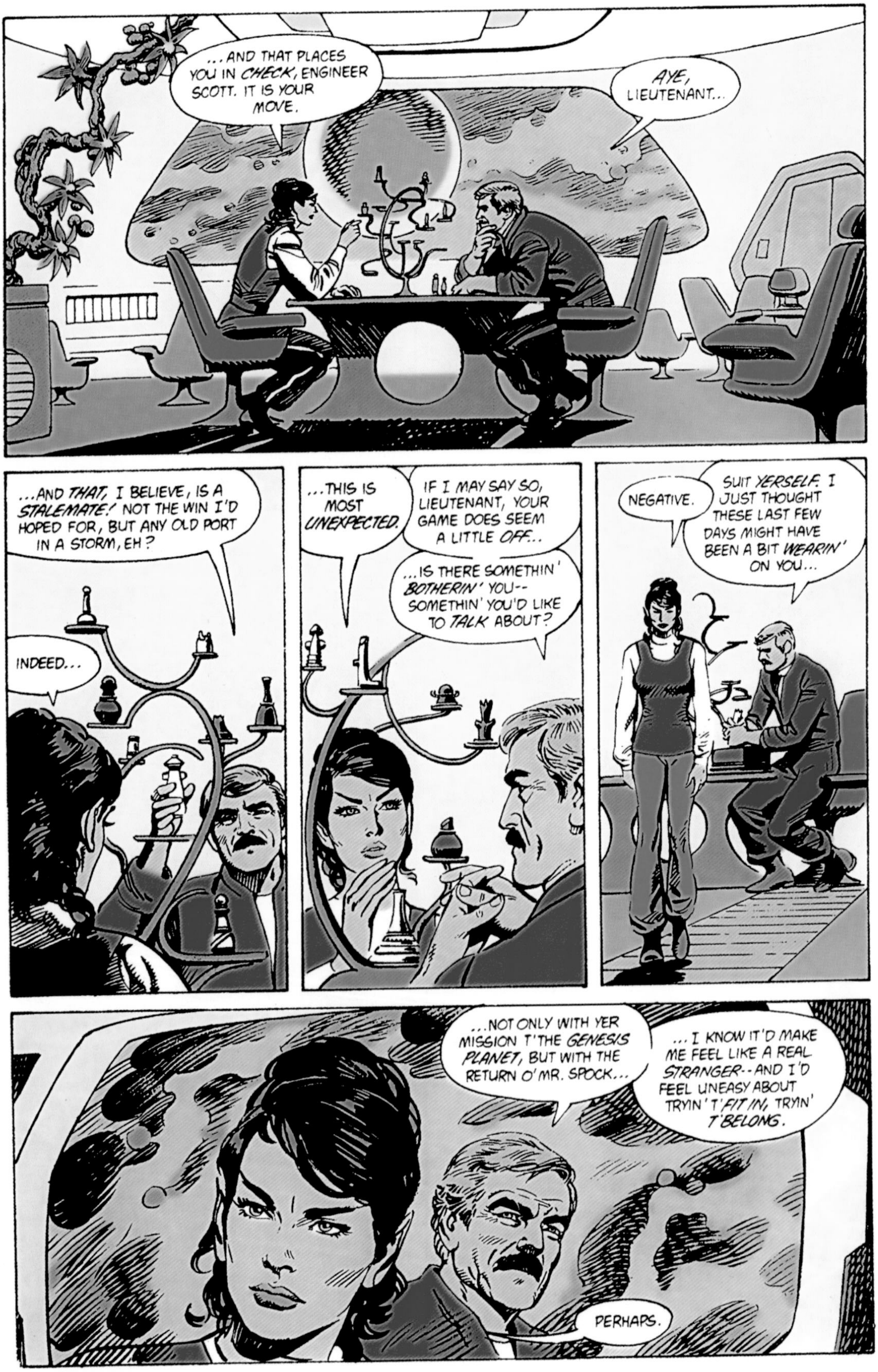
...AND THAT PLACES YOU IN CHECK, ENGINEER SCOTT. IT IS YOUR MOVE.
AYE, LIEUTENANT...
...AND THAT, I BELIEVE, IS A STALEMATE! NOT THE WIN I'D HOPED FOR, BUT ANY OLD PORT IN A STORM, EH?
INDEED...
...THIS IS MOST UNEXPECTED.
IF I MAY SAY SO, LIEUTENANT, YOUR GAME DOES SEEM A LITTLE OFF...
...IS THERE SOMETHIN' BOTHERIN' YOU-- SOMETHIN' YOU'D LIKE TO TALK ABOUT?
NEGATIVE.
SUIT YERSELF. I JUST THOUGHT THESE LAST FEW DAYS MIGHT HAVE BEEN A BIT WEARIN' ON YOU...
...NOT ONLY WITH YER MISSION T'THE GENESIS PLANET, BUT WITH THE RETURN O'MR. SPOCK...
...I KNOW IT'D MAKE ME FEEL LIKE A REAL STRANGER--AND I'D FEEL UNEASY ABOUT TRYIN' T'FIT IN, TRYIN' T'BELONG.
PERHAPS.

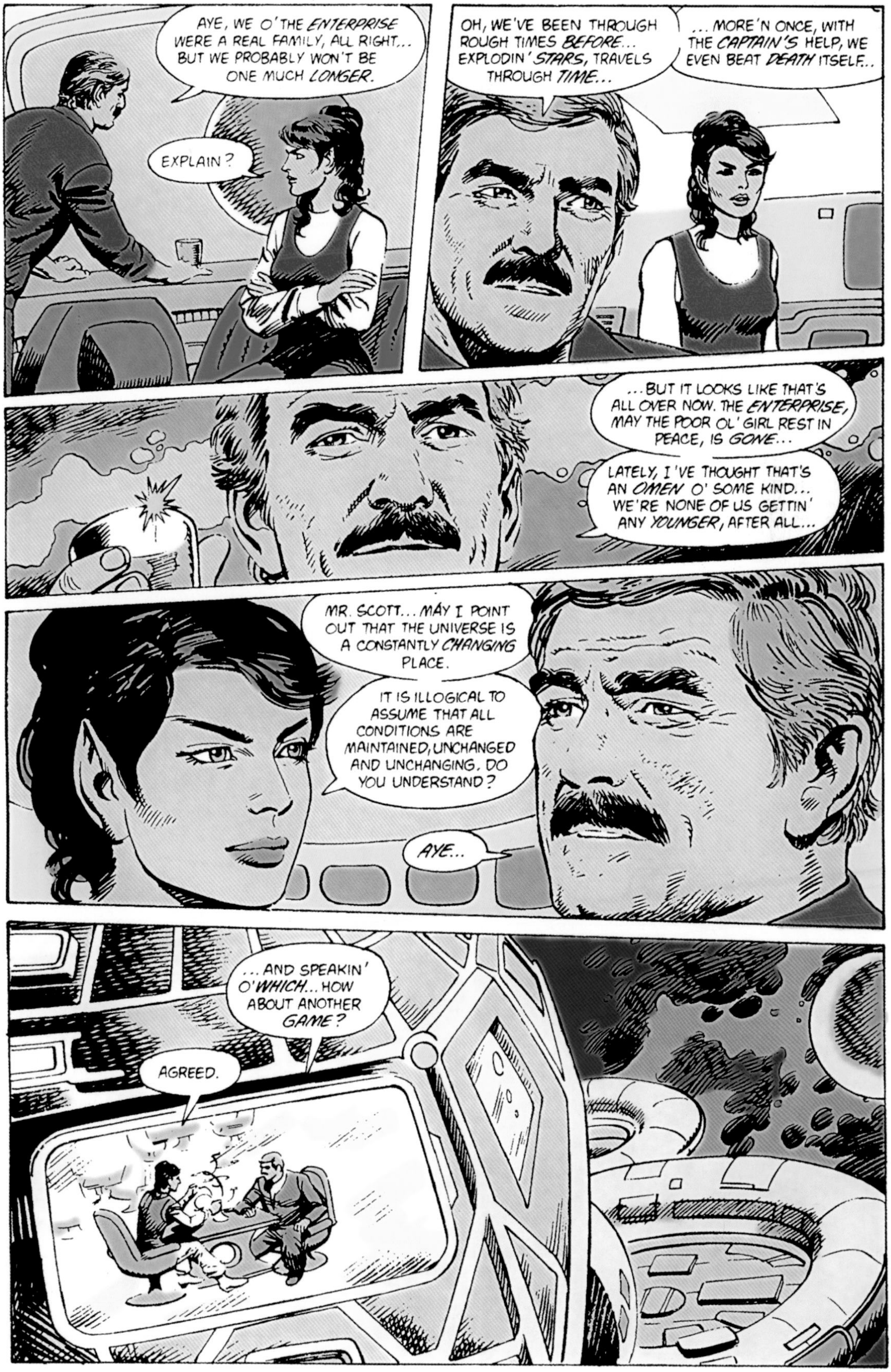
AYE, WE O' THE ENTERPRISE WERE A REAL FAMILY, ALL RIGHT... BUT WE PROBABLY WON'T BE ONE MUCH LONGER.
EXPLAIN?
OH, WE'VE BEEN THROUGH ROUGH TIMES BEFORE... EXPLODIN' STARS, TRAVELS THROUGH TIME...
...MORE'N ONCE, WITH THE CAPTAIN'S HELP, WE EVEN BEAT DEATH ITSELF...
...BUT IT LOOKS LIKE THAT'S ALL OVER NOW. THE ENTERPRISE, MAY THE POOR OL' GIRL REST IN PEACE, IS GONE...
LATELY, I'VE THOUGHT THAT'S AN OMEN O' SOME KIND... WE'RE NONE OF US GETTIN' ANY YOUNGER, AFTER ALL...
MR. SCOTT... MAY I POINT OUT THAT THE UNIVERSE IS A CONSTANTLY CHANGING PLACE.
IT IS ILLOGICAL TO ASSUME THAT ALL CONDITIONS ARE MAINTAINED, UNCHANGED AND UNCHANGING. DO YOU UNDERSTAND?
AYE...
...AND SPEAKIN' O' WHICH... HOW ABOUT ANOTHER GAME?
AGREED.

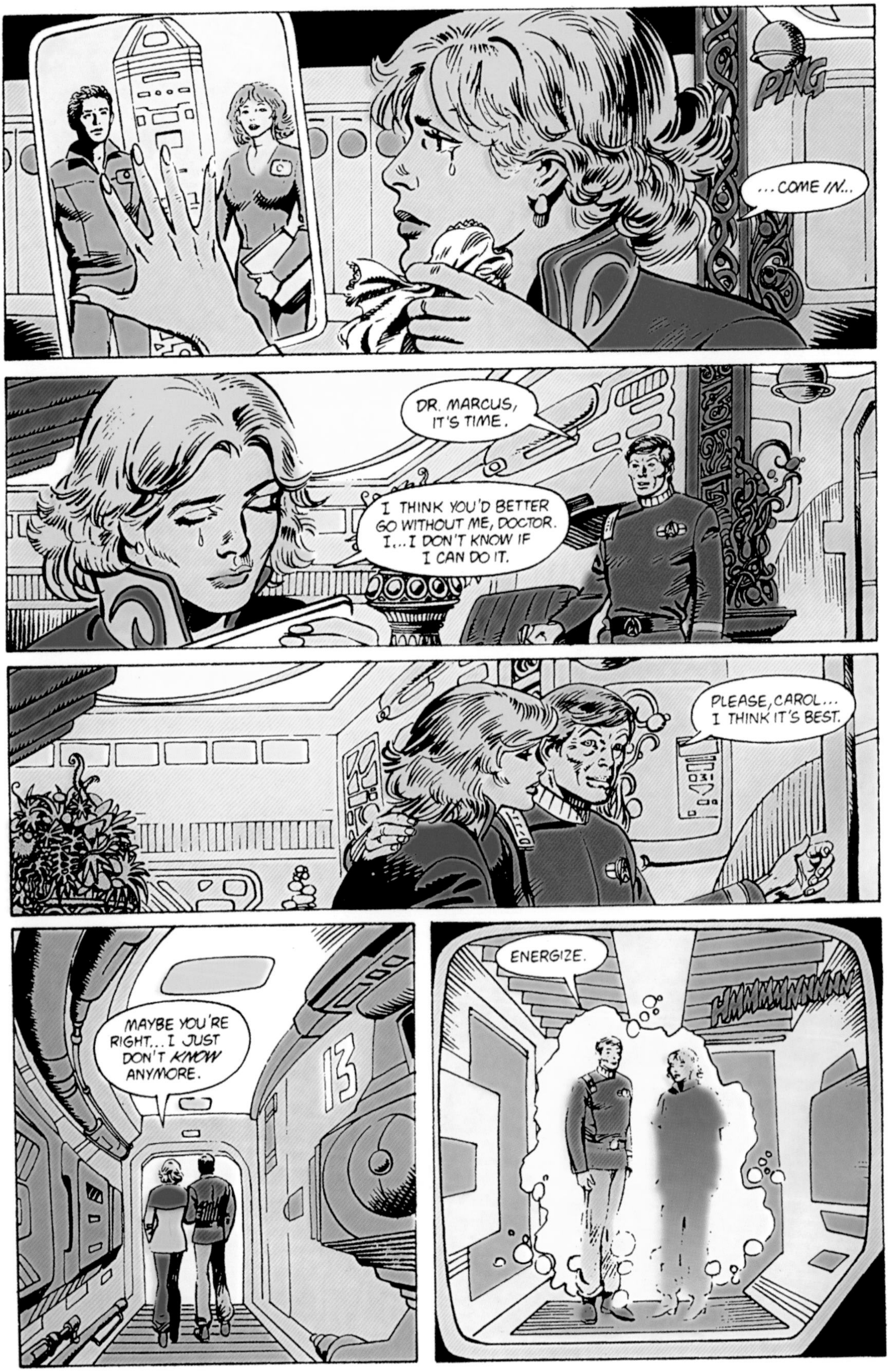
PING
...COME IN...
DR. MARCUS, IT'S TIME.
I THINK YOU'D BETTER GO WITHOUT ME, DOCTOR. I...I DON'T KNOW IF I CAN DO IT.
PLEASE, CAROL... I THINK IT'S BEST.
MAYBE YOU'RE RIGHT... I JUST DON'T KNOW ANYMORE.
ENERGIZE.

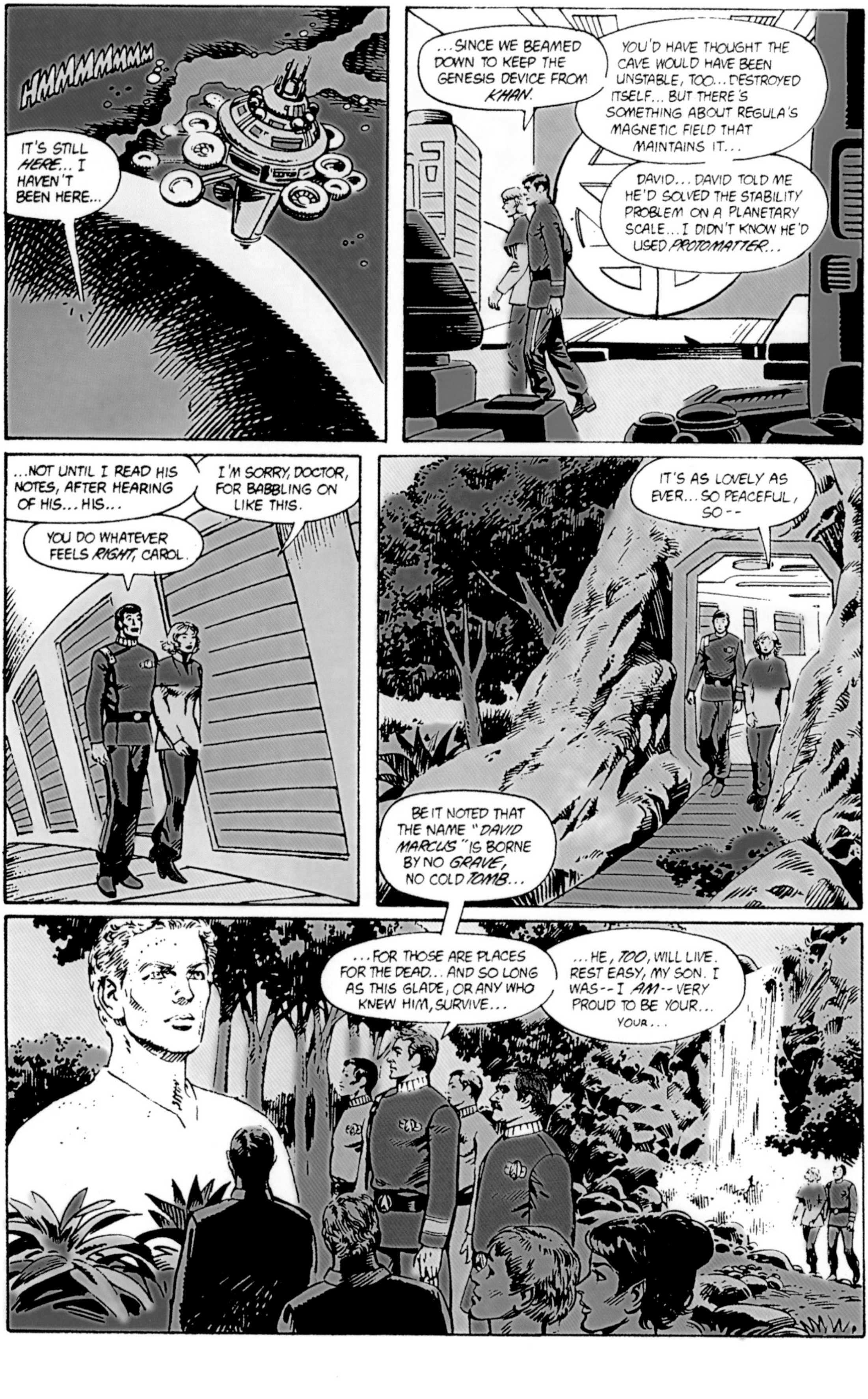
HMMMMMMM
IT'S STILL HERE... I HAVEN'T BEEN HERE...
...SINCE WE BEAMED DOWN TO KEEP THE GENESIS DEVICE FROM KHAN.
YOU'D HAVE THOUGHT THE CAVE WOULD HAVE BEEN UNSTABLE, TOO... DESTROYED ITSELF... BUT THERE'S SOMETHING ABOUT REGULA'S MAGNETIC FIELD THAT MAINTAINS IT...
DAVID... DAVID TOLD ME HE'D SOLVED THE STABILITY PROBLEM ON A PLANETARY SCALE... I DIDN'T KNOW HE'D USED PROTOMATTER...
...NOT UNTIL I READ HIS NOTES, AFTER HEARING OF HIS... HIS...
I'M SORRY, DOCTOR, FOR BABBLING ON LIKE THIS.
YOU DO WHATEVER FEELS RIGHT, CAROL.
IT'S AS LOVELY AS EVER... SO PEACEFUL, SO--
BE IT NOTED THAT THE NAME "DAVID MARCUS" IS BORNE BY NO GRAVE, NO COLD TOMB...
...FOR THOSE ARE PLACES FOR THE DEAD... AND SO LONG AS THIS GLADE, OR ANY WHO KNEW HIM, SURVIVE...
...HE, TOO, WILL LIVE. REST EASY, MY SON. I WAS--I AM--VERY PROUD TO BE YOUR... YOUR...

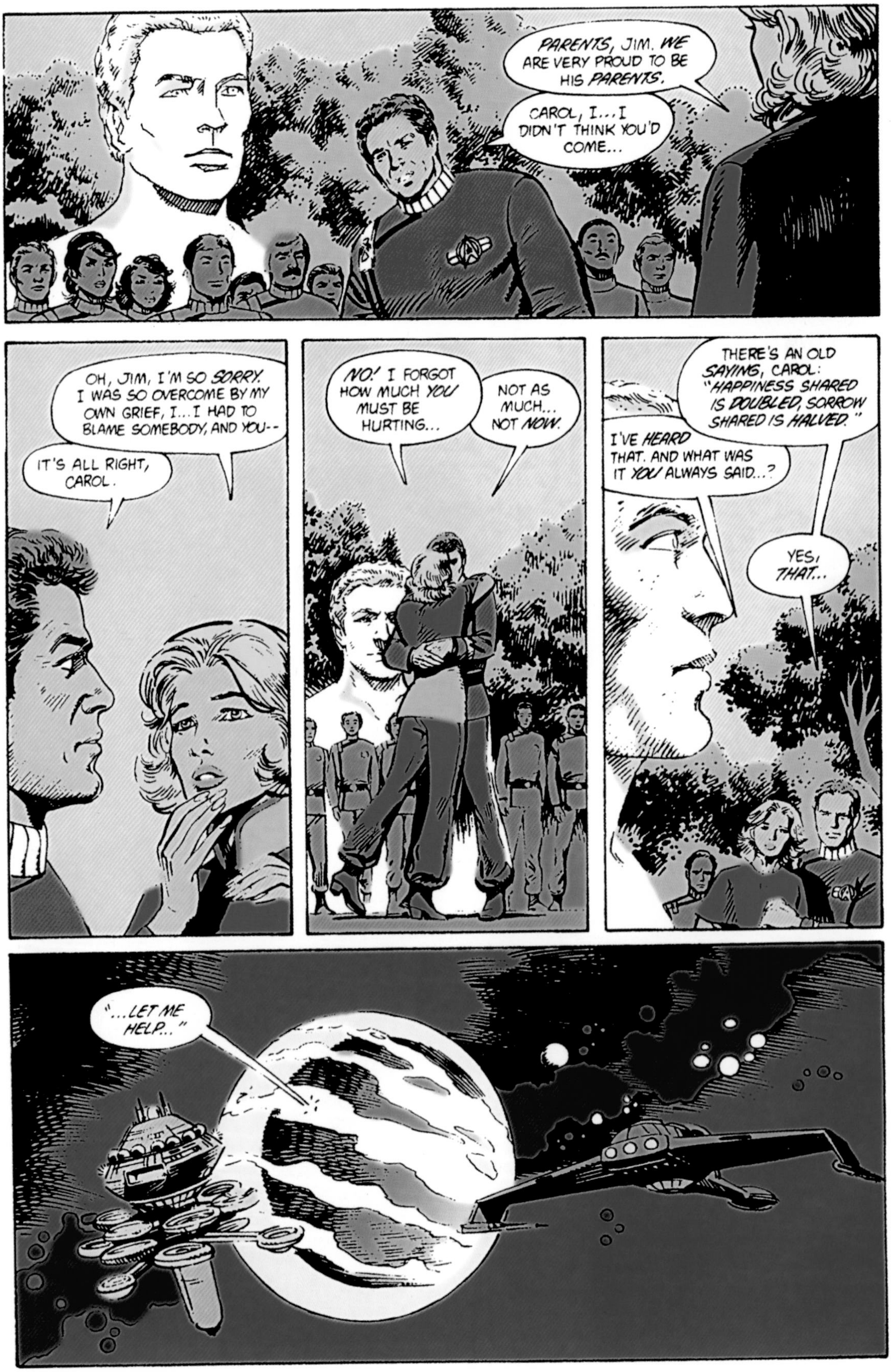
PARENTS, JIM. WE ARE VERY PROUD TO BE HIS PARENTS.
CAROL, I...I DIDN'T THINK YOU'D COME...
OH, JIM, I'M SO SORRY. I WAS SO OVERCOME BY MY OWN GRIEF, I...I HAD TO BLAME SOMEBODY, AND YOU--
IT'S ALL RIGHT, CAROL.
NO! I FORGOT HOW MUCH YOU MUST BE HURTING...
NOT AS MUCH... NOT NOW.
THERE'S AN OLD SAYING, CAROL: "HAPPINESS SHARED IS DOUBLED, SORROW SHARED IS HALVED."
I'VE HEARD THAT. AND WHAT WAS IT YOU ALWAYS SAID...?
YES, THAT...
"...LET ME HELP..."

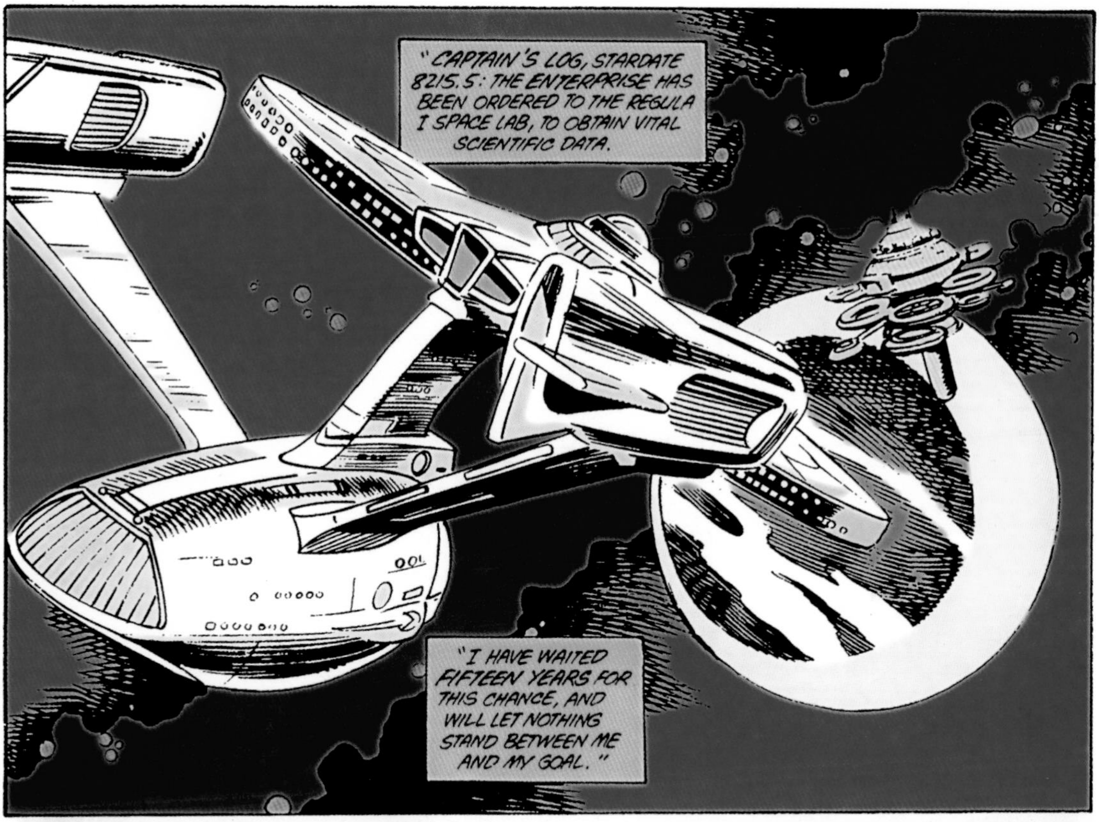
"CAPTAIN'S LOG, STARDATE 8215.5: THE ENTERPRISE HAS BEEN ORDERED TO THE REGULA I SPACE LAB, TO OBTAIN VITAL SCIENTIFIC DATA.
"I HAVE WAITED FIFTEEN YEARS FOR THIS CHANCE, AND WILL LET NOTHING STAND BETWEEN ME AND MY GOAL."

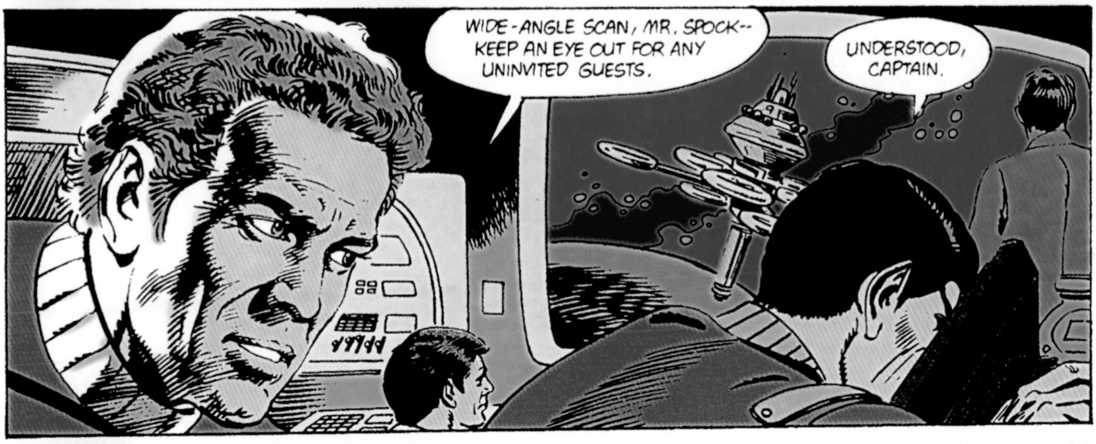
WIDE-ANGLE SCAN, MR. SPOCK-- KEEP AN EYE OUT FOR ANY UNINVITED GUESTS.
UNDERSTOOD, CAPTAIN.

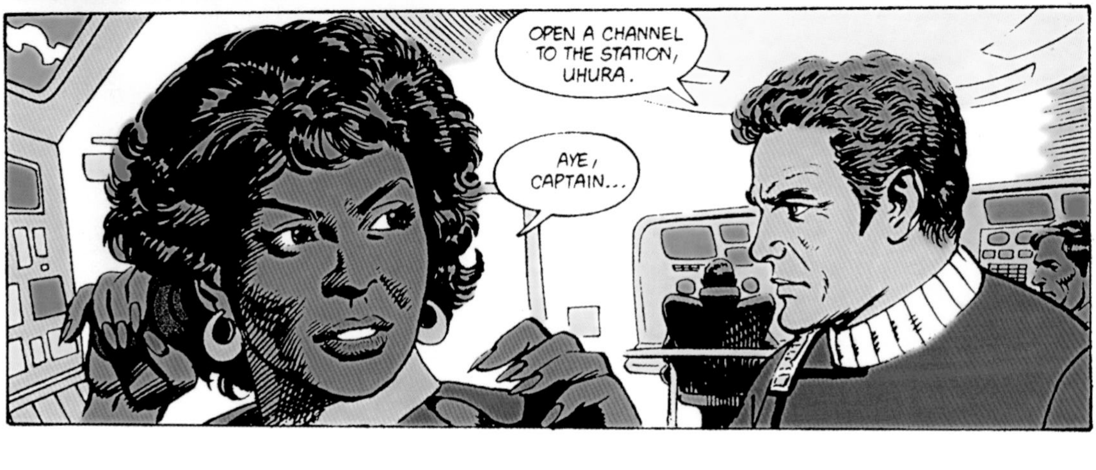
OPEN A CHANNEL TO THE STATION, UHURA.
AYE, CAPTAIN...

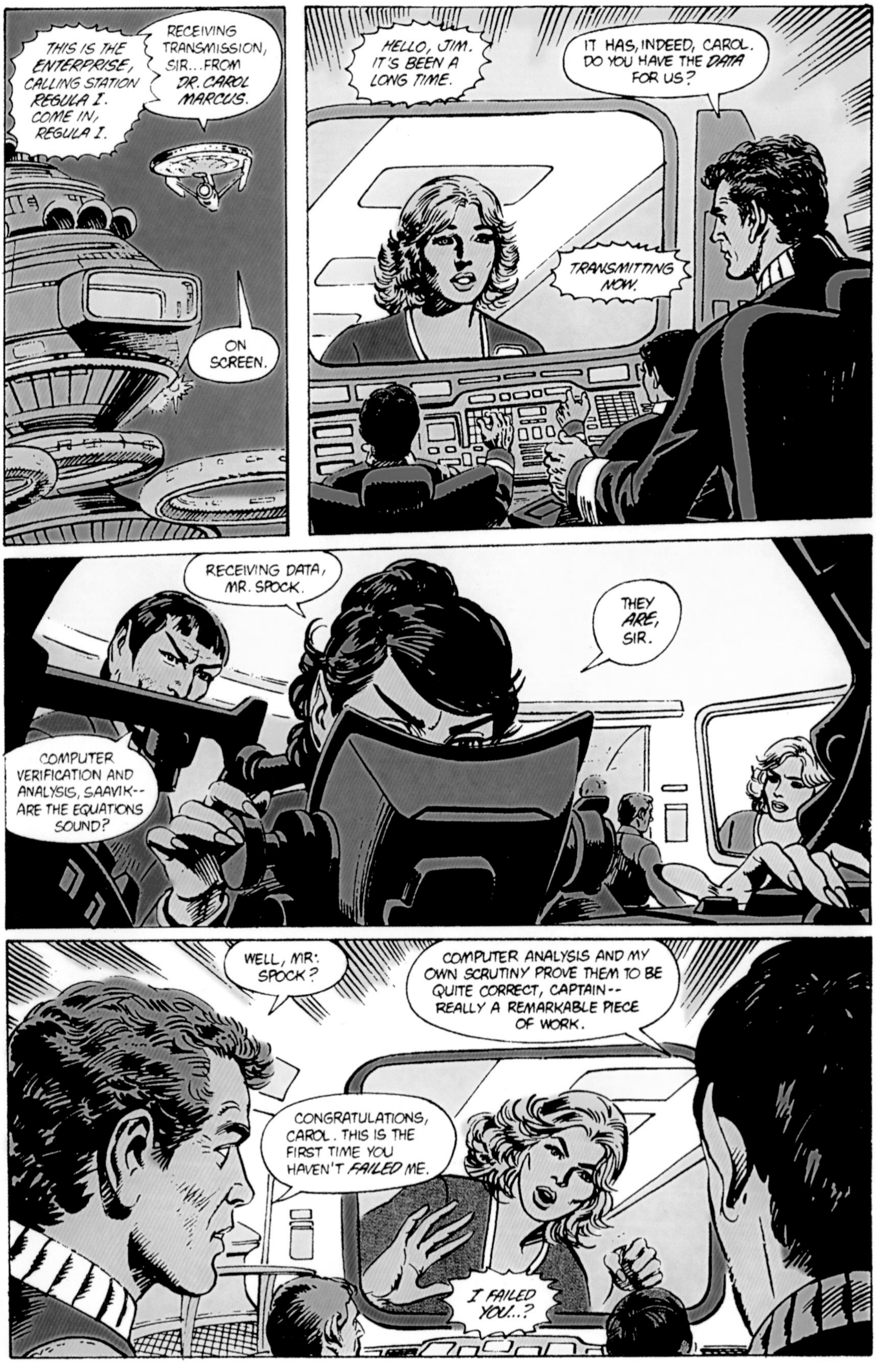
THIS IS THE ENTERPRISE, CALLING STATION REGULA I. COME IN, REGULA I.
RECEIVING TRANSMISSION, SIR...FROM DR. CAROL MARCUS.
ON SCREEN.
HELLO, JIM. IT'S BEEN A LONG TIME.
IT HAS, INDEED, CAROL. DO YOU HAVE THE DATA FOR US?
TRANSMITTING NOW.
RECEIVING DATA, MR. SPOCK.
COMPUTER VERIFICATION AND ANALYSIS, SAAVIK--ARE THE EQUATIONS SOUND?
THEY ARE, SIR.
WELL, MR. SPOCK?
COMPUTER ANALYSIS AND MY OWN SCRUTINY PROVE THEM TO BE QUITE CORRECT, CAPTAIN--REALLY A REMARKABLE PIECE OF WORK.
CONGRATULATIONS, CAROL. THIS IS THE FIRST TIME YOU HAVEN'T FAILED ME.
I FAILED YOU...?

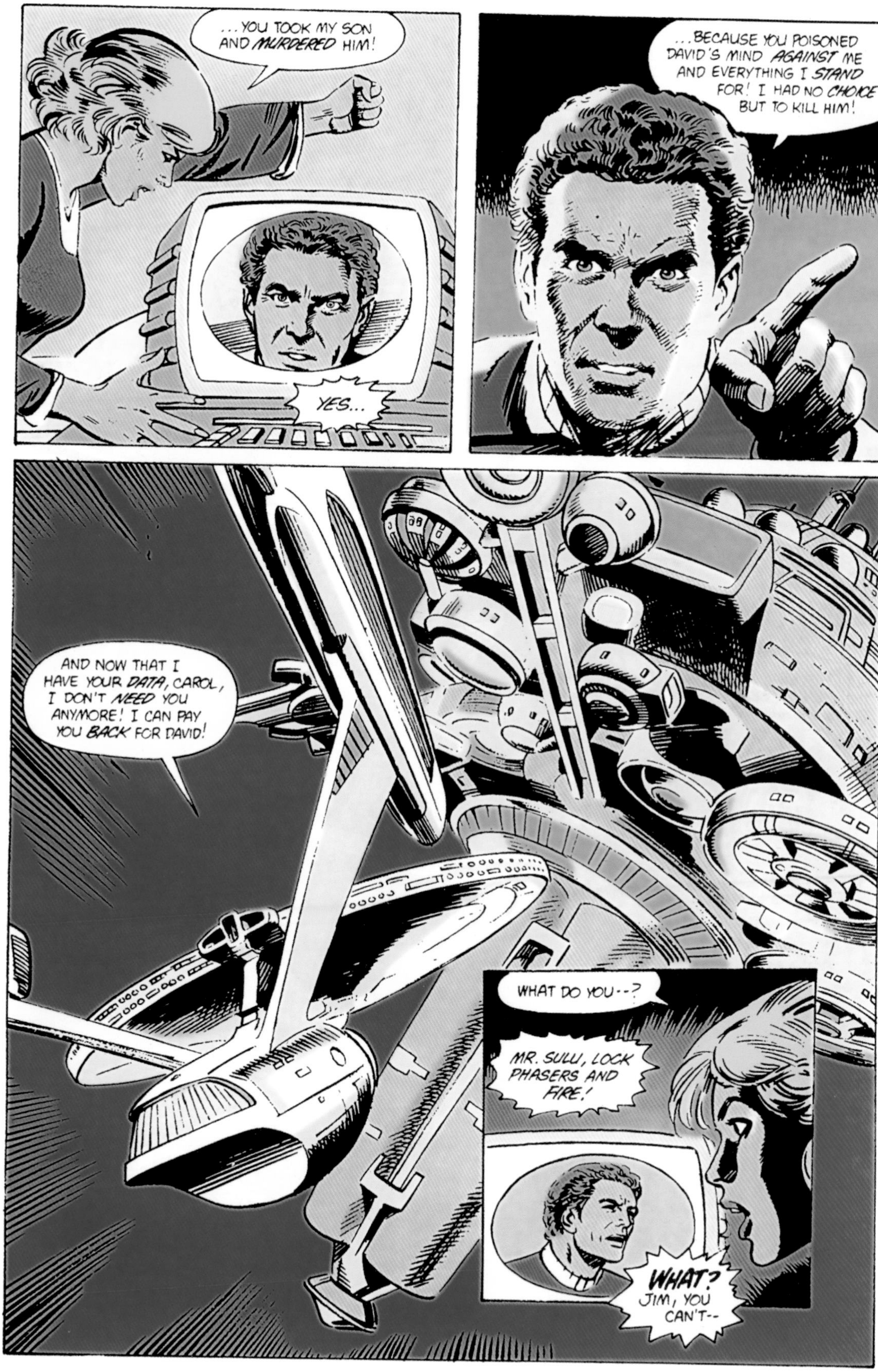
...YOU TOOK MY SON AND MURDERED HIM!
YES...
...BECAUSE YOU POISONED DAVID'S MIND AGAINST ME AND EVERYTHING I STAND FOR! I HAD NO CHOICE BUT TO KILL HIM!
AND NOW THAT I HAVE YOUR DATA, CAROL, I DON'T NEED YOU ANYMORE! I CAN PAY YOU BACK FOR DAVID!
WHAT DO YOU--?
MR. SULU, LOCK PHASERS AND FIRE!
WHAT? JIM, YOU CAN'T--

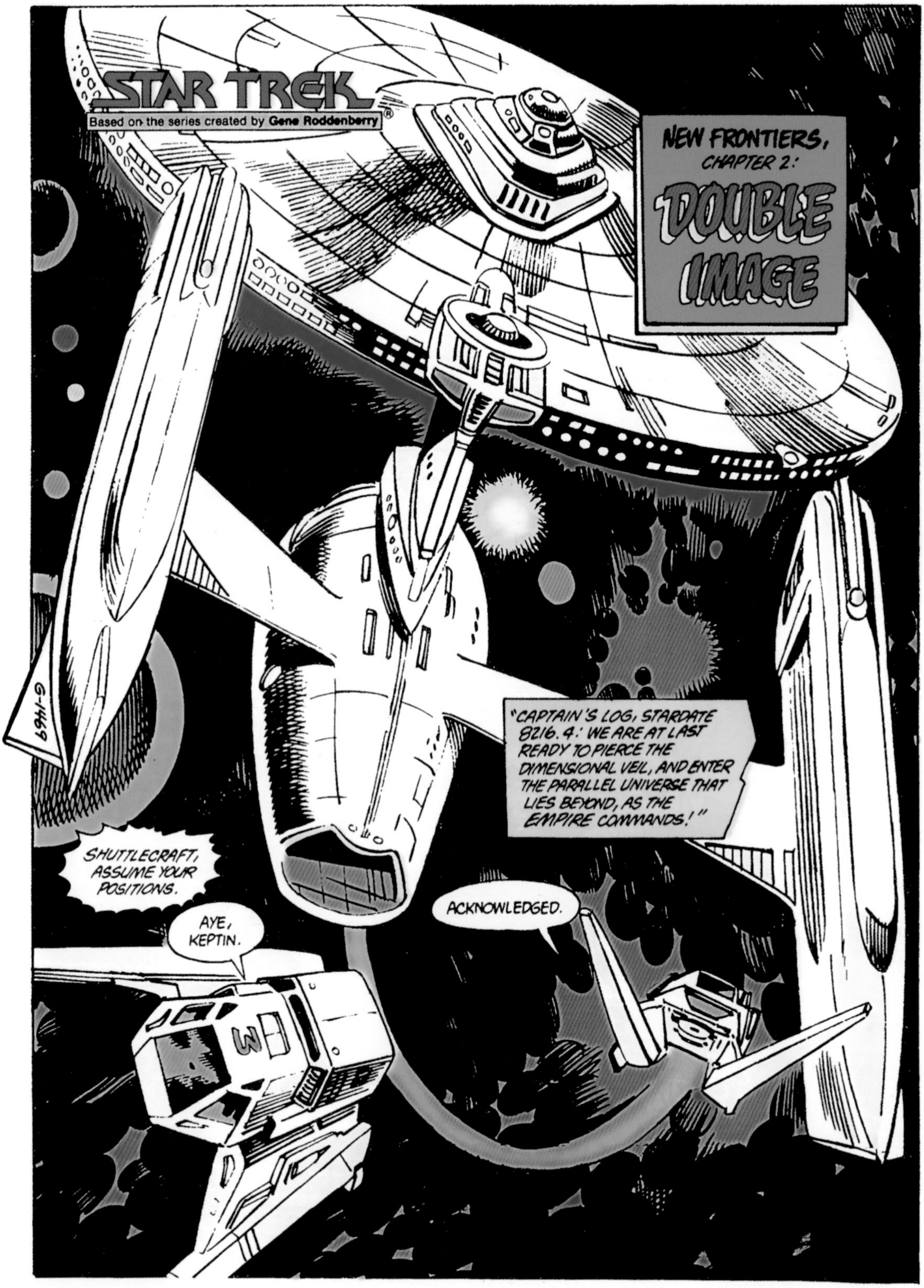
STAR TREK
Based on the series created by Gene Roddenberry®
NEW FRONTIERS, CHAPTER 2:
DOUBLE IMAGE
"CAPTAIN'S LOG, STARDATE 8216.4: WE ARE AT LAST READY TO PIERCE THE DIMENSIONAL VEIL, AND ENTER THE PARALLEL UNIVERSE THAT LIES BEYOND, AS THE EMPIRE COMMANDS!"
G-1469
SHUTTLECRAFT, ASSUME YOUR POSITIONS.
AYE, KEPTIN.
ACKNOWLEDGED.

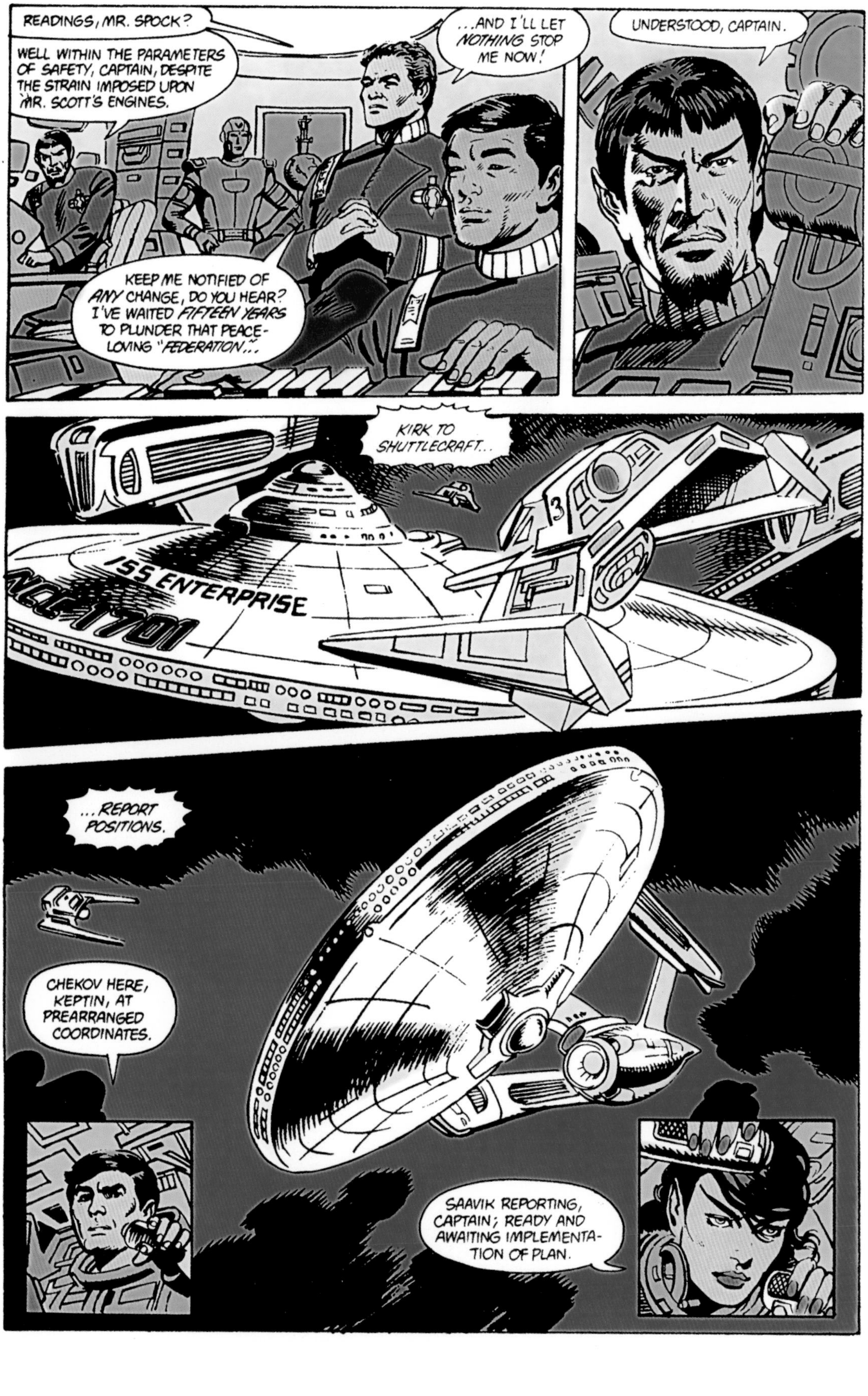
READINGS, MR. SPOCK?
WELL WITHIN THE PARAMETERS OF SAFETY, CAPTAIN, DESPITE THE STRAIN IMPOSED UPON MR. SCOTT'S ENGINES.
KEEP ME NOTIFIED OF ANY CHANGE, DO YOU HEAR? I'VE WAITED FIFTEEN YEARS TO PLUNDER THAT PEACE-LOVING "FEDERATION"...
...AND I'LL LET NOTHING STOP ME NOW!
UNDERSTOOD, CAPTAIN.
KIRK TO SHUTTLECRAFT...
ISS ENTERPRISE
NCC-1701
3
...REPORT POSITIONS.
CHEKOV HERE, KEPTIN, AT PREARRANGED COORDINATES.
SAAVIK REPORTING, CAPTAIN; READY AND AWAITING IMPLEMENTATION OF PLAN.

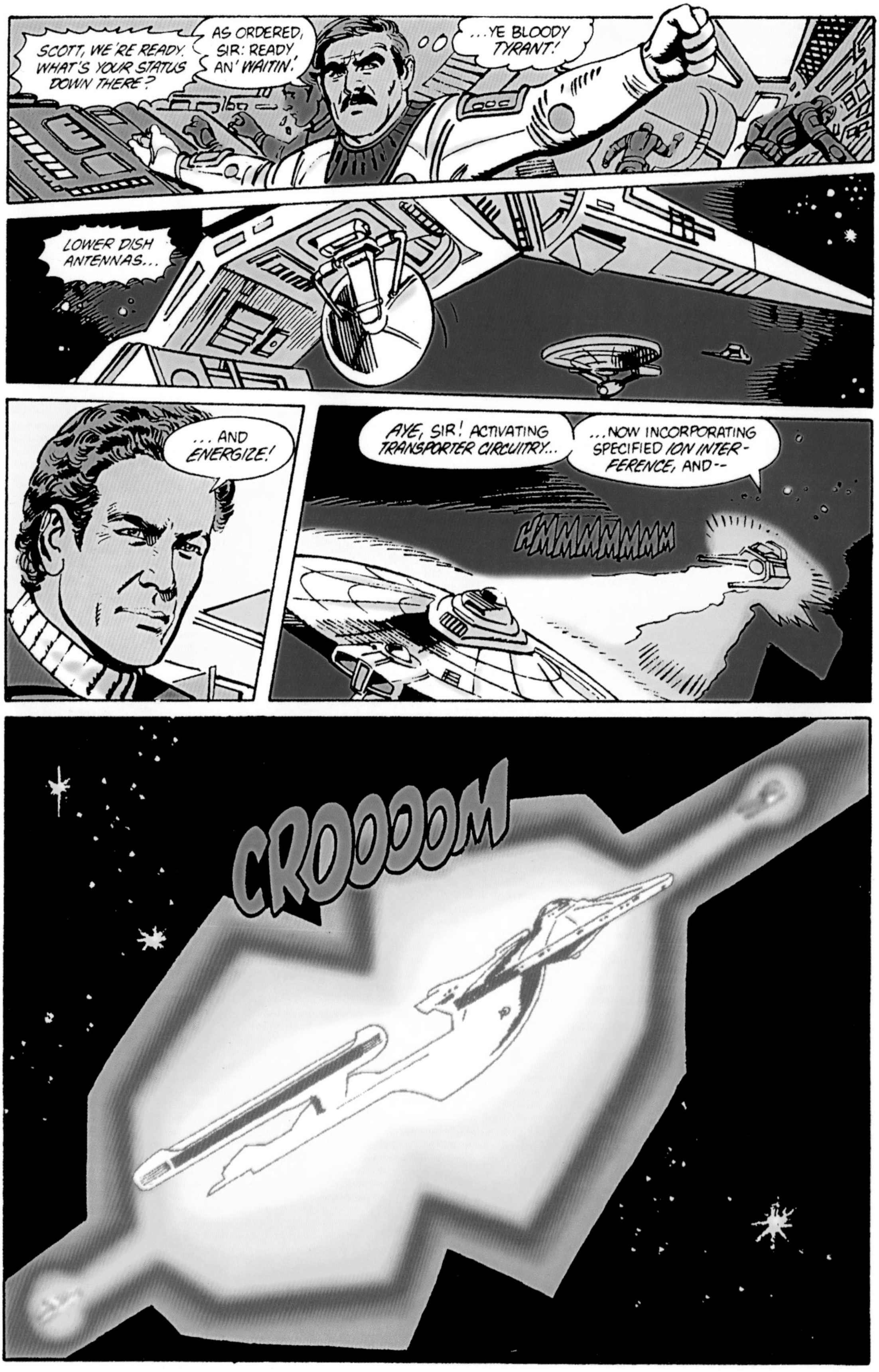
SCOTT, WE'RE READY. WHAT'S YOUR STATUS DOWN THERE?
AS ORDERED, SIR: READY AN' WAITIN'.
...YE BLOODY TYRANT!
LOWER DISH ANTENNAS...
... AND ENERGIZE!
AYE, SIR! ACTIVATING TRANSPORTER CIRCUITRY...
...NOW INCORPORATING SPECIFIED ION INTER-FERENCE, AND--
HMMMMMMMM
CROOOOM

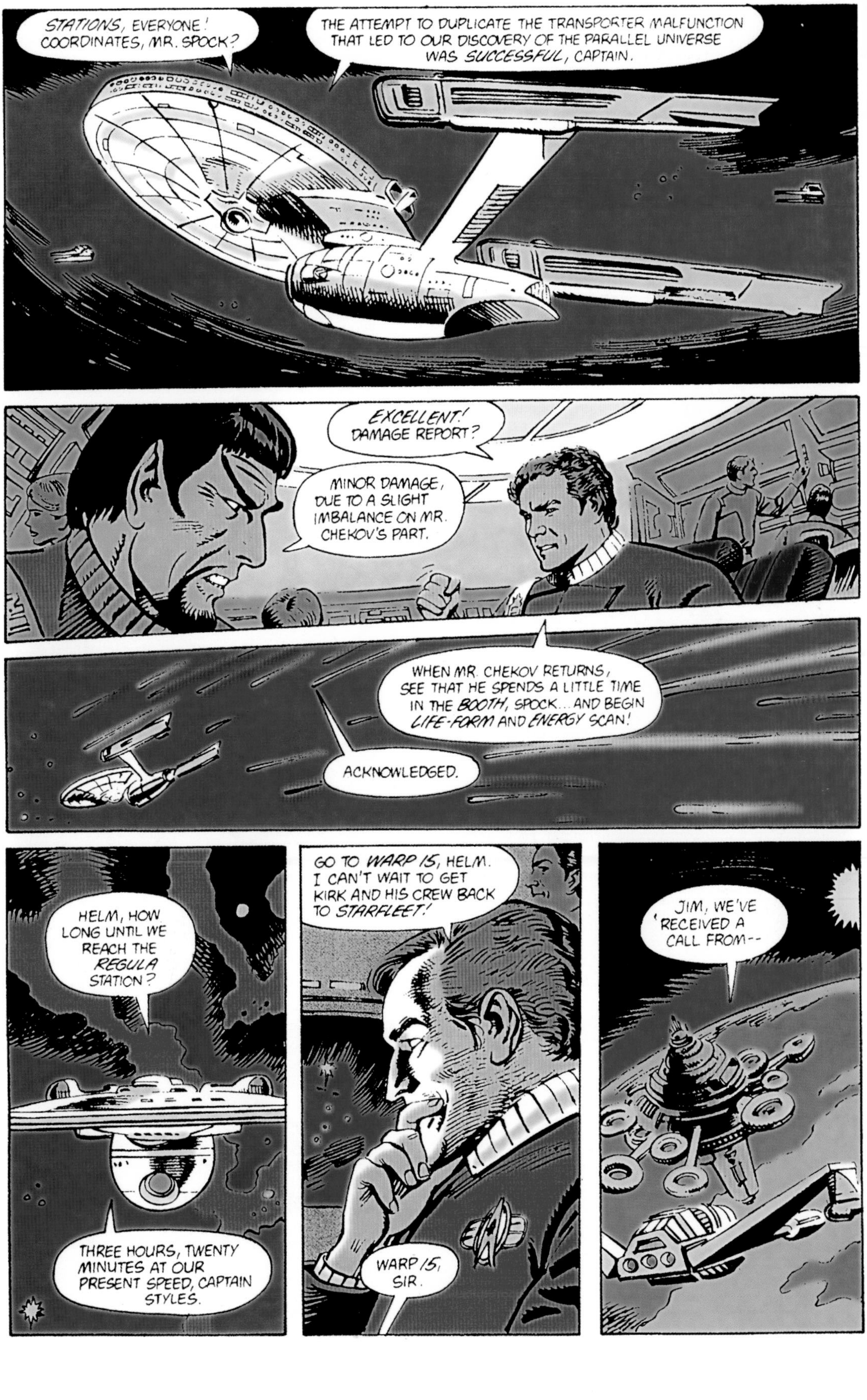
STATIONS, EVERYONE! COORDINATES, MR. SPOCK?
THE ATTEMPT TO DUPLICATE THE TRANSPORTER MALFUNCTION THAT LED TO OUR DISCOVERY OF THE PARALLEL UNIVERSE WAS SUCCESSFUL, CAPTAIN.
EXCELLENT! DAMAGE REPORT?
MINOR DAMAGE, DUE TO A SLIGHT IMBALANCE ON MR. CHEKOV'S PART.
WHEN MR. CHEKOV RETURNS, SEE THAT HE SPENDS A LITTLE TIME IN THE BOOTH, SPOCK... AND BEGIN LIFE-FORM AND ENERGY SCAN!
ACKNOWLEDGED.
HELM, HOW LONG UNTIL WE REACH THE REGULA STATION?
THREE HOURS, TWENTY MINUTES AT OUR PRESENT SPEED, CAPTAIN STYLES.
GO TO WARP 15, HELM. I CAN'T WAIT TO GET KIRK AND HIS CREW BACK TO STARFLEET!
WARP 15, SIR.
JIM, WE'VE RECEIVED A CALL FROM--

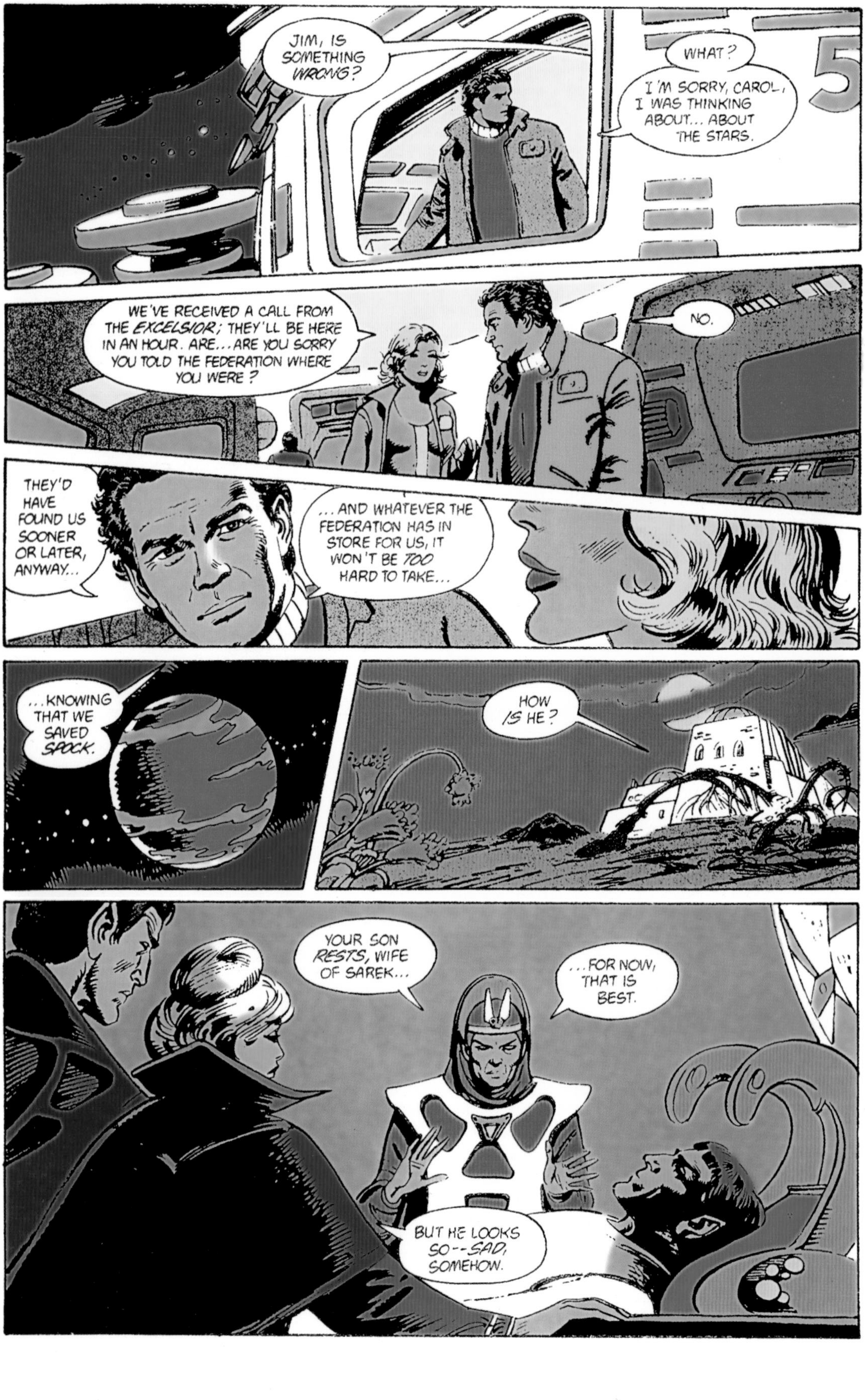
JIM, IS SOMETHING WRONG?
WHAT?
I'M SORRY, CAROL, I WAS THINKING ABOUT... ABOUT THE STARS.
WE'VE RECEIVED A CALL FROM THE EXCELSIOR; THEY'LL BE HERE IN AN HOUR. ARE... ARE YOU SORRY YOU TOLD THE FEDERATION WHERE YOU WERE?
NO.
THEY'D HAVE FOUND US SOONER OR LATER, ANYWAY...
...AND WHATEVER THE FEDERATION HAS IN STORE FOR US, IT WON'T BE TOO HARD TO TAKE...
...KNOWING THAT WE SAVED SPOCK.
HOW IS HE?
YOUR SON RESTS, WIFE OF SAREK...
...FOR NOW, THAT IS BEST.
BUT HE LOOKS SO--SAD, SOMEHOW.

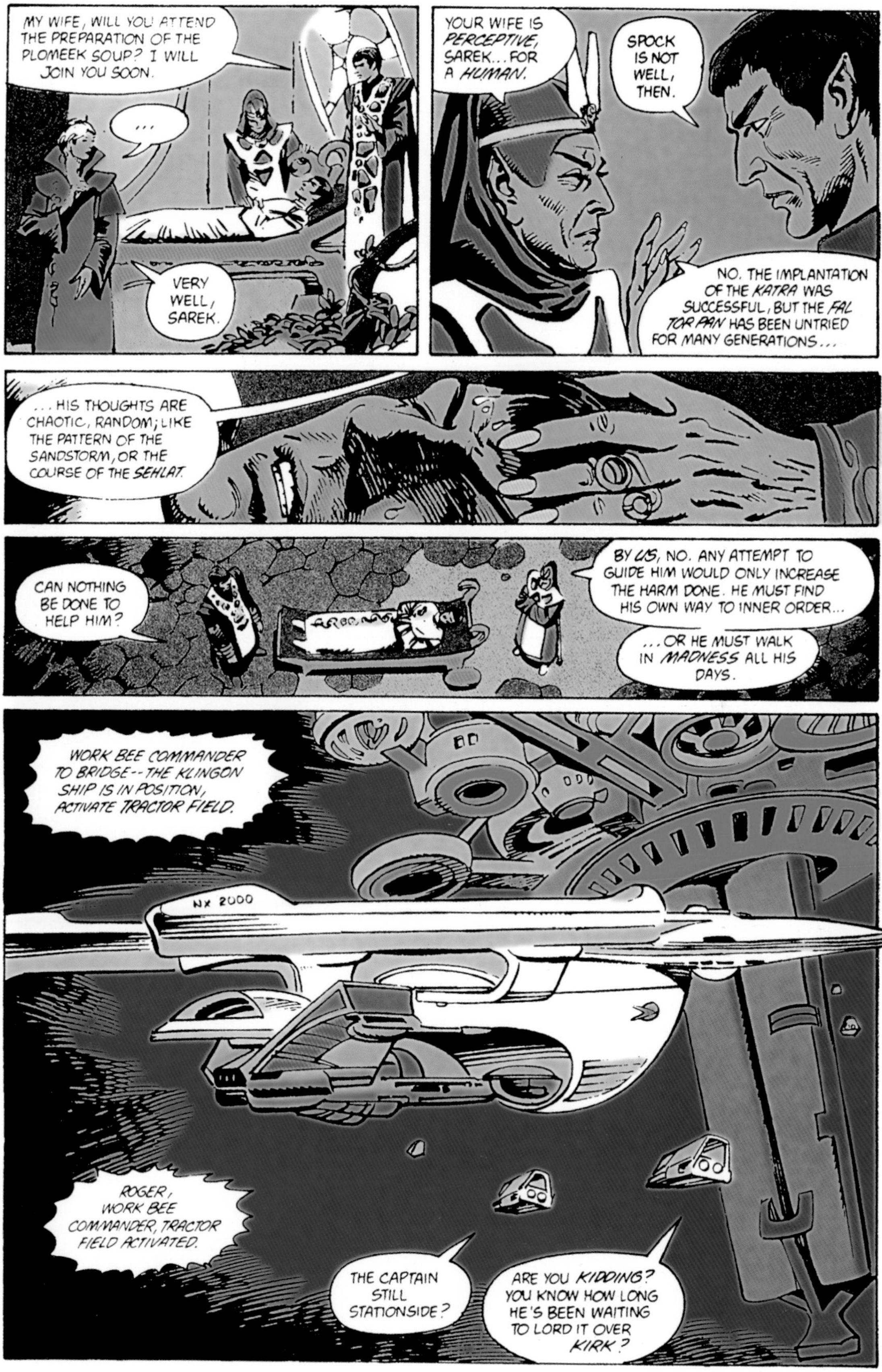
MY WIFE, WILL YOU ATTEND THE PREPARATION OF THE PLOMEEK SOUP? I WILL JOIN YOU SOON.
...
VERY WELL, SAREK.
YOUR WIFE IS *PERCEPTIVE*, SAREK... FOR A *HUMAN*.
SPOCK IS NOT WELL, THEN.
NO. THE IMPLANTATION OF THE *KATRA* WAS SUCCESSFUL, BUT THE *FAL TOR PAN* HAS BEEN UNTRIED FOR MANY GENERATIONS...
... HIS THOUGHTS ARE CHAOTIC, RANDOM; LIKE THE PATTERN OF THE SANDSTORM, OR THE COURSE OF THE *SEHLAT*.
CAN NOTHING BE DONE TO HELP HIM?
BY *US*, NO. ANY ATTEMPT TO GUIDE HIM WOULD ONLY INCREASE THE HARM DONE. HE MUST FIND HIS OWN WAY TO INNER ORDER...
... OR HE MUST WALK IN *MADNESS* ALL HIS DAYS.
WORK BEE COMMANDER TO BRIDGE--THE KLINGON SHIP IS IN POSITION, ACTIVATE TRACTOR FIELD.
NX 2000
ROGER, WORK BEE COMMANDER, TRACTOR FIELD ACTIVATED.
THE CAPTAIN STILL STATIONSIDE?
ARE YOU *KIDDING*? YOU KNOW HOW LONG HE'S BEEN WAITING TO LORD IT OVER *KIRK*?

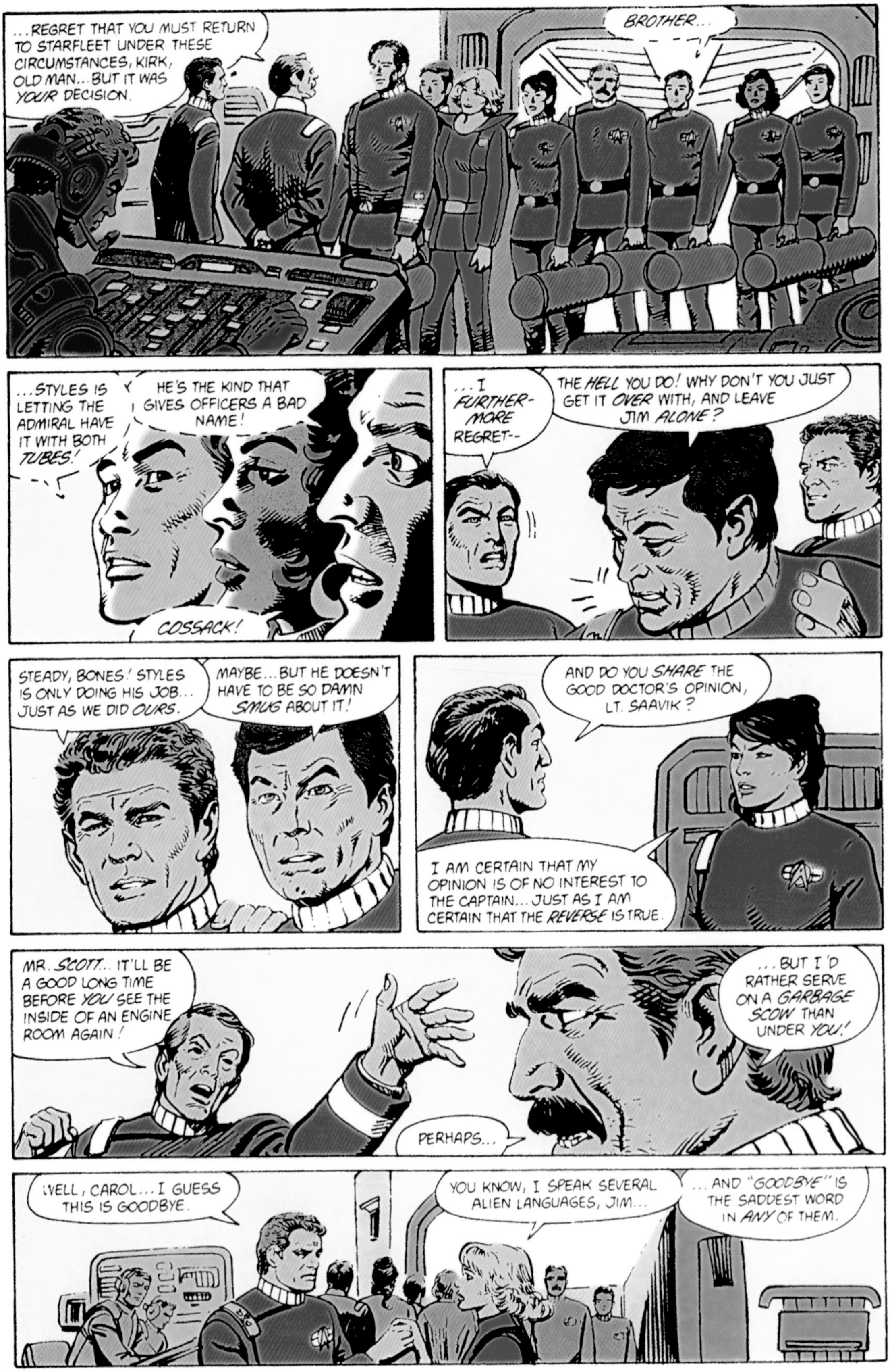

...REGRET THAT YOU MUST RETURN TO STARFLEET UNDER THESE CIRCUMSTANCES, KIRK, OLD MAN... BUT IT WAS YOUR DECISION.
BROTHER...
...STYLES IS LETTING THE ADMIRAL HAVE IT WITH BOTH TUBES!
HE'S THE KIND THAT GIVES OFFICERS A BAD NAME!
COSSACK!
...I FURTHERMORE REGRET--
THE HELL YOU DO! WHY DON'T YOU JUST GET IT OVER WITH, AND LEAVE JIM ALONE?
STEADY, BONES! STYLES IS ONLY DOING HIS JOB... JUST AS WE DID OURS.
MAYBE... BUT HE DOESN'T HAVE TO BE SO DAMN SMUG ABOUT IT!
AND DO YOU SHARE THE GOOD DOCTOR'S OPINION, LT. SAAVIK?
I AM CERTAIN THAT MY OPINION IS OF NO INTEREST TO THE CAPTAIN... JUST AS I AM CERTAIN THAT THE REVERSE IS TRUE.
MR. SCOTT... IT'LL BE A GOOD LONG TIME BEFORE YOU SEE THE INSIDE OF AN ENGINE ROOM AGAIN!
PERHAPS...
...BUT I'D RATHER SERVE ON A GARBAGE SCOW THAN UNDER YOU!
WELL, CAROL... I GUESS THIS IS GOODBYE.
YOU KNOW, I SPEAK SEVERAL ALIEN LANGUAGES, JIM...
...AND "GOODBYE" IS THE SADDEST WORD IN ANY OF THEM.

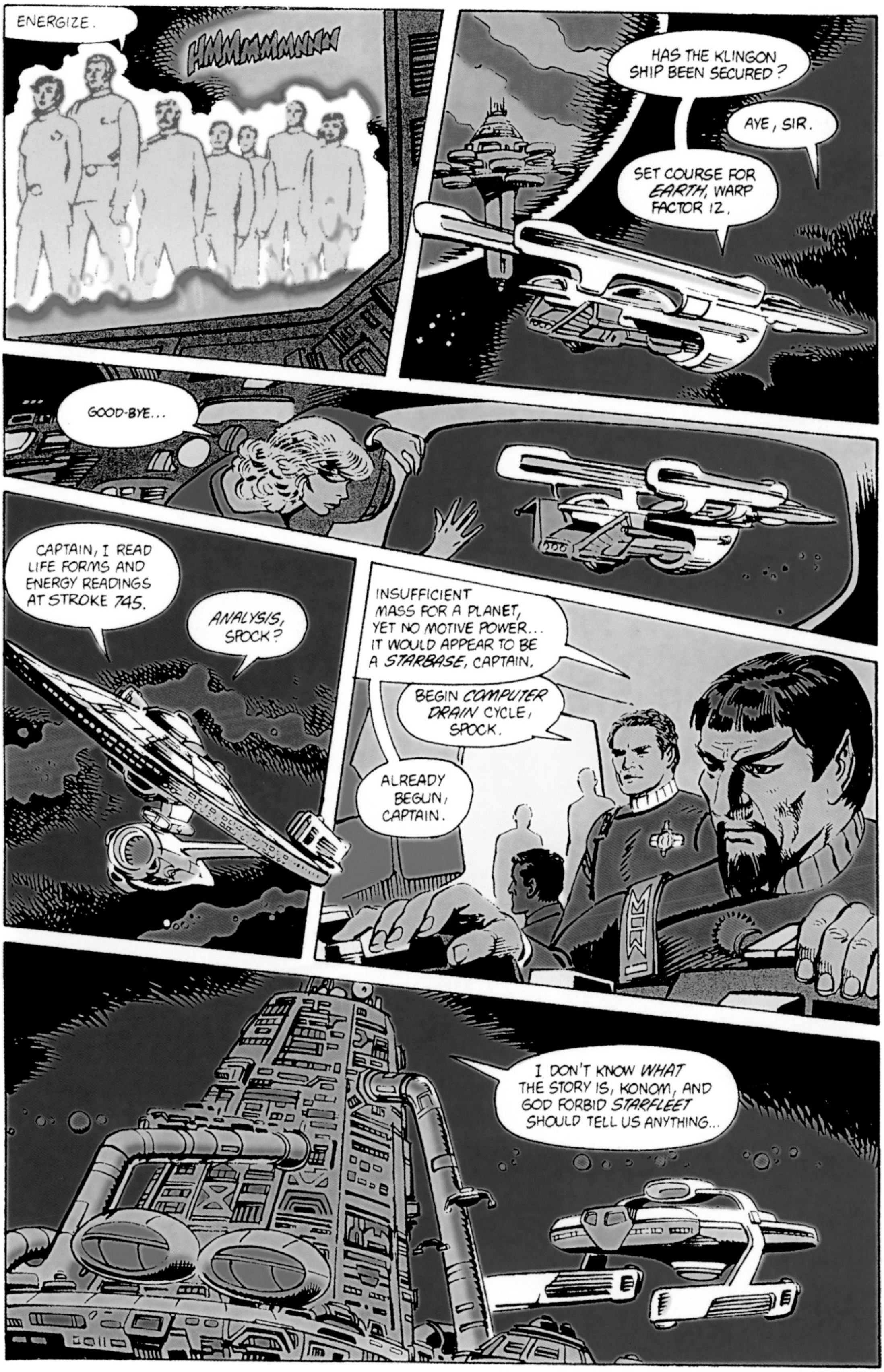
ENERGIZE.
HMMMMMMNNN
HAS THE KLINGON SHIP BEEN SECURED?
AYE, SIR.
SET COURSE FOR EARTH, WARP FACTOR 12.
GOOD-BYE...
CAPTAIN, I READ LIFE FORMS AND ENERGY READINGS AT STROKE 745.
ANALYSIS, SPOCK?
INSUFFICIENT MASS FOR A PLANET, YET NO MOTIVE POWER... IT WOULD APPEAR TO BE A STARBASE, CAPTAIN.
BEGIN COMPUTER DRAIN CYCLE, SPOCK.
ALREADY BEGUN, CAPTAIN.
I DON'T KNOW WHAT THE STORY IS, KONOM, AND GOD FORBID STARFLEET SHOULD TELL US ANYTHING...

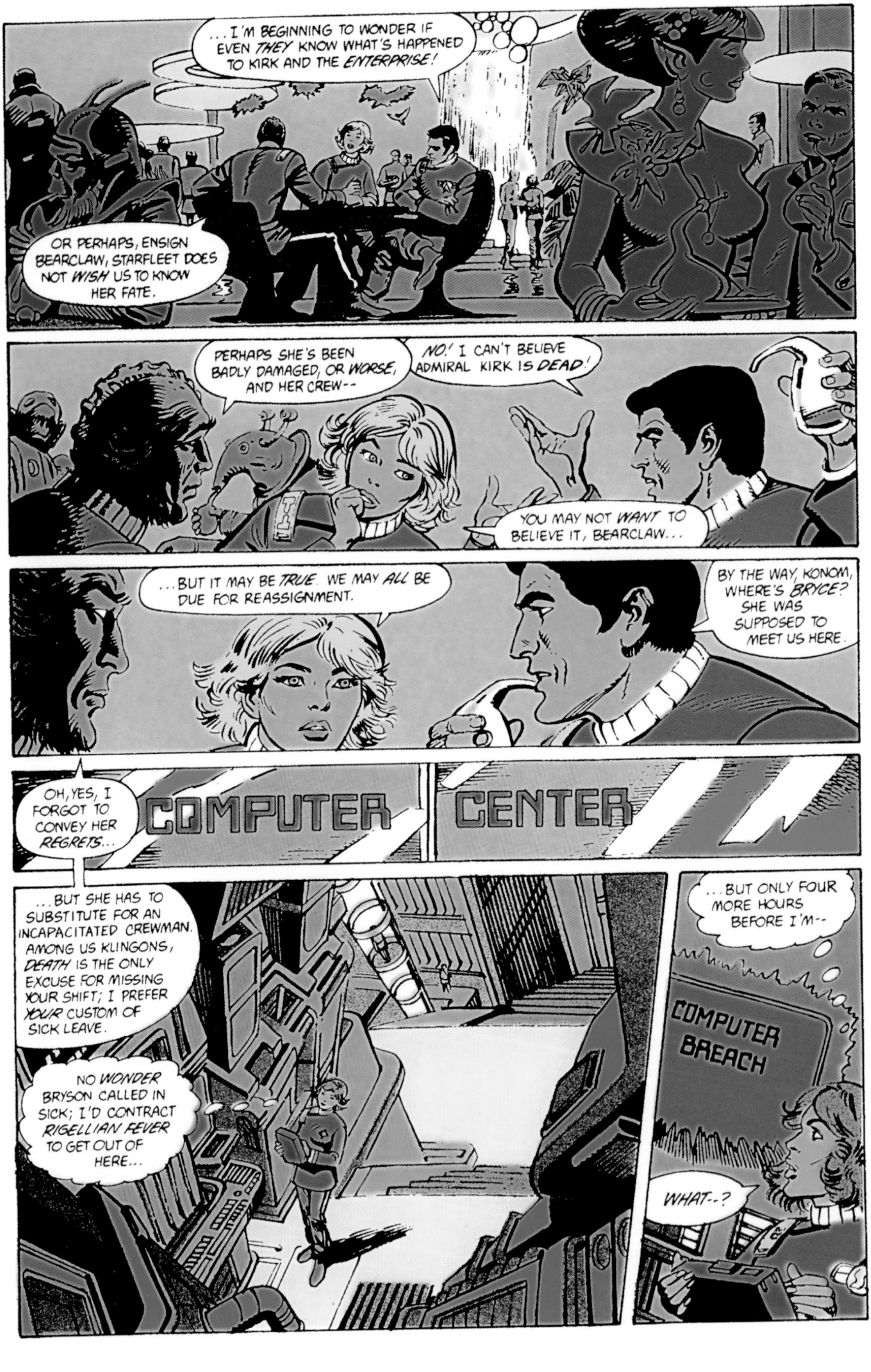

...I'M BEGINNING TO WONDER IF EVEN THEY KNOW WHAT'S HAPPENED TO KIRK AND THE ENTERPRISE!
OR PERHAPS, ENSIGN BEARCLAW, STARFLEET DOES NOT WISH US TO KNOW HER FATE.
PERHAPS SHE'S BEEN BADLY DAMAGED, OR WORSE, AND HER CREW--
NO! I CAN'T BELIEVE ADMIRAL KIRK IS DEAD!
YOU MAY NOT WANT TO BELIEVE IT, BEARCLAW...
...BUT IT MAY BE TRUE. WE MAY ALL BE DUE FOR REASSIGNMENT.
BY THE WAY, KONOM, WHERE'S BRYCE? SHE WAS SUPPOSED TO MEET US HERE.
OH, YES, I FORGOT TO CONVEY HER REGRETS...
COMPUTER CENTER
...BUT SHE HAS TO SUBSTITUTE FOR AN INCAPACITATED CREWMAN. AMONG US KLINGONS, DEATH IS THE ONLY EXCUSE FOR MISSING YOUR SHIFT; I PREFER YOUR CUSTOM OF SICK LEAVE.
NO WONDER BRYSON CALLED IN SICK; I'D CONTRACT RIGELLIAN FEVER TO GET OUT OF HERE...
...BUT ONLY FOUR MORE HOURS BEFORE I'M--
COMPUTER BREACH
WHAT--?

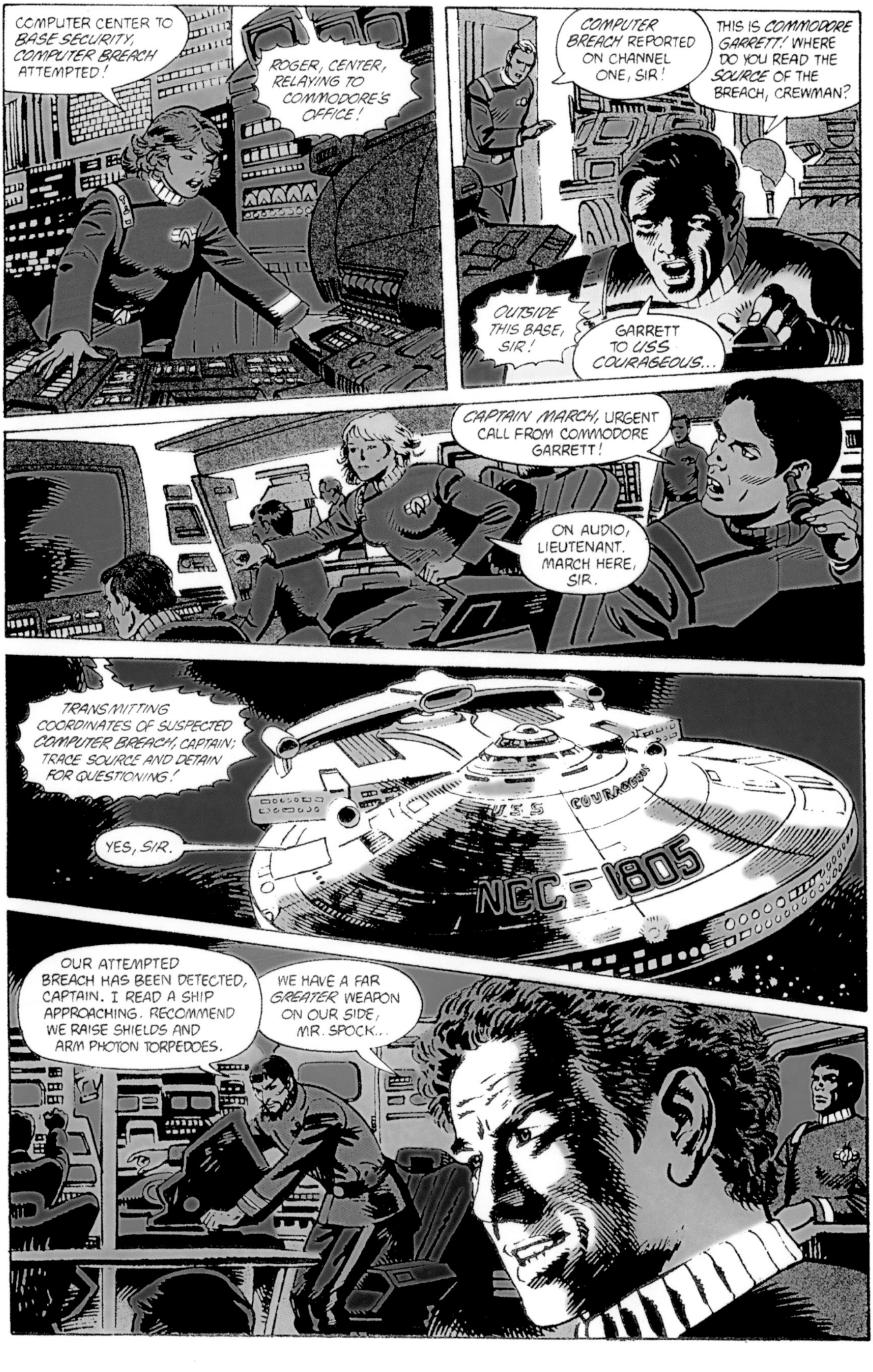
COMPUTER CENTER TO BASE SECURITY, COMPUTER BREACH ATTEMPTED!
ROGER, CENTER, RELAYING TO COMMODORE'S OFFICE!
COMPUTER BREACH REPORTED ON CHANNEL ONE, SIR!
THIS IS COMMODORE GARRETT! WHERE DO YOU READ THE SOURCE OF THE BREACH, CREWMAN?
OUTSIDE THIS BASE, SIR!
GARRETT TO USS COURAGEOUS...
CAPTAIN MARCH, URGENT CALL FROM COMMODORE GARRETT!
ON AUDIO, LIEUTENANT. MARCH HERE, SIR.
TRANSMITTING COORDINATES OF SUSPECTED COMPUTER BREACH, CAPTAIN; TRACE SOURCE AND DETAIN FOR QUESTIONING!
YES, SIR.
USS COURAGEOUS
NCC-1805
OUR ATTEMPTED BREACH HAS BEEN DETECTED, CAPTAIN. I READ A SHIP APPROACHING. RECOMMEND WE RAISE SHIELDS AND ARM PHOTON TORPEDOES.
WE HAVE A FAR GREATER WEAPON ON OUR SIDE, MR. SPOCK...

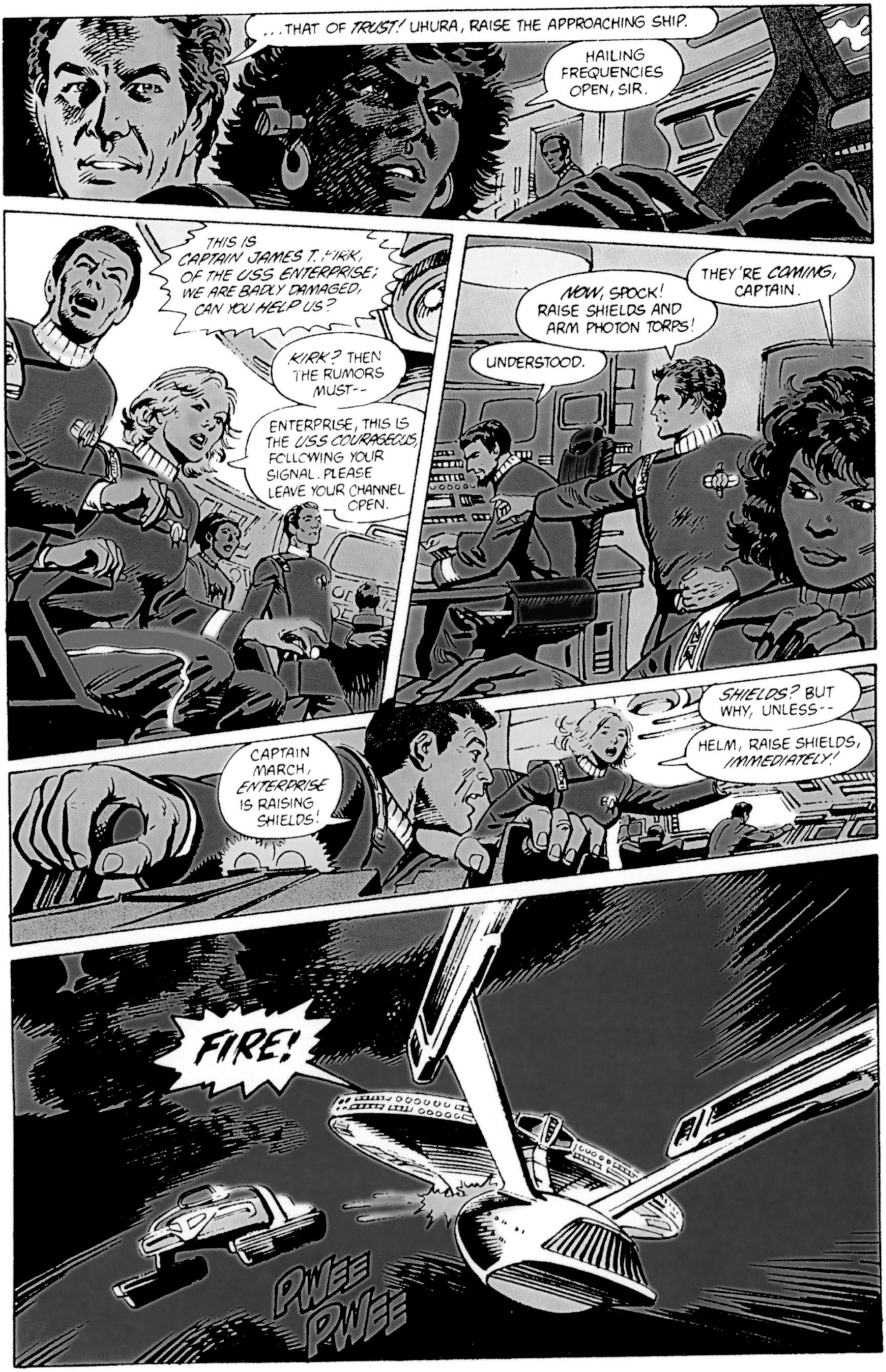

...THAT OF TRUST! UHURA, RAISE THE APPROACHING SHIP.
HAILING FREQUENCIES OPEN, SIR.
THIS IS CAPTAIN JAMES T. KIRK, OF THE USS ENTERPRISE; WE ARE BADLY DAMAGED, CAN YOU HELP US?
KIRK? THEN THE RUMORS MUST--
ENTERPRISE, THIS IS THE USS COURAGEOUS, FOLLOWING YOUR SIGNAL. PLEASE LEAVE YOUR CHANNEL OPEN.
THEY'RE COMING, CAPTAIN.
NOW, SPOCK! RAISE SHIELDS AND ARM PHOTON TORPS!
UNDERSTOOD.
CAPTAIN MARCH, ENTERPRISE IS RAISING SHIELDS!
SHIELDS? BUT WHY, UNLESS--
HELM, RAISE SHIELDS, IMMEDIATELY!
FIRE!
PWEE PWEE

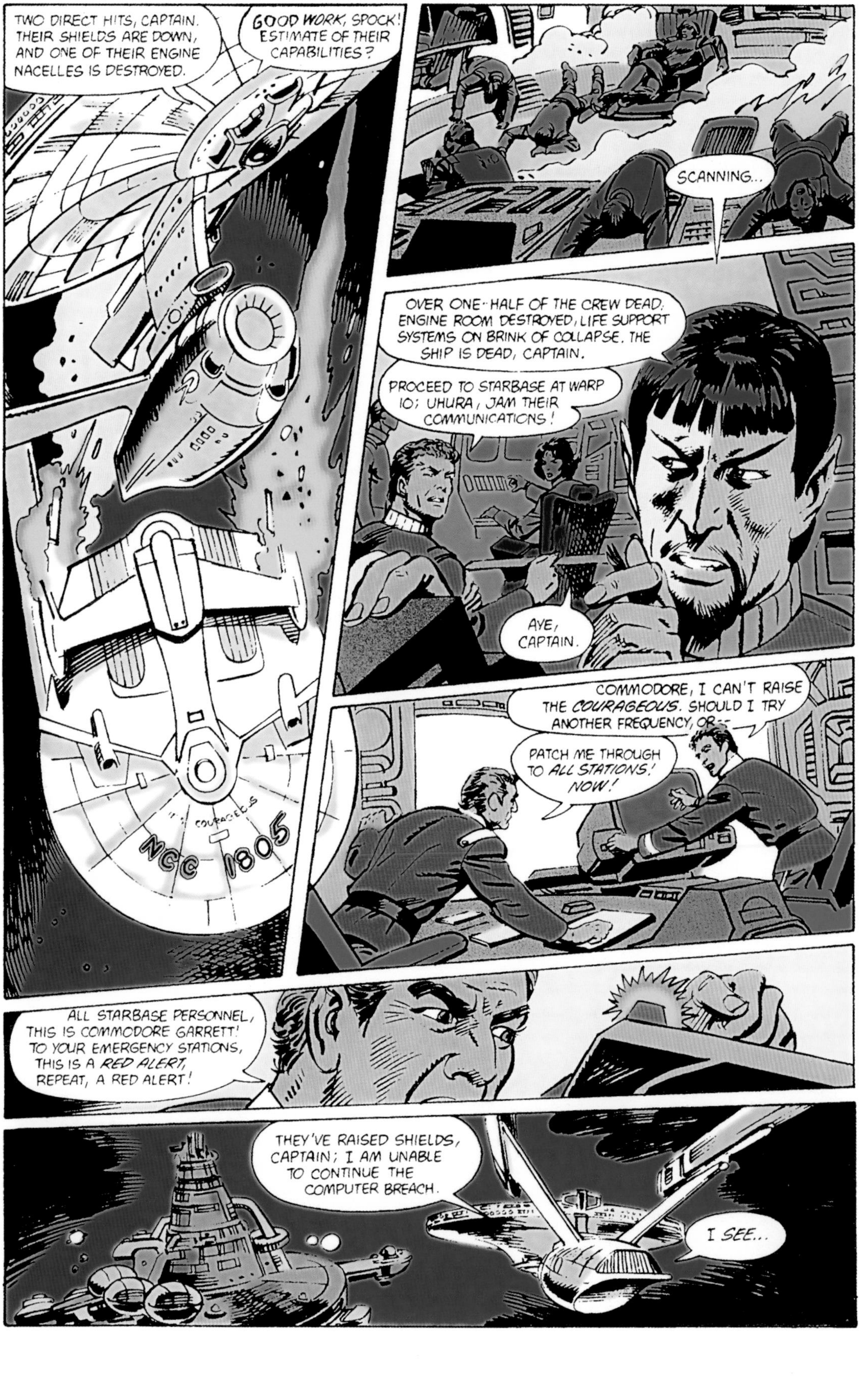
TWO DIRECT HITS, CAPTAIN. THEIR SHIELDS ARE DOWN, AND ONE OF THEIR ENGINE NACELLES IS DESTROYED.
GOOD WORK, SPOCK! ESTIMATE OF THEIR CAPABILITIES?
NCC 1805
SCANNING...
OVER ONE-HALF OF THE CREW DEAD; ENGINE ROOM DESTROYED, LIFE SUPPORT SYSTEMS ON BRINK OF COLLAPSE. THE SHIP IS DEAD, CAPTAIN.
PROCEED TO STARBASE AT WARP 10; UHURA, JAM THEIR COMMUNICATIONS!
AYE, CAPTAIN.
COMMODORE, I CAN'T RAISE THE *COURAGEOUS*. SHOULD I TRY ANOTHER FREQUENCY, OR--
PATCH ME THROUGH TO *ALL STATIONS*! NOW!
ALL STARBASE PERSONNEL, THIS IS COMMODORE GARRETT! TO YOUR EMERGENCY STATIONS, THIS IS A *RED ALERT*, REPEAT, A RED ALERT!
THEY'VE RAISED SHIELDS, CAPTAIN; I AM UNABLE TO CONTINUE THE COMPUTER BREACH.
I SEE...

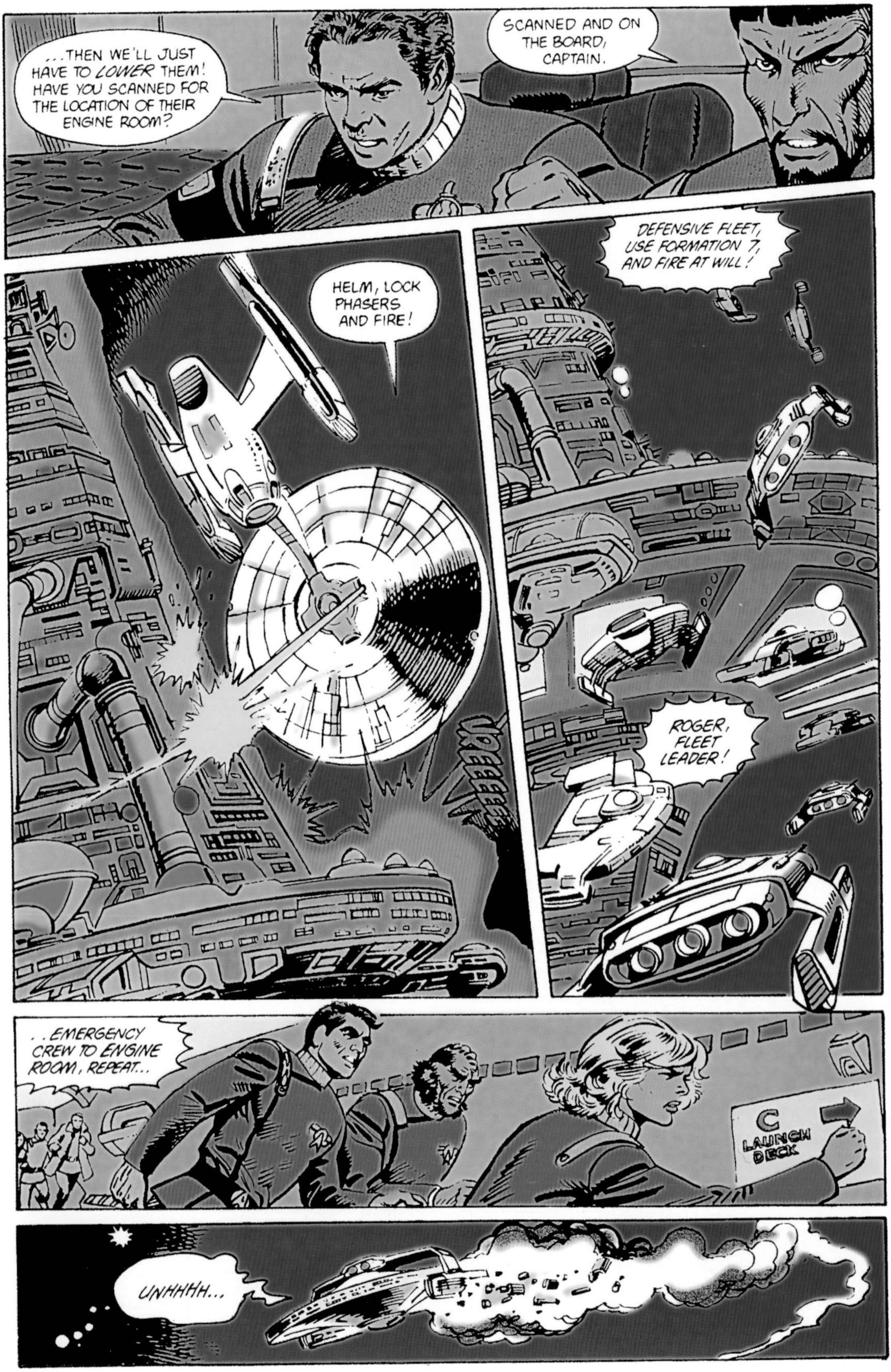
...THEN WE'LL JUST HAVE TO LOWER THEM! HAVE YOU SCANNED FOR THE LOCATION OF THEIR ENGINE ROOM?
SCANNED AND ON THE BOARD, CAPTAIN.
HELM, LOCK PHASERS AND FIRE!
DEFENSIVE FLEET, USE FORMATION 7, AND FIRE AT WILL!
ROGER, FLEET LEADER!
...EMERGENCY CREW TO ENGINE ROOM, REPEAT...
C
LAUNCH DECK
UNHHHH...

...C-COLLINS, DAMAGE REPORT...

COLLINS... HUGHES... ALL *DEAD*...

...BUT AT LEAST WE CAN RAISE THE *ALARM!*

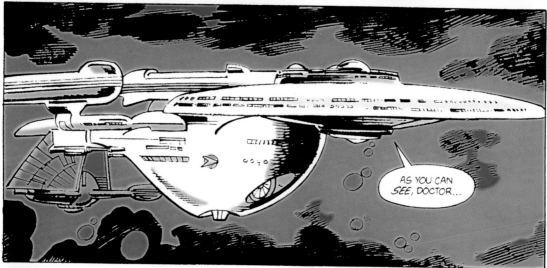

AS YOU CAN *SEE*, DOCTOR...

...*OUR* MEDICAL FACILITIES ARE SEVERAL TIMES THE *SIZE* OF ANYTHING *YOU'RE* USED TO-- AND SEVERAL TIMES MORE *EFFICIENT*, AS WELL!

I'M A *DOCTOR*, STYLES, NOT A *COMPUTER PROGRAMMER!* THIS PLACE WAS DESIGNED *BY* MACHINES, *FOR* MACHINES!

SEND A *HUMAN* PATIENT IN HERE, AND HE'D GET LOST IN THE *CIRCUITRY!*

BRIDGE TO CAPTAIN STYLES, EMERGENCY!

YES, MR. SANCHEZ, WHAT *IS* IT?

SIR, WE'VE RECEIVED A PRIORITY-1 DISTRESS CALL FROM THE *COURAGEOUS,* ASSIGNED TO STARBASE 13!

CHANGE COURSE FOR THE BASE, INCREASE SPEED TO *WARP 17!* I'LL BE THERE AT ONCE!

YOU CAN COME WITH ME TO THE BRIDGE IF YOU LIKE, KIRK... TO SEE HOW A *REAL* CAPTAIN HANDLES AN EMERGENCY!

YOUR... GENEROSITY IS OVERWHELMING, CAPTAIN.

YES, I *KNOW.*

STATUS, SPOCK?

THIS *"FLEET"* CONSISTS OF SHORT-RANGE CRAFT, ARMED WITH *PHASERS,* CAPTAIN. THEY MANEUVER TOO QUICKLY FOR US TO EASILY DESTROY THEM WITH PHASERS OR TORPEDOES...

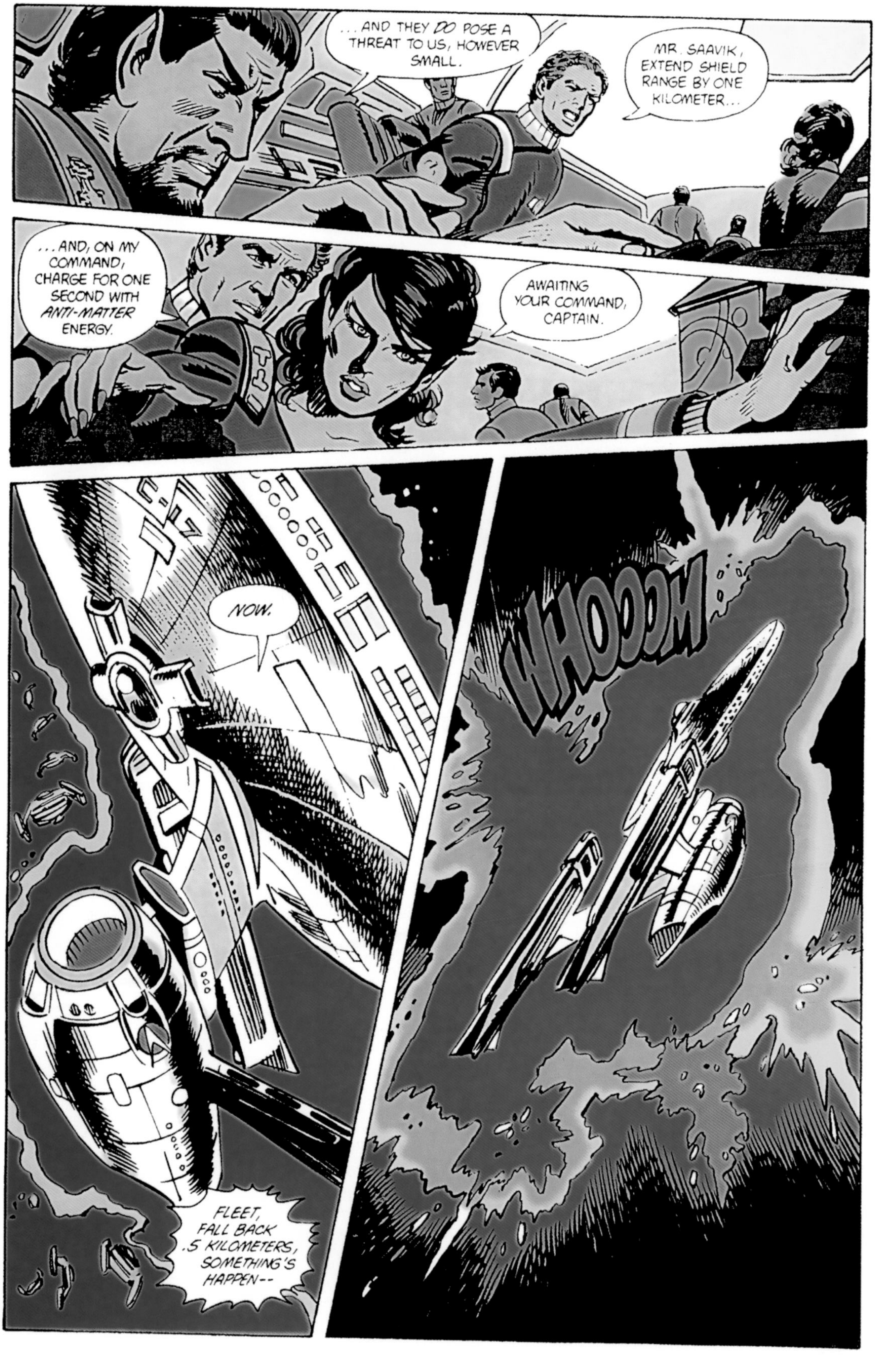
...AND THEY DO POSE A THREAT TO US, HOWEVER SMALL.
MR. SAAVIK, EXTEND SHIELD RANGE BY ONE KILOMETER...
...AND, ON MY COMMAND, CHARGE FOR ONE SECOND WITH ANTI-MATTER ENERGY.
AWAITING YOUR COMMAND, CAPTAIN.
NOW.
FLEET, FALL BACK .5 KILOMETERS, SOMETHING'S HAPPEN--
WHOOOM

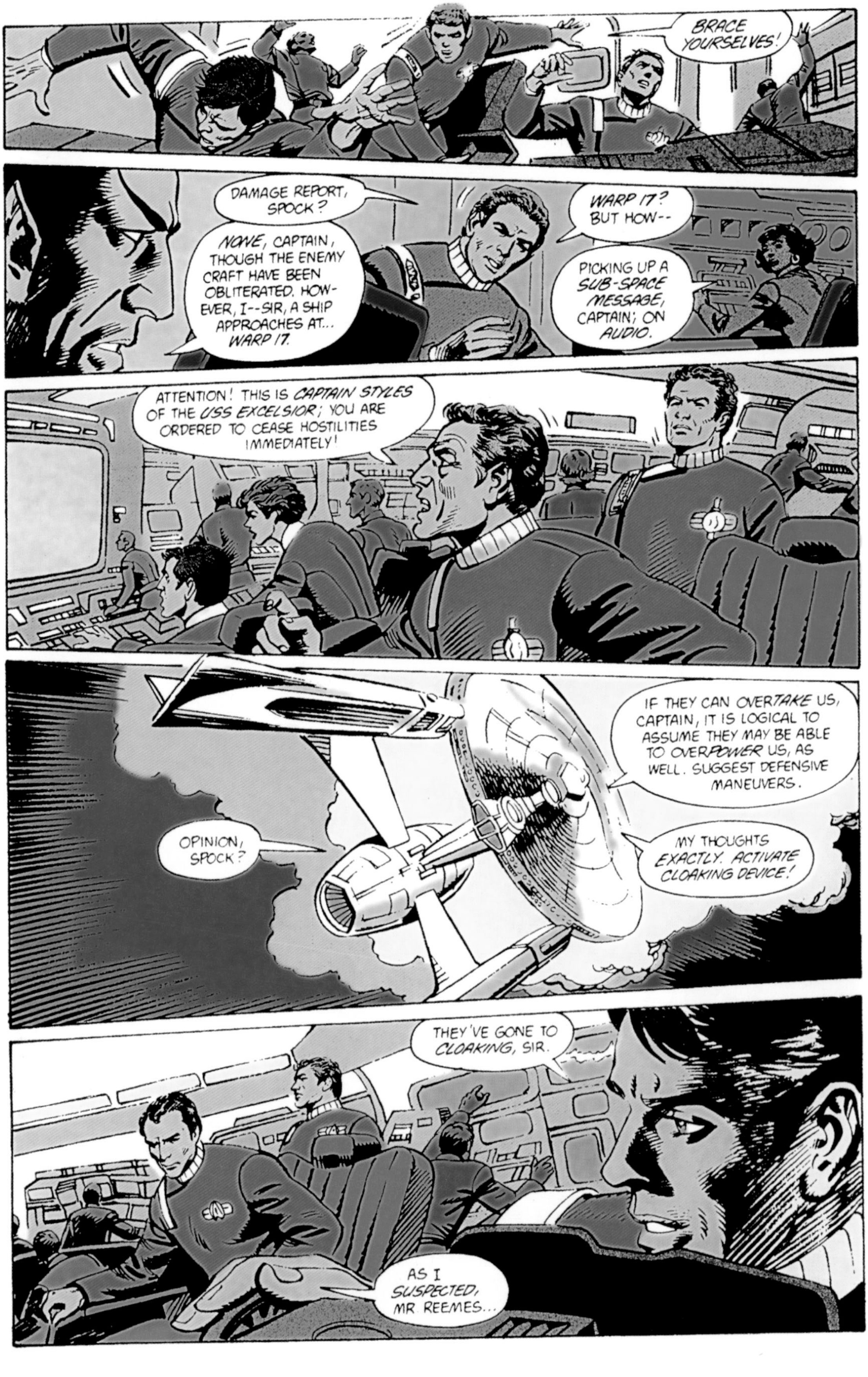
BRACE YOURSELVES!
DAMAGE REPORT, SPOCK?
NONE, CAPTAIN, THOUGH THE ENEMY CRAFT HAVE BEEN OBLITERATED. HOWEVER, I--SIR, A SHIP APPROACHES AT... WARP 17.
WARP 17? BUT HOW--
PICKING UP A SUB-SPACE MESSAGE, CAPTAIN; ON AUDIO.
ATTENTION! THIS IS CAPTAIN STYLES OF THE USS EXCELSIOR; YOU ARE ORDERED TO CEASE HOSTILITIES IMMEDIATELY!
OPINION, SPOCK?
IF THEY CAN OVERTAKE US, CAPTAIN, IT IS LOGICAL TO ASSUME THEY MAY BE ABLE TO OVERPOWER US, AS WELL. SUGGEST DEFENSIVE MANEUVERS.
MY THOUGHTS EXACTLY. ACTIVATE CLOAKING DEVICE!
THEY'VE GONE TO CLOAKING, SIR.
AS I SUSPECTED, MR REEMES...

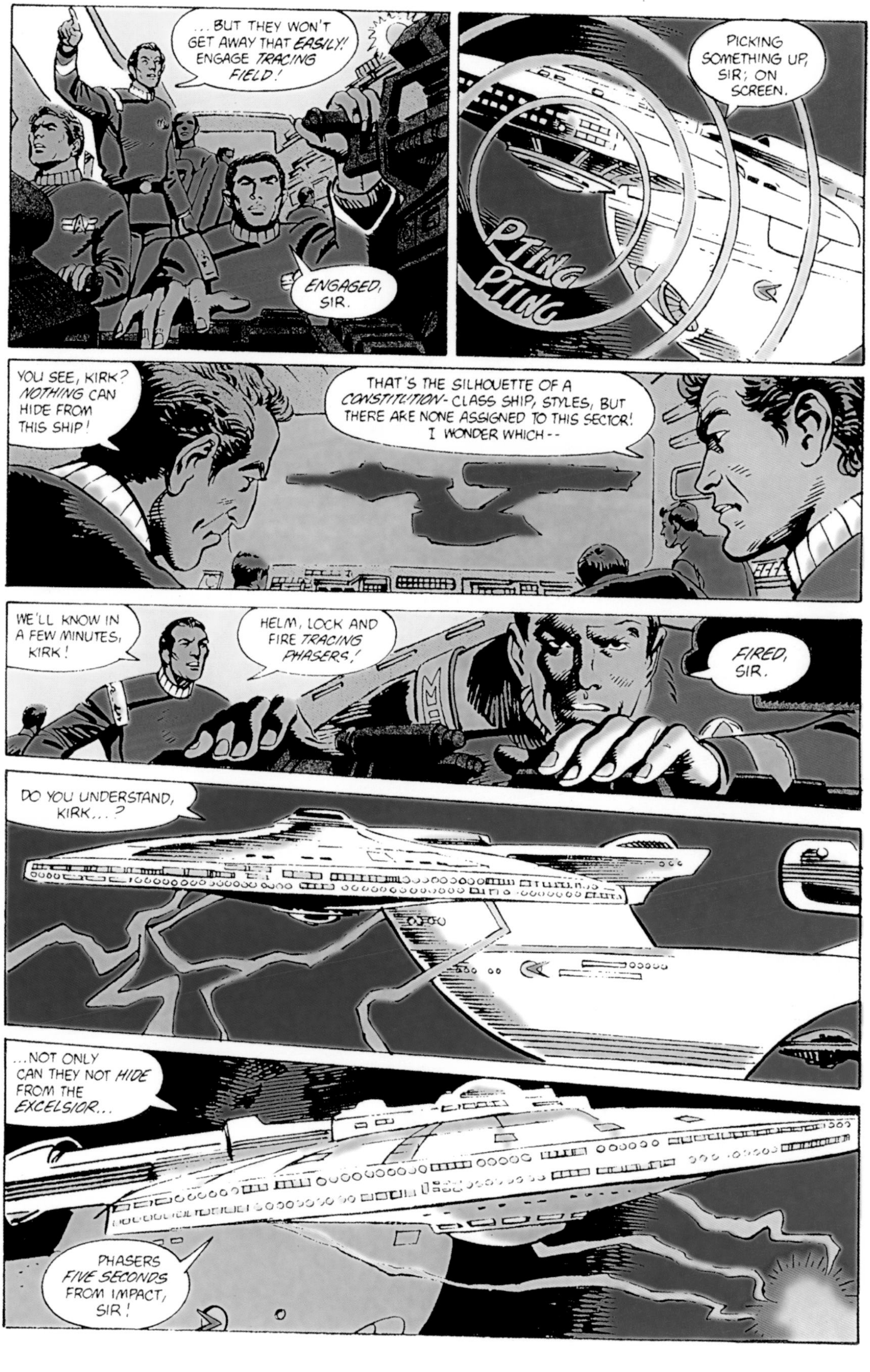
...BUT THEY WON'T GET AWAY THAT EASILY! ENGAGE TRACING FIELD!
ENGAGED, SIR.
PICKING SOMETHING UP, SIR; ON SCREEN.
PTING PTING
YOU SEE, KIRK? NOTHING CAN HIDE FROM THIS SHIP!
THAT'S THE SILHOUETTE OF A CONSTITUTION-CLASS SHIP, STYLES, BUT THERE ARE NONE ASSIGNED TO THIS SECTOR! I WONDER WHICH--
WE'LL KNOW IN A FEW MINUTES, KIRK!
HELM, LOCK AND FIRE TRACING PHASERS!
FIRED, SIR.
DO YOU UNDERSTAND, KIRK...?
...NOT ONLY CAN THEY NOT HIDE FROM THE EXCELSIOR...
PHASERS FIVE SECONDS FROM IMPACT, SIR!

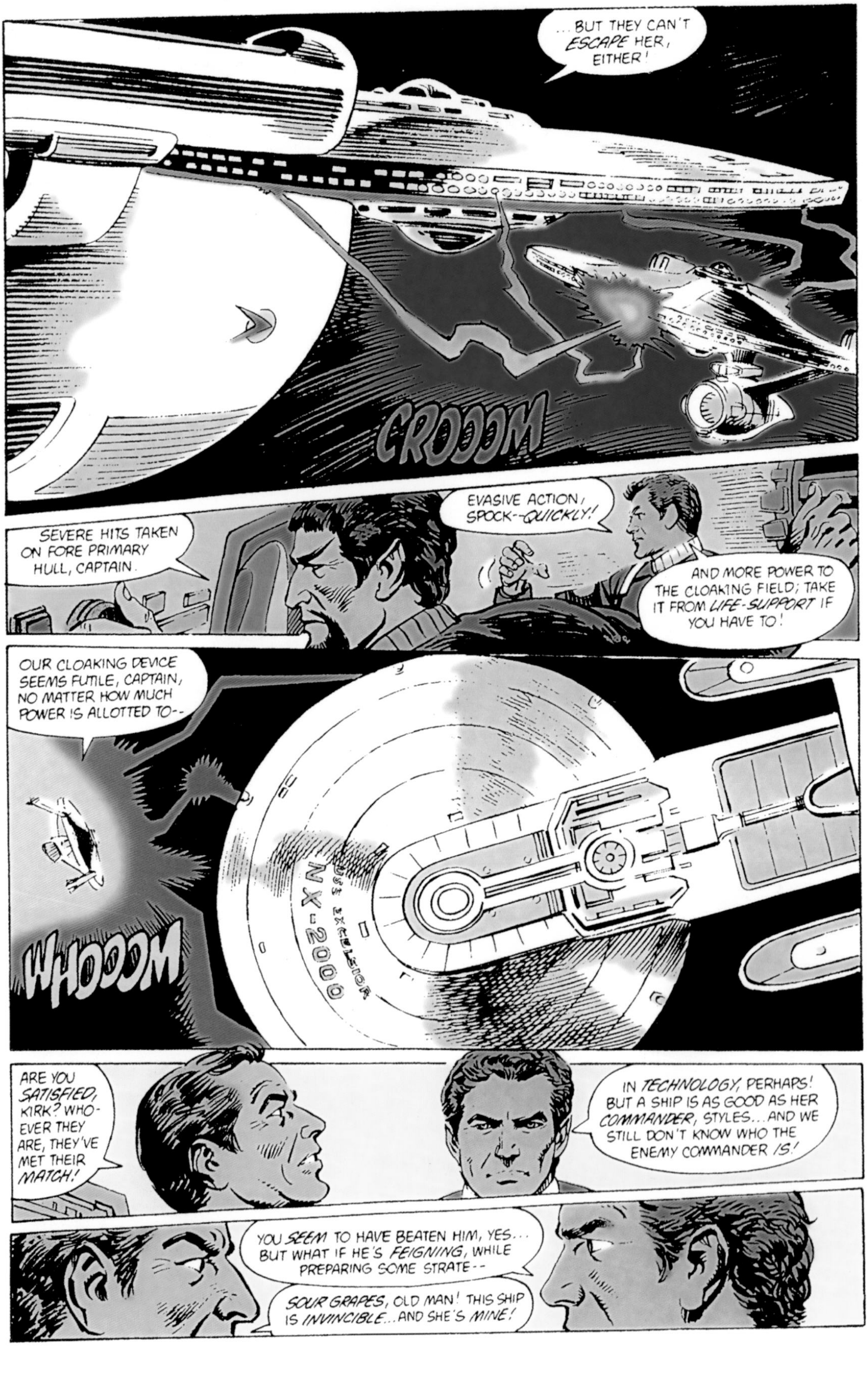
...BUT THEY CAN'T ESCAPE HER, EITHER!
CROOOM
SEVERE HITS TAKEN ON FORE PRIMARY HULL, CAPTAIN.
EVASIVE ACTION, SPOCK--QUICKLY!
AND MORE POWER TO THE CLOAKING FIELD; TAKE IT FROM LIFE-SUPPORT IF YOU HAVE TO!
OUR CLOAKING DEVICE SEEMS FUTILE, CAPTAIN, NO MATTER HOW MUCH POWER IS ALLOTTED TO--
WHOOOM
USS EXCELSIOR
NX-2000
ARE YOU SATISFIED, KIRK? WHOEVER THEY ARE, THEY'VE MET THEIR MATCH!
IN TECHNOLOGY, PERHAPS! BUT A SHIP IS AS GOOD AS HER COMMANDER, STYLES...AND WE STILL DON'T KNOW WHO THE ENEMY COMMANDER IS!
YOU SEEM TO HAVE BEATEN HIM, YES... BUT WHAT IF HE'S FEIGNING, WHILE PREPARING SOME STRATE--
SOUR GRAPES, OLD MAN! THIS SHIP IS INVINCIBLE...AND SHE'S MINE!

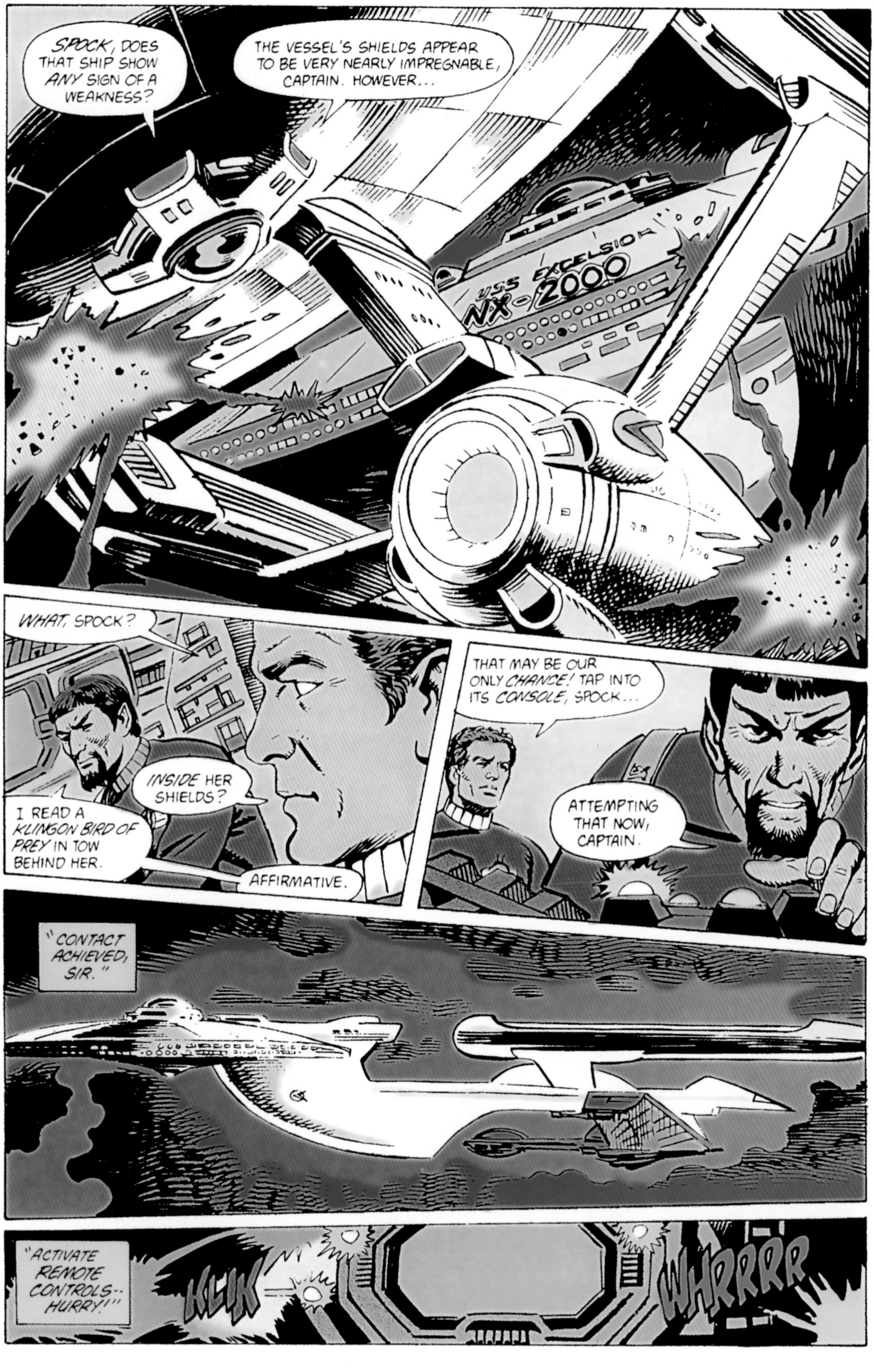
SPOCK, DOES THAT SHIP SHOW ANY SIGN OF A WEAKNESS?
THE VESSEL'S SHIELDS APPEAR TO BE VERY NEARLY IMPREGNABLE, CAPTAIN. HOWEVER...
USS EXCELSIOR
NX-2000
WHAT, SPOCK?
I READ A KLINGON BIRD OF PREY IN TOW BEHIND HER.
INSIDE HER SHIELDS?
AFFIRMATIVE.
THAT MAY BE OUR ONLY CHANCE! TAP INTO ITS CONSOLE, SPOCK...
ATTEMPTING THAT NOW, CAPTAIN.
"CONTACT ACHIEVED, SIR."
"ACTIVATE REMOTE CONTROLS-- HURRY!"
KLIK
WHRRRR

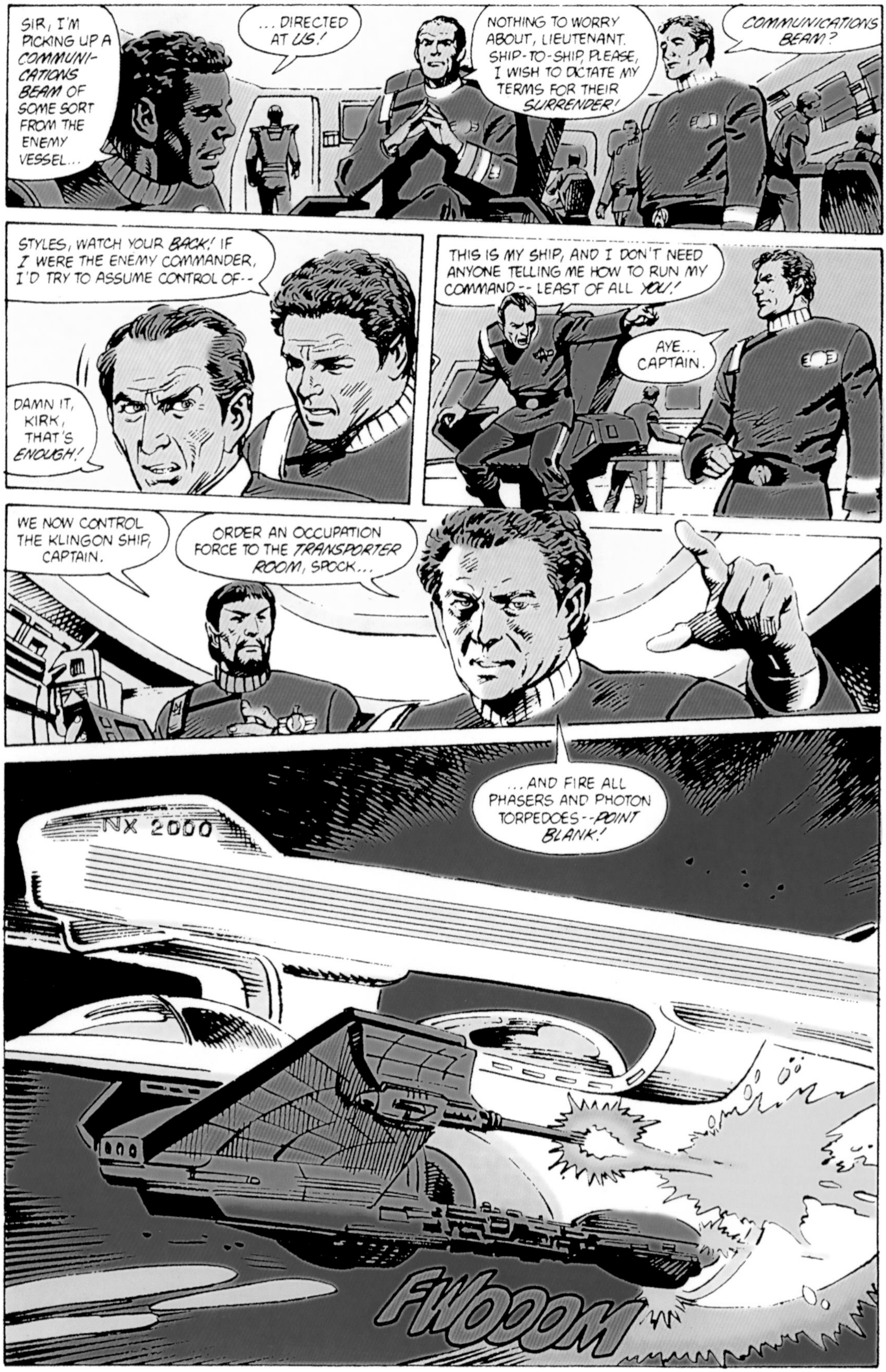
SIR, I'M PICKING UP A COMMUNICATIONS BEAM OF SOME SORT FROM THE ENEMY VESSEL...
...DIRECTED AT US!
NOTHING TO WORRY ABOUT, LIEUTENANT. SHIP-TO-SHIP, PLEASE, I WISH TO DICTATE MY TERMS FOR THEIR SURRENDER!
COMMUNICATIONS BEAM?
STYLES, WATCH YOUR BACK! IF I WERE THE ENEMY COMMANDER, I'D TRY TO ASSUME CONTROL OF--
DAMN IT, KIRK, THAT'S ENOUGH!
THIS IS MY SHIP, AND I DON'T NEED ANYONE TELLING ME HOW TO RUN MY COMMAND--LEAST OF ALL YOU!
AYE... CAPTAIN.
WE NOW CONTROL THE KLINGON SHIP, CAPTAIN.
ORDER AN OCCUPATION FORCE TO THE TRANSPORTER ROOM, SPOCK...
...AND FIRE ALL PHASERS AND PHOTON TORPEDOES--POINT BLANK!
NX 2000
FWOOOM

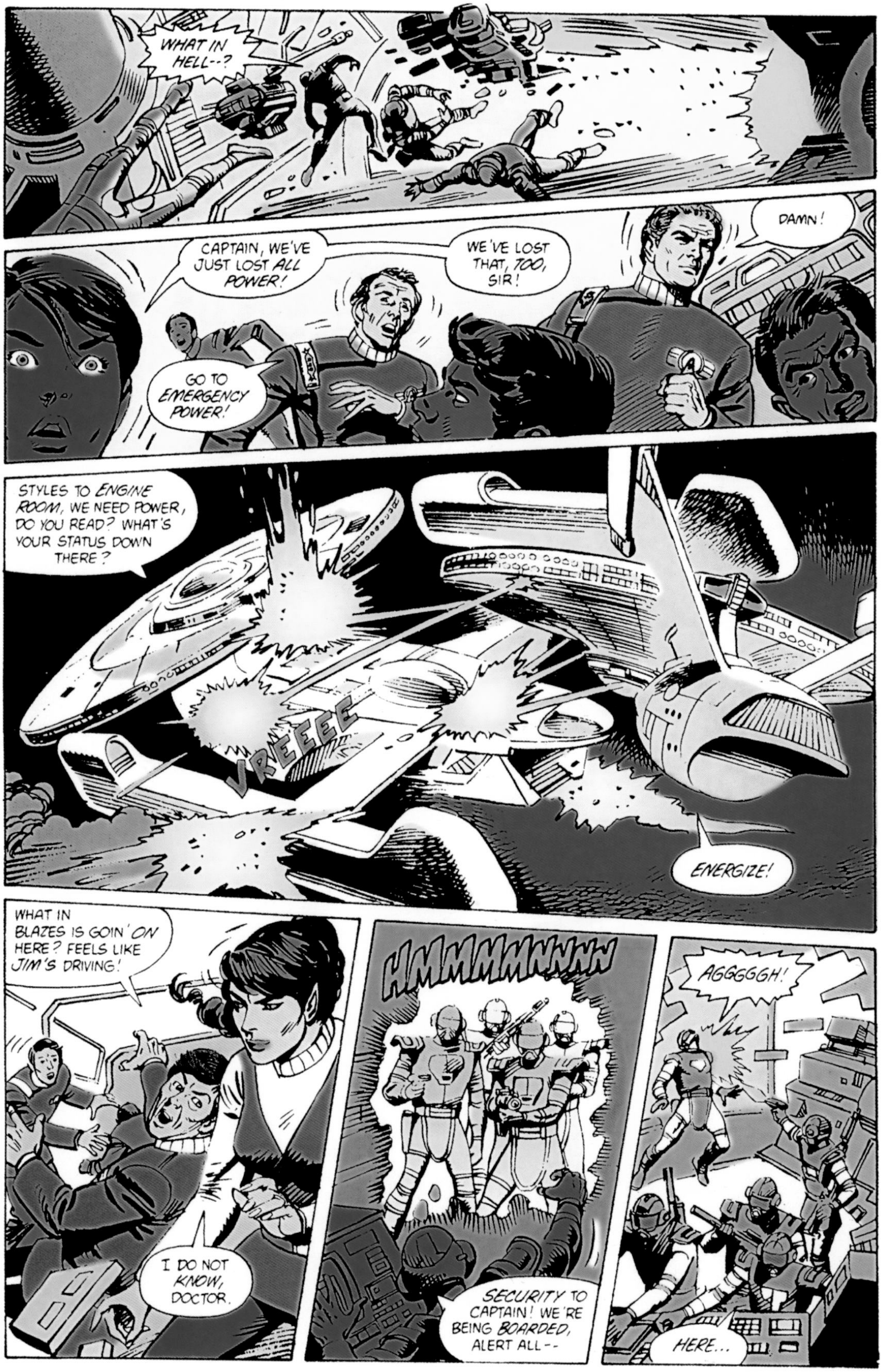
WHAT IN HELL--?
CAPTAIN, WE'VE JUST LOST ALL POWER!
GO TO EMERGENCY POWER!
WE'VE LOST THAT, TOO, SIR!
DAMN!
STYLES TO ENGINE ROOM, WE NEED POWER, DO YOU READ? WHAT'S YOUR STATUS DOWN THERE?
VREEEE
ENERGIZE!
WHAT IN BLAZES IS GOIN' ON HERE? FEELS LIKE JIM'S DRIVING!
I DO NOT KNOW, DOCTOR.
HMMMMNNNN
SECURITY TO CAPTAIN! WE'RE BEING BOARDED, ALERT ALL--
AGGGGGH!
HERE...

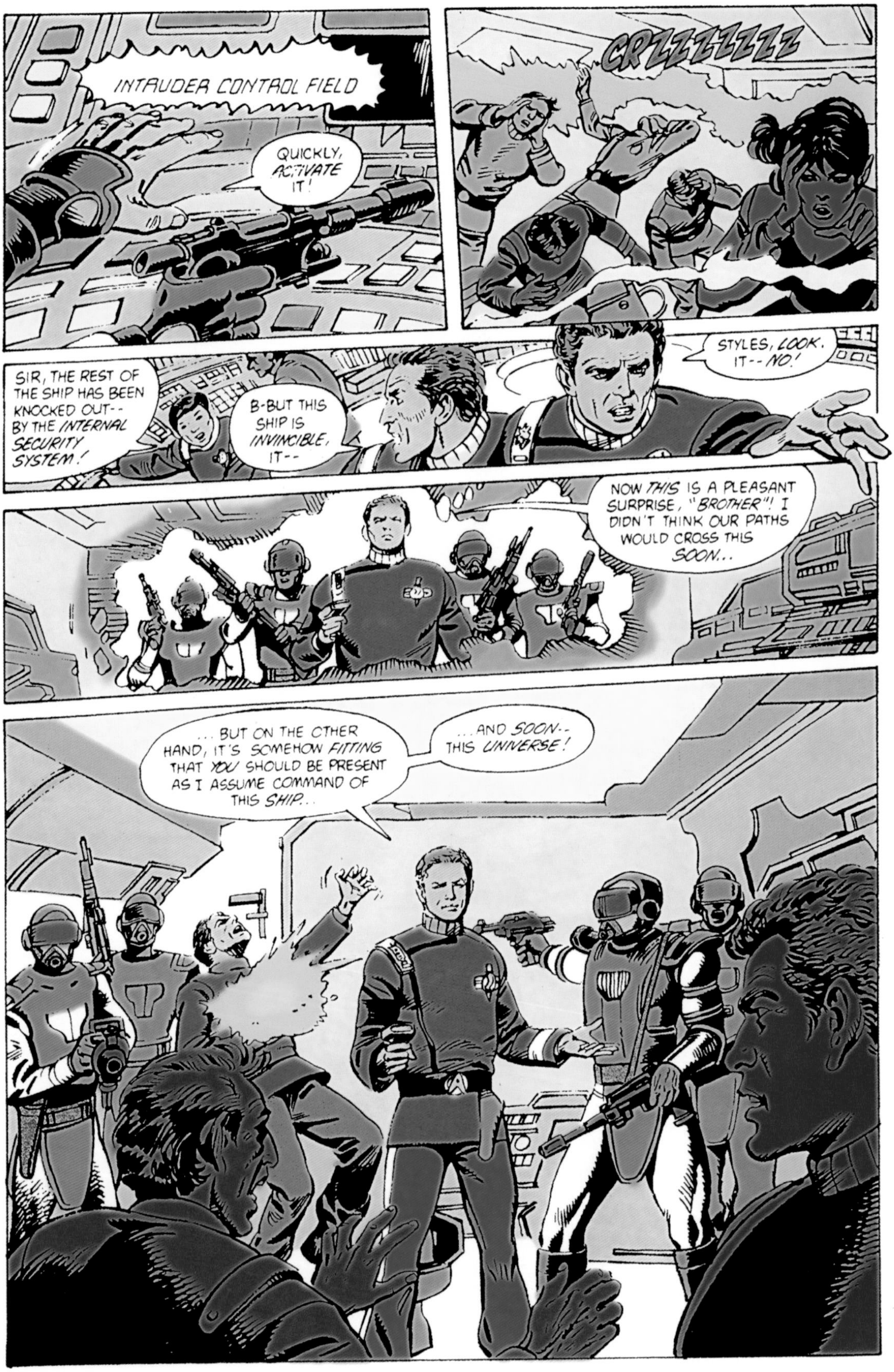
INTRUDER CONTROL FIELD
QUICKLY, ACTIVATE IT!
CRZZZZZZZ
SIR, THE REST OF THE SHIP HAS BEEN KNOCKED OUT-- BY THE INTERNAL SECURITY SYSTEM!
B-BUT THIS SHIP IS INVINCIBLE, IT--
STYLES, LOOK. IT--NO!
NOW THIS IS A PLEASANT SURPRISE, "BROTHER"! I DIDN'T THINK OUR PATHS WOULD CROSS THIS SOON...
...BUT ON THE OTHER HAND, IT'S SOMEHOW FITTING THAT YOU SHOULD BE PRESENT AS I ASSUME COMMAND OF THIS SHIP...
...AND SOON-- THIS UNIVERSE!

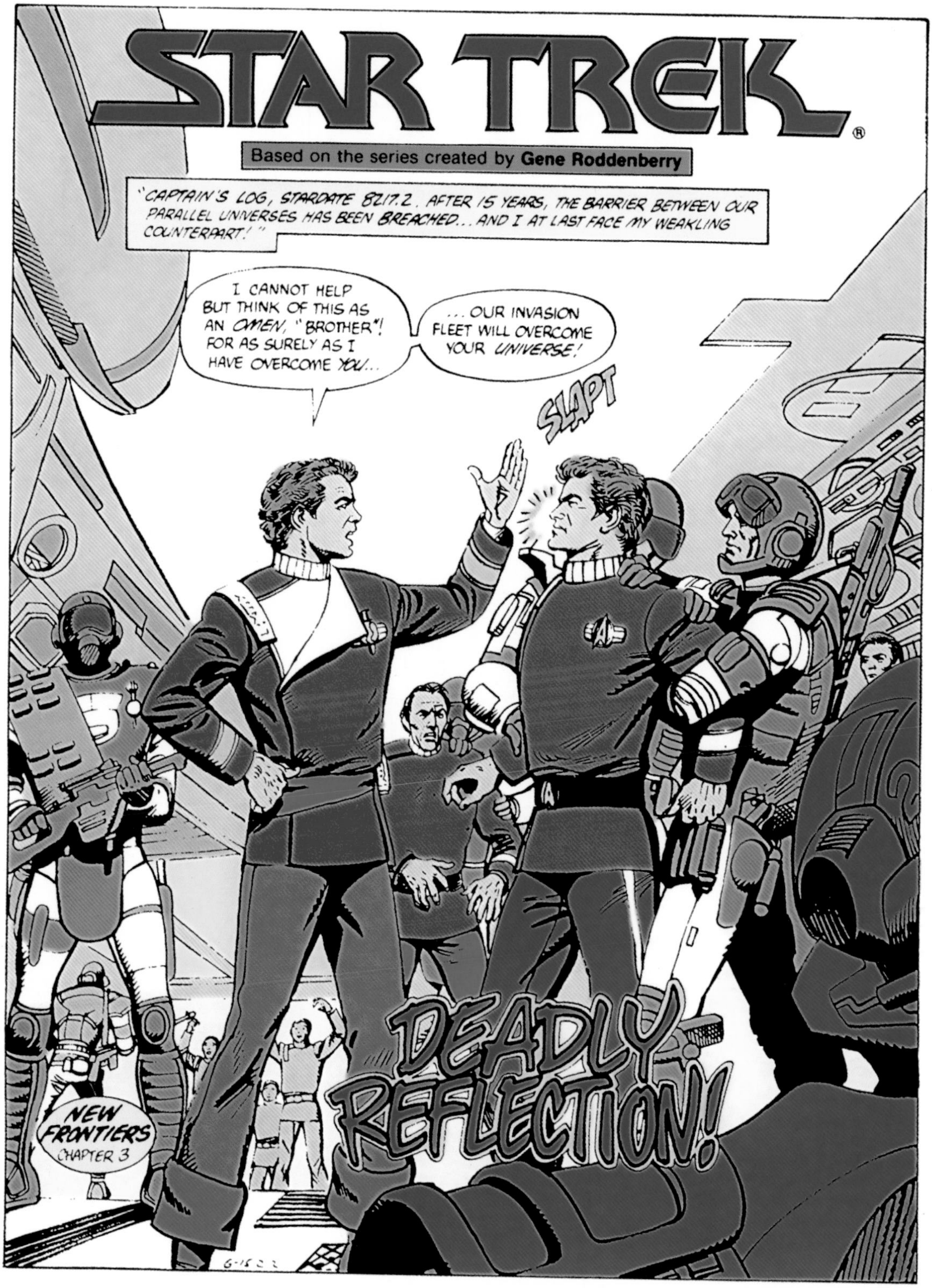
STAR TREK®
Based on the series created by Gene Roddenberry
"CAPTAIN'S LOG, STARDATE 8217.2. AFTER 15 YEARS, THE BARRIER BETWEEN OUR PARALLEL UNIVERSES HAS BEEN BREACHED... AND I AT LAST FACE MY WEAKLING COUNTERPART!"
I CANNOT HELP BUT THINK OF THIS AS AN OMEN, "BROTHER"! FOR AS SURELY AS I HAVE OVERCOME YOU...
...OUR INVASION FLEET WILL OVERCOME YOUR UNIVERSE!
SLAPT
NEW FRONTIERS CHAPTER 3
DEADLY REFLECTION!

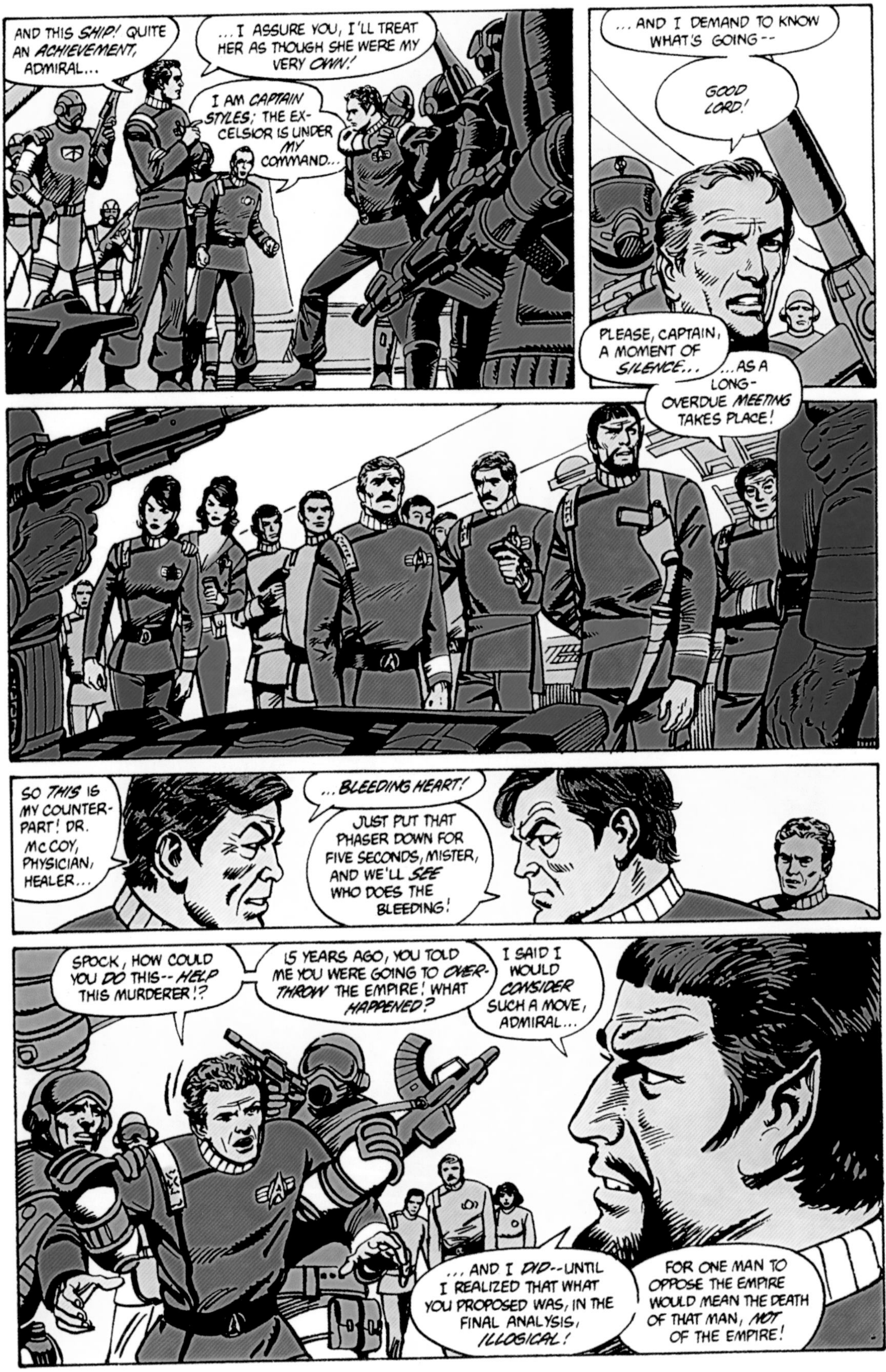
AND THIS SHIP! QUITE AN ACHIEVEMENT, ADMIRAL...
...I ASSURE YOU, I'LL TREAT HER AS THOUGH SHE WERE MY VERY OWN!
I AM CAPTAIN STYLES; THE EXCELSIOR IS UNDER MY COMMAND...
...AND I DEMAND TO KNOW WHAT'S GOING--
GOOD LORD!
PLEASE, CAPTAIN, A MOMENT OF SILENCE...
...AS A LONG-OVERDUE MEETING TAKES PLACE!
SO THIS IS MY COUNTERPART! DR. McCOY, PHYSICIAN, HEALER...
...BLEEDING HEART!
JUST PUT THAT PHASER DOWN FOR FIVE SECONDS, MISTER, AND WE'LL SEE WHO DOES THE BLEEDING!
SPOCK, HOW COULD YOU DO THIS--HELP THIS MURDERER!?
15 YEARS AGO, YOU TOLD ME YOU WERE GOING TO OVERTHROW THE EMPIRE! WHAT HAPPENED?
I SAID I WOULD CONSIDER SUCH A MOVE, ADMIRAL...
...AND I DID--UNTIL I REALIZED THAT WHAT YOU PROPOSED WAS, IN THE FINAL ANALYSIS, ILLOGICAL!
FOR ONE MAN TO OPPOSE THE EMPIRE WOULD MEAN THE DEATH OF THAT MAN, NOT OF THE EMPIRE!

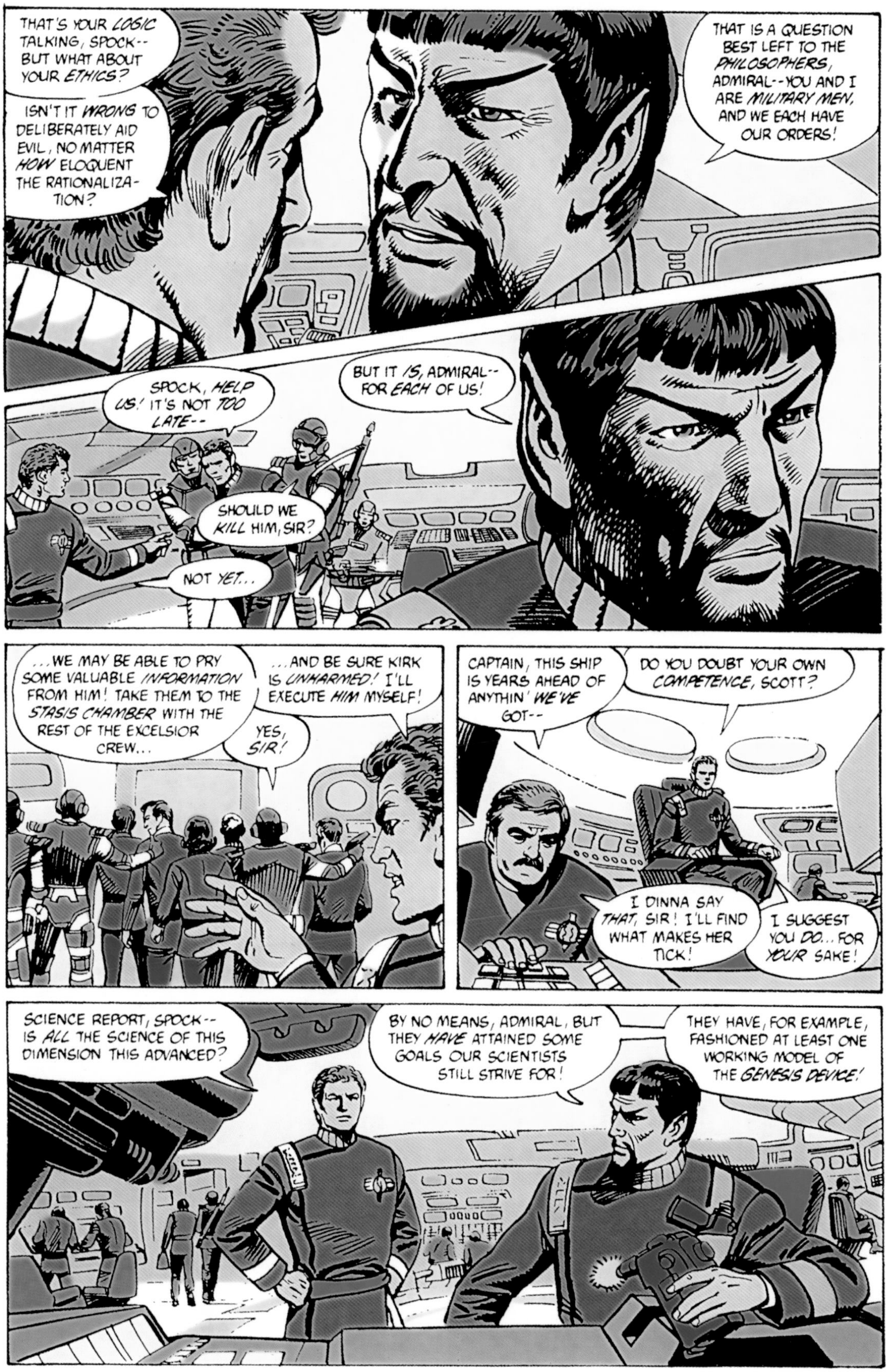
THAT'S YOUR LOGIC TALKING, SPOCK-- BUT WHAT ABOUT YOUR ETHICS?
ISN'T IT WRONG TO DELIBERATELY AID EVIL, NO MATTER HOW ELOQUENT THE RATIONALIZATION?
THAT IS A QUESTION BEST LEFT TO THE PHILOSOPHERS, ADMIRAL--YOU AND I ARE MILITARY MEN, AND WE EACH HAVE OUR ORDERS!
SPOCK, HELP US! IT'S NOT TOO LATE--
BUT IT IS, ADMIRAL-- FOR EACH OF US!
SHOULD WE KILL HIM, SIR?
NOT YET...
...WE MAY BE ABLE TO PRY SOME VALUABLE INFORMATION FROM HIM! TAKE THEM TO THE STASIS CHAMBER WITH THE REST OF THE EXCELSIOR CREW...
...AND BE SURE KIRK IS UNHARMED! I'LL EXECUTE HIM MYSELF!
YES, SIR!
CAPTAIN, THIS SHIP IS YEARS AHEAD OF ANYTHIN' WE'VE GOT--
DO YOU DOUBT YOUR OWN COMPETENCE, SCOTT?
I DINNA SAY THAT, SIR! I'LL FIND WHAT MAKES HER TICK!
I SUGGEST YOU DO... FOR YOUR SAKE!
SCIENCE REPORT, SPOCK-- IS ALL THE SCIENCE OF THIS DIMENSION THIS ADVANCED?
BY NO MEANS, ADMIRAL, BUT THEY HAVE ATTAINED SOME GOALS OUR SCIENTISTS STILL STRIVE FOR!
THEY HAVE, FOR EXAMPLE, FASHIONED AT LEAST ONE WORKING MODEL OF THE GENESIS DEVICE!

GENESIS! SPOCK, SHOW ME!

THE SALIENT DATA IS CONTAINED IN A TOP-SECURITY REPORT FILED, I BELIEVE, BY YOUR *COUNTERPART*, CAPTAIN...

...IT WAS THE PREMATURE DETONATION OF THE DEVICE THAT RESULTED IN THE CREATION OF THE GENESIS PLANET...

TO FULLY UNDER-STAND THE EVENTS ON WHICH I REPORT, IT IS NECESSARY TO REVIEW THE THEORETICAL DATA ON THE GENESIS DEVICE...

THE GENESIS PLANET? SPOCK, THE RECORD TAPES OF THE KLINGON BIRD OF PREY REPORT THAT THE GENESIS PLANET *SELF-DESTRUCTED*!

TRUE, CAPTAIN...

...BUT THOSE SAME TAPES REVEAL THAT THE GENESIS PLANET REVIVED THIS DIMENSION'S *SPOCK*...

...AND THAT SPOCK'S GENES MAY YET CARRY THE SECRET OF GENESIS!

PRECISELY...

...BUT THE RISK OF RETRIEVING HIM WOULD BE CONSIDERABLE.

BUT *WORTH* IT, SPOCK! WHERE *IS* YOUR COUNTERPART?

ON *VULCAN*, CAPTAIN.

THEN IT'S OBVIOUS THAT *YOU* ARE THE BEST MAN TO RETRIEVE HIM, SPOCK...

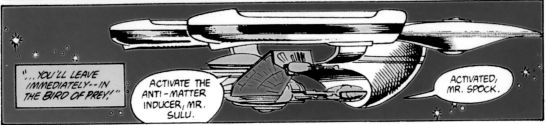

"...YOU'LL LEAVE IMMEDIATELY--IN THE BIRD OF PREY!"

ACTIVATE THE ANTI-MATTER INDUCER, MR. SULU.

ACTIVATED, MR. SPOCK.

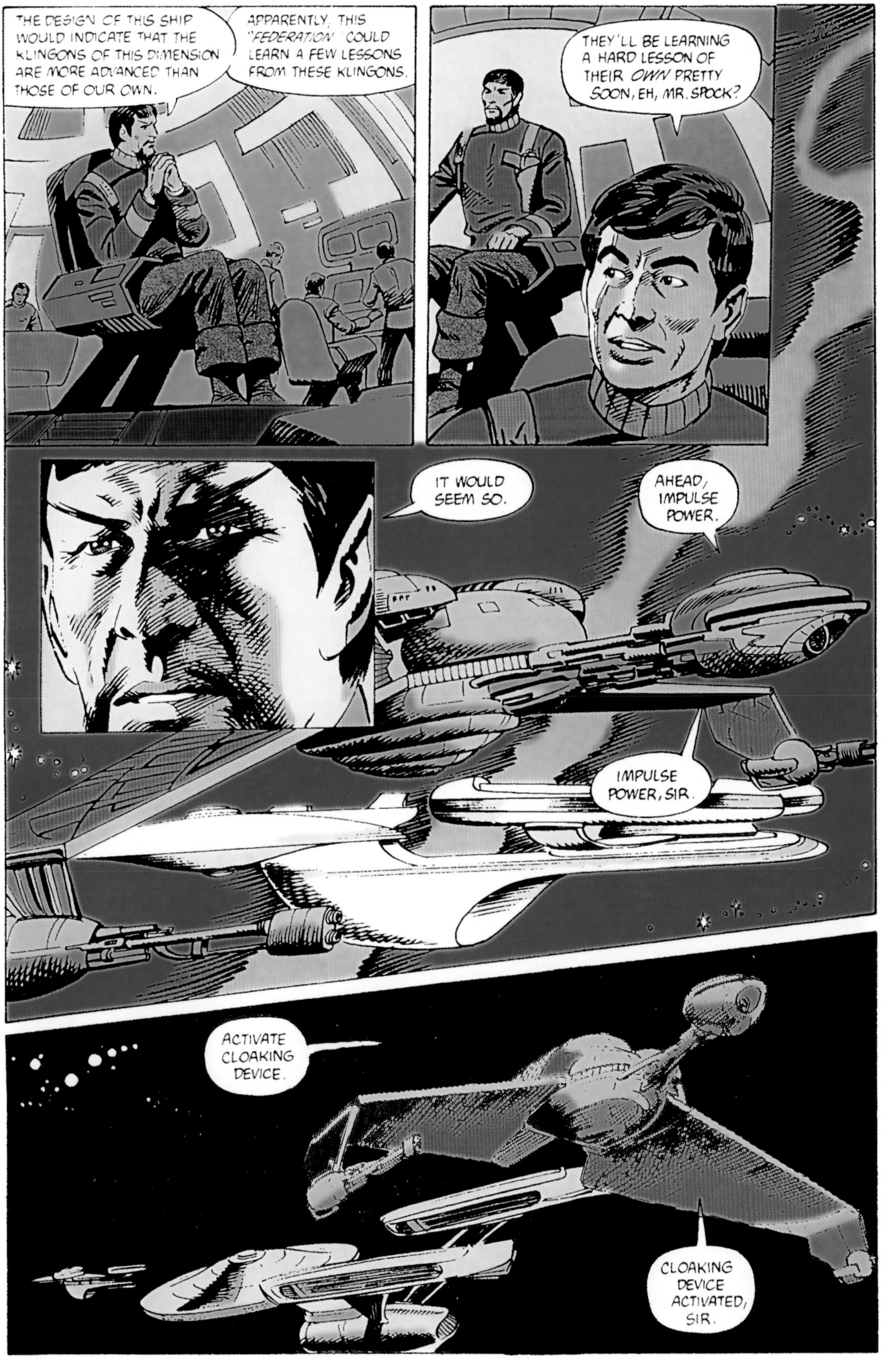
THE DESIGN OF THIS SHIP WOULD INDICATE THAT THE KLINGONS OF THIS DIMENSION ARE MORE ADVANCED THAN THOSE OF OUR OWN.
APPARENTLY, THIS "FEDERATION" COULD LEARN A FEW LESSONS FROM THESE KLINGONS.
THEY'LL BE LEARNING A HARD LESSON OF THEIR OWN PRETTY SOON, EH, MR. SPOCK?
IT WOULD SEEM SO.
AHEAD, IMPULSE POWER.
IMPULSE POWER, SIR.
ACTIVATE CLOAKING DEVICE.
CLOAKING DEVICE ACTIVATED, SIR.

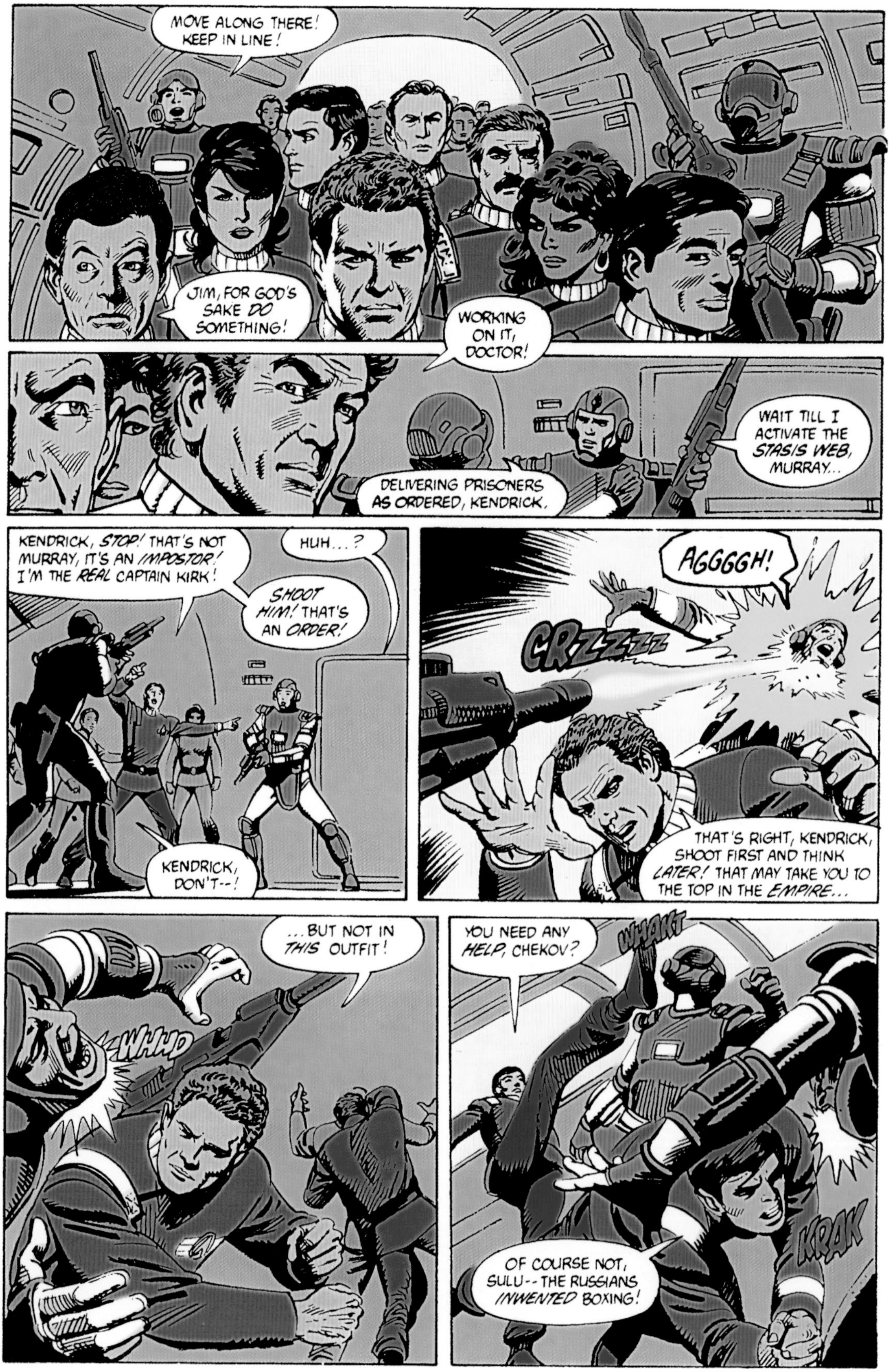
MOVE ALONG THERE! KEEP IN LINE!
JIM, FOR GOD'S SAKE DO SOMETHING!
WORKING ON IT, DOCTOR!
DELIVERING PRISONERS AS ORDERED, KENDRICK.
WAIT TILL I ACTIVATE THE STASIS WEB, MURRAY...
KENDRICK, STOP! THAT'S NOT MURRAY, IT'S AN IMPOSTOR! I'M THE REAL CAPTAIN KIRK!
HUH...?
SHOOT HIM! THAT'S AN ORDER!
KENDRICK, DON'T--!
AGGGGH!
CRZZZZZ
THAT'S RIGHT, KENDRICK, SHOOT FIRST AND THINK LATER! THAT MAY TAKE YOU TO THE TOP IN THE EMPIRE...
...BUT NOT IN THIS OUTFIT!
WHUD
YOU NEED ANY HELP, CHEKOV?
WHAKT
OF COURSE NOT, SULU--THE RUSSIANS INWENTED BOXING!
KRAK

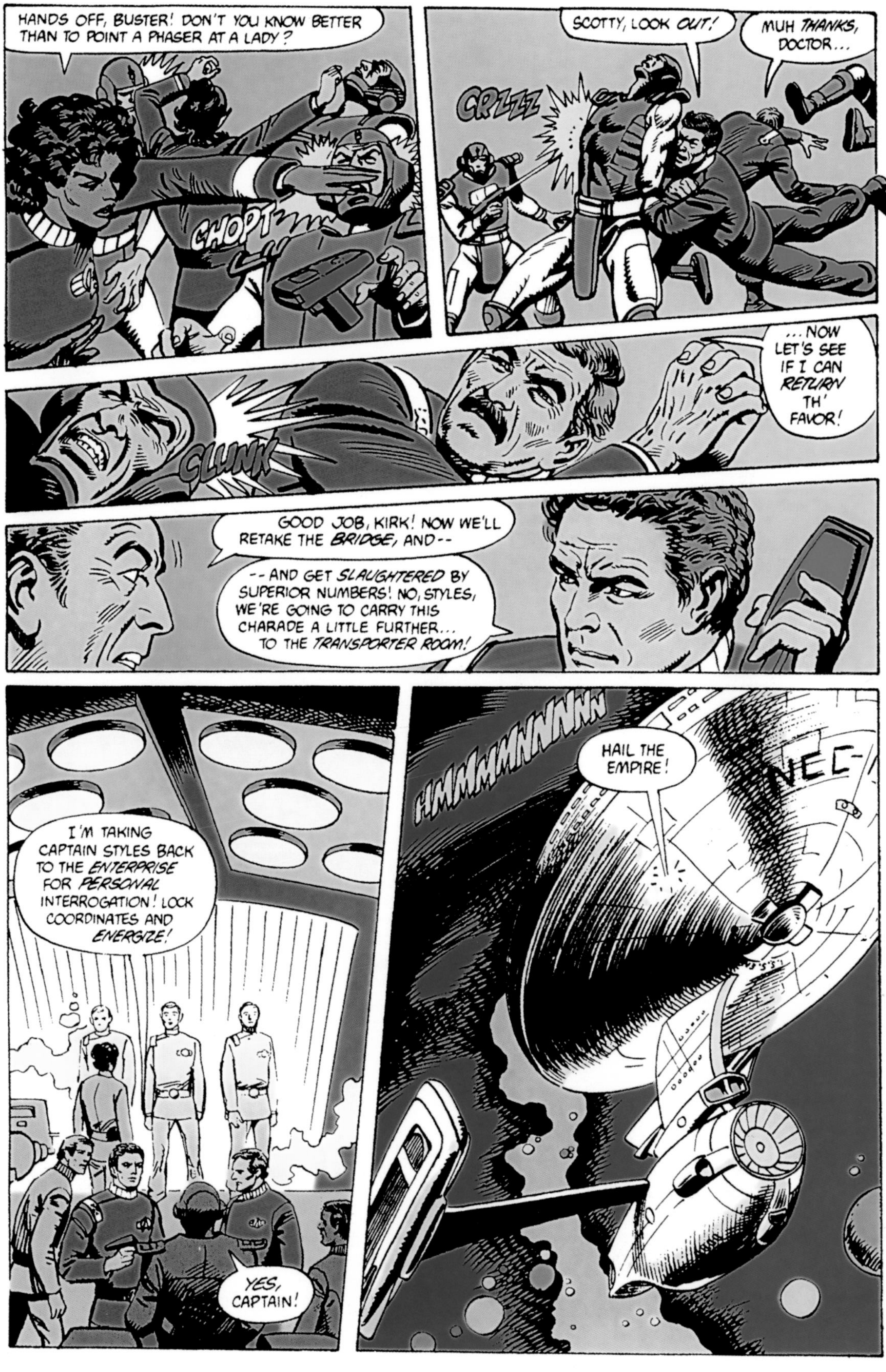
HANDS OFF, BUSTER! DON'T YOU KNOW BETTER THAN TO POINT A PHASER AT A LADY?
CHOPT
SCOTTY, LOOK OUT!
CRZZZ
MUH THANKS, DOCTOR...
...NOW LET'S SEE IF I CAN RETURN TH' FAVOR!
CLUNK
GOOD JOB, KIRK! NOW WE'LL RETAKE THE BRIDGE, AND--
--AND GET SLAUGHTERED BY SUPERIOR NUMBERS! NO, STYLES, WE'RE GOING TO CARRY THIS CHARADE A LITTLE FURTHER... TO THE TRANSPORTER ROOM!
I'M TAKING CAPTAIN STYLES BACK TO THE ENTERPRISE FOR PERSONAL INTERROGATION! LOCK COORDINATES AND ENERGIZE!
YES, CAPTAIN!
HMMMMNNNNN
HAIL THE EMPIRE!
NCC-

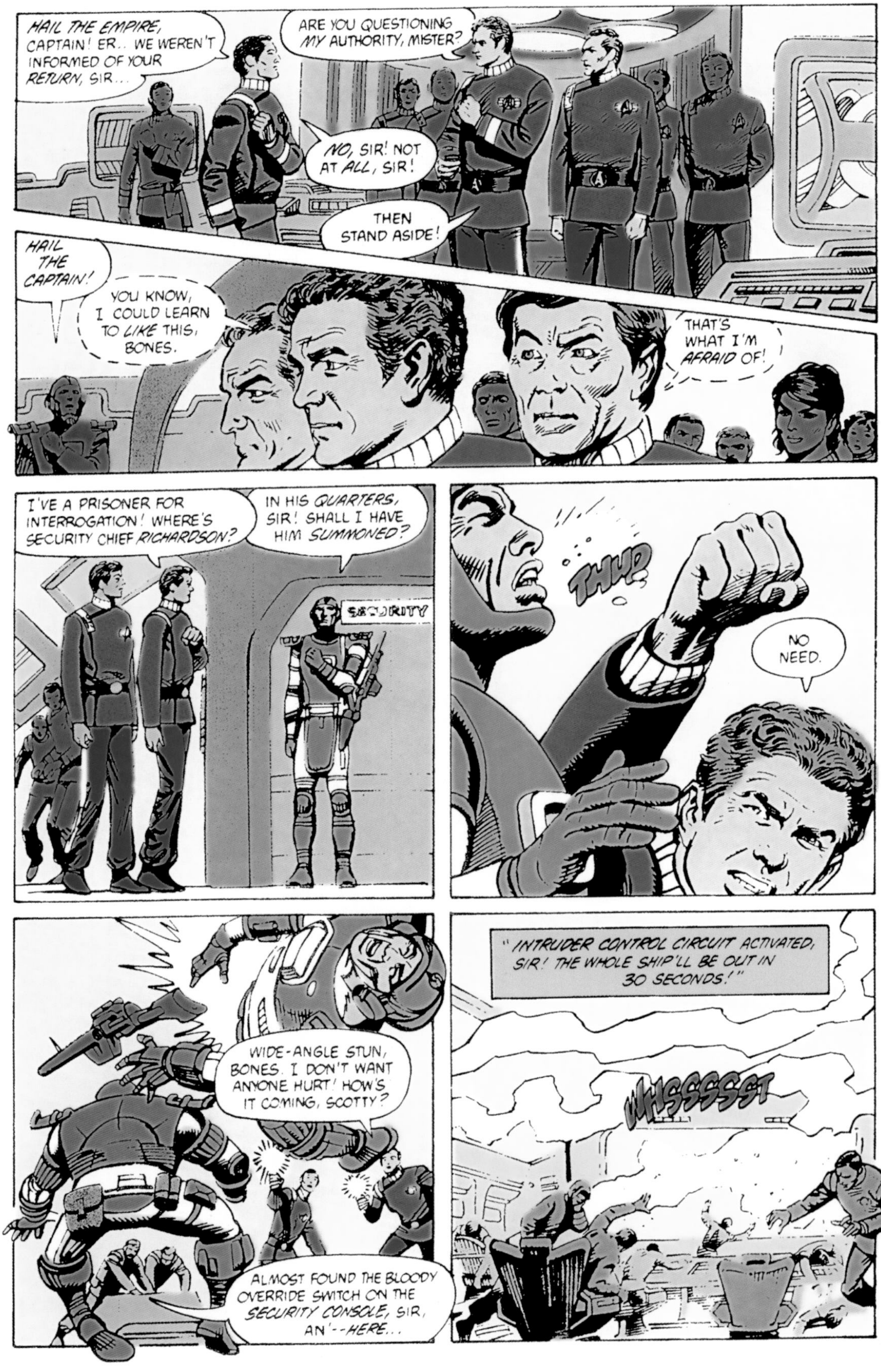
HAIL THE EMPIRE, CAPTAIN! ER.. WE WEREN'T INFORMED OF YOUR RETURN, SIR...
ARE YOU QUESTIONING MY AUTHORITY, MISTER?
NO, SIR! NOT AT ALL, SIR!
THEN STAND ASIDE!
HAIL THE CAPTAIN!
YOU KNOW, I COULD LEARN TO LIKE THIS, BONES.
THAT'S WHAT I'M AFRAID OF!
I'VE A PRISONER FOR INTERROGATION! WHERE'S SECURITY CHIEF RICHARDSON?
IN HIS QUARTERS, SIR! SHALL I HAVE HIM SUMMONED?
SECURITY
THUD
NO NEED.
WIDE-ANGLE STUN, BONES. I DON'T WANT ANYONE HURT! HOW'S IT COMING, SCOTTY?
ALMOST FOUND THE BLOODY OVERRIDE SWITCH ON THE SECURITY CONSOLE, SIR, AN'--HERE...
"INTRUDER CONTROL CIRCUIT ACTIVATED, SIR! THE WHOLE SHIP'LL BE OUT IN 30 SECONDS!"
WHSSSSST

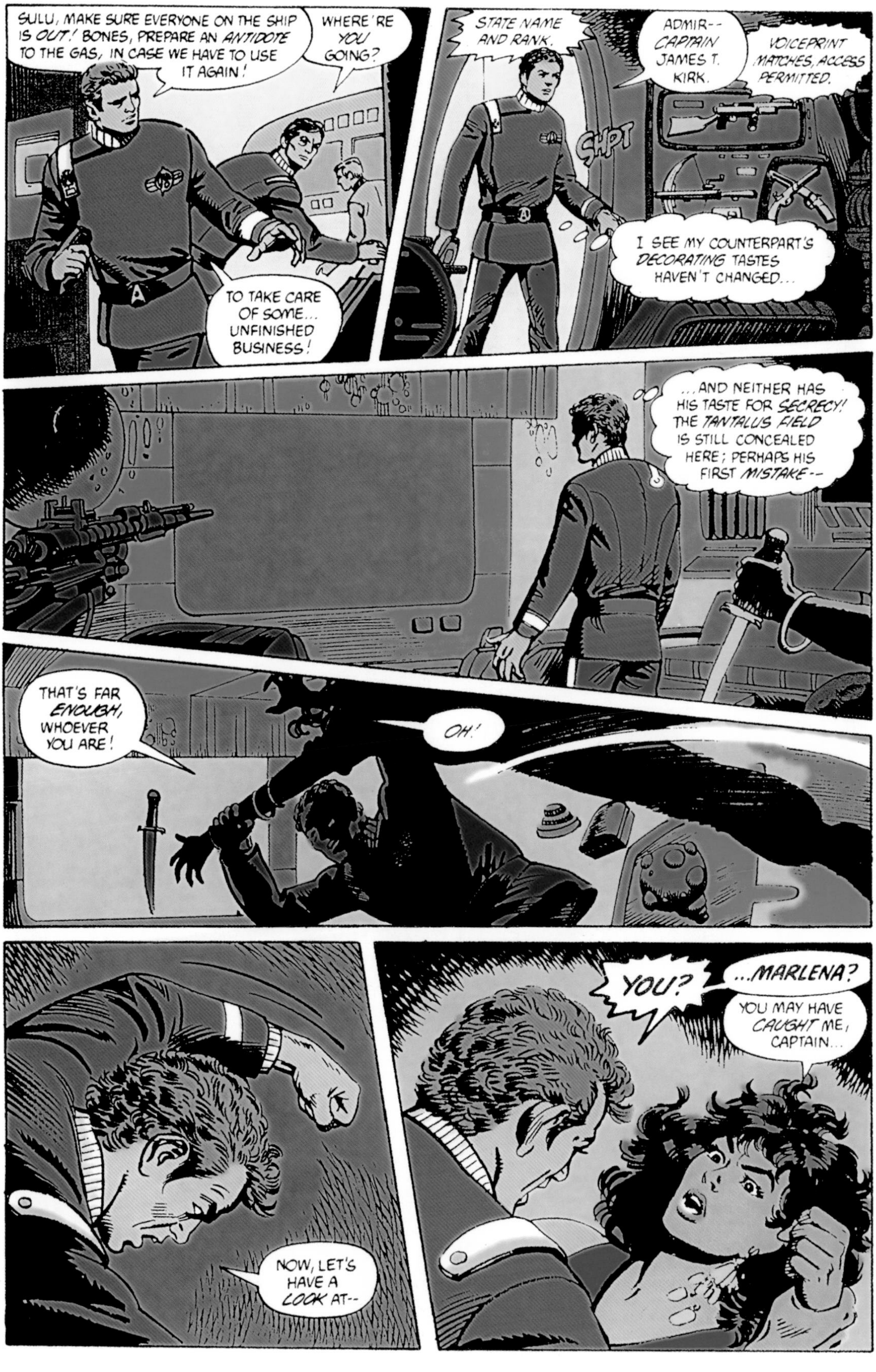
SULU, MAKE SURE EVERYONE ON THE SHIP IS OUT! BONES, PREPARE AN ANTIDOTE TO THE GAS, IN CASE WE HAVE TO USE IT AGAIN!
WHERE'RE YOU GOING?
TO TAKE CARE OF SOME... UNFINISHED BUSINESS!
STATE NAME AND RANK.
ADMIR-- CAPTAIN JAMES T. KIRK.
VOICEPRINT MATCHES, ACCESS PERMITTED.
SHPT
I SEE MY COUNTERPART'S DECORATING TASTES HAVEN'T CHANGED...
...AND NEITHER HAS HIS TASTE FOR SECRECY! THE TANTALUS FIELD IS STILL CONCEALED HERE; PERHAPS HIS FIRST MISTAKE--
THAT'S FAR ENOUGH, WHOEVER YOU ARE!
OH!
NOW, LET'S HAVE A LOOK AT--
YOU?
...MARLENA?
YOU MAY HAVE CAUGHT ME, CAPTAIN...

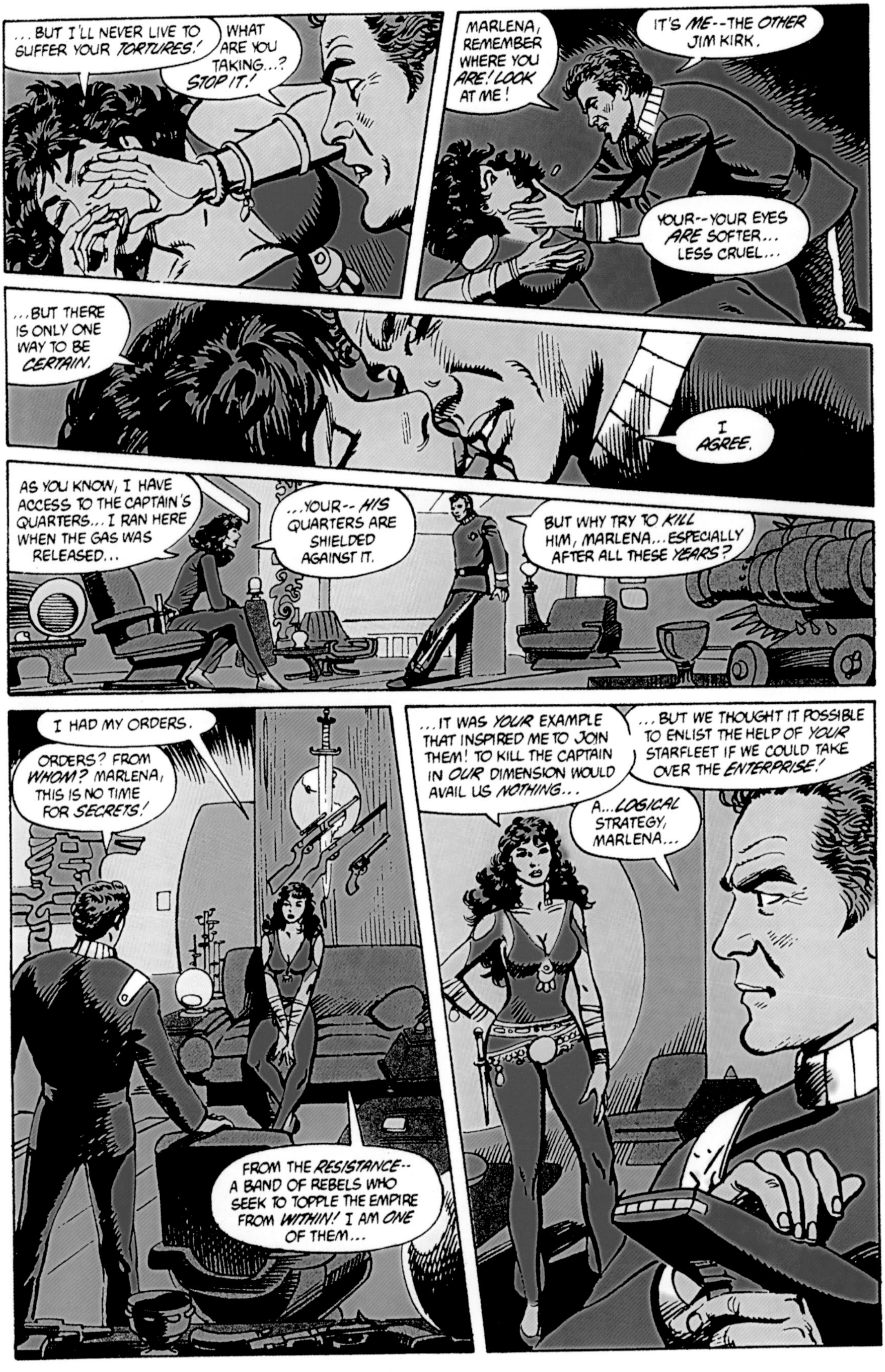
...BUT I'LL NEVER LIVE TO SUFFER YOUR TORTURES!
WHAT ARE YOU TAKING...? STOP IT!
MARLENA, REMEMBER WHERE YOU ARE! LOOK AT ME!
IT'S ME--THE OTHER JIM KIRK.
YOUR--YOUR EYES ARE SOFTER... LESS CRUEL...
...BUT THERE IS ONLY ONE WAY TO BE CERTAIN.
I AGREE.
AS YOU KNOW, I HAVE ACCESS TO THE CAPTAIN'S QUARTERS... I RAN HERE WHEN THE GAS WAS RELEASED...
...YOUR-- HIS QUARTERS ARE SHIELDED AGAINST IT.
BUT WHY TRY TO KILL HIM, MARLENA... ESPECIALLY AFTER ALL THESE YEARS?
I HAD MY ORDERS.
ORDERS? FROM WHOM? MARLENA, THIS IS NO TIME FOR SECRETS!
FROM THE RESISTANCE-- A BAND OF REBELS WHO SEEK TO TOPPLE THE EMPIRE FROM WITHIN! I AM ONE OF THEM...
...IT WAS YOUR EXAMPLE THAT INSPIRED ME TO JOIN THEM! TO KILL THE CAPTAIN IN OUR DIMENSION WOULD AVAIL US NOTHING...
...BUT WE THOUGHT IT POSSIBLE TO ENLIST THE HELP OF YOUR STARFLEET IF WE COULD TAKE OVER THE ENTERPRISE!
A...LOGICAL STRATEGY, MARLENA...

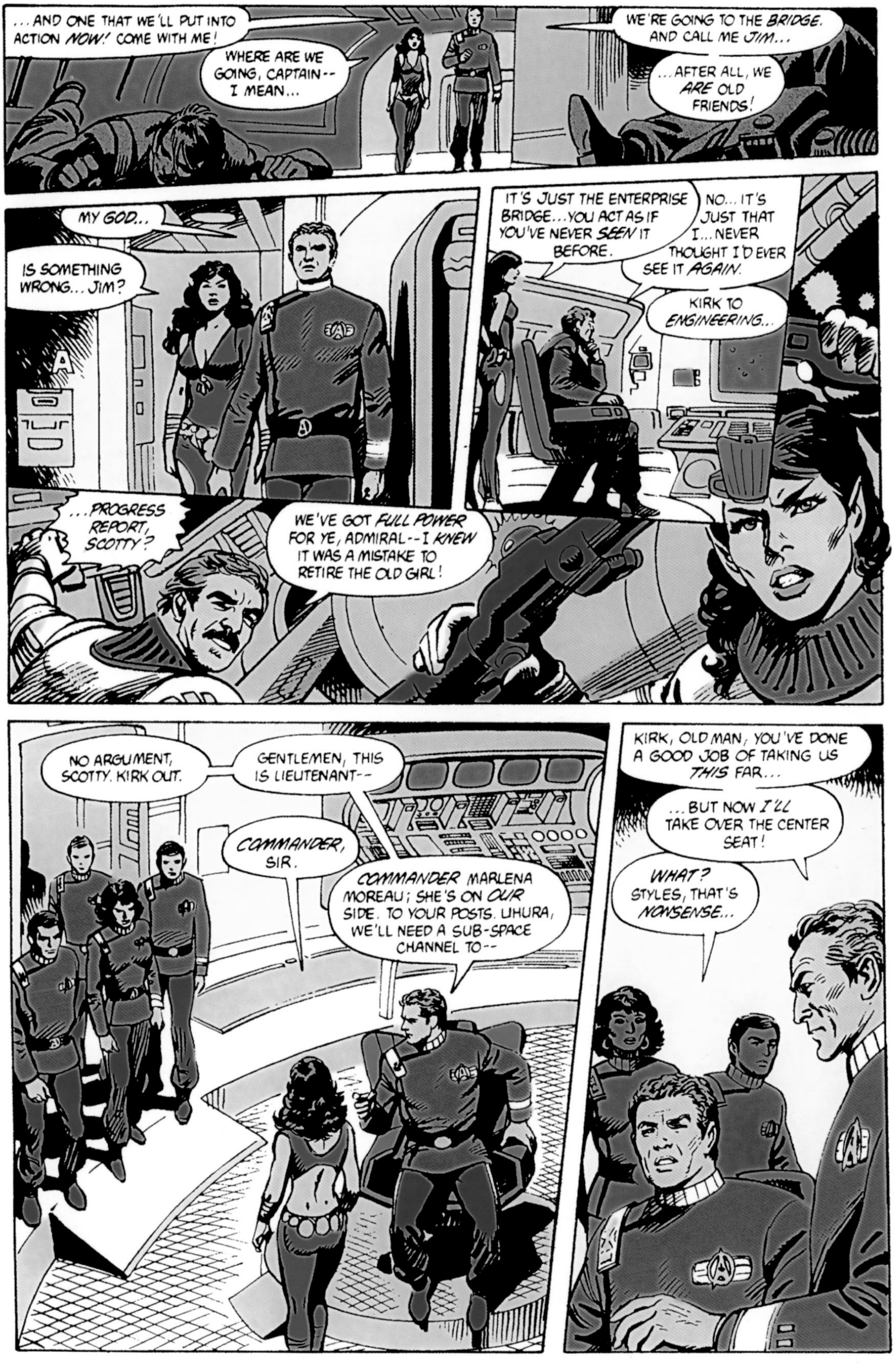
...AND ONE THAT WE'LL PUT INTO ACTION NOW! COME WITH ME!
WHERE ARE WE GOING, CAPTAIN-- I MEAN...
WE'RE GOING TO THE BRIDGE. AND CALL ME JIM...
...AFTER ALL, WE ARE OLD FRIENDS!
MY GOD...
IS SOMETHING WRONG... JIM?
IT'S JUST THE ENTERPRISE BRIDGE... YOU ACT AS IF YOU'VE NEVER SEEN IT BEFORE.
NO... IT'S JUST THAT I... NEVER THOUGHT I'D EVER SEE IT AGAIN.
KIRK TO ENGINEERING...
...PROGRESS REPORT, SCOTTY?
WE'VE GOT FULL POWER FOR YE, ADMIRAL--I KNEW IT WAS A MISTAKE TO RETIRE THE OLD GIRL!
NO ARGUMENT, SCOTTY. KIRK OUT.
GENTLEMEN, THIS IS LIEUTENANT--
COMMANDER, SIR.
COMMANDER MARLENA MOREAU; SHE'S ON OUR SIDE. TO YOUR POSTS. UHURA, WE'LL NEED A SUB-SPACE CHANNEL TO--
KIRK, OLD MAN, YOU'VE DONE A GOOD JOB OF TAKING US THIS FAR...
...BUT NOW I'LL TAKE OVER THE CENTER SEAT!
WHAT? STYLES, THAT'S NONSENSE...

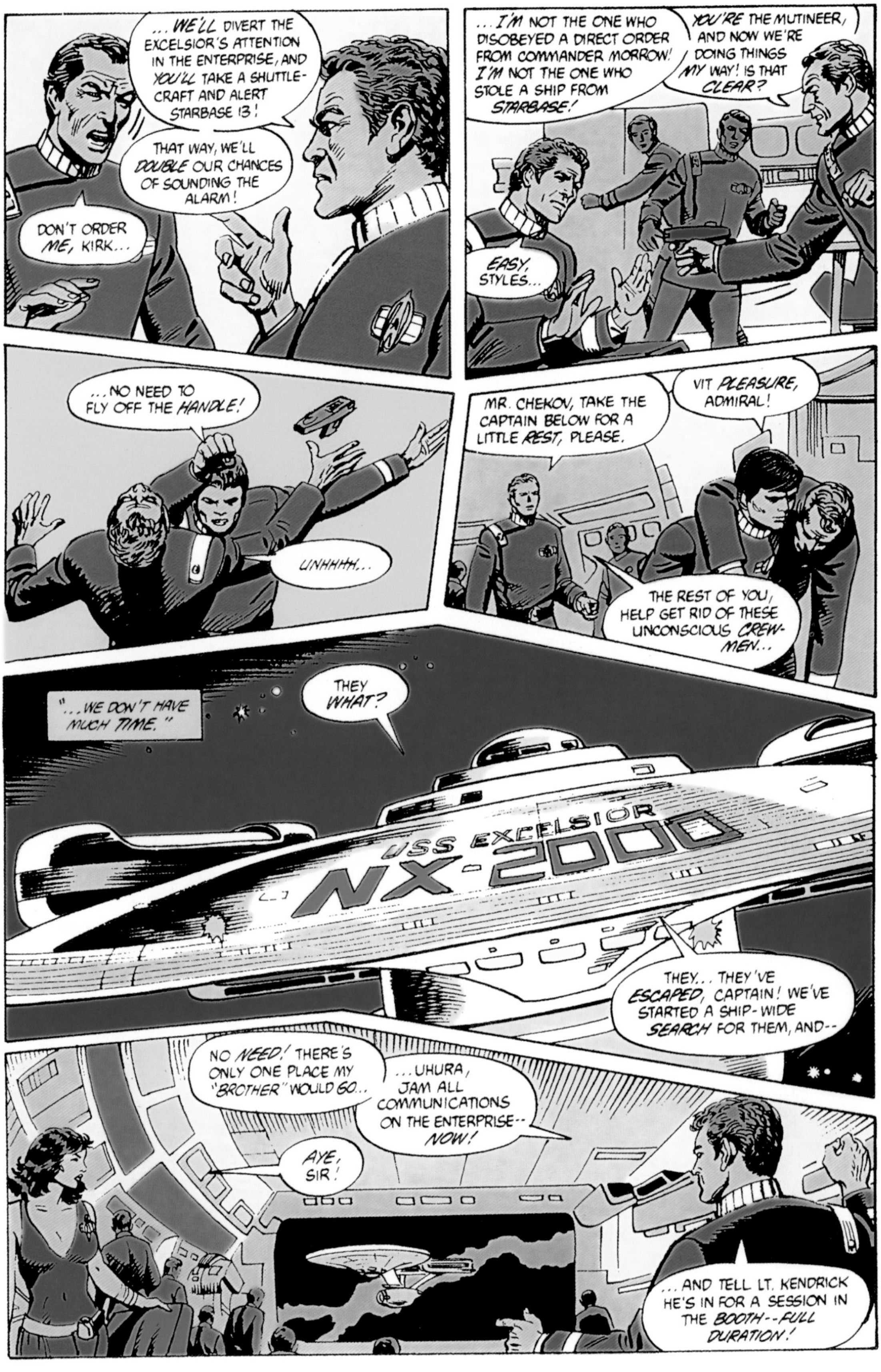

...WE'LL DIVERT THE EXCELSIOR'S ATTENTION IN THE ENTERPRISE, AND YOU'LL TAKE A SHUTTLE-CRAFT AND ALERT STARBASE 13!
THAT WAY, WE'LL DOUBLE OUR CHANCES OF SOUNDING THE ALARM!
DON'T ORDER ME, KIRK...
...I'M NOT THE ONE WHO DISOBEYED A DIRECT ORDER FROM COMMANDER MORROW! I'M NOT THE ONE WHO STOLE A SHIP FROM STARBASE!
YOU'RE THE MUTINEER, AND NOW WE'RE DOING THINGS MY WAY! IS THAT CLEAR?
EASY, STYLES...
...NO NEED TO FLY OFF THE HANDLE!
UNHHHH...
MR. CHEKOV, TAKE THE CAPTAIN BELOW FOR A LITTLE REST, PLEASE.
VIT PLEASURE, ADMIRAL!
THE REST OF YOU, HELP GET RID OF THESE UNCONSCIOUS CREW-MEN...
"...WE DON'T HAVE MUCH TIME."
THEY WHAT?
USS EXCELSIOR
NX-2000
THEY... THEY'VE ESCAPED, CAPTAIN! WE'VE STARTED A SHIP-WIDE SEARCH FOR THEM, AND--
NO NEED! THERE'S ONLY ONE PLACE MY "BROTHER" WOULD GO...
...UHURA, JAM ALL COMMUNICATIONS ON THE ENTERPRISE--NOW!
AYE, SIR!
...AND TELL LT. KENDRICK HE'S IN FOR A SESSION IN THE BOOTH--FULL DURATION!

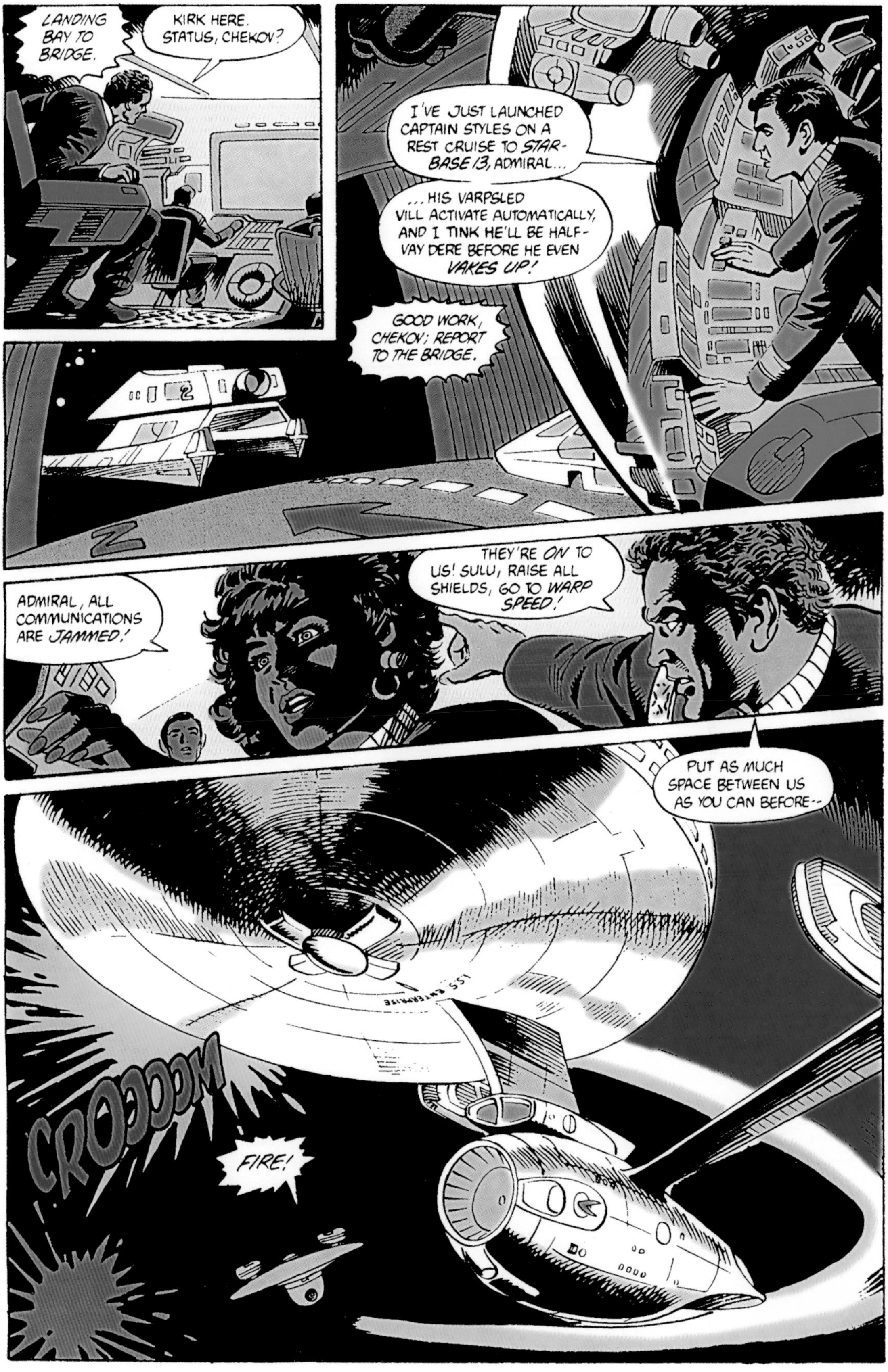
LANDING BAY TO BRIDGE.
KIRK HERE. STATUS, CHEKOV?
I'VE JUST LAUNCHED CAPTAIN STYLES ON A REST CRUISE TO STAR-BASE 13, ADMIRAL...
...HIS VARPSLED VILL ACTIVATE AUTOMATICALLY, AND I TINK HE'LL BE HALF-VAY DERE BEFORE HE EVEN VAKES UP!
GOOD WORK, CHEKOV; REPORT TO THE BRIDGE.
ADMIRAL, ALL COMMUNICATIONS ARE JAMMED!
THEY'RE ON TO US! SULU, RAISE ALL SHIELDS, GO TO WARP SPEED!
PUT AS MUCH SPACE BETWEEN US AS YOU CAN BEFORE--
I.S.S. ENTERPRISE
CROOOOM
FIRE!

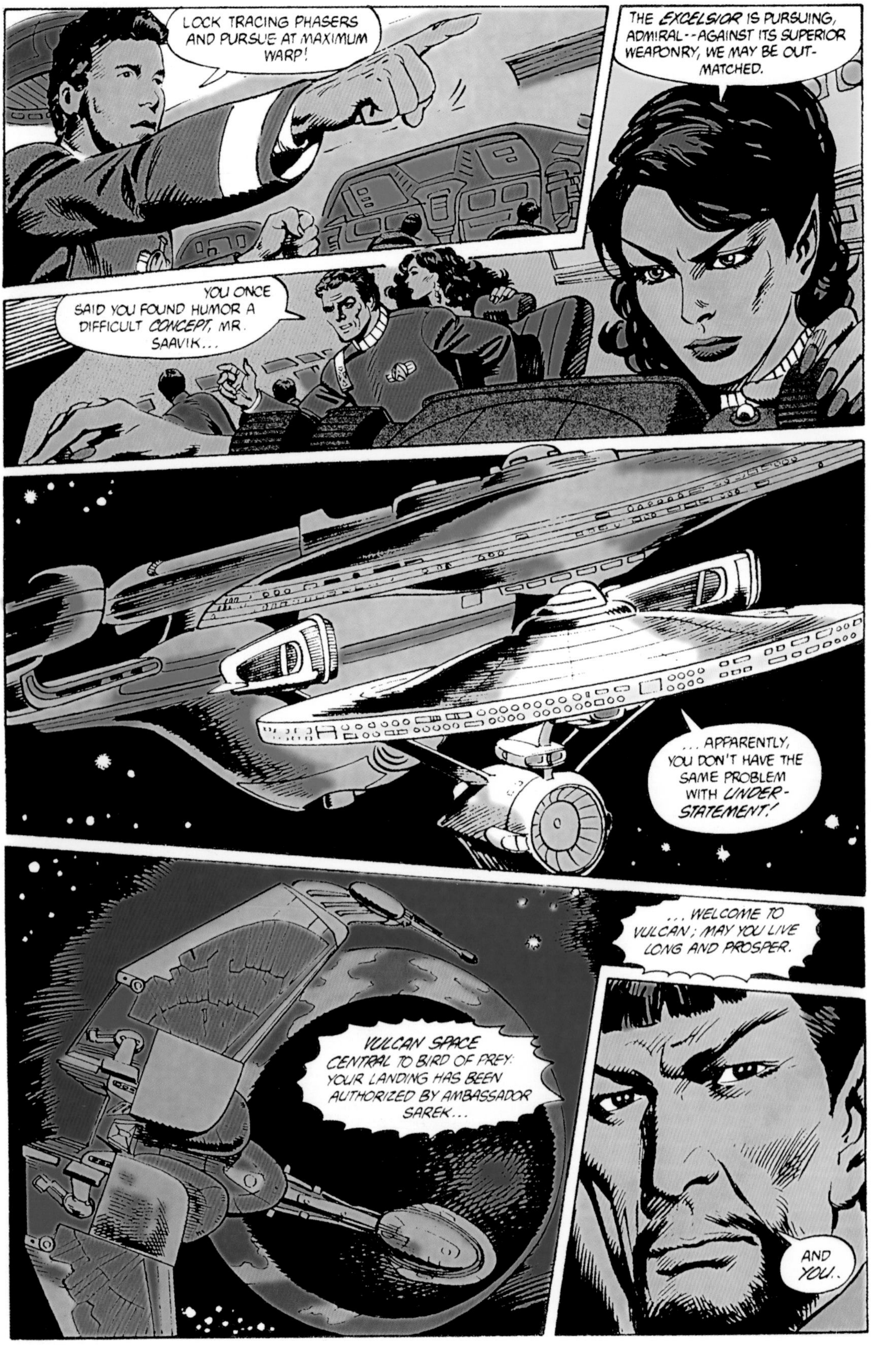
LOCK TRACING PHASERS AND PURSUE AT MAXIMUM WARP!
THE EXCELSIOR IS PURSUING, ADMIRAL--AGAINST ITS SUPERIOR WEAPONRY, WE MAY BE OUT-MATCHED.
YOU ONCE SAID YOU FOUND HUMOR A DIFFICULT CONCEPT, MR. SAAVIK...
...APPARENTLY, YOU DON'T HAVE THE SAME PROBLEM WITH UNDER-STATEMENT!
VULCAN SPACE CENTRAL TO BIRD OF PREY: YOUR LANDING HAS BEEN AUTHORIZED BY AMBASSADOR SAREK...
...WELCOME TO VULCAN; MAY YOU LIVE LONG AND PROSPER.
AND YOU.

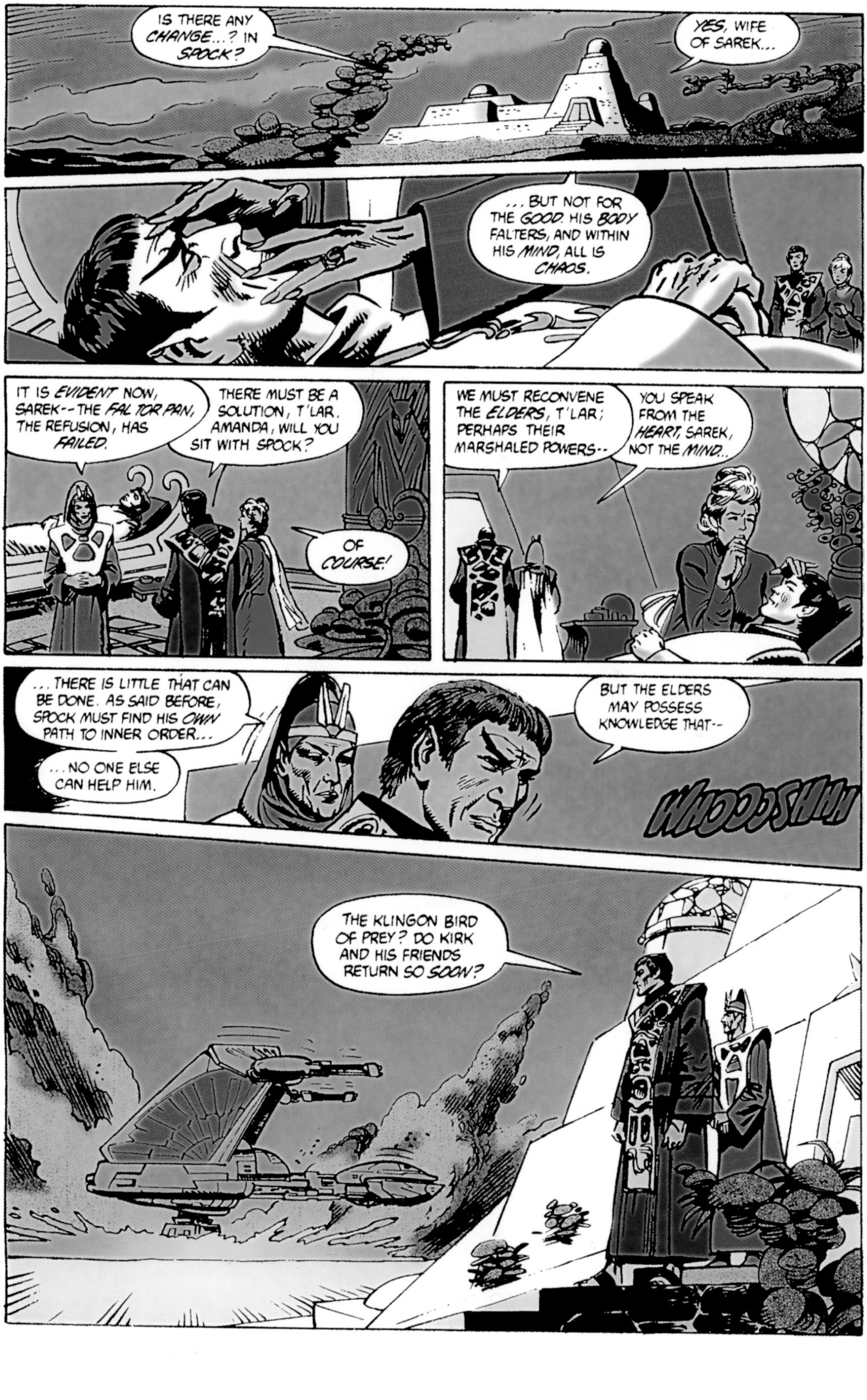
IS THERE ANY CHANGE...? IN SPOCK?
YES, WIFE OF SAREK...
...BUT NOT FOR THE GOOD. HIS BODY FALTERS, AND WITHIN HIS MIND, ALL IS CHAOS.
IT IS EVIDENT NOW, SAREK--THE FAL TOR PAN, THE REFUSION, HAS FAILED.
THERE MUST BE A SOLUTION, T'LAR. AMANDA, WILL YOU SIT WITH SPOCK?
OF COURSE!
WE MUST RECONVENE THE ELDERS, T'LAR; PERHAPS THEIR MARSHALED POWERS--
YOU SPEAK FROM THE HEART, SAREK, NOT THE MIND...
...THERE IS LITTLE THAT CAN BE DONE. AS SAID BEFORE, SPOCK MUST FIND HIS OWN PATH TO INNER ORDER...
...NO ONE ELSE CAN HELP HIM.
BUT THE ELDERS MAY POSSESS KNOWLEDGE THAT--
THE KLINGON BIRD OF PREY? DO KIRK AND HIS FRIENDS RETURN SO SOON?

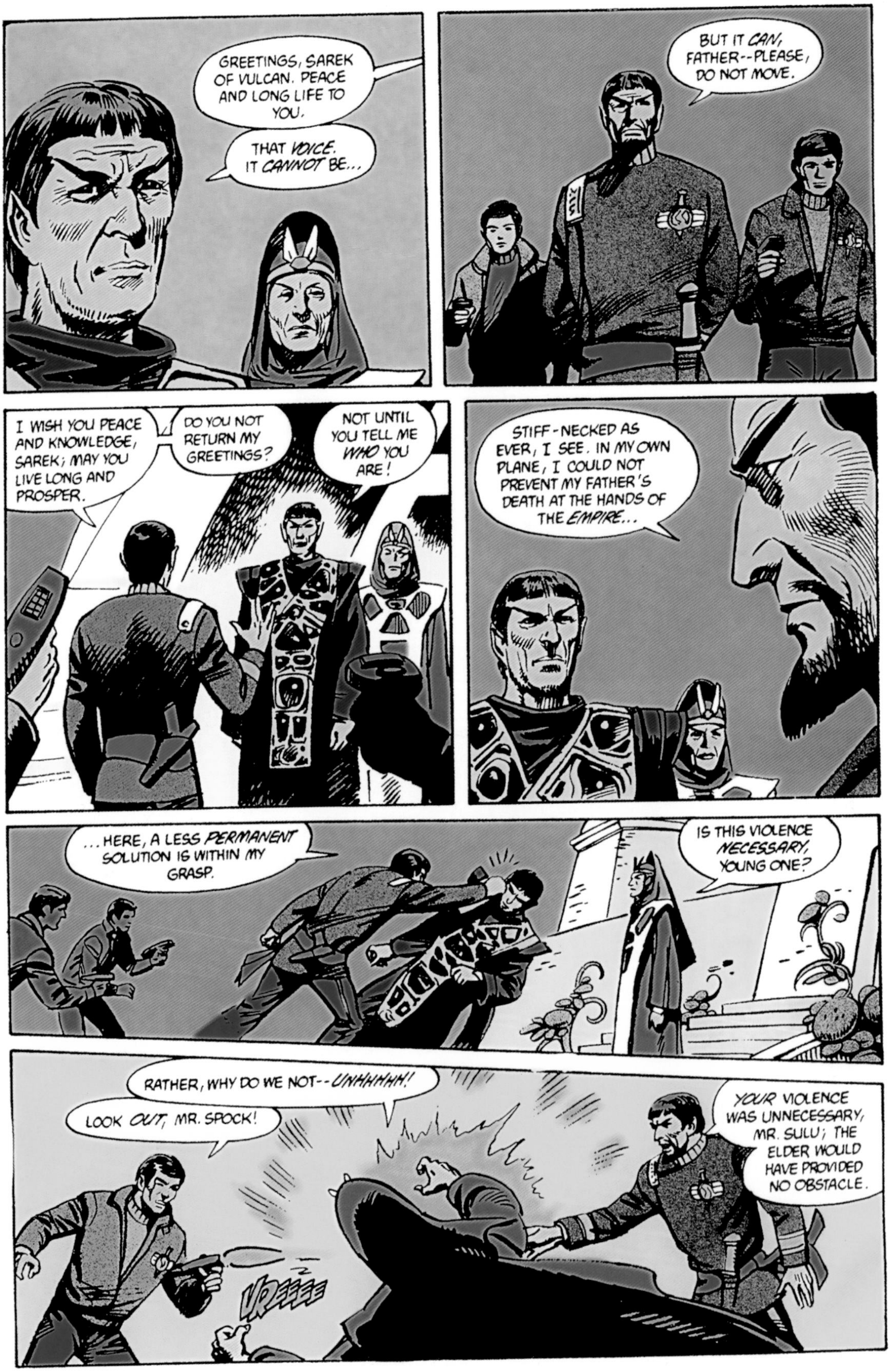
GREETINGS, SAREK OF VULCAN. PEACE AND LONG LIFE TO YOU.
THAT VOICE. IT CANNOT BE...
BUT IT CAN, FATHER--PLEASE, DO NOT MOVE.
I WISH YOU PEACE AND KNOWLEDGE, SAREK; MAY YOU LIVE LONG AND PROSPER.
DO YOU NOT RETURN MY GREETINGS?
NOT UNTIL YOU TELL ME WHO YOU ARE!
STIFF-NECKED AS EVER, I SEE. IN MY OWN PLANE, I COULD NOT PREVENT MY FATHER'S DEATH AT THE HANDS OF THE EMPIRE...
...HERE, A LESS PERMANENT SOLUTION IS WITHIN MY GRASP.
IS THIS VIOLENCE NECESSARY, YOUNG ONE?
RATHER, WHY DO WE NOT--UNHHHHH!
LOOK OUT, MR. SPOCK!
YOUR VIOLENCE WAS UNNECESSARY, MR. SULU; THE ELDER WOULD HAVE PROVIDED NO OBSTACLE.
VREEEE

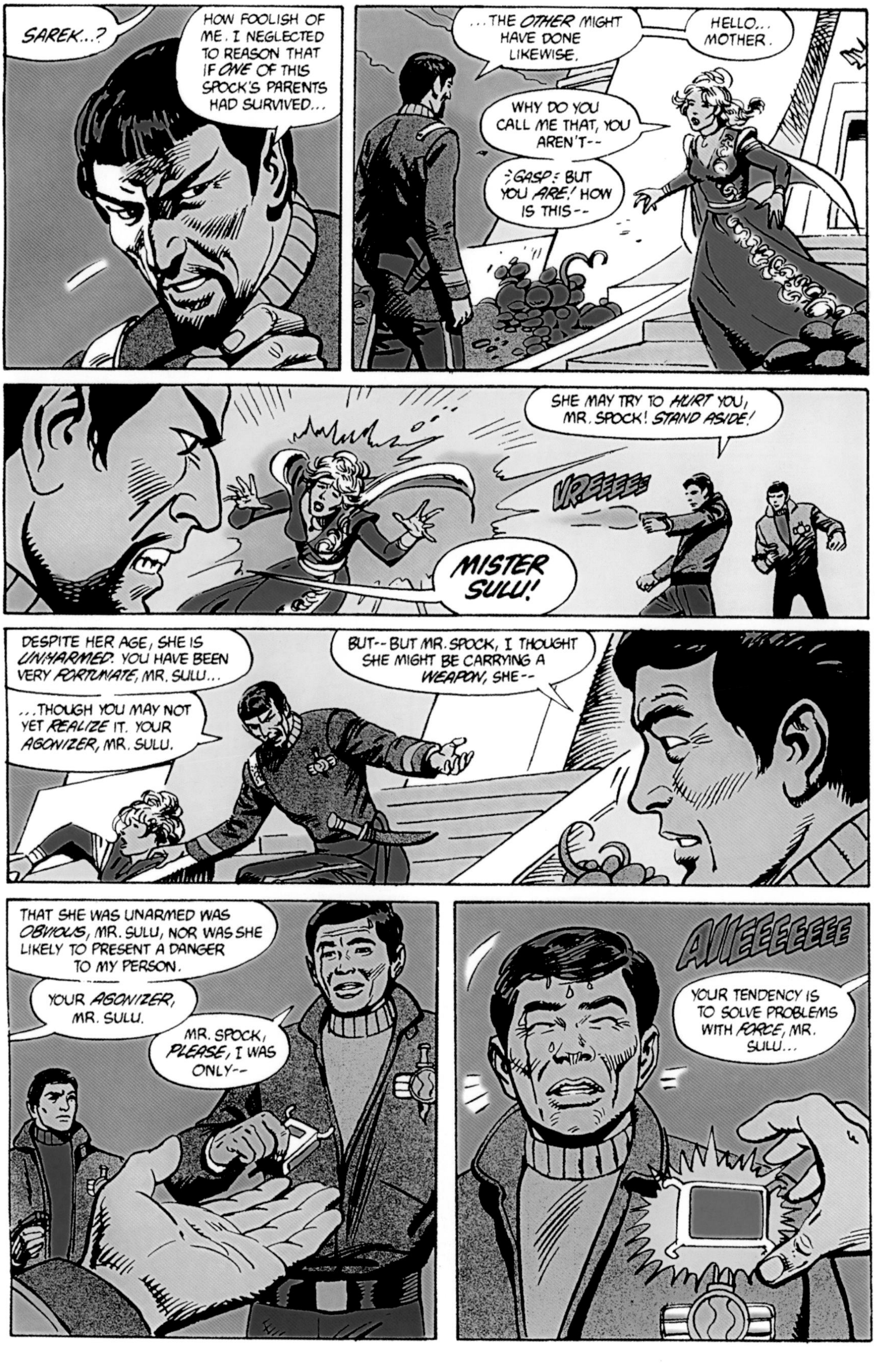
SAREK...?
HOW FOOLISH OF ME. I NEGLECTED TO REASON THAT IF ONE OF THIS SPOCK'S PARENTS HAD SURVIVED...
...THE OTHER MIGHT HAVE DONE LIKEWISE.
HELLO... MOTHER.
WHY DO YOU CALL ME THAT, YOU AREN'T--
:GASP: BUT YOU ARE! HOW IS THIS--
SHE MAY TRY TO HURT YOU, MR. SPOCK! STAND ASIDE!
VREEEE
MISTER SULU!
DESPITE HER AGE, SHE IS UNHARMED. YOU HAVE BEEN VERY FORTUNATE, MR. SULU...
...THOUGH YOU MAY NOT YET REALIZE IT. YOUR AGONIZER, MR. SULU.
BUT--BUT MR. SPOCK, I THOUGHT SHE MIGHT BE CARRYING A WEAPON, SHE--
THAT SHE WAS UNARMED WAS OBVIOUS, MR. SULU, NOR WAS SHE LIKELY TO PRESENT A DANGER TO MY PERSON.
YOUR AGONIZER, MR. SULU.
MR. SPOCK, PLEASE, I WAS ONLY--
AIIEEEEEEE
YOUR TENDENCY IS TO SOLVE PROBLEMS WITH FORCE, MR. SULU...

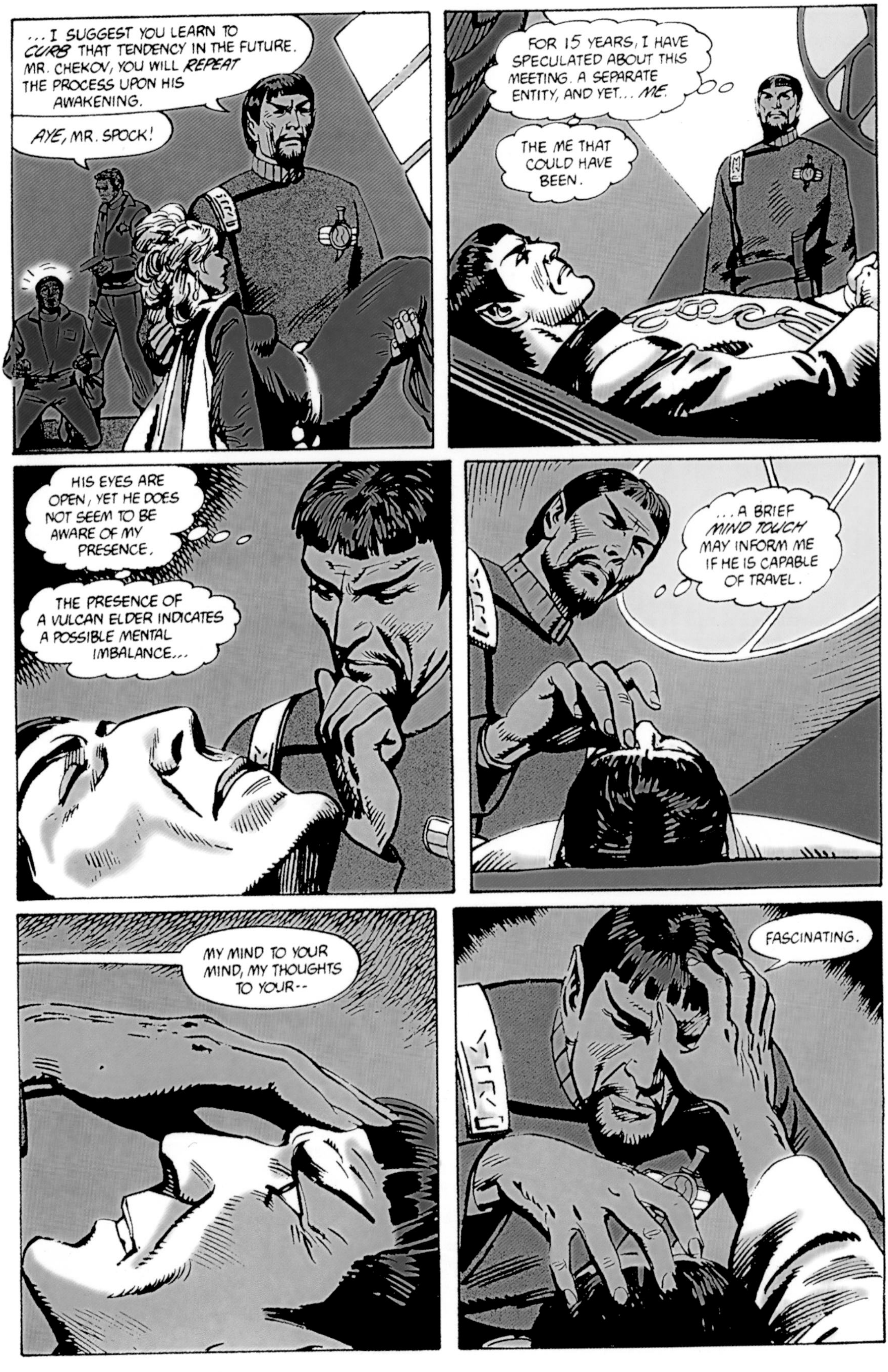
... I SUGGEST YOU LEARN TO CURB THAT TENDENCY IN THE FUTURE. MR. CHEKOV, YOU WILL REPEAT THE PROCESS UPON HIS AWAKENING.
AYE, MR. SPOCK!
FOR 15 YEARS, I HAVE SPECULATED ABOUT THIS MEETING. A SEPARATE ENTITY, AND YET... ME.
THE ME THAT COULD HAVE BEEN.
HIS EYES ARE OPEN, YET HE DOES NOT SEEM TO BE AWARE OF MY PRESENCE.
THE PRESENCE OF A VULCAN ELDER INDICATES A POSSIBLE MENTAL IMBALANCE...
... A BRIEF MIND TOUCH MAY INFORM ME IF HE IS CAPABLE OF TRAVEL.
MY MIND TO YOUR MIND, MY THOUGHTS TO YOUR--
FASCINATING.

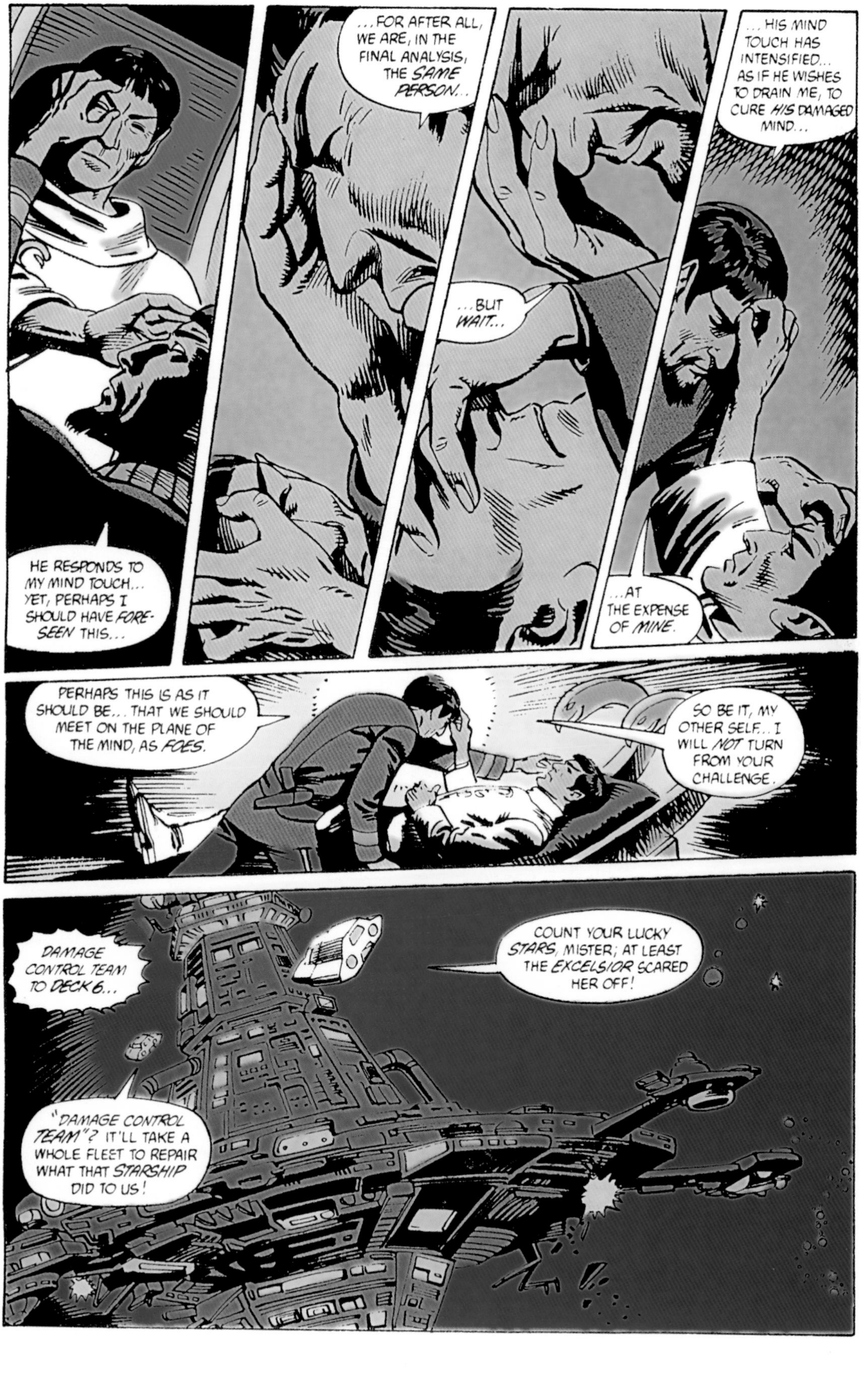
HE RESPONDS TO MY MIND TOUCH... YET, PERHAPS I SHOULD HAVE FORE-SEEN THIS...
...FOR AFTER ALL, WE ARE, IN THE FINAL ANALYSIS, THE SAME PERSON...
...BUT WAIT...
...HIS MIND TOUCH HAS INTENSIFIED... AS IF HE WISHES TO DRAIN ME, TO CURE HIS DAMAGED MIND...
...AT THE EXPENSE OF MINE.
PERHAPS THIS IS AS IT SHOULD BE... THAT WE SHOULD MEET ON THE PLANE OF THE MIND, AS FOES.
SO BE IT, MY OTHER SELF... I WILL NOT TURN FROM YOUR CHALLENGE.
DAMAGE CONTROL TEAM TO DECK 6...
COUNT YOUR LUCKY STARS, MISTER; AT LEAST THE EXCELSIOR SCARED HER OFF!
"DAMAGE CONTROL TEAM"? IT'LL TAKE A WHOLE FLEET TO REPAIR WHAT THAT STARSHIP DID TO US!

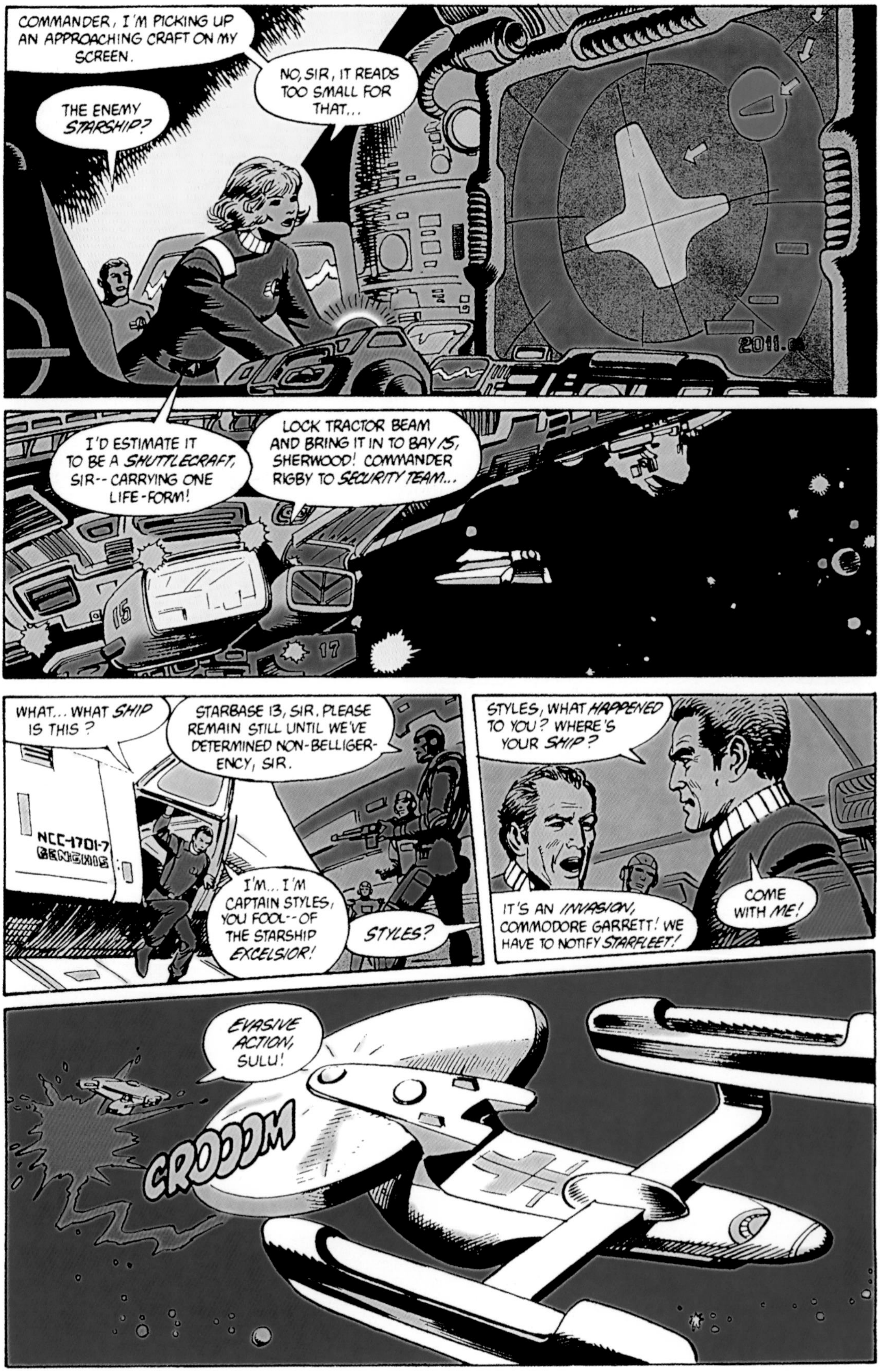
COMMANDER, I'M PICKING UP AN APPROACHING CRAFT ON MY SCREEN.
THE ENEMY STARSHIP?
NO, SIR, IT READS TOO SMALL FOR THAT...
I'D ESTIMATE IT TO BE A SHUTTLECRAFT, SIR-- CARRYING ONE LIFE-FORM!
LOCK TRACTOR BEAM AND BRING IT IN TO BAY 15, SHERWOOD! COMMANDER RIGBY TO SECURITY TEAM...
15
17
WHAT... WHAT SHIP IS THIS?
STARBASE 13, SIR, PLEASE REMAIN STILL UNTIL WE'VE DETERMINED NON-BELLIGERENCY, SIR.
NCC-1701-7
GENGHIS
I'M... I'M CAPTAIN STYLES, YOU FOOL-- OF THE STARSHIP EXCELSIOR!
STYLES?
STYLES, WHAT HAPPENED TO YOU? WHERE'S YOUR SHIP?
IT'S AN INVASION, COMMODORE GARRETT! WE HAVE TO NOTIFY STARFLEET!
COME WITH ME!
EVASIVE ACTION, SULU!
CROOOM

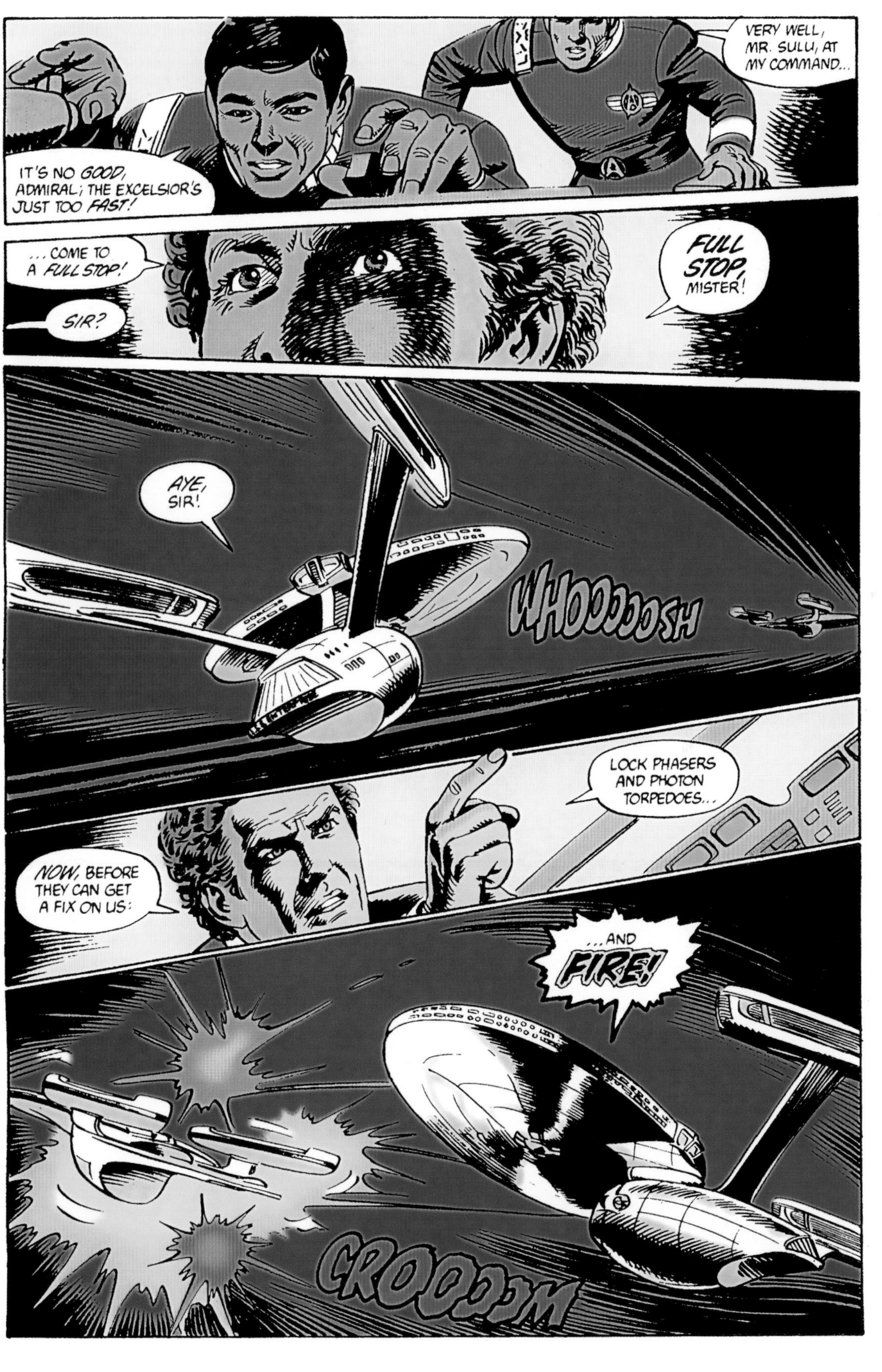
VERY WELL, MR. SULU, AT MY COMMAND...
IT'S NO GOOD, ADMIRAL; THE EXCELSIOR'S JUST TOO FAST!
...COME TO A FULL STOP!
SIR?
FULL STOP, MISTER!
AYE, SIR!
WHOOOOOOSH
LOCK PHASERS AND PHOTON TORPEDOES...
NOW, BEFORE THEY CAN GET A FIX ON US:
...AND FIRE!
CROOOOM

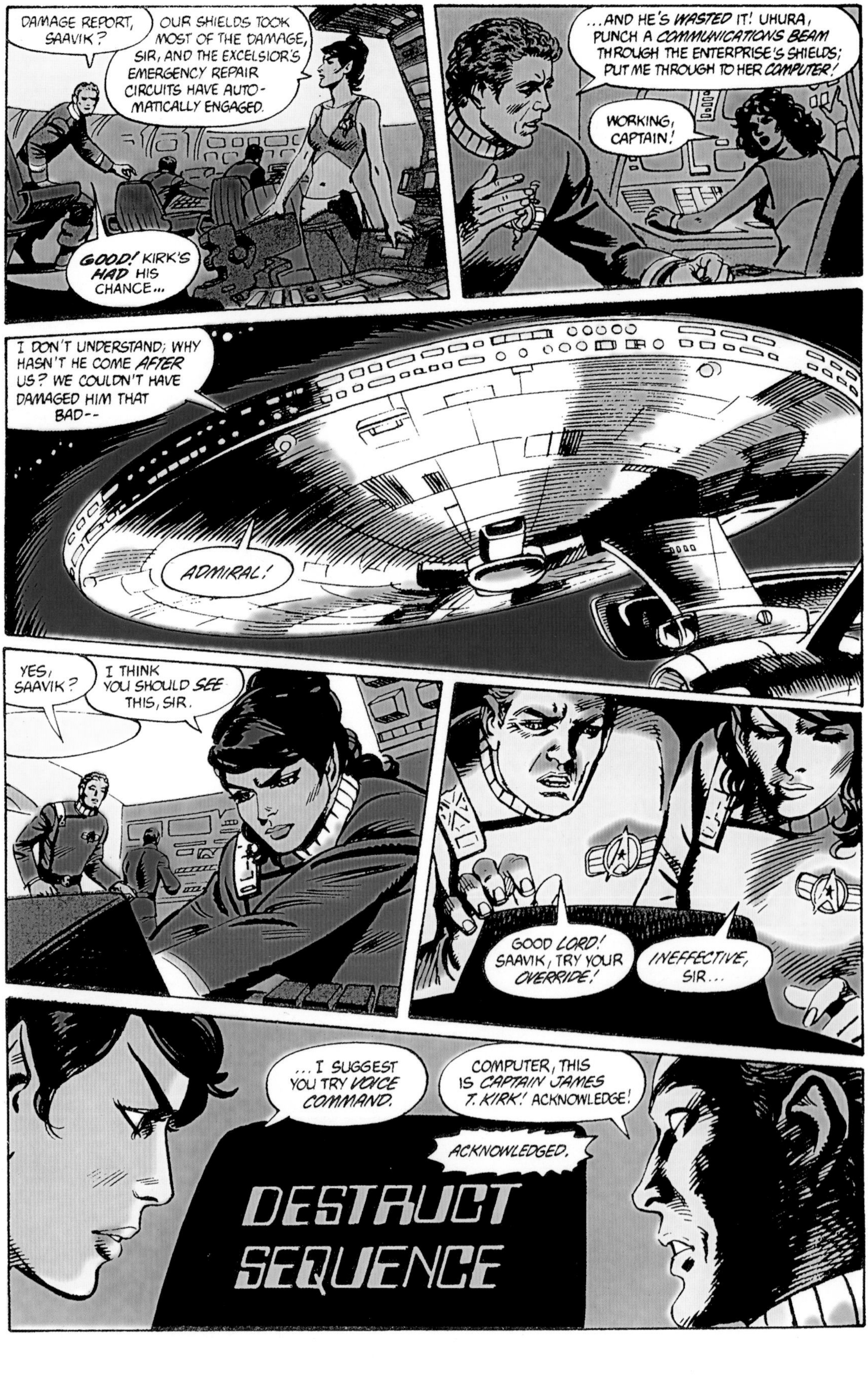
DAMAGE REPORT, SAAVIK?
OUR SHIELDS TOOK MOST OF THE DAMAGE, SIR, AND THE EXCELSIOR'S EMERGENCY REPAIR CIRCUITS HAVE AUTO-MATICALLY ENGAGED.
GOOD! KIRK'S HAD HIS CHANCE...
...AND HE'S WASTED IT! UHURA, PUNCH A COMMUNICATIONS BEAM THROUGH THE ENTERPRISE'S SHIELDS; PUT ME THROUGH TO HER COMPUTER!
WORKING, CAPTAIN!
I DON'T UNDERSTAND; WHY HASN'T HE COME AFTER US? WE COULDN'T HAVE DAMAGED HIM THAT BAD--
ADMIRAL!
YES, SAAVIK?
I THINK YOU SHOULD SEE THIS, SIR.
GOOD LORD! SAAVIK, TRY YOUR OVERRIDE!
INEFFECTIVE, SIR...
...I SUGGEST YOU TRY VOICE COMMAND.
COMPUTER, THIS IS CAPTAIN JAMES T. KIRK! ACKNOWLEDGE!
ACKNOWLEDGED.
DESTRUCT SEQUENCE

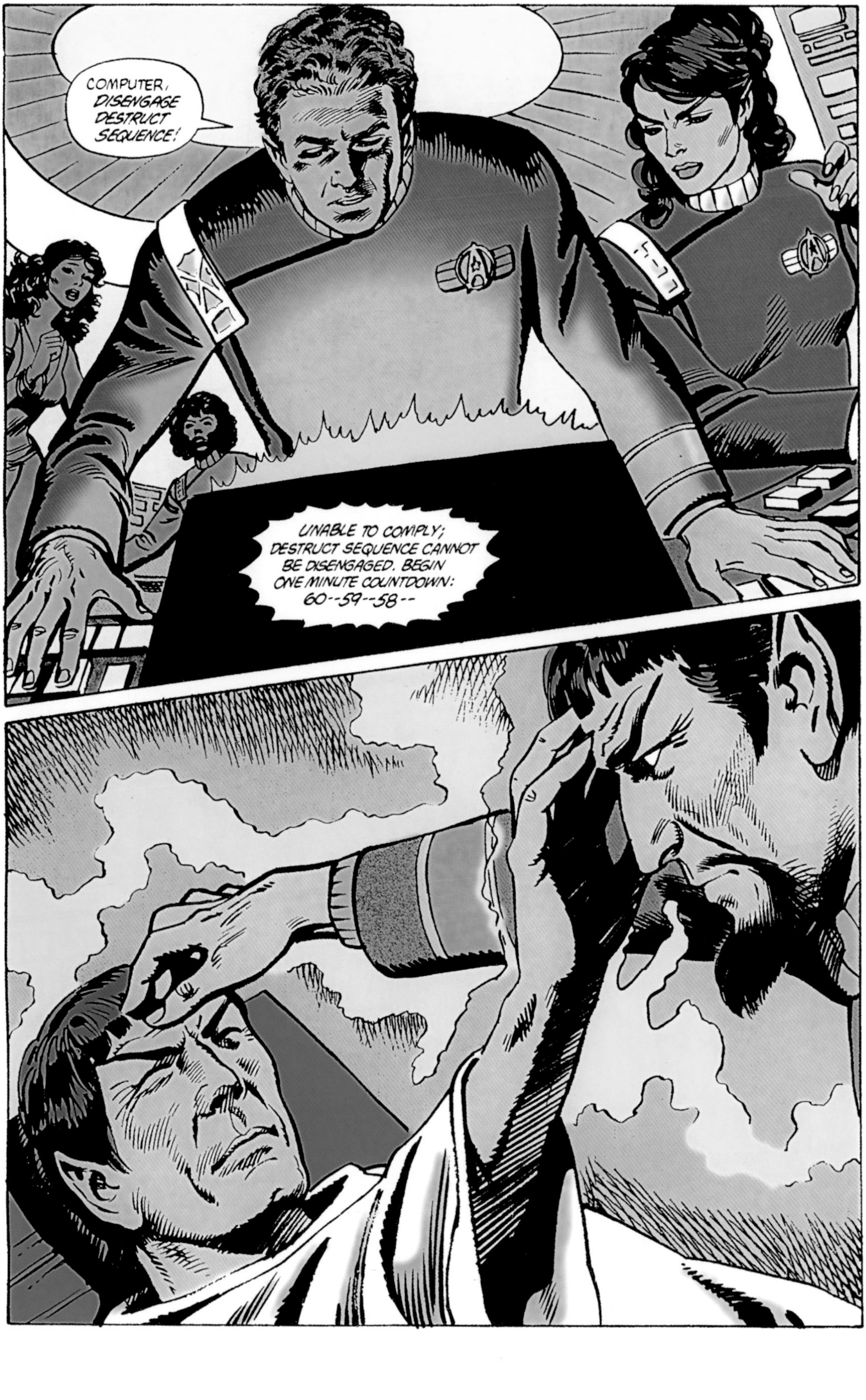
COMPUTER, DISENGAGE DESTRUCT SEQUENCE!
UNABLE TO COMPLY; DESTRUCT SEQUENCE CANNOT BE DISENGAGED. BEGIN ONE MINUTE COUNTDOWN: 60--59--58--

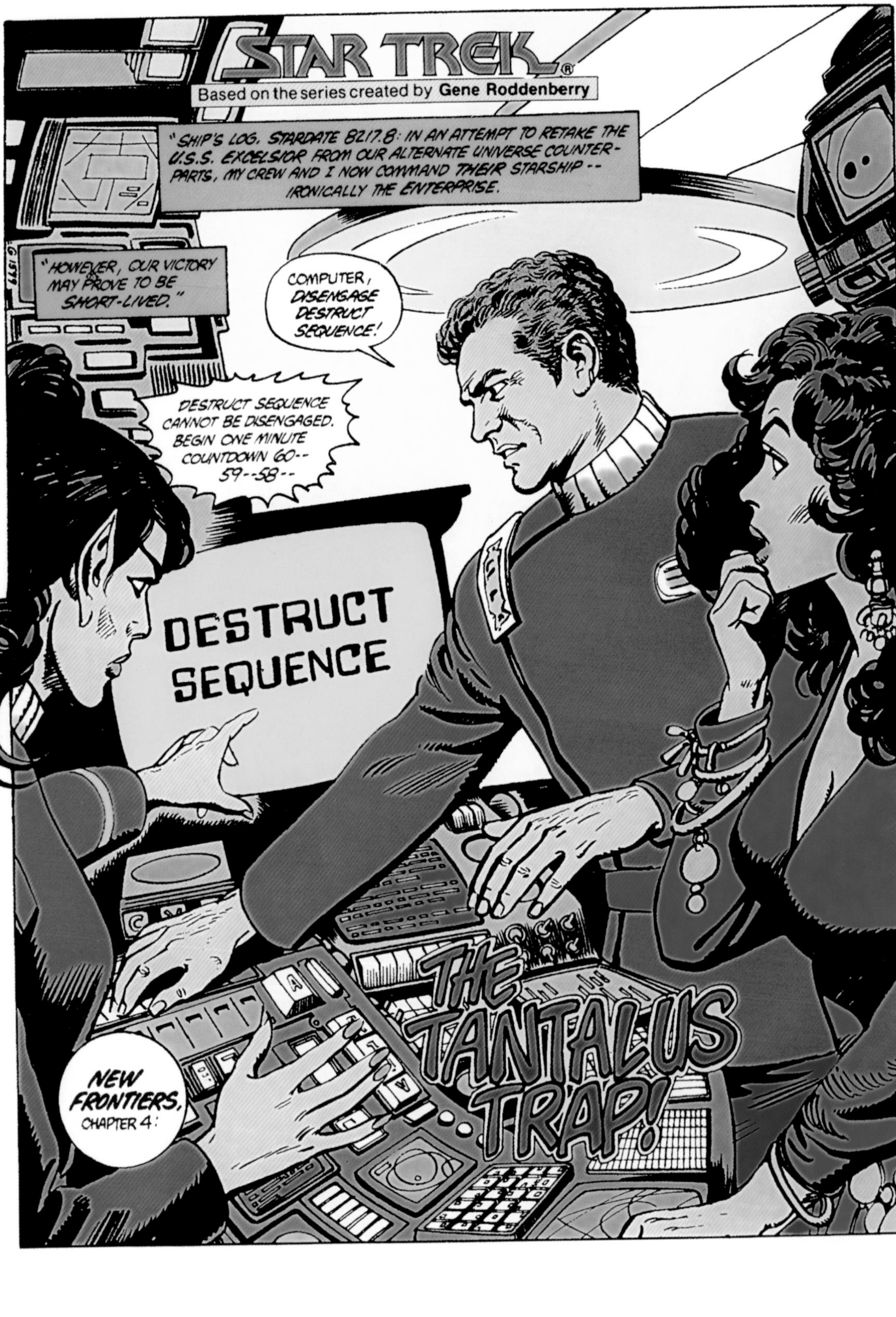
STAR TREK®
Based on the series created by Gene Roddenberry
"SHIP'S LOG, STARDATE 8217.8: IN AN ATTEMPT TO RETAKE THE U.S.S. EXCELSIOR FROM OUR ALTERNATE UNIVERSE COUNTERPARTS, MY CREW AND I NOW COMMAND THEIR STARSHIP -- IRONICALLY THE ENTERPRISE.
"HOWEVER, OUR VICTORY MAY PROVE TO BE SHORT-LIVED."
COMPUTER, DISENGAGE DESTRUCT SEQUENCE!
DESTRUCT SEQUENCE CANNOT BE DISENGAGED. BEGIN ONE MINUTE COUNTDOWN 60-- 59--58--
DESTRUCT SEQUENCE
NEW FRONTIERS, CHAPTER 4:
THE TANTALUS TRAP!

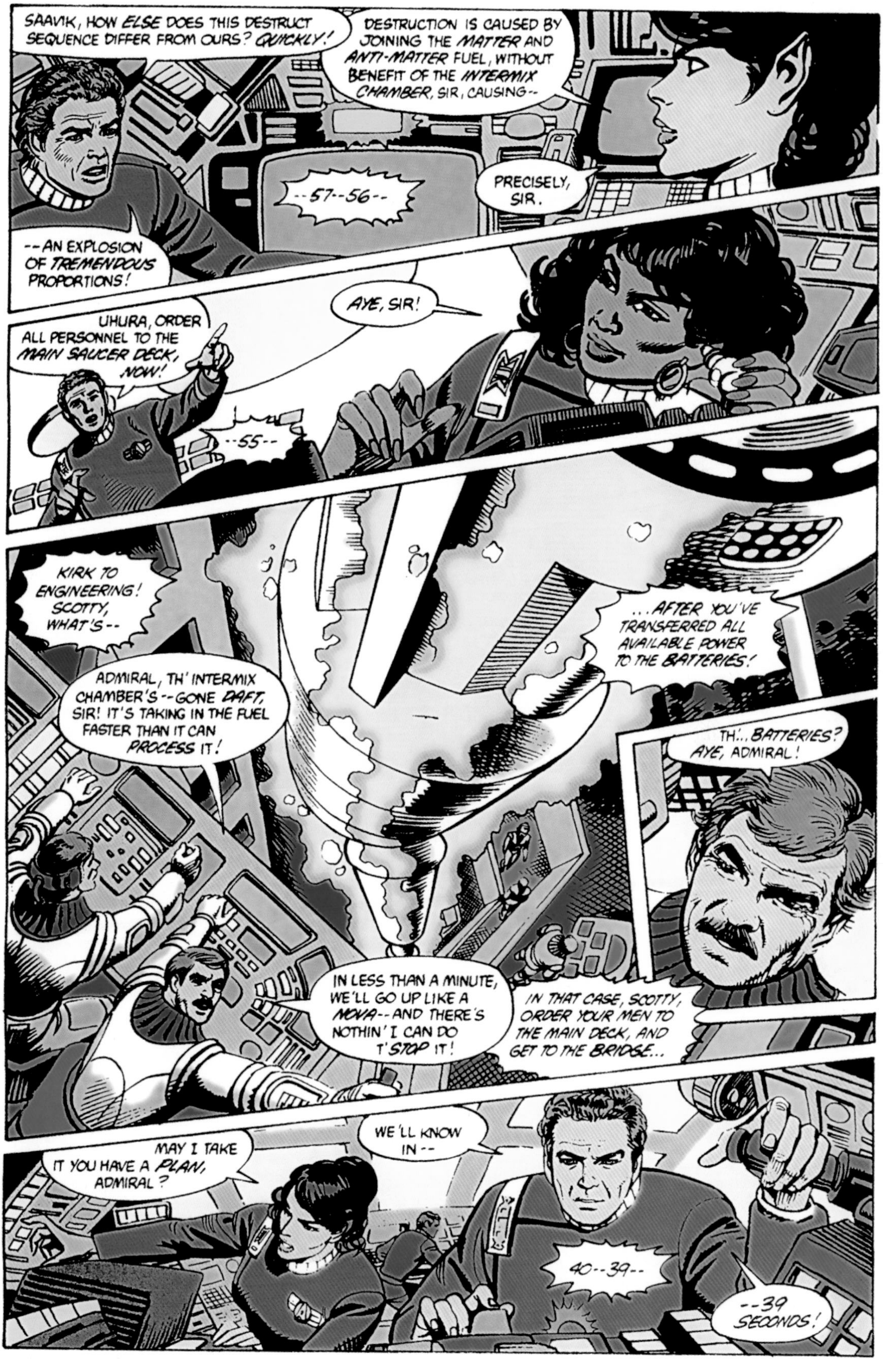
SAAVIK, HOW ELSE DOES THIS DESTRUCT SEQUENCE DIFFER FROM OURS? QUICKLY!
DESTRUCTION IS CAUSED BY JOINING THE MATTER AND ANTI-MATTER FUEL, WITHOUT BENEFIT OF THE INTERMIX CHAMBER, SIR, CAUSING--
--57--56--
PRECISELY, SIR.
--AN EXPLOSION OF TREMENDOUS PROPORTIONS!
UHURA, ORDER ALL PERSONNEL TO THE MAIN SAUCER DECK, NOW!
AYE, SIR!
--55--
KIRK TO ENGINEERING! SCOTTY, WHAT'S--
ADMIRAL, TH' INTERMIX CHAMBER'S--GONE DAFT, SIR! IT'S TAKING IN THE FUEL FASTER THAN IT CAN PROCESS IT!
IN LESS THAN A MINUTE, WE'LL GO UP LIKE A NOVA--AND THERE'S NOTHIN' I CAN DO T'STOP IT!
IN THAT CASE, SCOTTY, ORDER YOUR MEN TO THE MAIN DECK, AND GET TO THE BRIDGE...
...AFTER YOU'VE TRANSFERRED ALL AVAILABLE POWER TO THE BATTERIES!
TH'.. BATTERIES? AYE, ADMIRAL!
MAY I TAKE IT YOU HAVE A PLAN, ADMIRAL?
WE'LL KNOW IN--
40--39--
--39 SECONDS!

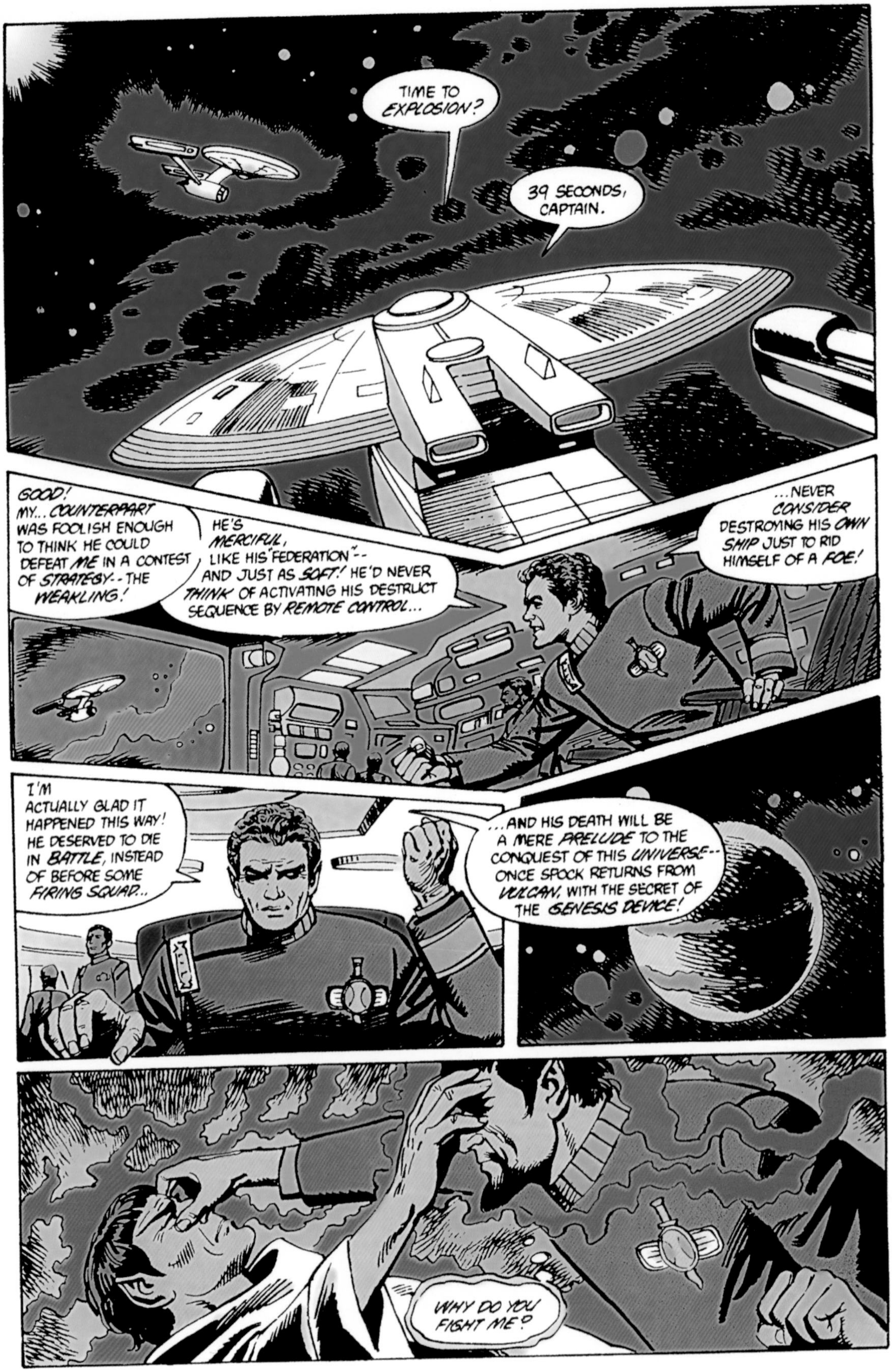

TIME TO EXPLOSION?
39 SECONDS, CAPTAIN.
GOOD! MY... COUNTERPART WAS FOOLISH ENOUGH TO THINK HE COULD DEFEAT ME IN A CONTEST OF STRATEGY-- THE WEAKLING!
HE'S MERCIFUL, LIKE HIS "FEDERATION"-- AND JUST AS SOFT! HE'D NEVER THINK OF ACTIVATING HIS DESTRUCT SEQUENCE BY REMOTE CONTROL...
...NEVER CONSIDER DESTROYING HIS OWN SHIP JUST TO RID HIMSELF OF A FOE!
I'M ACTUALLY GLAD IT HAPPENED THIS WAY! HE DESERVED TO DIE IN BATTLE, INSTEAD OF BEFORE SOME FIRING SQUAD...
...AND HIS DEATH WILL BE A MERE PRELUDE TO THE CONQUEST OF THIS UNIVERSE-- ONCE SPOCK RETURNS FROM VULCAN, WITH THE SECRET OF THE GENESIS DEVICE!
WHY DO YOU FIGHT ME?

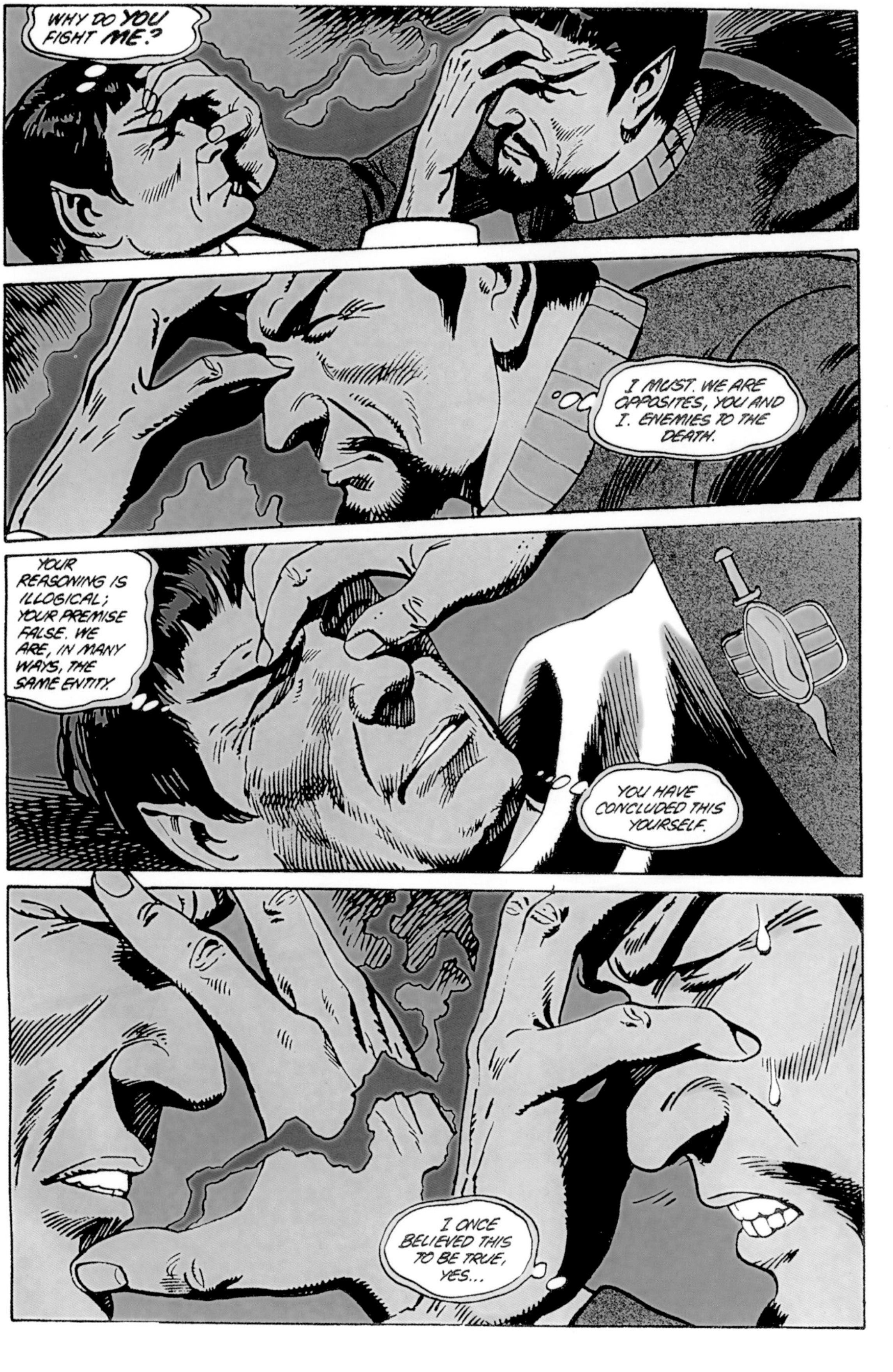
WHY DO YOU FIGHT ME?
I MUST. WE ARE OPPOSITES, YOU AND I. ENEMIES TO THE DEATH.
YOUR REASONING IS ILLOGICAL; YOUR PREMISE FALSE. WE ARE, IN MANY WAYS, THE SAME ENTITY.
YOU HAVE CONCLUDED THIS YOURSELF.
I ONCE BELIEVED THIS TO BE TRUE, YES...

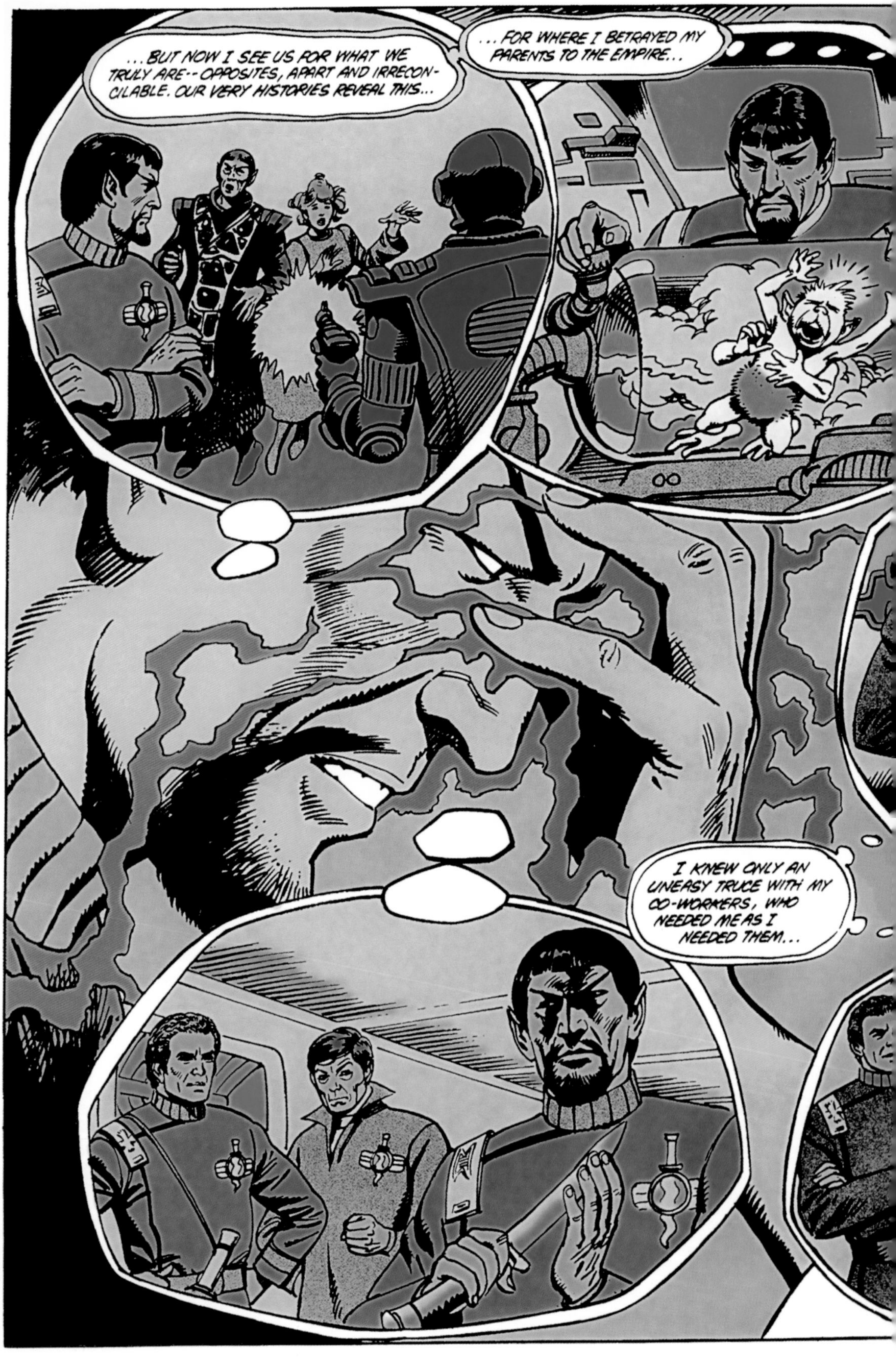
...BUT NOW I SEE US FOR WHAT WE TRULY ARE--OPPOSITES, APART AND IRRECONCILABLE. OUR VERY HISTORIES REVEAL THIS...
...FOR WHERE I BETRAYED MY PARENTS TO THE EMPIRE...
I KNEW ONLY AN UNEASY TRUCE WITH MY CO-WORKERS, WHO NEEDED ME AS I NEEDED THEM...

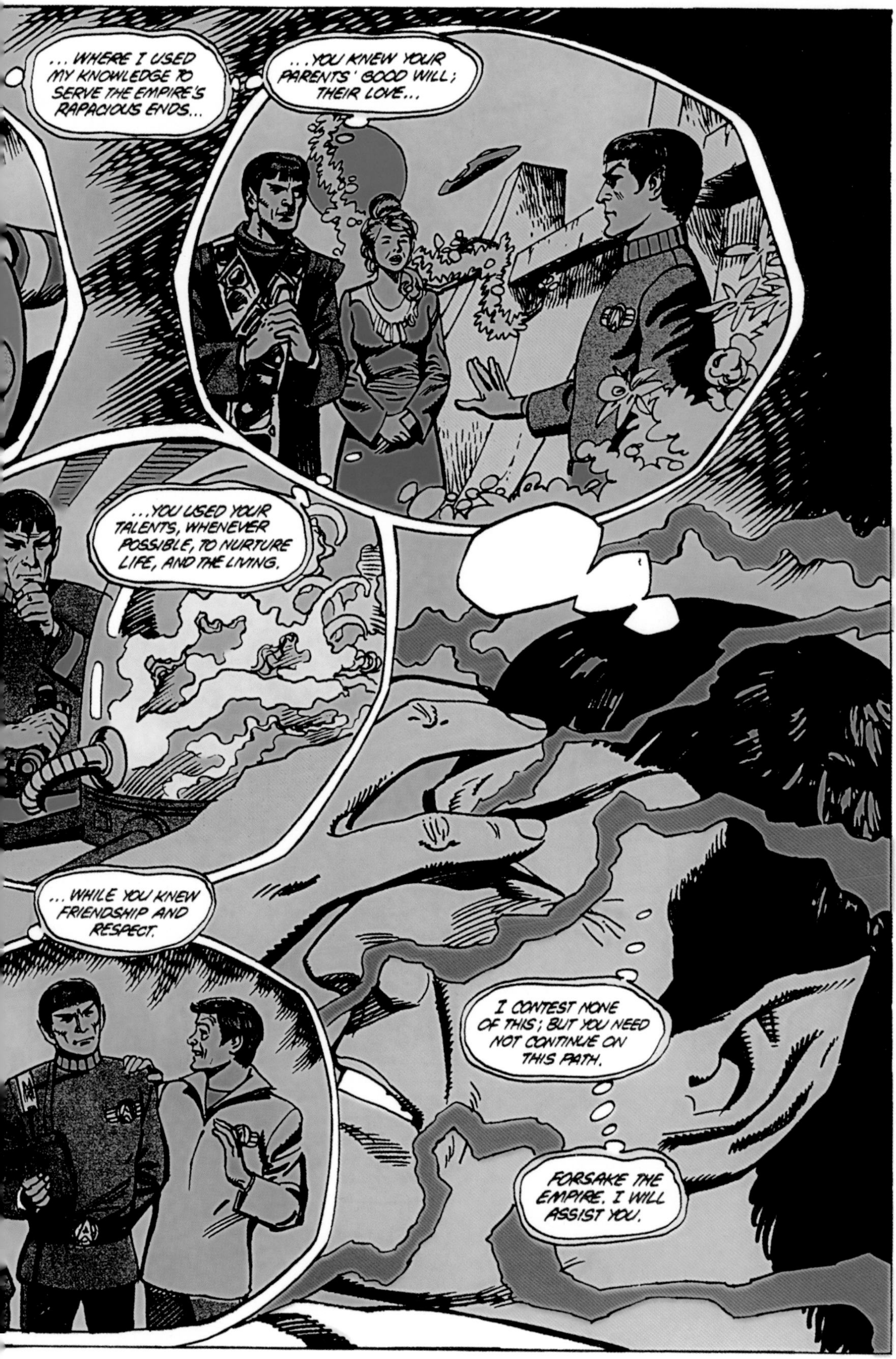
...WHERE I USED MY KNOWLEDGE TO SERVE THE EMPIRE'S RAPACIOUS ENDS...
...YOU KNEW YOUR PARENTS' GOOD WILL; THEIR LOVE...
...YOU USED YOUR TALENTS, WHENEVER POSSIBLE, TO NURTURE LIFE, AND THE LIVING.
...WHILE YOU KNEW FRIENDSHIP AND RESPECT.
I CONTEST NONE OF THIS; BUT YOU NEED NOT CONTINUE ON THIS PATH.
FORSAKE THE EMPIRE. I WILL ASSIST YOU.

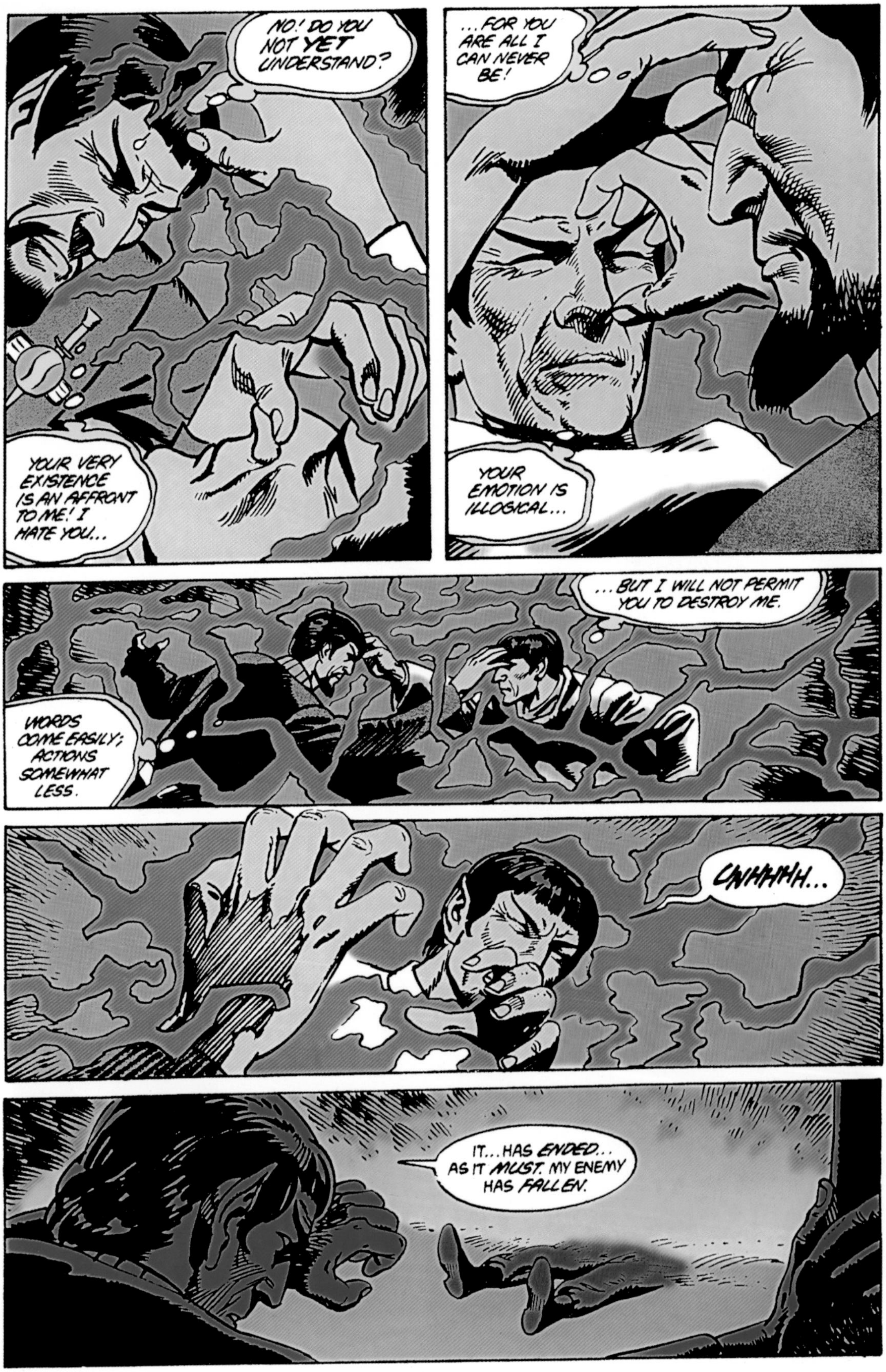
NO! DO YOU NOT YET UNDERSTAND?
YOUR VERY EXISTENCE IS AN AFFRONT TO ME! I HATE YOU...
...FOR YOU ARE ALL I CAN NEVER BE!
YOUR EMOTION IS ILLOGICAL...
...BUT I WILL NOT PERMIT YOU TO DESTROY ME.
WORDS COME EASILY; ACTIONS SOMEWHAT LESS.
UNHHHH...
IT...HAS ENDED... AS IT MUST. MY ENEMY HAS FALLEN.

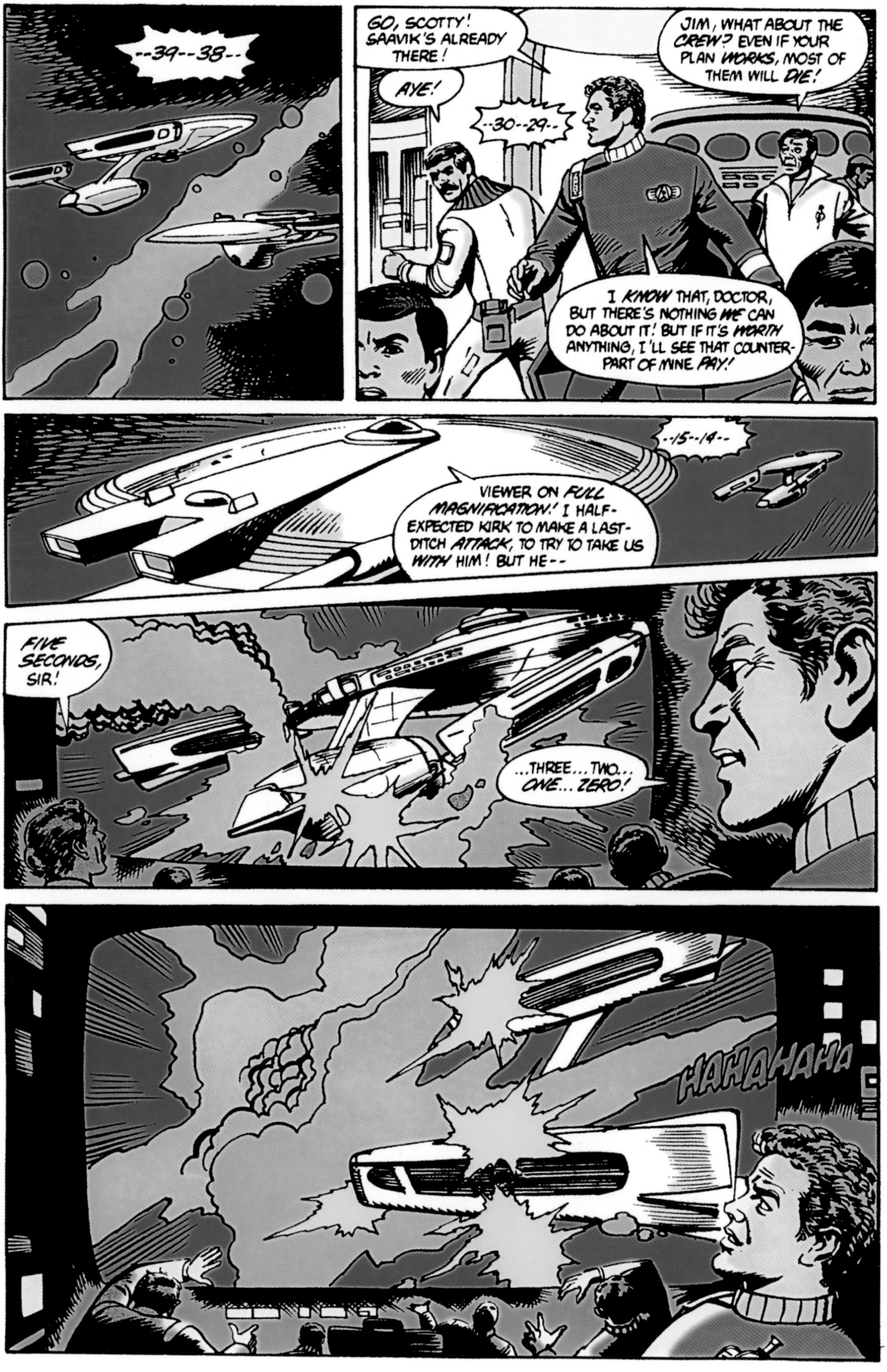
--39--38--
GO, SCOTTY! SAAVIK'S ALREADY THERE!
AYE!
--30--29--
JIM, WHAT ABOUT THE CREW? EVEN IF YOUR PLAN WORKS, MOST OF THEM WILL DIE!
I KNOW THAT, DOCTOR, BUT THERE'S NOTHING WE CAN DO ABOUT IT! BUT IF IT'S WORTH ANYTHING, I'LL SEE THAT COUNTERPART OF MINE PAY!
--15--14--
VIEWER ON FULL MAGNIFICATION! I HALF-EXPECTED KIRK TO MAKE A LAST-DITCH ATTACK, TO TRY TO TAKE US WITH HIM! BUT HE--
FIVE SECONDS, SIR!
...THREE...TWO... ONE...ZERO!
HAHAHAHA

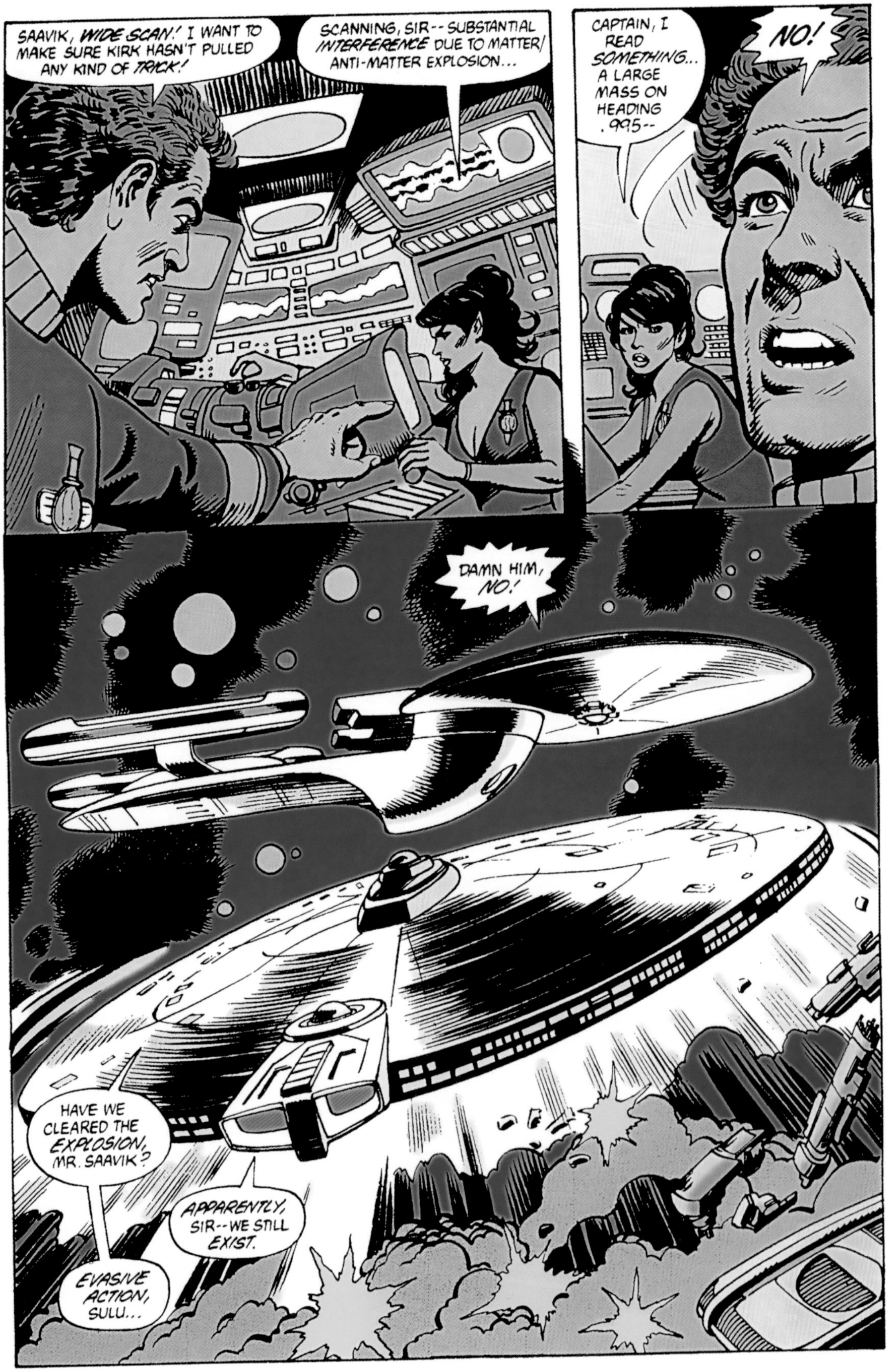
SAAVIK, WIDE SCAN! I WANT TO MAKE SURE KIRK HASN'T PULLED ANY KIND OF TRICK!
SCANNING, SIR-- SUBSTANTIAL INTERFERENCE DUE TO MATTER/ ANTI-MATTER EXPLOSION...
CAPTAIN, I READ SOMETHING... A LARGE MASS ON HEADING .995--
NO!
DAMN HIM, NO!
HAVE WE CLEARED THE EXPLOSION, MR. SAAVIK?
APPARENTLY, SIR--WE STILL EXIST.
EVASIVE ACTION, SULU...

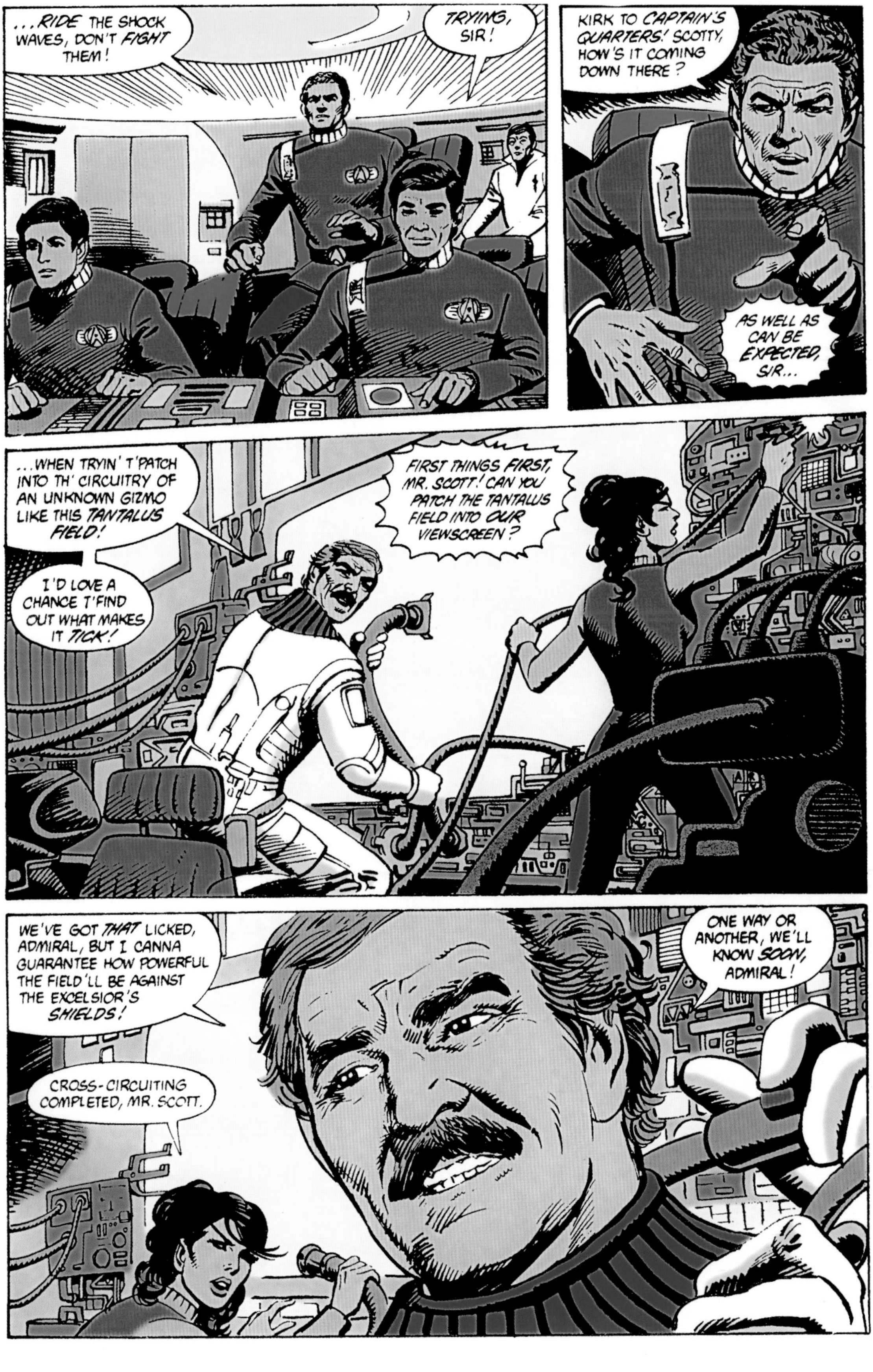
...RIDE THE SHOCK WAVES, DON'T FIGHT THEM!
TRYING, SIR!
KIRK TO CAPTAIN'S QUARTERS! SCOTTY, HOW'S IT COMING DOWN THERE?
AS WELL AS CAN BE EXPECTED, SIR...
...WHEN TRYIN' T'PATCH INTO TH' CIRCUITRY OF AN UNKNOWN GIZMO LIKE THIS TANTALUS FIELD!
I'D LOVE A CHANCE T'FIND OUT WHAT MAKES IT TICK!
FIRST THINGS FIRST, MR. SCOTT! CAN YOU PATCH THE TANTALUS FIELD INTO OUR VIEWSCREEN?
WE'VE GOT THAT LICKED, ADMIRAL, BUT I CANNA GUARANTEE HOW POWERFUL THE FIELD'LL BE AGAINST THE EXCELSIOR'S SHIELDS!
CROSS-CIRCUITING COMPLETED, MR. SCOTT.
ONE WAY OR ANOTHER, WE'LL KNOW SOON, ADMIRAL!

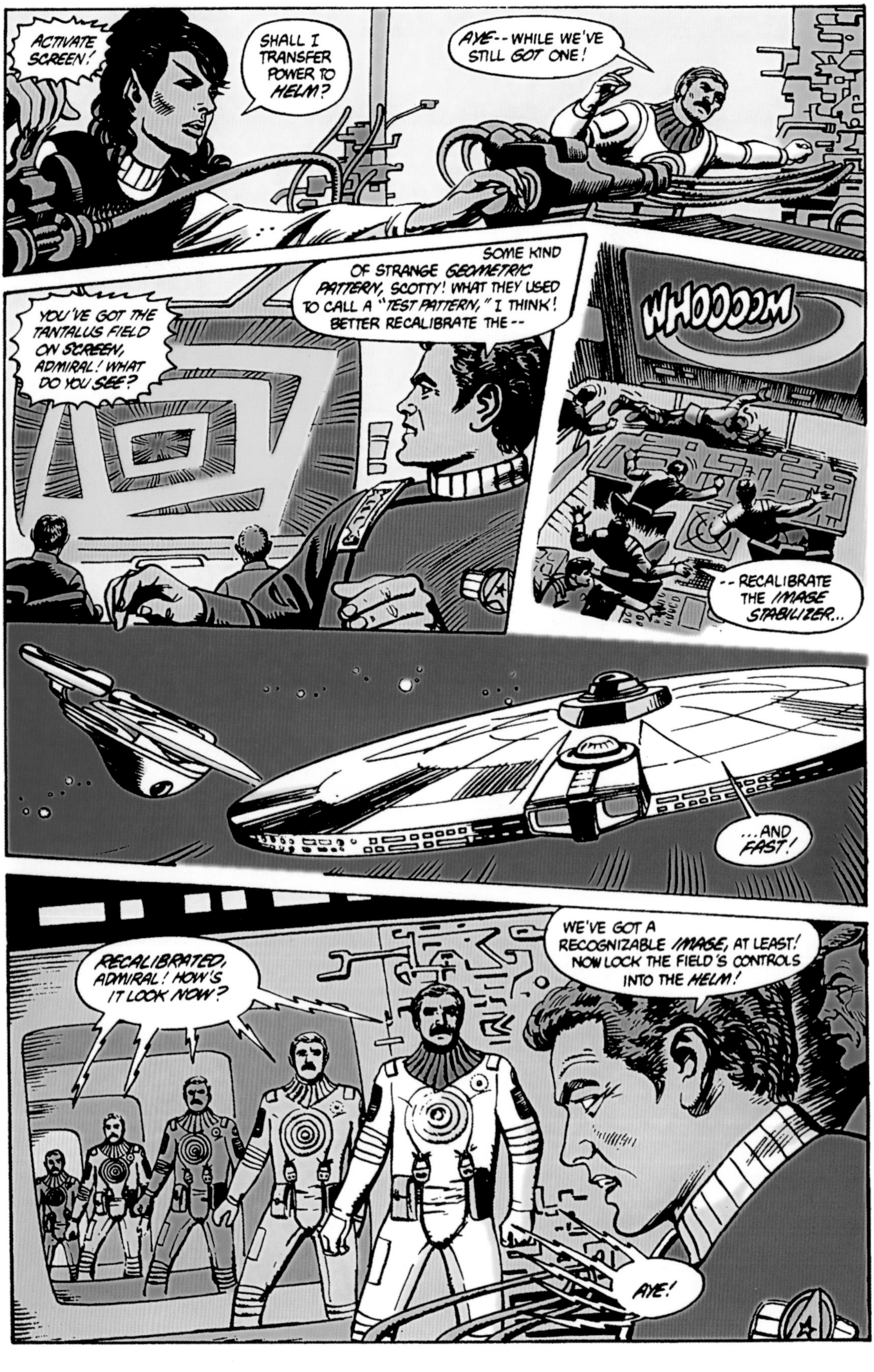
ACTIVATE SCREEN!
SHALL I TRANSFER POWER TO HELM?
AYE--WHILE WE'VE STILL GOT ONE!
YOU'VE GOT THE TANTALUS FIELD ON SCREEN, ADMIRAL! WHAT DO YOU SEE?
SOME KIND OF STRANGE GEOMETRIC PATTERN, SCOTTY! WHAT THEY USED TO CALL A "TEST PATTERN," I THINK! BETTER RECALIBRATE THE--
WHOOOOM
--RECALIBRATE THE IMAGE STABILIZER...
...AND FAST!
RECALIBRATED, ADMIRAL! HOW'S IT LOOK NOW?
WE'VE GOT A RECOGNIZABLE IMAGE, AT LEAST! NOW LOCK THE FIELD'S CONTROLS INTO THE HELM!
AYE!

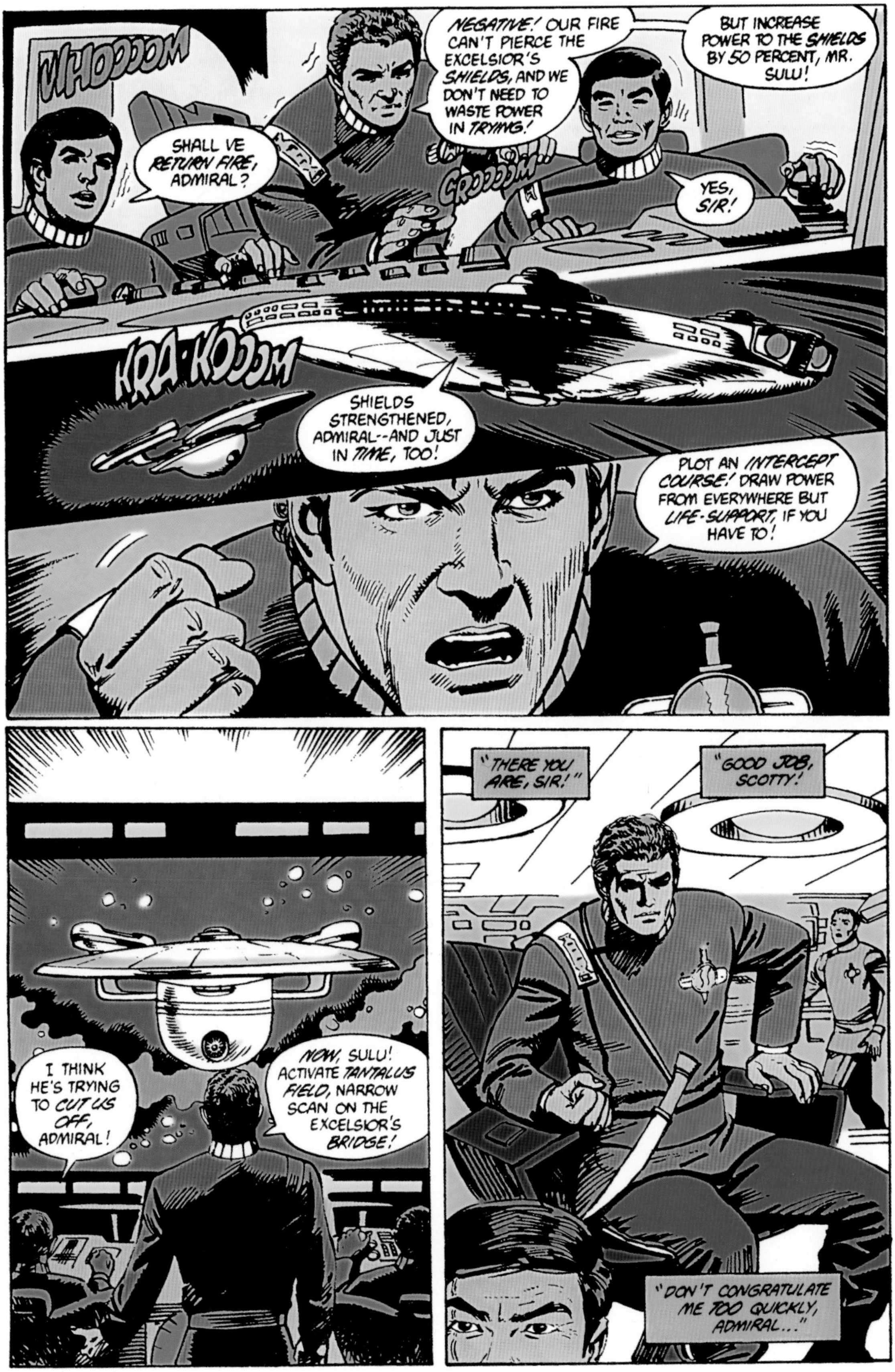
WHOOOOOM
SHALL VE RETURN FIRE, ADMIRAL?
NEGATIVE! OUR FIRE CAN'T PIERCE THE EXCELSIOR'S SHIELDS, AND WE DON'T NEED TO WASTE POWER IN TRYING!
BUT INCREASE POWER TO THE SHIELDS BY 50 PERCENT, MR. SULU!
GROOOOM
YES, SIR!
KRA-KOOOM
SHIELDS STRENGTHENED, ADMIRAL--AND JUST IN TIME, TOO!
PLOT AN INTERCEPT COURSE! DRAW POWER FROM EVERYWHERE BUT LIFE-SUPPORT, IF YOU HAVE TO!
I THINK HE'S TRYING TO CUT US OFF, ADMIRAL!
NOW, SULU! ACTIVATE TANTALUS FIELD, NARROW SCAN ON THE EXCELSIOR'S BRIDGE!
"THERE YOU ARE, SIR!"
"GOOD JOB, SCOTTY!"
"DON'T CONGRATULATE ME TOO QUICKLY, ADMIRAL..."

...WE'VE *TAPPED* INTO THE *TANTALUS FIELD'S* *SPYING ABILITY,* RIGHT ENOUGH-- BUT I CAN'T *GUARANTEE* THE *DISINTEGRATION FUNCTION'LL* WORK--NOT AGAINST THEIR *SHIELDS!*

I DON'T WANT TO *DESTROY* THE *WHOLE SHIP,* SCOTTY...

...JUST A FEW *KEY* COMPONENTS!

YOU-- THEIR *CAPTAIN,* SIR?

NO, SULU-- AS MUCH AS I'D *LIKE* TO!

SWITCH TO *EXCELSIOR'S* *ENGINE ROOM,* FOCUS ON THEIR *POWER SUPPLY CONVERTER!*

AYE, SIR.

ACTIVATE *DISINTEGRATION* FUNCTION.

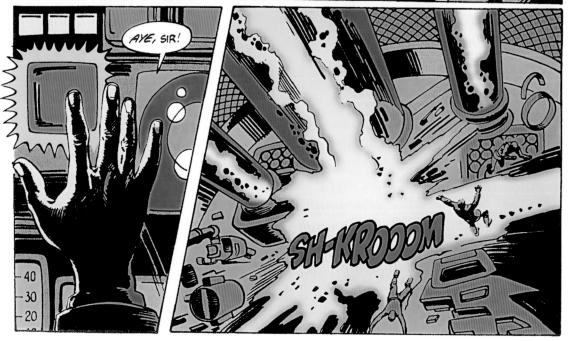

AYE, SIR!

SH-KROOOM

40
30
20

FIRE *FULL PHASERS* AND *PHOTON TORPEDOES!*

ARE YOU DEAF? *FIRE!*

WE'VE JUST LOST *ALL POWER* TO THE *WEAPONS,* SIR...

...AND... TO THE *SCREEN,* TOO!

ENGINEERING, WHAT'S HAPPENING?

DAMMIT, WHAT'S GOING *ON?*

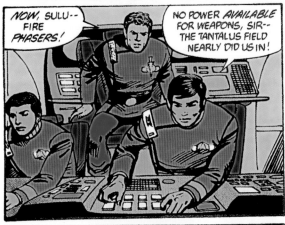

NOW, SULU-- FIRE *PHASERS!*

NO POWER *AVAILABLE* FOR WEAPONS, SIR-- THE TANTALUS FIELD NEARLY DID US IN!

KIRK TO CAPTAIN'S QUARTERS! MR. SCOTT, MR. SAAVIK, REPORT TO *PRIMARY DOCKING PORT* IMMEDIATELY!

BONES, SULU, CHEKOV, YOU'LL COME WITH *ME...*

...UHURA, YOU HAVE THE *CONN--*

--OR AT LEAST, WHAT'S *LEFT* OF IT!

Y-YES, SIR!

WELL, BETTER LATE THAN *NEVER!*

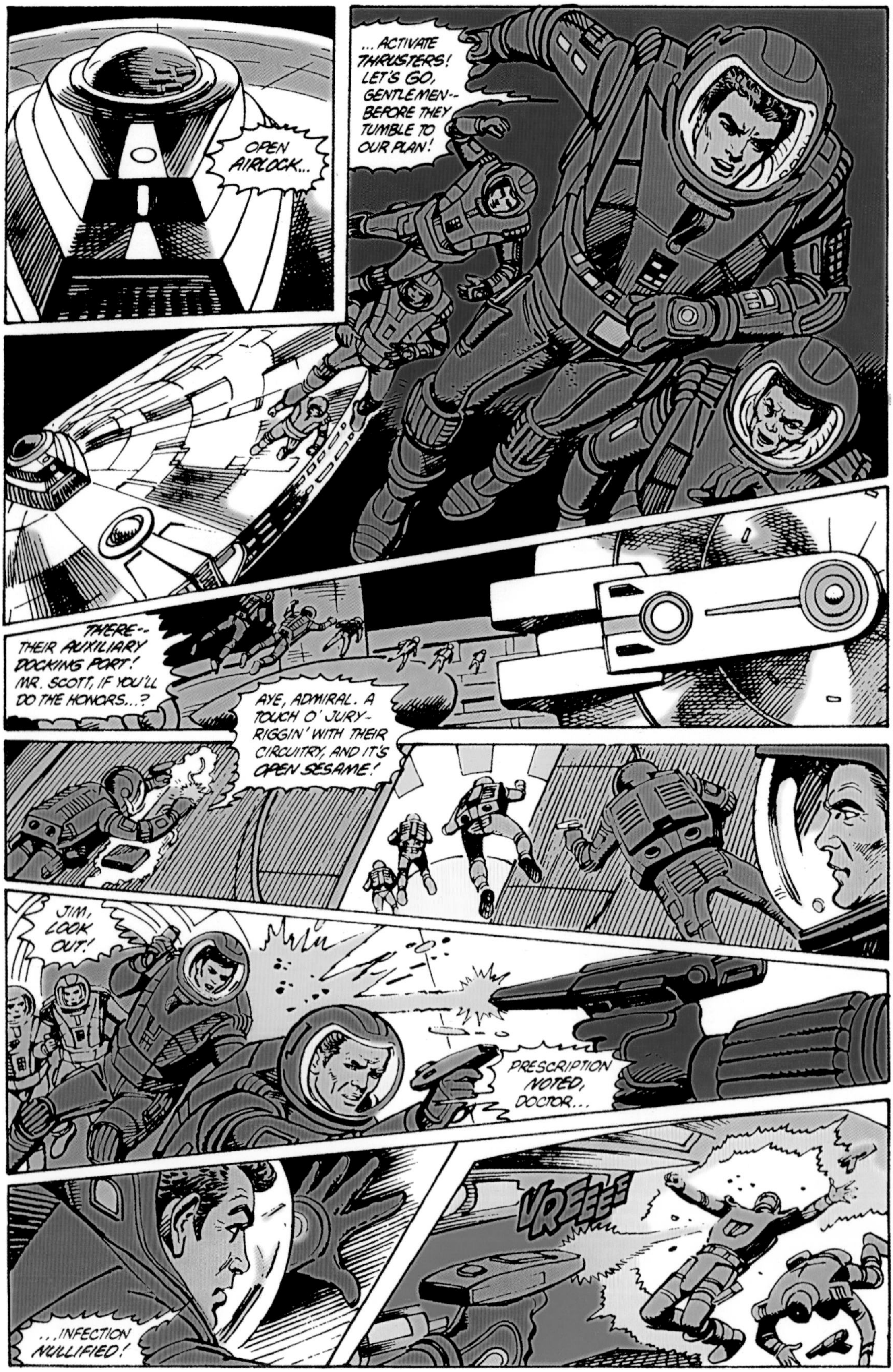

OPEN AIRLOCK...
... ACTIVATE THRUSTERS! LET'S GO, GENTLEMEN-- BEFORE THEY TUMBLE TO OUR PLAN!
THERE-- THEIR AUXILIARY DOCKING PORT! MR. SCOTT, IF YOU'LL DO THE HONORS...?
AYE, ADMIRAL. A TOUCH O' JURY-RIGGIN' WITH THEIR CIRCUITRY, AND IT'S OPEN SESAME!
JIM, LOOK OUT!
PRESCRIPTION NOTED, DOCTOR...
...INFECTION NULLIFIED!
VREEEE

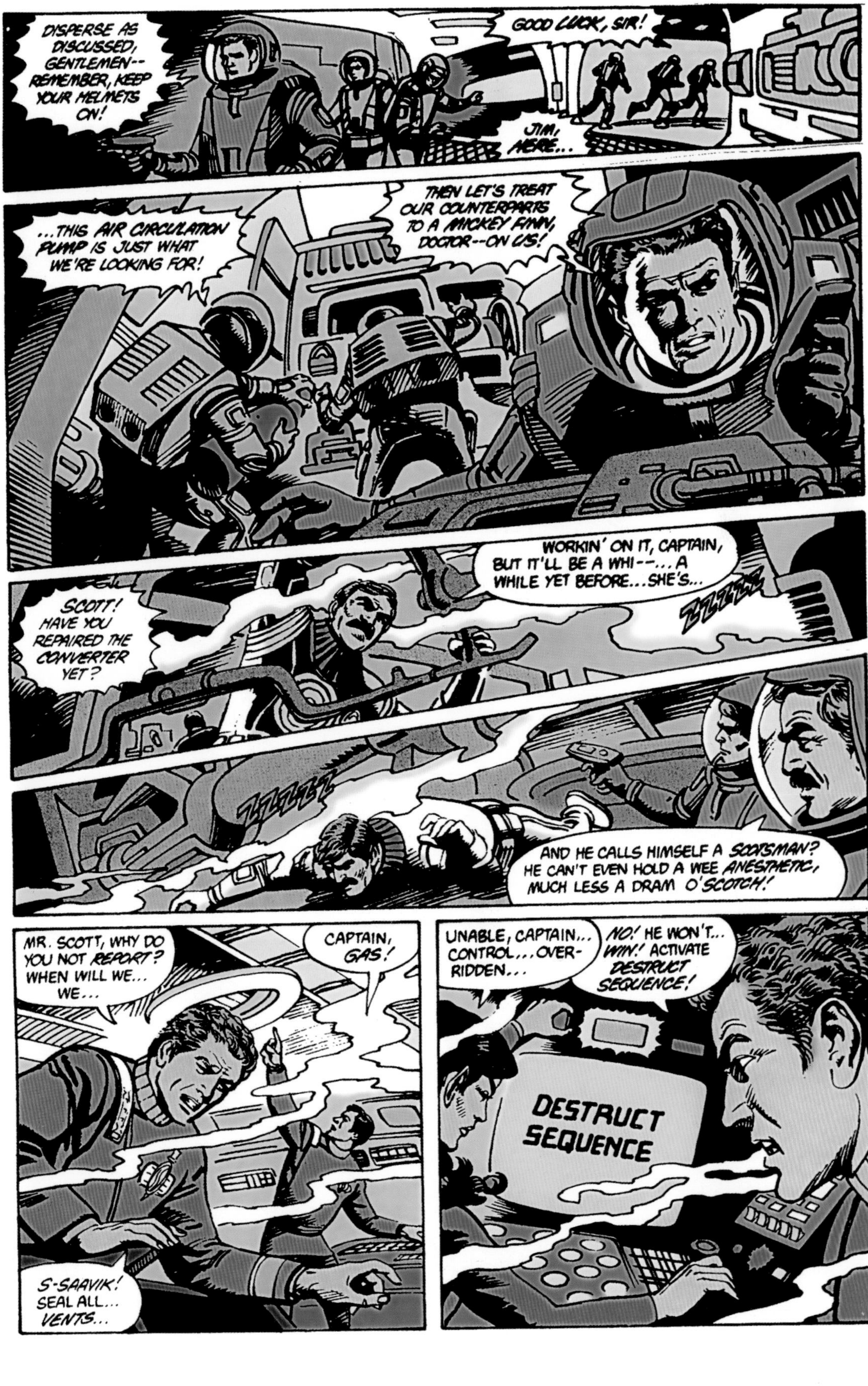
DISPERSE AS DISCUSSED, GENTLEMEN-- REMEMBER, KEEP YOUR HELMETS ON!
GOOD LUCK, SIR!
JIM, HERE...
...THIS AIR CIRCULATION PUMP IS JUST WHAT WE'RE LOOKING FOR!
THEN LET'S TREAT OUR COUNTERPARTS TO A MICKEY FINN, DOCTOR--ON US!
SCOTT! HAVE YOU REPAIRED THE CONVERTER YET?
WORKIN' ON IT, CAPTAIN, BUT IT'LL BE A WHI--... A WHILE YET BEFORE... SHE'S...
ZZZZZ
ZZZZZ
AND HE CALLS HIMSELF A SCOTSMAN? HE CAN'T EVEN HOLD A WEE ANESTHETIC, MUCH LESS A DRAM O'SCOTCH!
MR. SCOTT, WHY DO YOU NOT REPORT? WHEN WILL WE... WE...
CAPTAIN, GAS!
S-SAAVIK! SEAL ALL... VENTS...
UNABLE, CAPTAIN... CONTROL... OVER-RIDDEN...
NO! HE WON'T... WIN! ACTIVATE DESTRUCT SEQUENCE!
DESTRUCT SEQUENCE

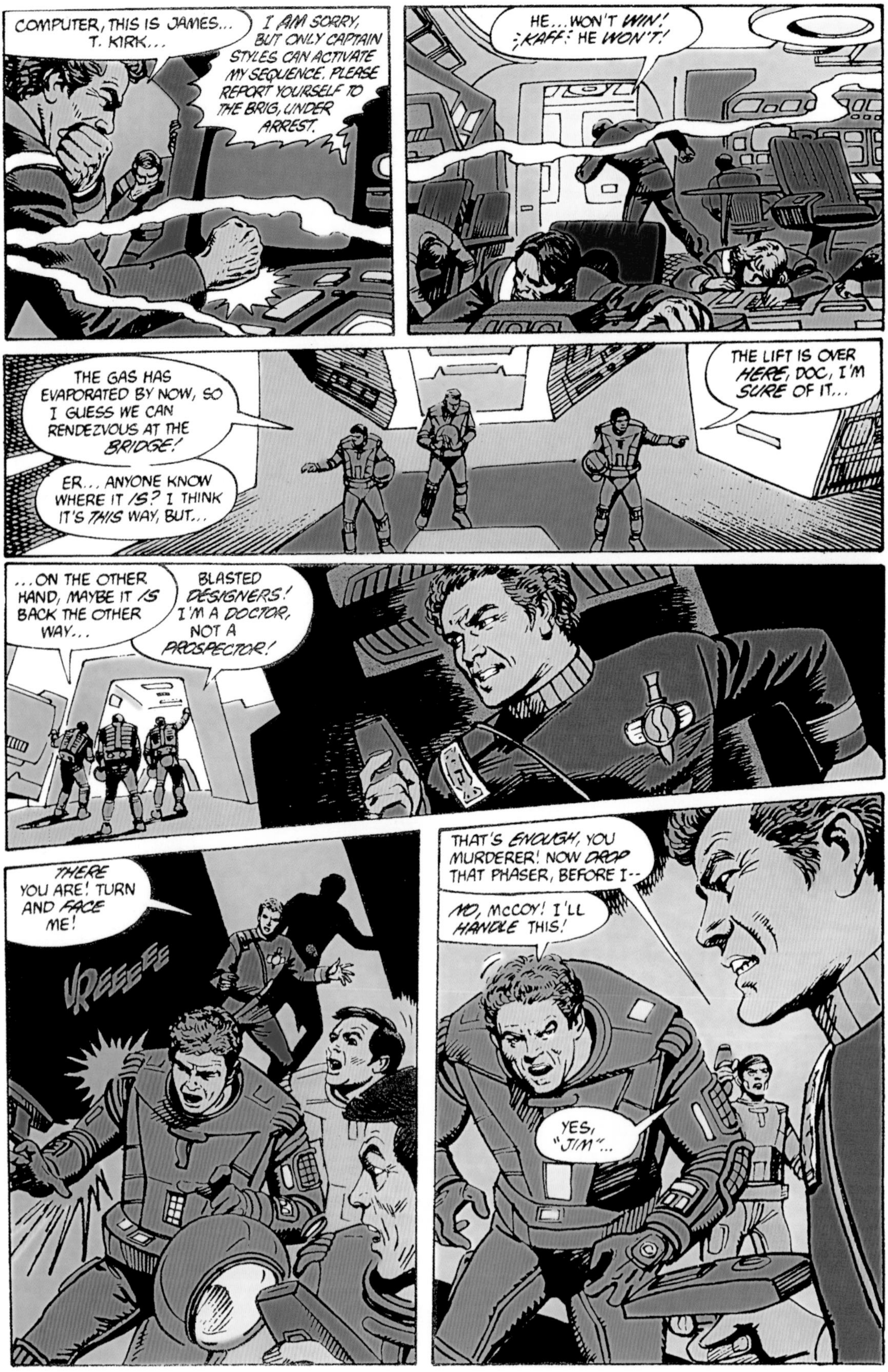

COMPUTER, THIS IS JAMES... T. KIRK...
I AM SORRY, BUT ONLY CAPTAIN STYLES CAN ACTIVATE MY SEQUENCE. PLEASE REPORT YOURSELF TO THE BRIG, UNDER ARREST.
HE...WON'T WIN! ;KAFF; HE WON'T!
THE GAS HAS EVAPORATED BY NOW, SO I GUESS WE CAN RENDEZVOUS AT THE BRIDGE!
ER... ANYONE KNOW WHERE IT IS? I THINK IT'S THIS WAY, BUT...
THE LIFT IS OVER HERE, DOC, I'M SURE OF IT...
...ON THE OTHER HAND, MAYBE IT IS BACK THE OTHER WAY...
BLASTED DESIGNERS! I'M A DOCTOR, NOT A PROSPECTOR!
THERE YOU ARE! TURN AND FACE ME!
VREEEEEE
THAT'S ENOUGH, YOU MURDERER! NOW DROP THAT PHASER, BEFORE I--
NO, McCOY! I'LL HANDLE THIS!
YES, "JIM"...

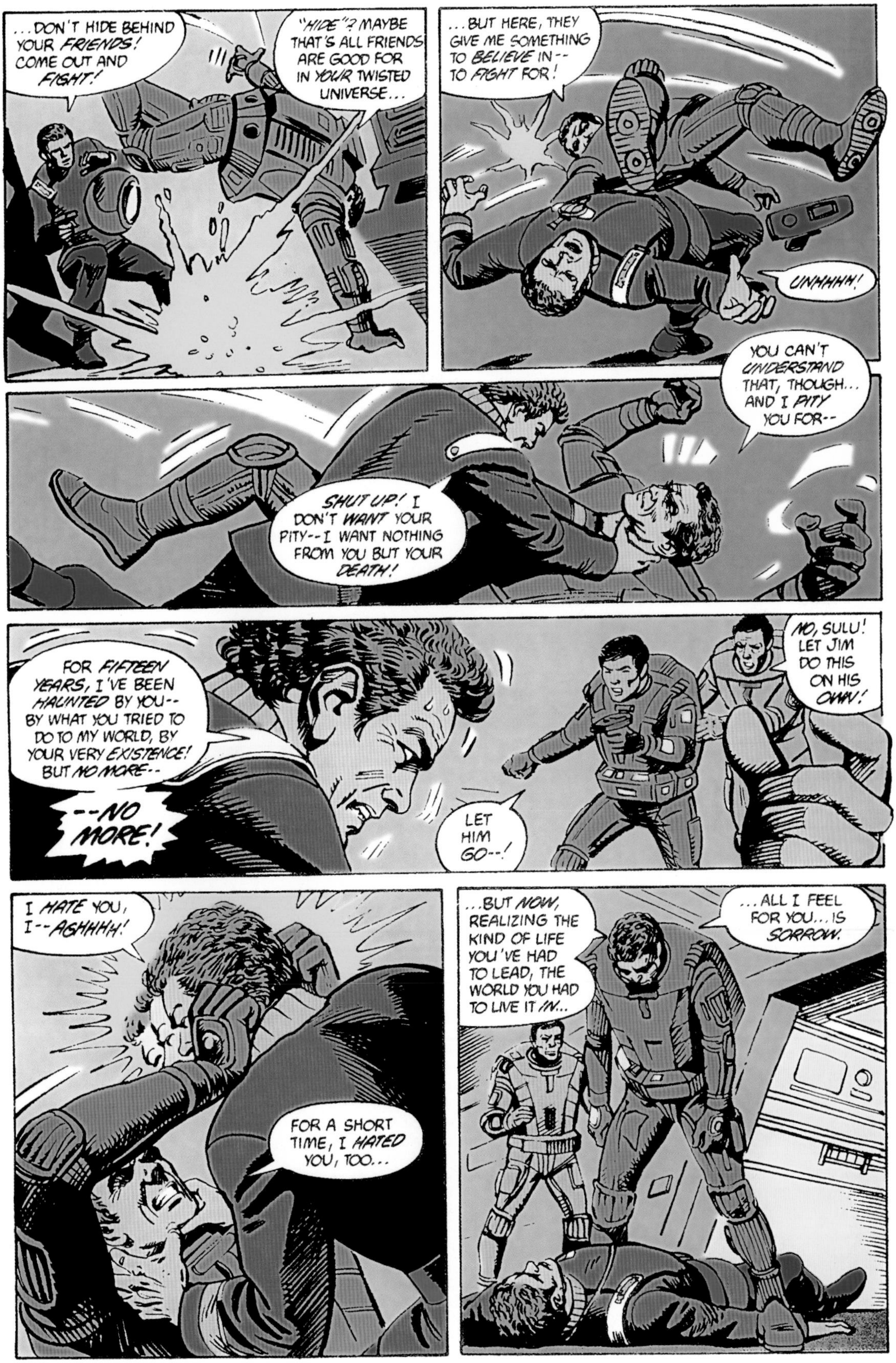
...DON'T HIDE BEHIND YOUR FRIENDS! COME OUT AND FIGHT!
"HIDE"? MAYBE THAT'S ALL FRIENDS ARE GOOD FOR IN YOUR TWISTED UNIVERSE...
...BUT HERE, THEY GIVE ME SOMETHING TO BELIEVE IN-- TO FIGHT FOR!
UNHHHH!
YOU CAN'T UNDERSTAND THAT, THOUGH... AND I PITY YOU FOR--
SHUT UP! I DON'T WANT YOUR PITY--I WANT NOTHING FROM YOU BUT YOUR DEATH!
FOR FIFTEEN YEARS, I'VE BEEN HAUNTED BY YOU-- BY WHAT YOU TRIED TO DO TO MY WORLD, BY YOUR VERY EXISTENCE! BUT NO MORE--
--NO MORE!
NO, SULU! LET JIM DO THIS ON HIS OWN!
LET HIM GO--!
I HATE YOU, I--AGHHHH!
FOR A SHORT TIME, I HATED YOU, TOO...
...BUT NOW, REALIZING THE KIND OF LIFE YOU'VE HAD TO LEAD, THE WORLD YOU HAD TO LIVE IT IN...
...ALL I FEEL FOR YOU... IS SORROW.

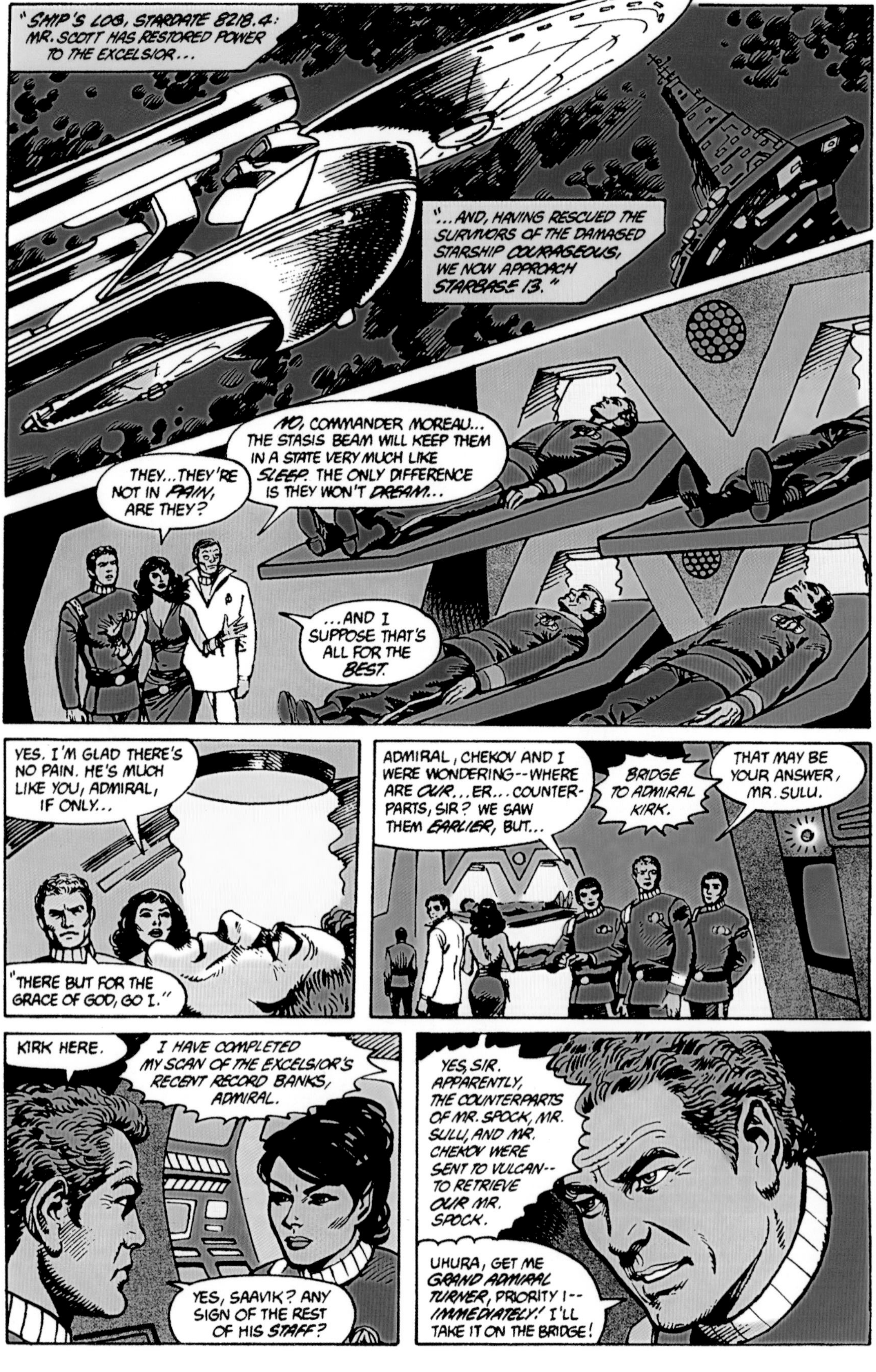
"SHIP'S LOG, STARDATE 8218.4: MR. SCOTT HAS RESTORED POWER TO THE EXCELSIOR...
"...AND, HAVING RESCUED THE SURVIVORS OF THE DAMAGED STARSHIP COURAGEOUS, WE NOW APPROACH STARBASE 13."
THEY...THEY'RE NOT IN PAIN, ARE THEY?
NO, COMMANDER MOREAU... THE STASIS BEAM WILL KEEP THEM IN A STATE VERY MUCH LIKE SLEEP. THE ONLY DIFFERENCE IS THEY WON'T DREAM...
...AND I SUPPOSE THAT'S ALL FOR THE BEST.
YES. I'M GLAD THERE'S NO PAIN. HE'S MUCH LIKE YOU, ADMIRAL, IF ONLY...
"THERE BUT FOR THE GRACE OF GOD, GO I."
ADMIRAL, CHEKOV AND I WERE WONDERING--WHERE ARE OUR...ER...COUNTER-PARTS, SIR? WE SAW THEM EARLIER, BUT...
BRIDGE TO ADMIRAL KIRK.
THAT MAY BE YOUR ANSWER, MR. SULU.
KIRK HERE.
I HAVE COMPLETED MY SCAN OF THE EXCELSIOR'S RECENT RECORD BANKS, ADMIRAL.
YES, SAAVIK? ANY SIGN OF THE REST OF HIS STAFF?
YES, SIR. APPARENTLY, THE COUNTERPARTS OF MR. SPOCK, MR. SULU, AND MR. CHEKOV WERE SENT TO VULCAN-- TO RETRIEVE OUR MR. SPOCK.
UHURA, GET ME GRAND ADMIRAL TURNER, PRIORITY I-- IMMEDIATELY! I'LL TAKE IT ON THE BRIDGE!

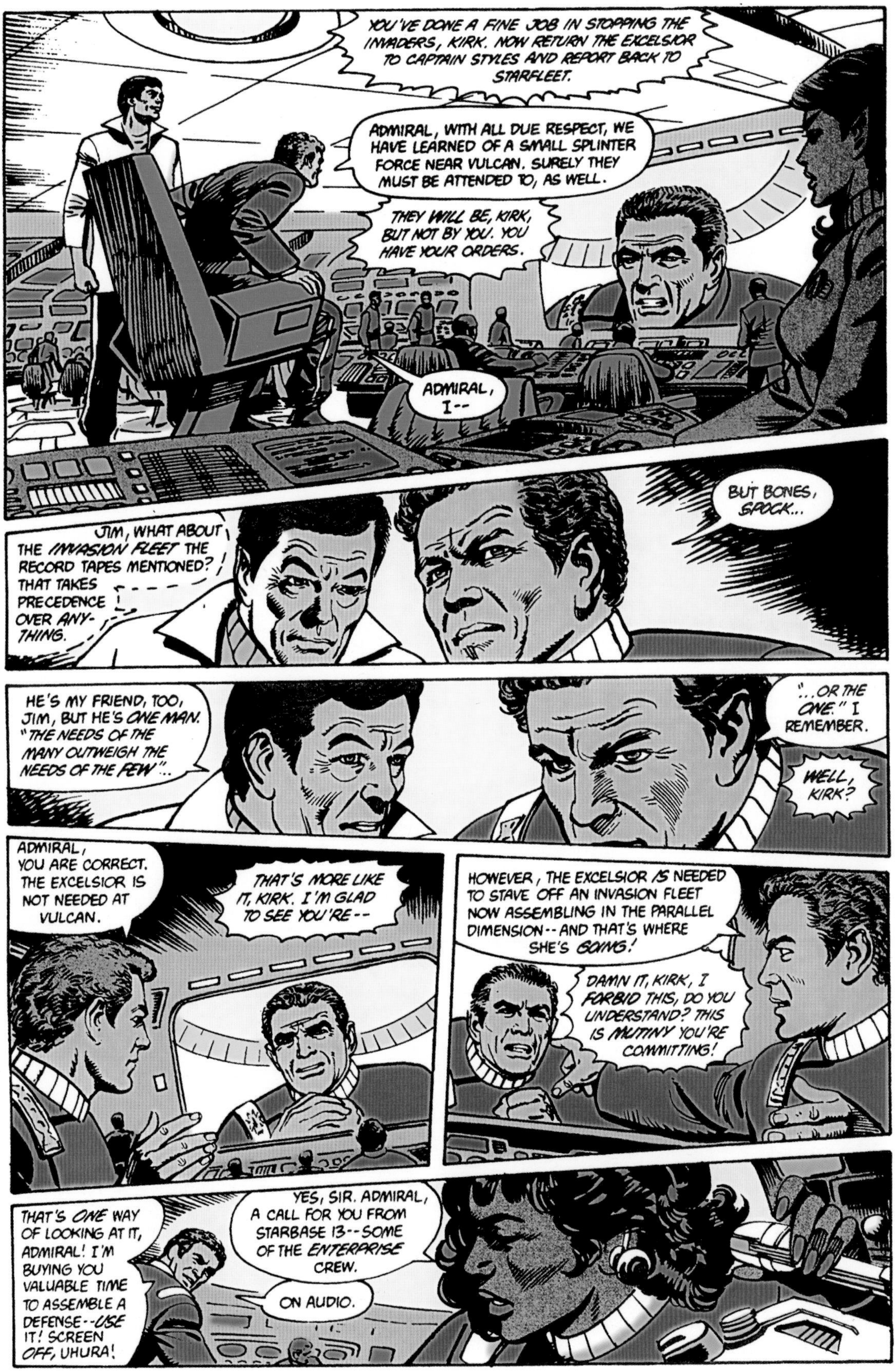

YOU'VE DONE A FINE JOB IN STOPPING THE INVADERS, KIRK. NOW RETURN THE EXCELSIOR TO CAPTAIN STYLES AND REPORT BACK TO STARFLEET.
ADMIRAL, WITH ALL DUE RESPECT, WE HAVE LEARNED OF A SMALL SPLINTER FORCE NEAR VULCAN. SURELY THEY MUST BE ATTENDED TO, AS WELL.
THEY WILL BE, KIRK, BUT NOT BY YOU. YOU HAVE YOUR ORDERS.
ADMIRAL, I--
JIM, WHAT ABOUT THE INVASION FLEET THE RECORD TAPES MENTIONED? THAT TAKES PRECEDENCE OVER ANYTHING.
BUT BONES, SPOCK...
HE'S MY FRIEND, TOO, JIM, BUT HE'S ONE MAN. "THE NEEDS OF THE MANY OUTWEIGH THE NEEDS OF THE FEW"...
"...OR THE ONE." I REMEMBER.
WELL, KIRK?
ADMIRAL, YOU ARE CORRECT. THE EXCELSIOR IS NOT NEEDED AT VULCAN.
THAT'S MORE LIKE IT, KIRK. I'M GLAD TO SEE YOU'RE--
HOWEVER, THE EXCELSIOR IS NEEDED TO STAVE OFF AN INVASION FLEET NOW ASSEMBLING IN THE PARALLEL DIMENSION--AND THAT'S WHERE SHE'S GOING!
DAMN IT, KIRK, I FORBID THIS, DO YOU UNDERSTAND? THIS IS MUTINY YOU'RE COMMITTING!
THAT'S ONE WAY OF LOOKING AT IT, ADMIRAL! I'M BUYING YOU VALUABLE TIME TO ASSEMBLE A DEFENSE--USE IT! SCREEN OFF, UHURA!
YES, SIR. ADMIRAL, A CALL FOR YOU FROM STARBASE 13--SOME OF THE ENTERPRISE CREW.
ON AUDIO.

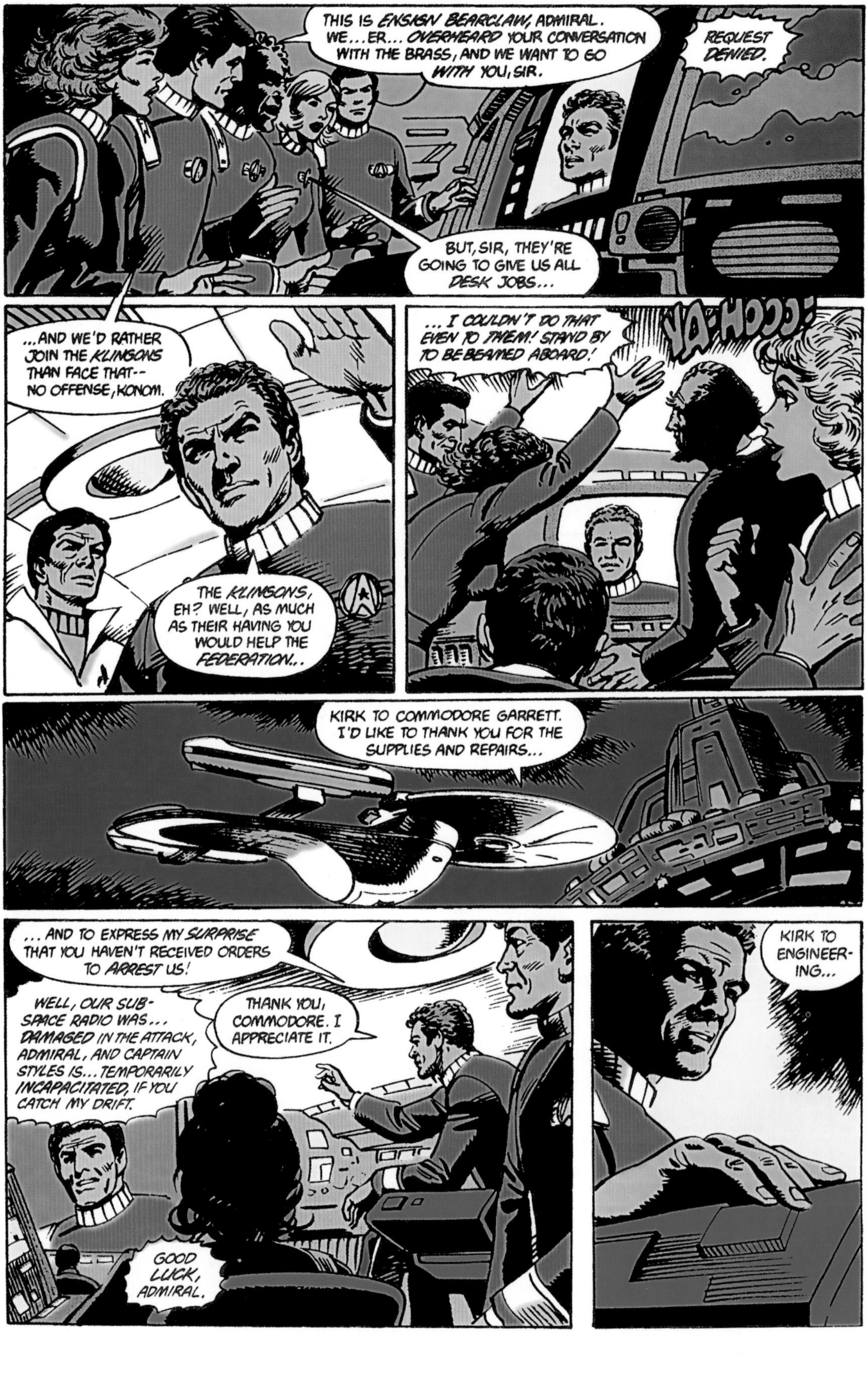

THIS IS ENSIGN BEARCLAW, ADMIRAL. WE...ER... OVERHEARD YOUR CONVERSATION WITH THE BRASS, AND WE WANT TO GO WITH YOU, SIR.
REQUEST DENIED.
BUT, SIR, THEY'RE GOING TO GIVE US ALL DESK JOBS...
...AND WE'D RATHER JOIN THE KLINGONS THAN FACE THAT-- NO OFFENSE, KONOM.
THE KLINGONS, EH? WELL, AS MUCH AS THEIR HAVING YOU WOULD HELP THE FEDERATION...
...I COULDN'T DO THAT EVEN TO THEM! STAND BY TO BE BEAMED ABOARD!
YA-HOOO!
KIRK TO COMMODORE GARRETT. I'D LIKE TO THANK YOU FOR THE SUPPLIES AND REPAIRS...
...AND TO EXPRESS MY SURPRISE THAT YOU HAVEN'T RECEIVED ORDERS TO ARREST US!
WELL, OUR SUB-SPACE RADIO WAS... DAMAGED IN THE ATTACK, ADMIRAL, AND CAPTAIN STYLES IS... TEMPORARILY INCAPACITATED, IF YOU CATCH MY DRIFT.
THANK YOU, COMMODORE. I APPRECIATE IT.
GOOD LUCK, ADMIRAL.
KIRK TO ENGINEER-ING...

...READY TO LIVE UP TO YOUR REPUTATION AS A *MIRACLE WORKER*, MR. SCOTT?

MR. SAAVIK TOLD ME SHE'S GOT THE WHOLE THING NAILED DOWN, AN' I BELIEVE *HER*...

...AS FOR MY PART, I CAN GIVE YE ALL THE POWER YE *WANT*... AND A TRIFLE *MORE*, BESIDES!

STATUS, MR. SAAVIK?

THE CALCULATIONS THAT LED TO OUR COUNTERPARTS' DIMENSIONAL BREACH ARE EXTRAORDINARILY *COMPLEX*, ADMIRAL...

WE'LL NEED IT, SCOTTY. WELL DONE.

...BUT QUITE CAPABLE OF DUPLICATION BY THE *EXCELSIOR*, DUE TO HER *TRANSWARP ENGINES*. WE MAY DEPART AT ANY TIME.

EXCELLENT; PREPARE FOR DEPARTURE.

I ONLY HOPE I'M DOING THE RIGHT THING, BONES. ALL I CAN THINK OF IS *SPOCK*.

ME, TOO, JIM, BUT *STARFLEET*'LL LOOK AFTER HIM. ONLY YOU CAN DO WHAT HAS TO BE DONE NOW.

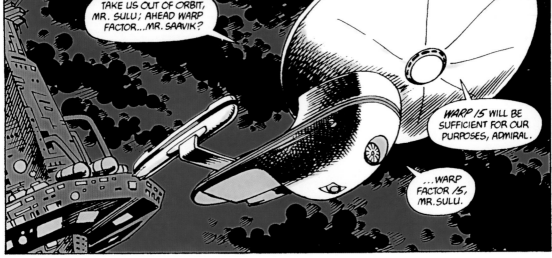

TAKE US OUT OF ORBIT, MR. SULU; AHEAD WARP FACTOR...MR. SAAVIK?

WARP 15 WILL BE SUFFICIENT FOR OUR PURPOSES, ADMIRAL.

...WARP FACTOR *15*, MR. SULU.

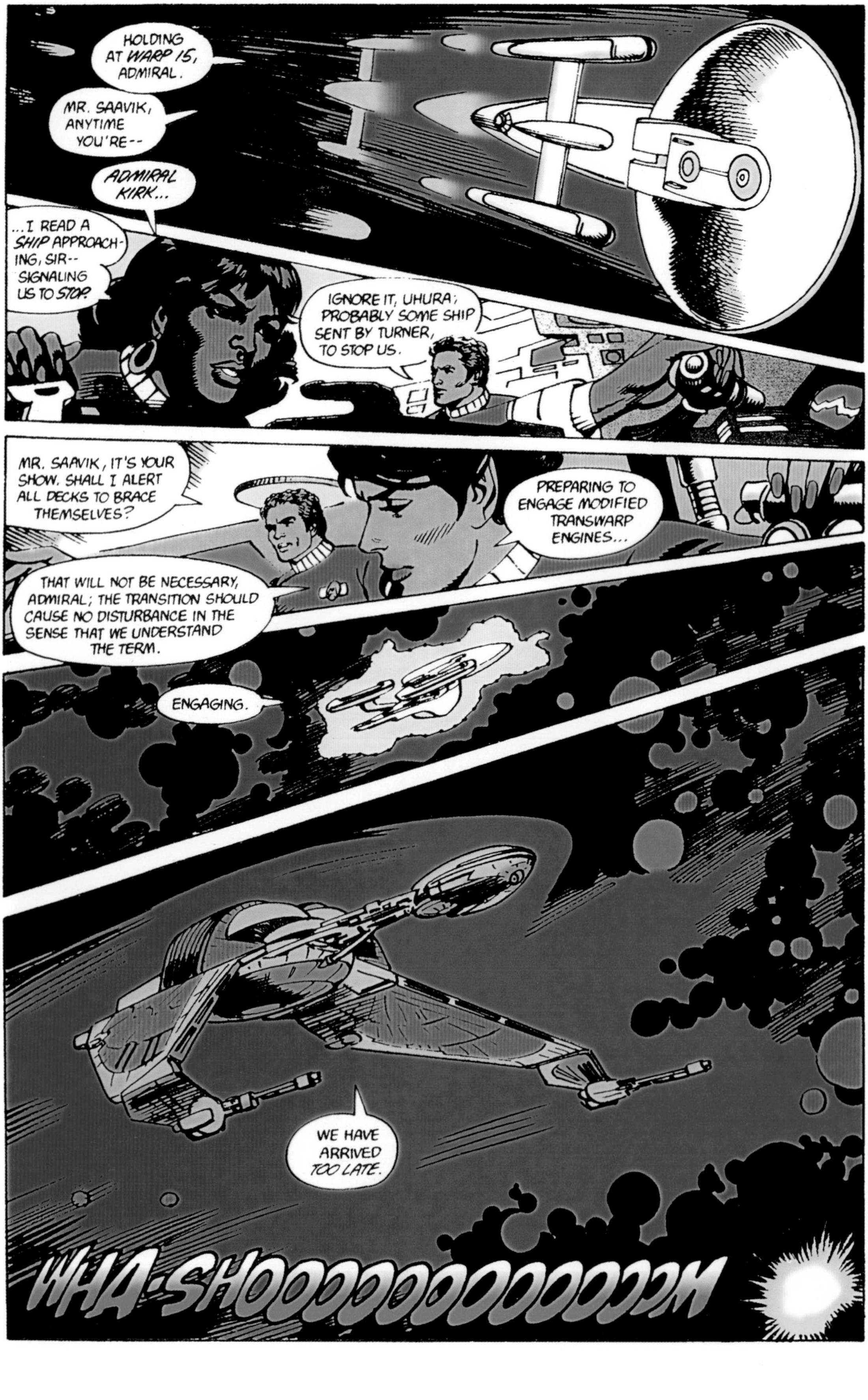
HOLDING AT WARP 15, ADMIRAL.
MR. SAAVIK, ANYTIME YOU'RE--
ADMIRAL KIRK...
...I READ A SHIP APPROACHING, SIR-- SIGNALING US TO STOP.
IGNORE IT, UHURA; PROBABLY SOME SHIP SENT BY TURNER, TO STOP US.
MR. SAAVIK, IT'S YOUR SHOW. SHALL I ALERT ALL DECKS TO BRACE THEMSELVES?
PREPARING TO ENGAGE MODIFIED TRANSWARP ENGINES...
THAT WILL NOT BE NECESSARY, ADMIRAL; THE TRANSITION SHOULD CAUSE NO DISTURBANCE IN THE SENSE THAT WE UNDERSTAND THE TERM.
ENGAGING.
WE HAVE ARRIVED TOO LATE.
WHA-SHOOOOOOOOOOOOOM

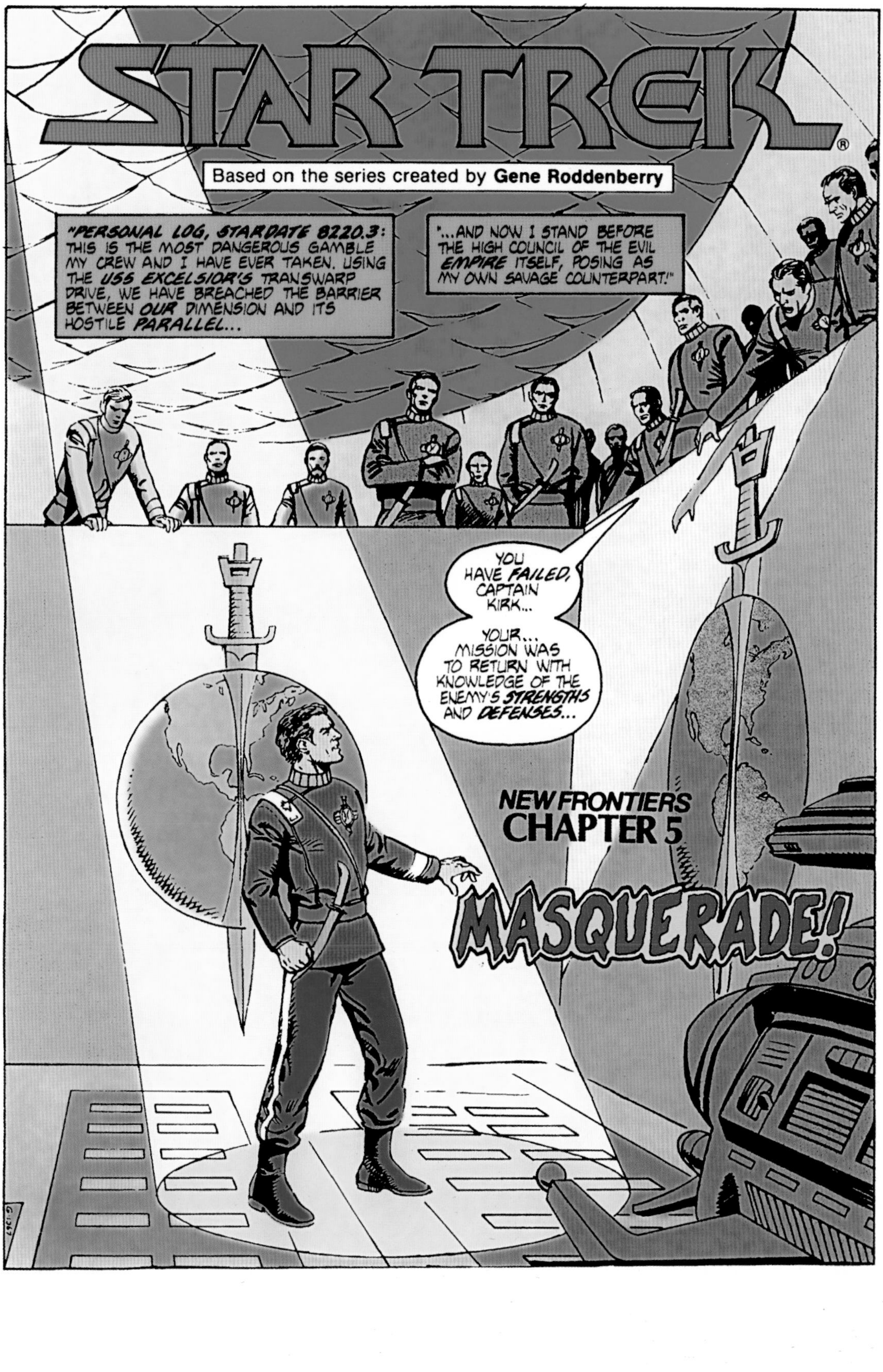
STAR TREK®
Based on the series created by Gene Roddenberry
"PERSONAL LOG, STARDATE 8220.3: THIS IS THE MOST DANGEROUS GAMBLE MY CREW AND I HAVE EVER TAKEN. USING THE USS EXCELSIOR'S TRANSWARP DRIVE, WE HAVE BREACHED THE BARRIER BETWEEN OUR DIMENSION AND ITS HOSTILE PARALLEL...
"...AND NOW I STAND BEFORE THE HIGH COUNCIL OF THE EVIL EMPIRE ITSELF, POSING AS MY OWN SAVAGE COUNTERPART!"
YOU HAVE FAILED, CAPTAIN KIRK...
YOUR... MISSION WAS TO RETURN WITH KNOWLEDGE OF THE ENEMY'S STRENGTHS AND DEFENSES...
NEW FRONTIERS CHAPTER 5
MASQUERADE!

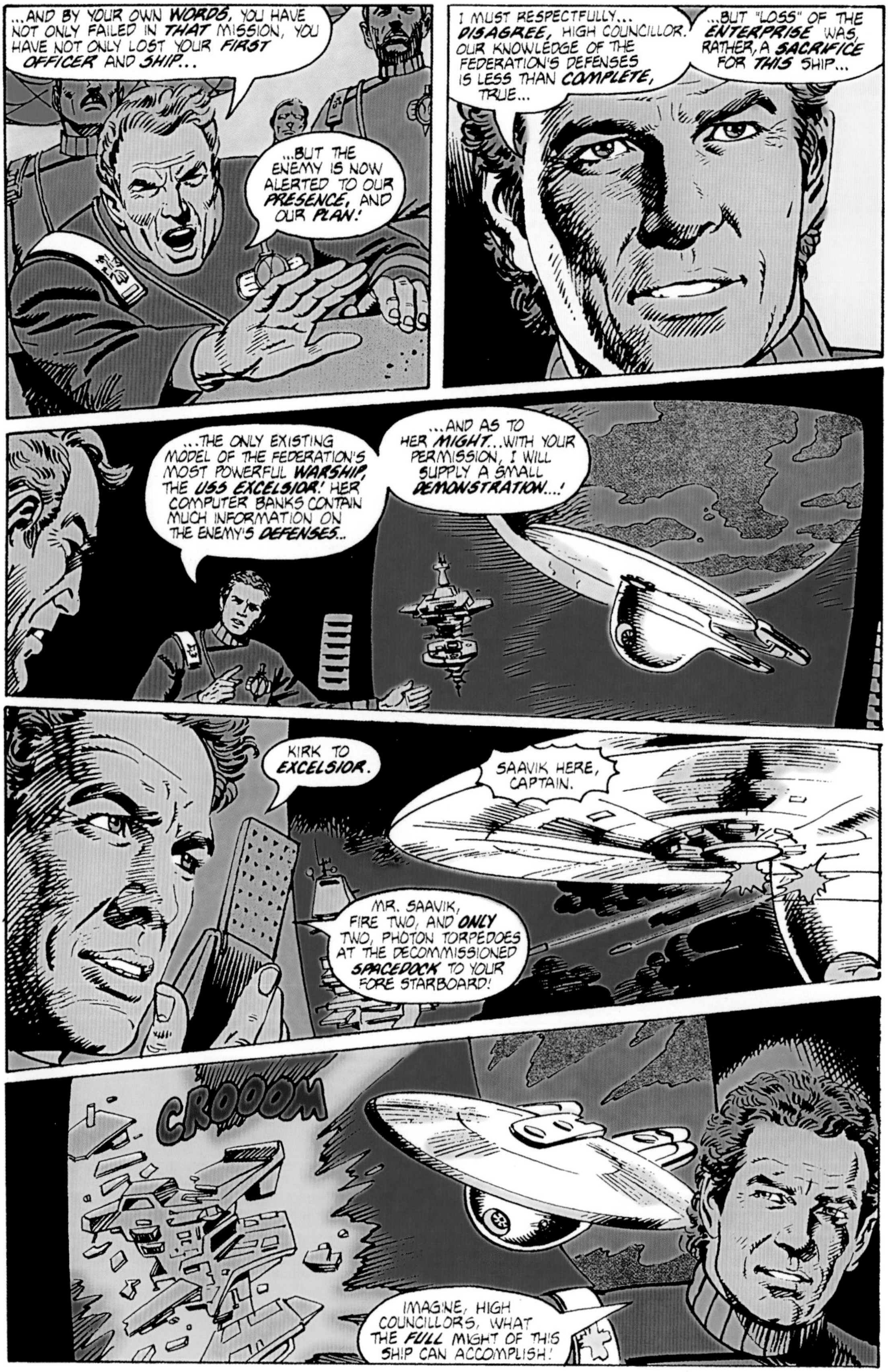
...AND BY YOUR OWN WORDS, YOU HAVE NOT ONLY FAILED IN THAT MISSION, YOU HAVE NOT ONLY LOST YOUR FIRST OFFICER AND SHIP...
...BUT THE ENEMY IS NOW ALERTED TO OUR PRESENCE, AND OUR PLAN!
I MUST RESPECTFULLY... DISAGREE, HIGH COUNCILLOR. OUR KNOWLEDGE OF THE FEDERATION'S DEFENSES IS LESS THAN COMPLETE, TRUE...
...BUT "LOSS" OF THE ENTERPRISE WAS, RATHER, A SACRIFICE FOR THIS SHIP...
...THE ONLY EXISTING MODEL OF THE FEDERATION'S MOST POWERFUL WARSHIP, THE USS EXCELSIOR! HER COMPUTER BANKS CONTAIN MUCH INFORMATION ON THE ENEMY'S DEFENSES...
...AND AS TO HER MIGHT...WITH YOUR PERMISSION, I WILL SUPPLY A SMALL DEMONSTRATION...!
KIRK TO EXCELSIOR.
SAAVIK HERE, CAPTAIN.
MR. SAAVIK, FIRE TWO, AND ONLY TWO, PHOTON TORPEDOES AT THE DECOMMISSIONED SPACEDOCK TO YOUR FORE STARBOARD!
CROOOM
IMAGINE, HIGH COUNCILLORS, WHAT THE FULL MIGHT OF THIS SHIP CAN ACCOMPLISH!

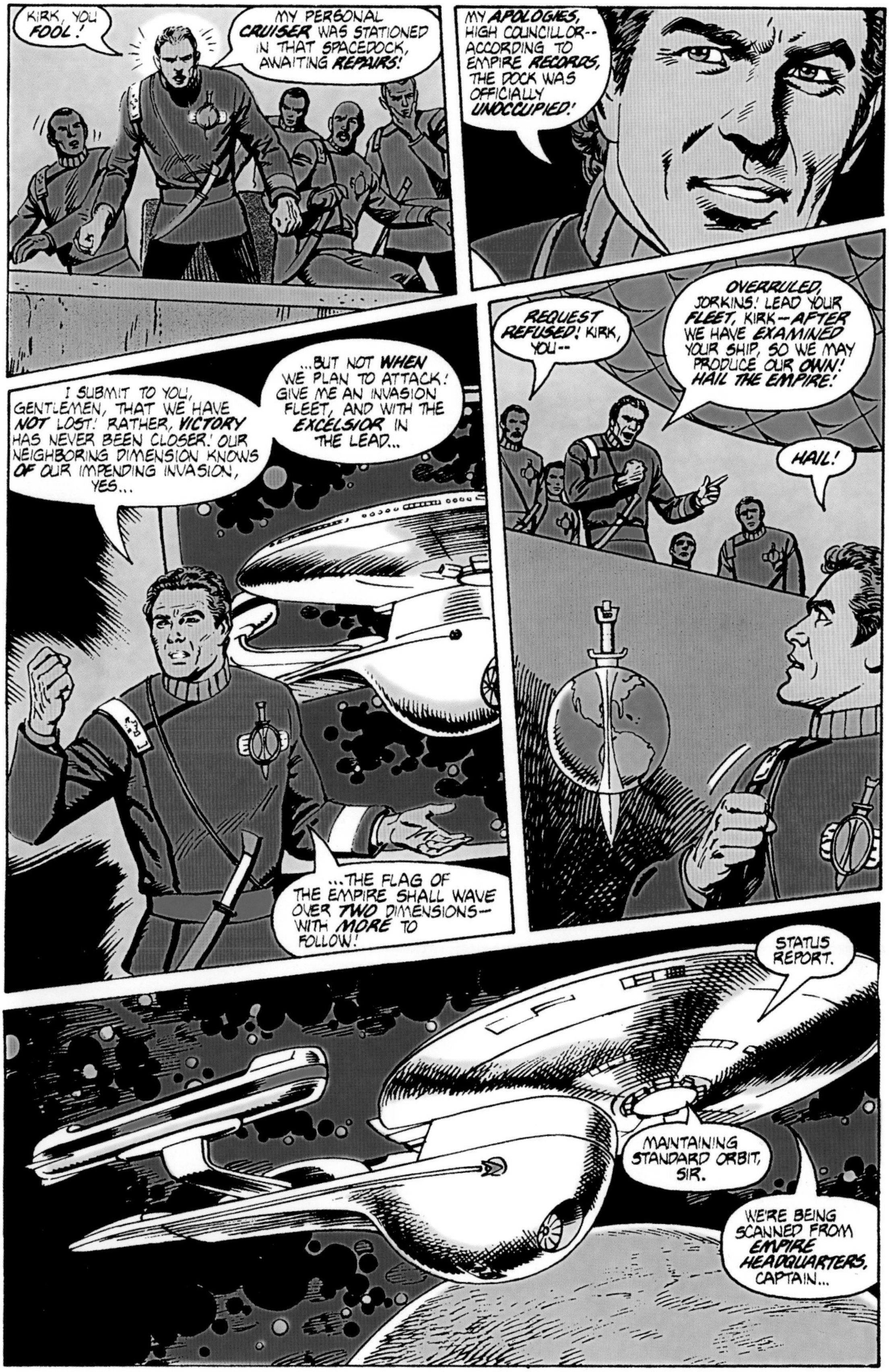
KIRK, YOU FOOL!
MY PERSONAL CRUISER WAS STATIONED IN THAT SPACEDOCK, AWAITING REPAIRS!
MY APOLOGIES, HIGH COUNCILLOR-- ACCORDING TO EMPIRE RECORDS, THE DOCK WAS OFFICIALLY UNOCCUPIED!
I SUBMIT TO YOU, GENTLEMEN, THAT WE HAVE NOT LOST! RATHER, VICTORY HAS NEVER BEEN CLOSER! OUR NEIGHBORING DIMENSION KNOWS OF OUR IMPENDING INVASION, YES...
...BUT NOT WHEN WE PLAN TO ATTACK! GIVE ME AN INVASION FLEET, AND WITH THE EXCELSIOR IN THE LEAD...
...THE FLAG OF THE EMPIRE SHALL WAVE OVER TWO DIMENSIONS-- WITH MORE TO FOLLOW!
REQUEST REFUSED! KIRK, YOU--
OVERRULED, JORKINS! LEAD YOUR FLEET, KIRK--AFTER WE HAVE EXAMINED YOUR SHIP, SO WE MAY PRODUCE OUR OWN! HAIL THE EMPIRE!
HAIL!
STATUS REPORT.
MAINTAINING STANDARD ORBIT, SIR.
WE'RE BEING SCANNED FROM EMPIRE HEADQUARTERS, CAPTAIN...

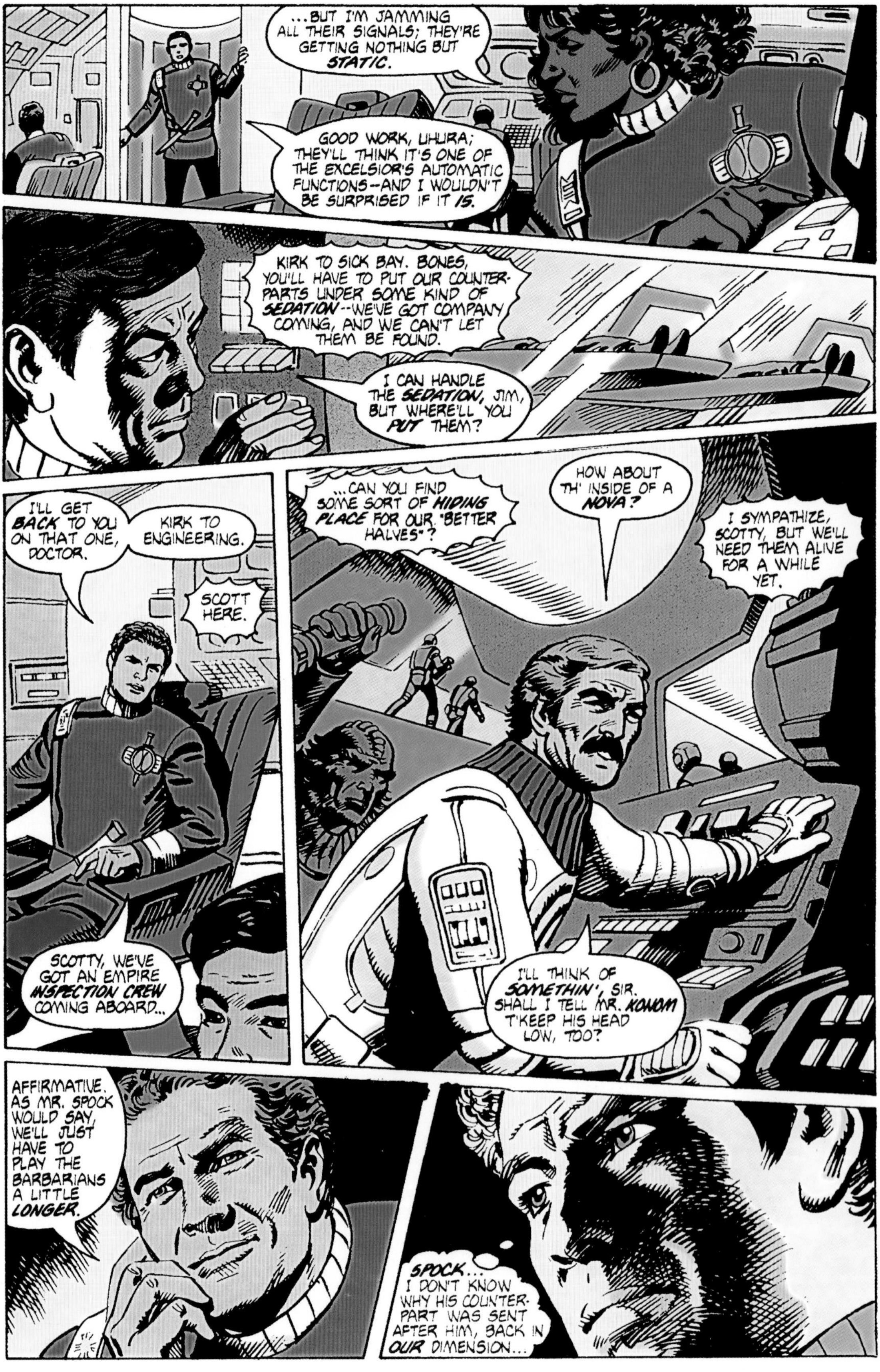
...BUT I'M JAMMING ALL THEIR SIGNALS; THEY'RE GETTING NOTHING BUT STATIC.
GOOD WORK, UHURA; THEY'LL THINK IT'S ONE OF THE EXCELSIOR'S AUTOMATIC FUNCTIONS--AND I WOULDN'T BE SURPRISED IF IT IS.
KIRK TO SICK BAY. BONES, YOU'LL HAVE TO PUT OUR COUNTER-PARTS UNDER SOME KIND OF SEDATION--WE'VE GOT COMPANY COMING, AND WE CAN'T LET THEM BE FOUND.
I CAN HANDLE THE SEDATION, JIM, BUT WHERE'LL YOU PUT THEM?
I'LL GET BACK TO YOU ON THAT ONE, DOCTOR.
KIRK TO ENGINEERING.
SCOTT HERE.
SCOTTY, WE'VE GOT AN EMPIRE INSPECTION CREW COMING ABOARD...
...CAN YOU FIND SOME SORT OF HIDING PLACE FOR OUR "BETTER HALVES"?
HOW ABOUT TH' INSIDE OF A NOVA?
I SYMPATHIZE, SCOTTY, BUT WE'LL NEED THEM ALIVE FOR A WHILE YET.
I'LL THINK OF SOMETHIN', SIR. SHALL I TELL MR. KONOM T'KEEP HIS HEAD LOW, TOO?
AFFIRMATIVE. AS MR. SPOCK WOULD SAY, WE'LL JUST HAVE TO PLAY THE BARBARIANS A LITTLE LONGER.
SPOCK... I DON'T KNOW WHY HIS COUNTER-PART WAS SENT AFTER HIM, BACK IN OUR DIMENSION...

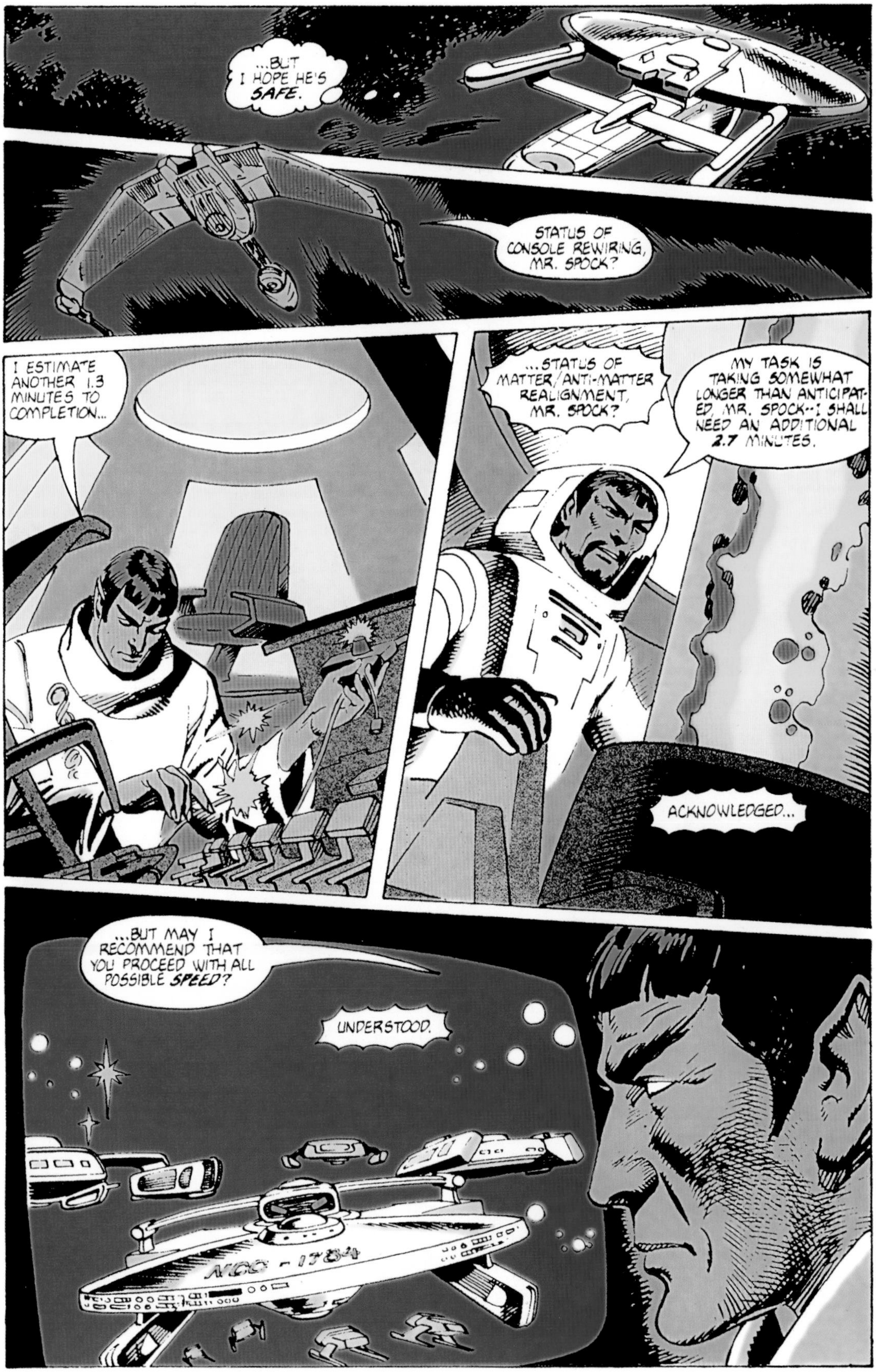
...BUT I HOPE HE'S SAFE.
STATUS OF CONSOLE REWIRING, MR. SPOCK?
I ESTIMATE ANOTHER 1.3 MINUTES TO COMPLETION...
...STATUS OF MATTER/ANTI-MATTER REALIGNMENT, MR. SPOCK?
MY TASK IS TAKING SOMEWHAT LONGER THAN ANTICIPATED, MR. SPOCK--I SHALL NEED AN ADDITIONAL 2.7 MINUTES.
ACKNOWLEDGED...
...BUT MAY I RECOMMEND THAT YOU PROCEED WITH ALL POSSIBLE SPEED?
UNDERSTOOD.
NCC-1784

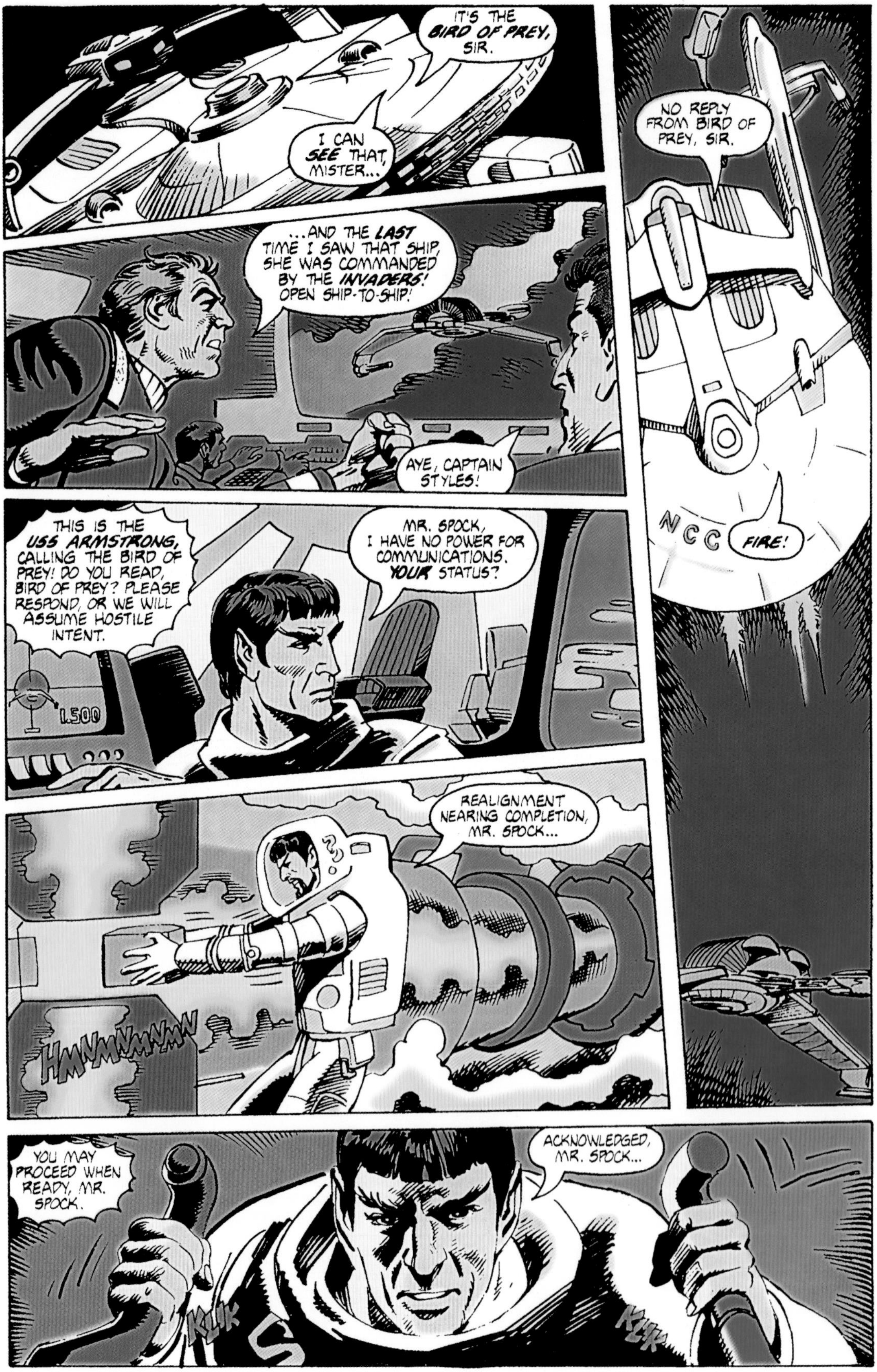

IT'S THE BIRD OF PREY, SIR.
I CAN SEE THAT, MISTER...
...AND THE LAST TIME I SAW THAT SHIP, SHE WAS COMMANDED BY THE INVADERS! OPEN SHIP-TO-SHIP!
AYE, CAPTAIN STYLES!
NO REPLY FROM BIRD OF PREY, SIR.
NCC
FIRE!
THIS IS THE USS ARMSTRONG, CALLING THE BIRD OF PREY! DO YOU READ, BIRD OF PREY? PLEASE RESPOND, OR WE WILL ASSUME HOSTILE INTENT.
MR. SPOCK, I HAVE NO POWER FOR COMMUNICATIONS. YOUR STATUS?
1.500
REALIGNMENT NEARING COMPLETION, MR. SPOCK...
HMNMNMNMN
YOU MAY PROCEED WHEN READY, MR. SPOCK.
ACKNOWLEDGED, MR. SPOCK...
KLIK
KLIK

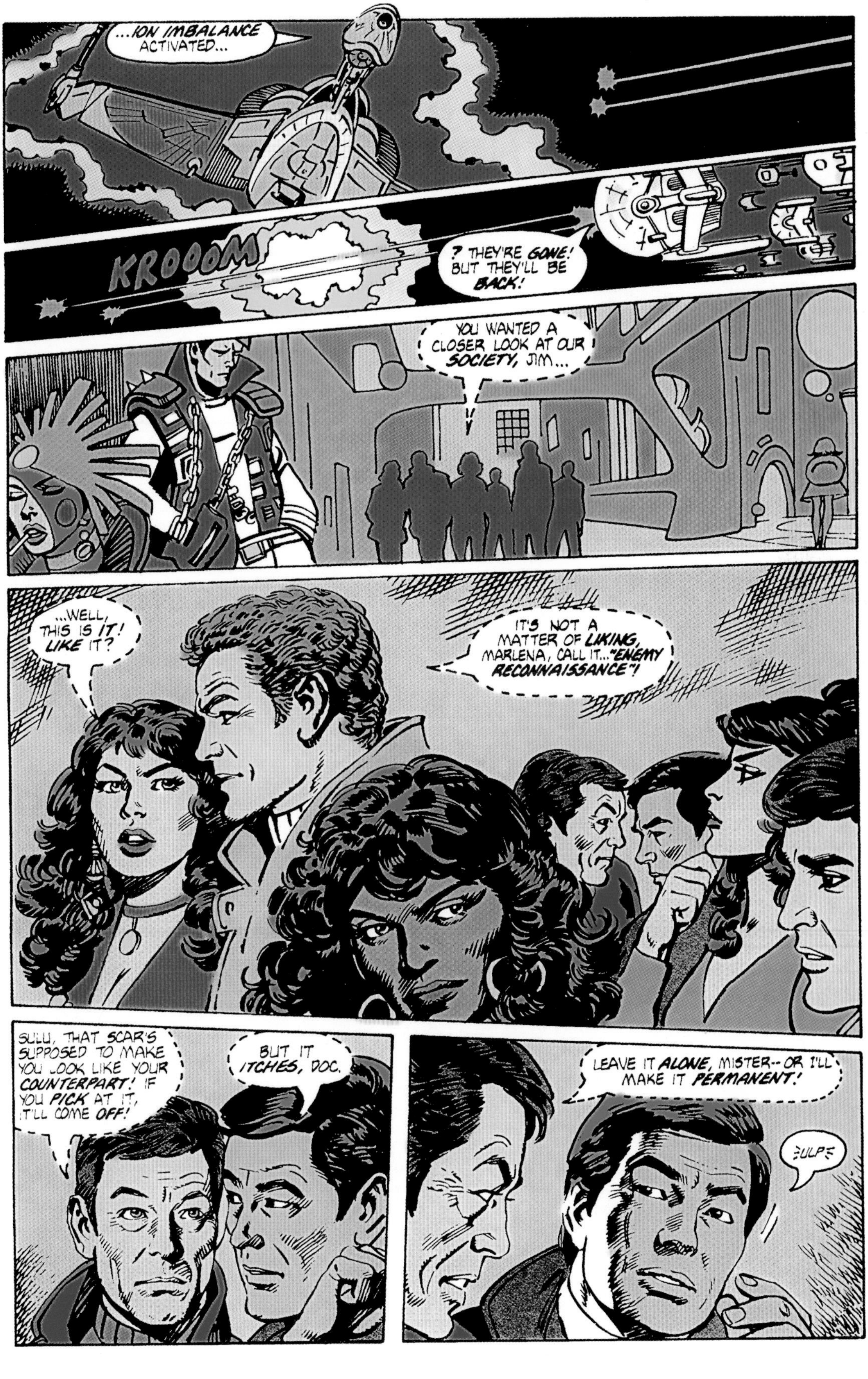
...ION IMBALANCE ACTIVATED...
KROOOM
? THEY'RE GONE! BUT THEY'LL BE BACK!
YOU WANTED A CLOSER LOOK AT OUR SOCIETY, JIM...
...WELL, THIS IS IT! LIKE IT?
IT'S NOT A MATTER OF LIKING, MARLENA, CALL IT..."ENEMY RECONNAISSANCE"!
SULU, THAT SCAR'S SUPPOSED TO MAKE YOU LOOK LIKE YOUR COUNTERPART! IF YOU PICK AT IT, IT'LL COME OFF!
BUT IT ITCHES, DOC.
LEAVE IT ALONE, MISTER--OR I'LL MAKE IT PERMANENT!
GULP

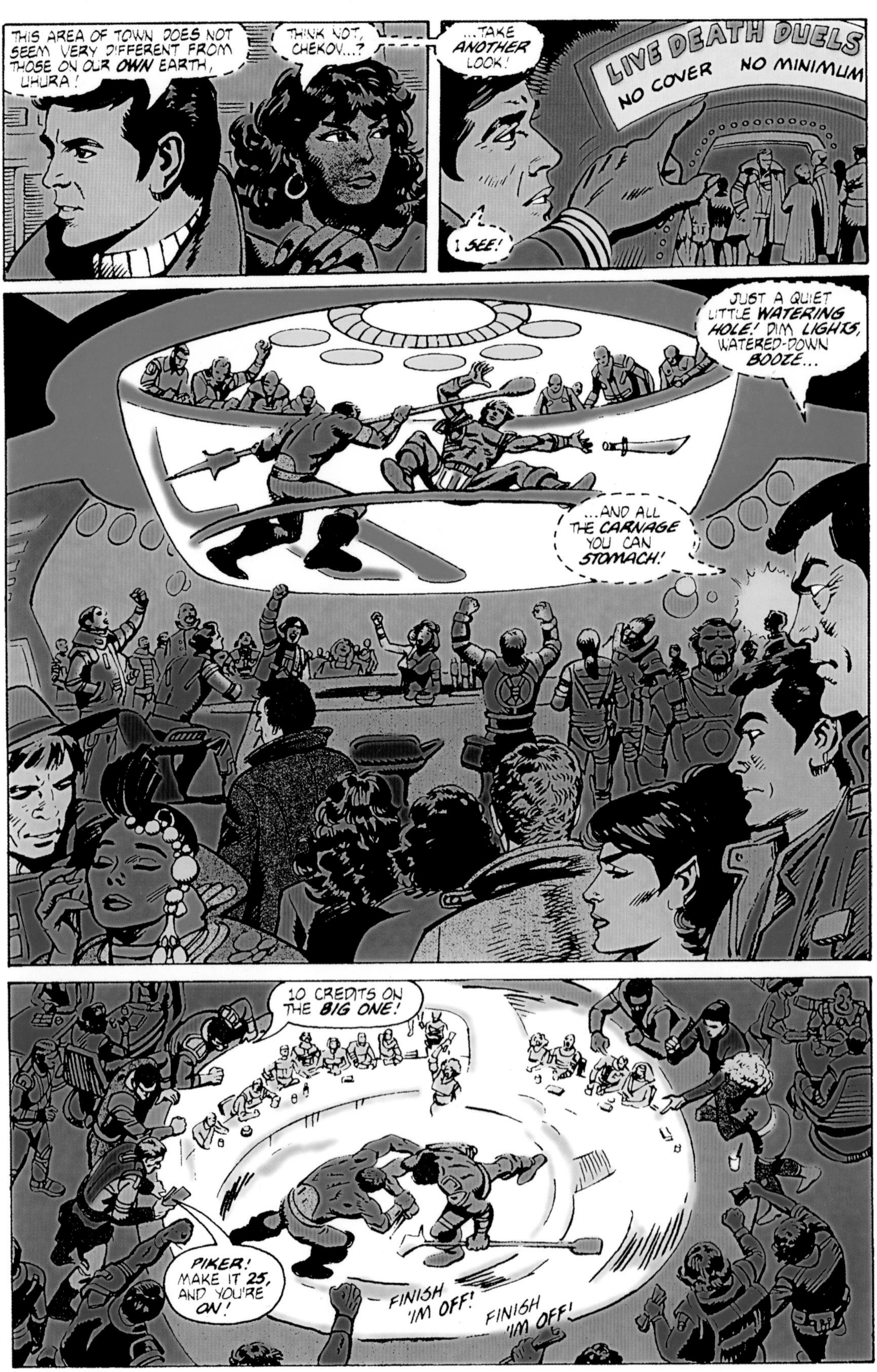

THIS AREA OF TOWN DOES NOT SEEM VERY DIFFERENT FROM THOSE ON OUR OWN EARTH, UHURA!
THINK NOT, CHEKOV...?
...TAKE ANOTHER LOOK!
LIVE DEATH DUELS
NO COVER NO MINIMUM
I SEE!
JUST A QUIET LITTLE WATERING HOLE! DIM LIGHTS, WATERED-DOWN BOOZE...
...AND ALL THE CARNAGE YOU CAN STOMACH!
10 CREDITS ON THE BIG ONE!
PIKER! MAKE IT 25, AND YOU'RE ON!
FINISH 'IM OFF!
FINISH 'IM OFF!

CARE TO PLACE A WAGER ON THE *NEXT EVENT?* THE HOUSE IS OFFERING ODDS OF--

WE'LL WAIT FOR THE *MAIN EVENT,* THANKS! SAURIAN BRANDY ALL AROUND.

MAKE MINE *WODKA!*

MR. SAAVIK, HAVE YOU FOUND OUT HOW *THIS* EARTH'S HISTORY DIFFERS FROM OUR *OWN?*

YES, CAPTAIN...

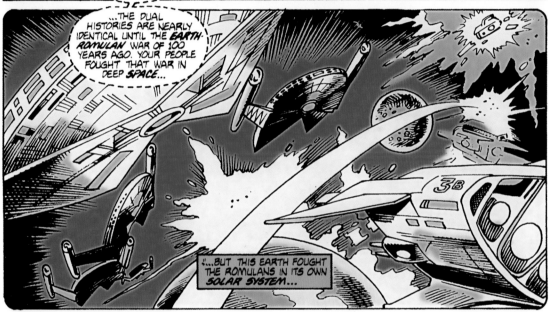

...THE DUAL HISTORIES ARE NEARLY IDENTICAL UNTIL THE *EARTH-ROMULAN* WAR OF 100 YEARS AGO. YOUR PEOPLE FOUGHT THAT WAR IN DEEP *SPACE...*

"...BUT THIS EARTH FOUGHT THE ROMULANS IN ITS OWN *SOLAR SYSTEM...*

"...AND *LOST.* THE ROMULANS CONQUERED EARTH, AND HELD IT IN SLAVERY FOR NEARLY A *DECADE...*

"...UNTIL A BAND OF EARTHMEN UNITED *AGAINST* THEIR CONQUERORS, AND FREED THEIR PLANET. BUT THE RESISTANCE DID NOT DISBAND WHEN THE BATTLE WAS WON...

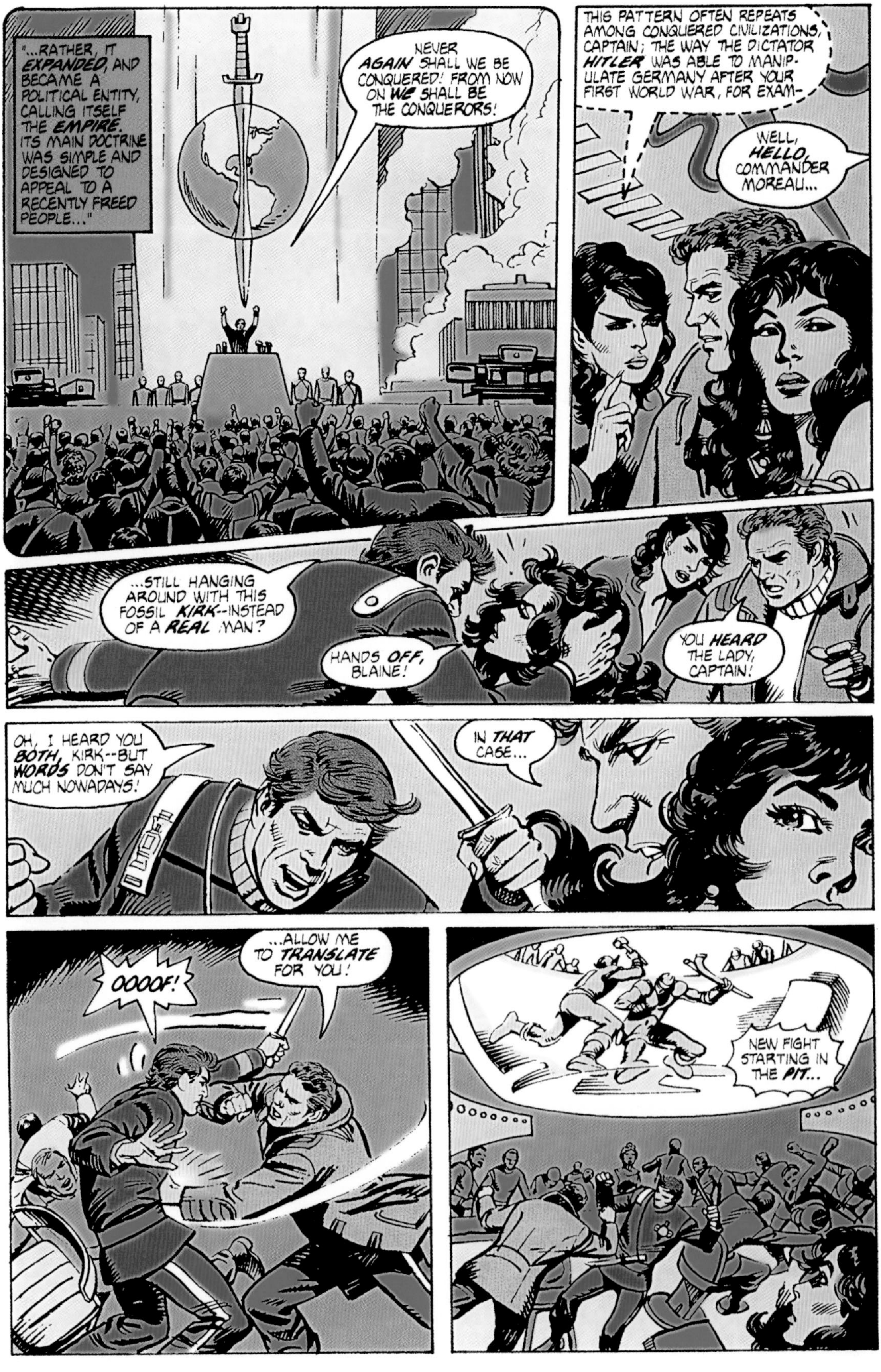
"...RATHER, IT EXPANDED, AND BECAME A POLITICAL ENTITY, CALLING ITSELF THE EMPIRE. ITS MAIN DOCTRINE WAS SIMPLE AND DESIGNED TO APPEAL TO A RECENTLY FREED PEOPLE..."
NEVER AGAIN SHALL WE BE CONQUERED! FROM NOW ON WE SHALL BE THE CONQUERORS!
THIS PATTERN OFTEN REPEATS AMONG CONQUERED CIVILIZATIONS, CAPTAIN; THE WAY THE DICTATOR HITLER WAS ABLE TO MANIPULATE GERMANY AFTER YOUR FIRST WORLD WAR, FOR EXAM-
WELL, HELLO, COMMANDER MOREAU...
...STILL HANGING AROUND WITH THIS FOSSIL KIRK--INSTEAD OF A REAL MAN?
HANDS OFF, BLAINE!
YOU HEARD THE LADY, CAPTAIN!
OH, I HEARD YOU BOTH, KIRK--BUT WORDS DON'T SAY MUCH NOWADAYS!
IN THAT CASE...
OOOOF!
...ALLOW ME TO TRANSLATE FOR YOU!
NEW FIGHT STARTING IN THE PIT...

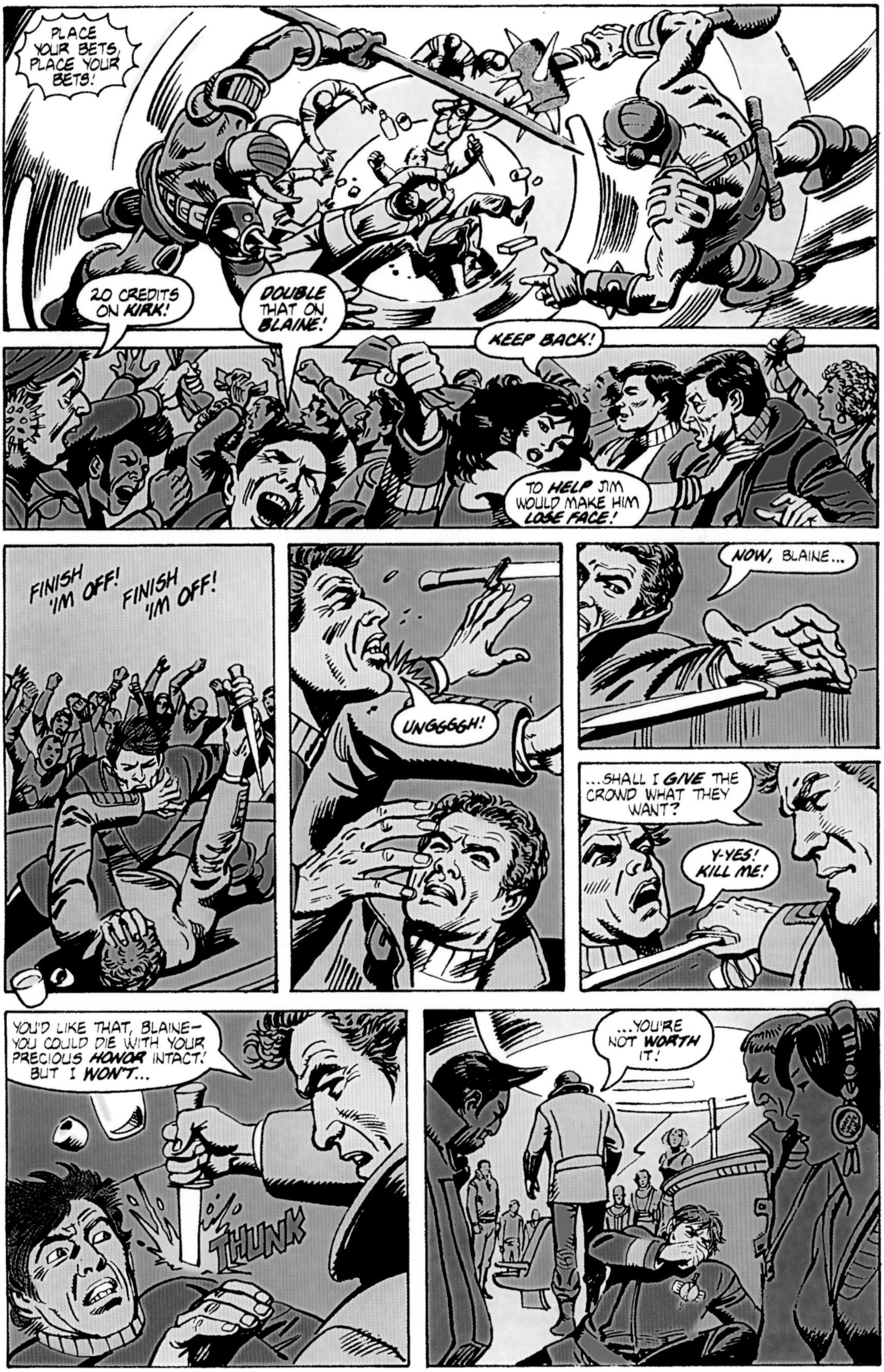
PLACE YOUR BETS, PLACE YOUR BETS!
20 CREDITS ON KIRK!
DOUBLE THAT ON BLAINE!
KEEP BACK!
TO HELP JIM WOULD MAKE HIM LOSE FACE!
FINISH 'IM OFF! FINISH 'IM OFF!
UNGGGGH!
NOW, BLAINE...
...SHALL I GIVE THE CROWD WHAT THEY WANT?
Y-YES! KILL ME!
YOU'D LIKE THAT, BLAINE– YOU COULD DIE WITH YOUR PRECIOUS HONOR INTACT! BUT I WON'T...
THUNK
...YOU'RE NOT WORTH IT!

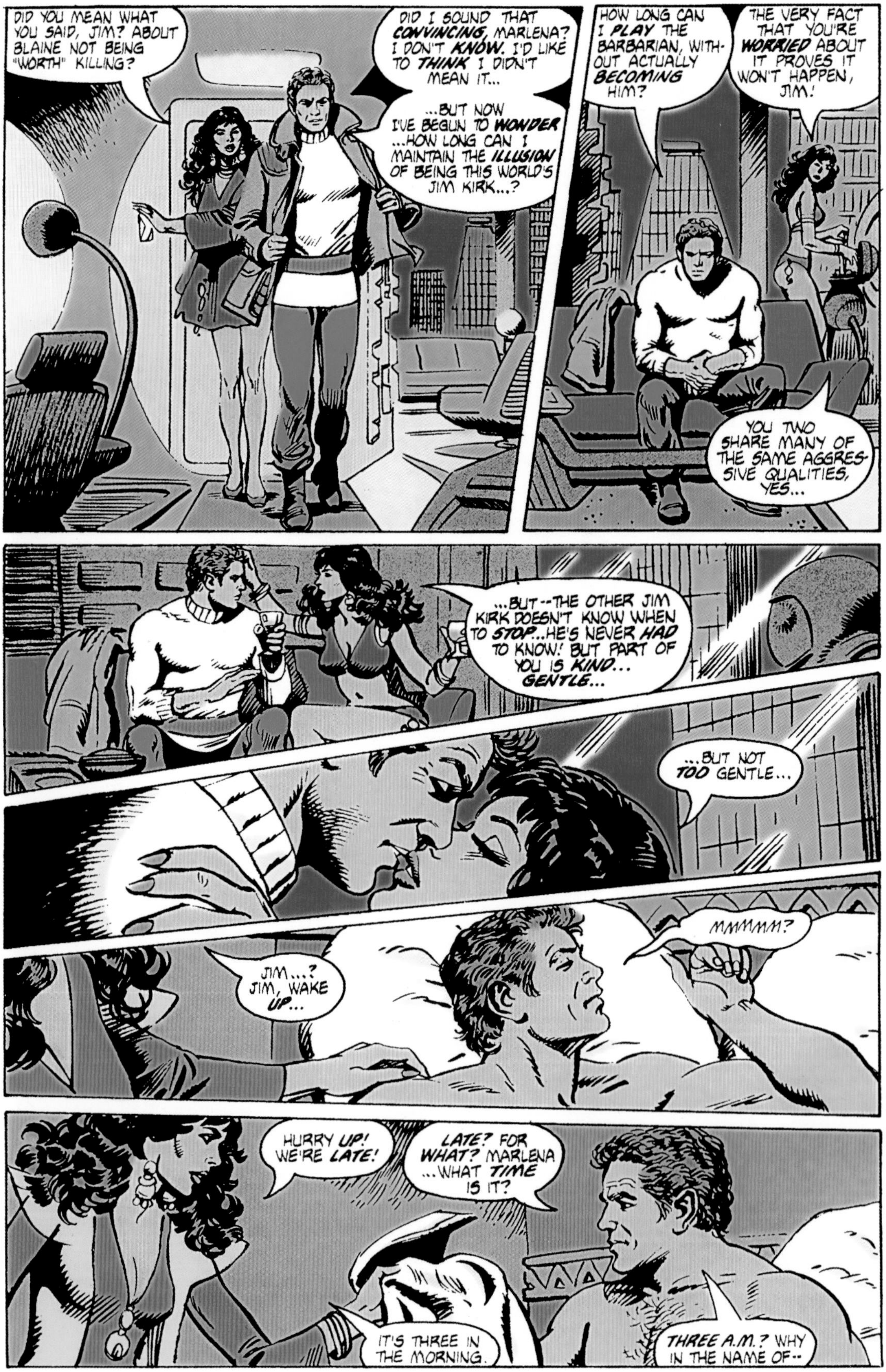
DID YOU MEAN WHAT YOU SAID, JIM? ABOUT BLAINE NOT BEING "WORTH" KILLING?
DID I SOUND THAT CONVINCING, MARLENA? I DON'T KNOW. I'D LIKE TO THINK I DIDN'T MEAN IT...
...BUT NOW I'VE BEGUN TO WONDER ...HOW LONG CAN I MAINTAIN THE ILLUSION OF BEING THIS WORLD'S JIM KIRK...?
HOW LONG CAN I PLAY THE BARBARIAN, WITHOUT ACTUALLY BECOMING HIM?
THE VERY FACT THAT YOU'RE WORRIED ABOUT IT PROVES IT WON'T HAPPEN, JIM!
YOU TWO SHARE MANY OF THE SAME AGGRESSIVE QUALITIES, YES...
...BUT--THE OTHER JIM KIRK DOESN'T KNOW WHEN TO STOP...HE'S NEVER HAD TO KNOW! BUT PART OF YOU IS KIND... GENTLE...
...BUT NOT TOO GENTLE...
MMMMM?
JIM...? JIM, WAKE UP...
HURRY UP! WE'RE LATE!
LATE? FOR WHAT? MARLENA ...WHAT TIME IS IT?
IT'S THREE IN THE MORNING.
THREE A.M.? WHY IN THE NAME OF--

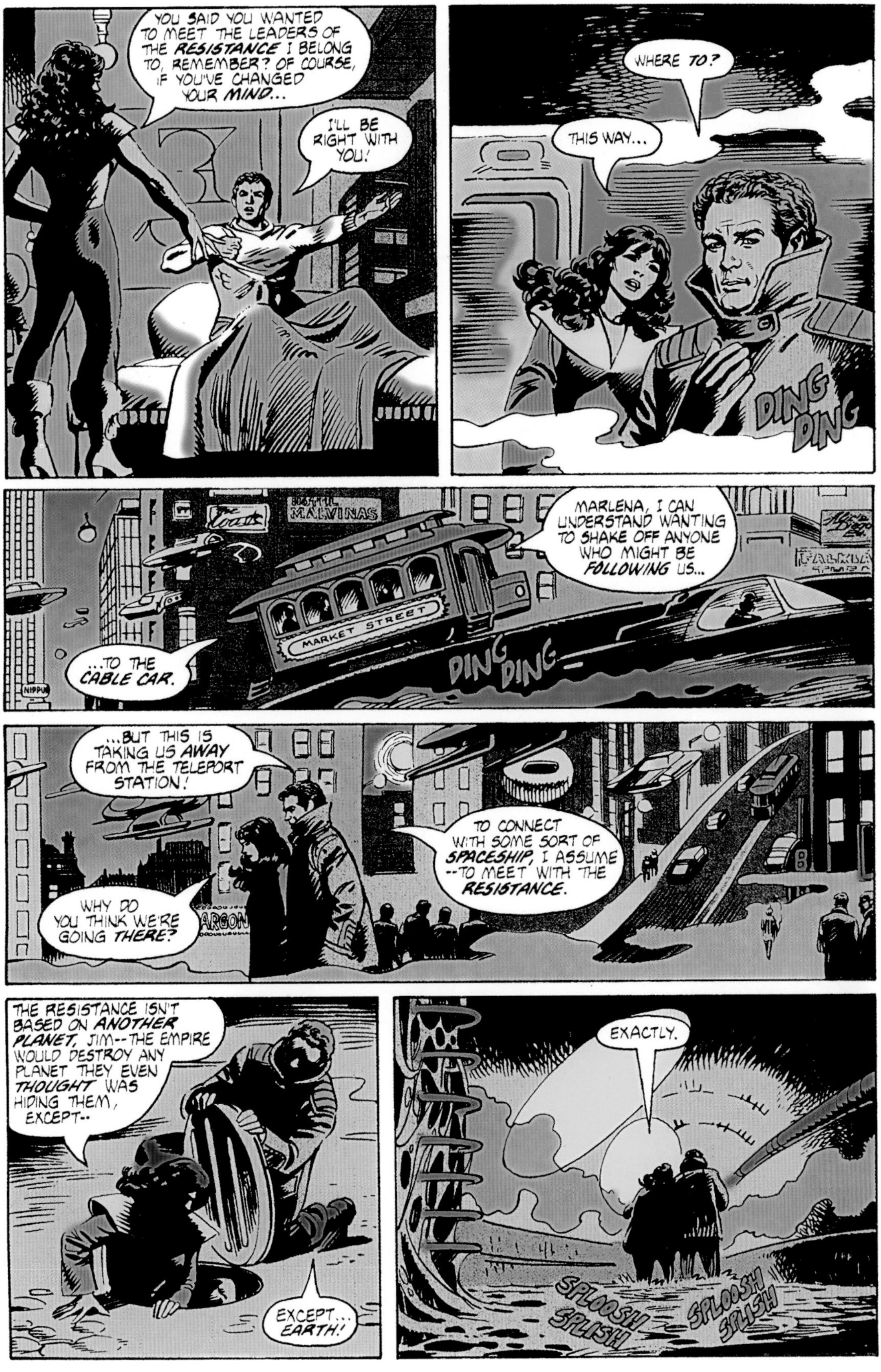
YOU SAID YOU WANTED TO MEET THE LEADERS OF THE RESISTANCE I BELONG TO, REMEMBER? OF COURSE, IF YOU'VE CHANGED YOUR MIND...
I'LL BE RIGHT WITH YOU!
WHERE TO?
THIS WAY...
DING DING
MALVINAS
MARLENA, I CAN UNDERSTAND WANTING TO SHAKE OFF ANYONE WHO MIGHT BE FOLLOWING US...
MARKET STREET
...TO THE CABLE CAR.
DING DING
...BUT THIS IS TAKING US AWAY FROM THE TELEPORT STATION!
TO CONNECT WITH SOME SORT OF SPACESHIP, I ASSUME --TO MEET WITH THE RESISTANCE.
WHY DO YOU THINK WE'RE GOING THERE?
ARGON
THE RESISTANCE ISN'T BASED ON ANOTHER PLANET, JIM--THE EMPIRE WOULD DESTROY ANY PLANET THEY EVEN THOUGHT WAS HIDING THEM, EXCEPT--
EXCEPT... EARTH!
EXACTLY.
SPLOOSH SPLISH
SPLOOSH SPLISH

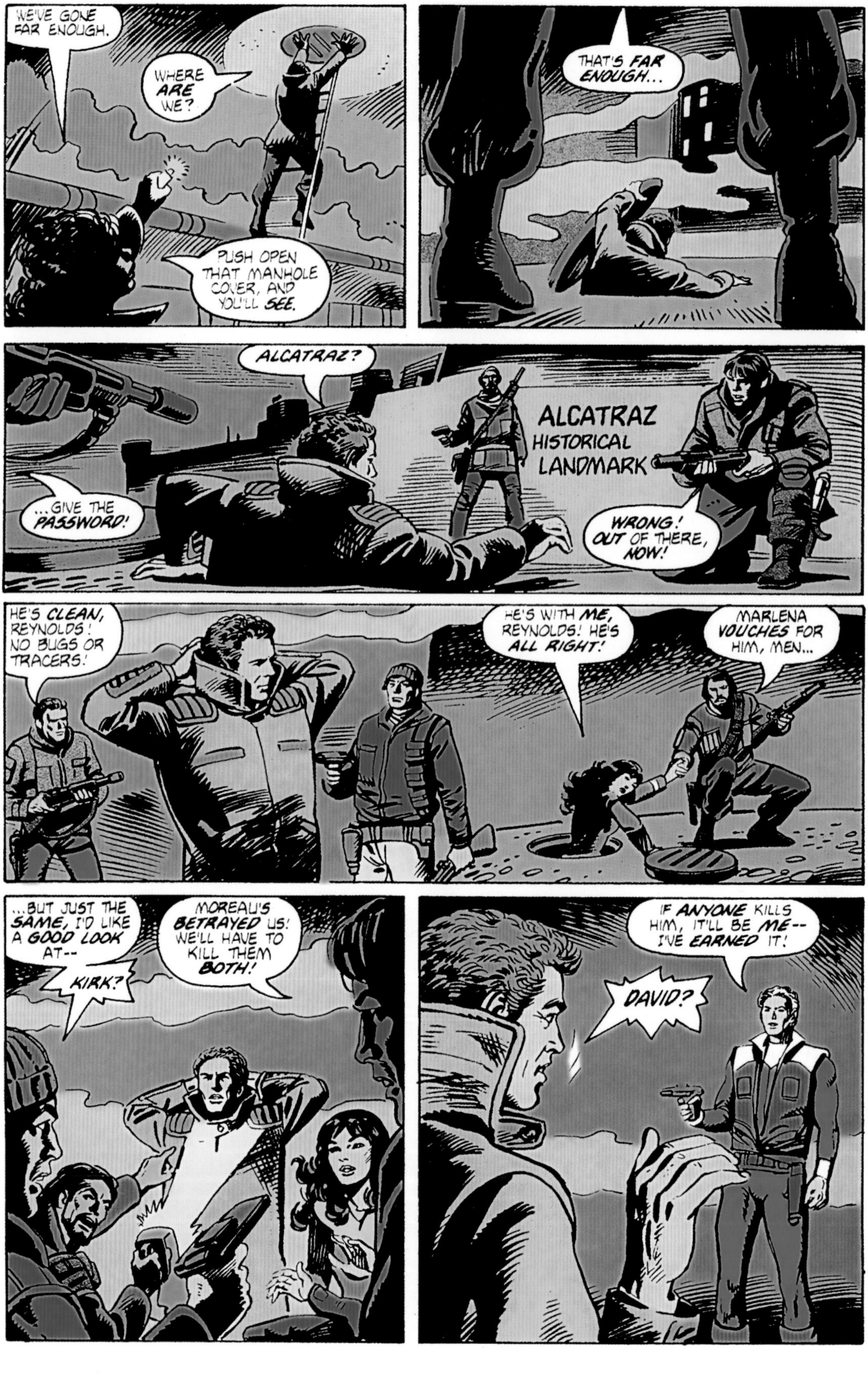
WE'VE GONE FAR ENOUGH.
WHERE ARE WE?
PUSH OPEN THAT MANHOLE COVER, AND YOU'LL SEE.
THAT'S FAR ENOUGH...
ALCATRAZ?
ALCATRAZ HISTORICAL LANDMARK
...GIVE THE PASSWORD!
WRONG! OUT OF THERE, NOW!
HE'S CLEAN, REYNOLDS! NO BUGS OR TRACERS!
HE'S WITH ME, REYNOLDS! HE'S ALL RIGHT!
MARLENA VOUCHES FOR HIM, MEN...
...BUT JUST THE SAME, I'D LIKE A GOOD LOOK AT--
KIRK?
MOREAU'S BETRAYED US! WE'LL HAVE TO KILL THEM BOTH!
IF ANYONE KILLS HIM, IT'LL BE ME-- I'VE EARNED IT!
DAVID?

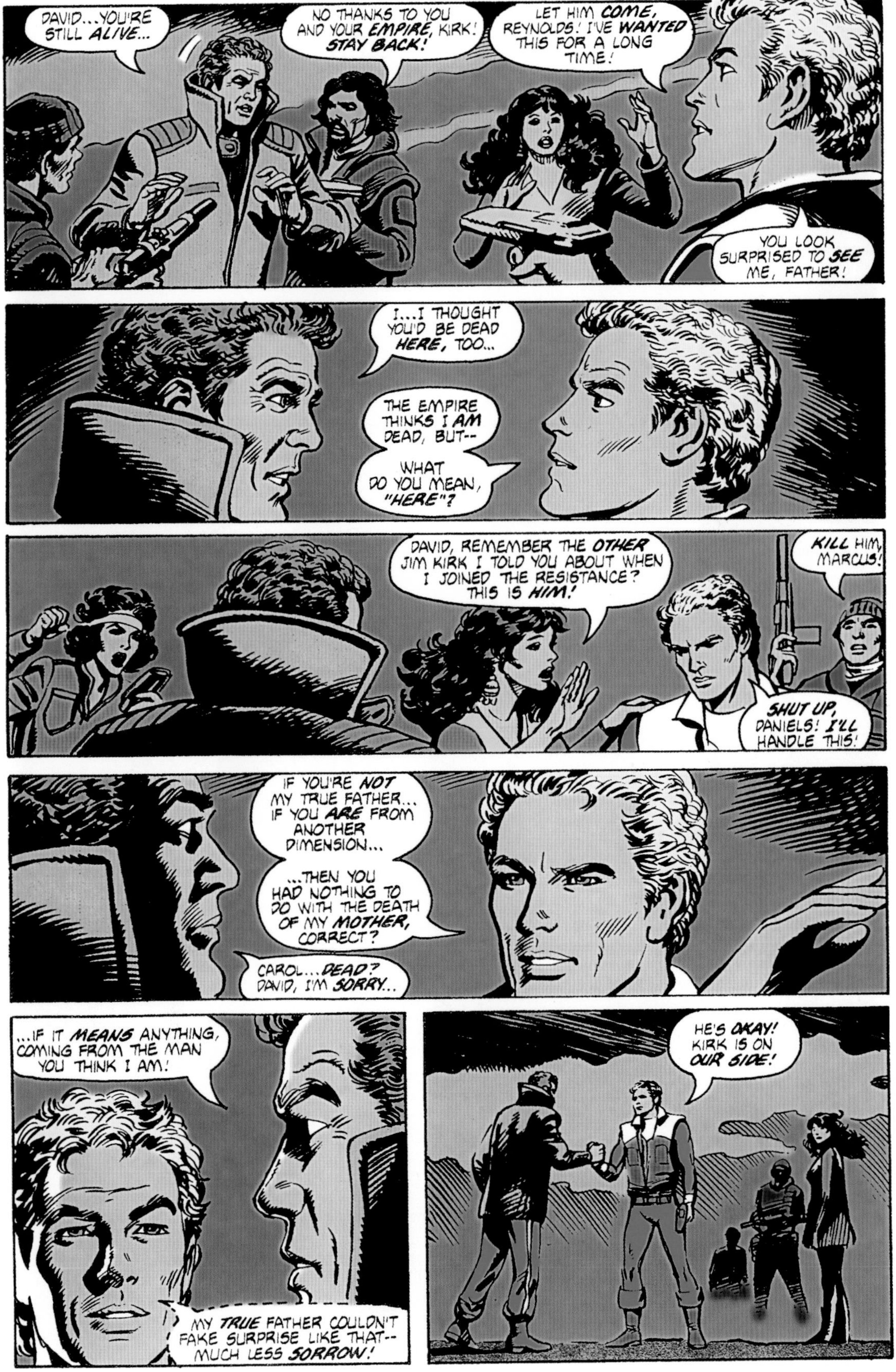
DAVID... YOU'RE STILL ALIVE...
NO THANKS TO YOU AND YOUR EMPIRE, KIRK! STAY BACK!
LET HIM COME, REYNOLDS! I'VE WANTED THIS FOR A LONG TIME!
YOU LOOK SURPRISED TO SEE ME, FATHER!
I...I THOUGHT YOU'D BE DEAD HERE, TOO...
THE EMPIRE THINKS I AM DEAD, BUT--
WHAT DO YOU MEAN, "HERE"?
DAVID, REMEMBER THE OTHER JIM KIRK I TOLD YOU ABOUT WHEN I JOINED THE RESISTANCE? THIS IS HIM!
KILL HIM, MARCUS!
SHUT UP, DANIELS! I'LL HANDLE THIS!
IF YOU'RE NOT MY TRUE FATHER... IF YOU ARE FROM ANOTHER DIMENSION...
...THEN YOU HAD NOTHING TO DO WITH THE DEATH OF MY MOTHER, CORRECT?
CAROL... DEAD? DAVID, I'M SORRY...
...IF IT MEANS ANYTHING, COMING FROM THE MAN YOU THINK I AM!
MY TRUE FATHER COULDN'T FAKE SURPRISE LIKE THAT-- MUCH LESS SORROW!
HE'S OKAY! KIRK IS ON OUR SIDE!

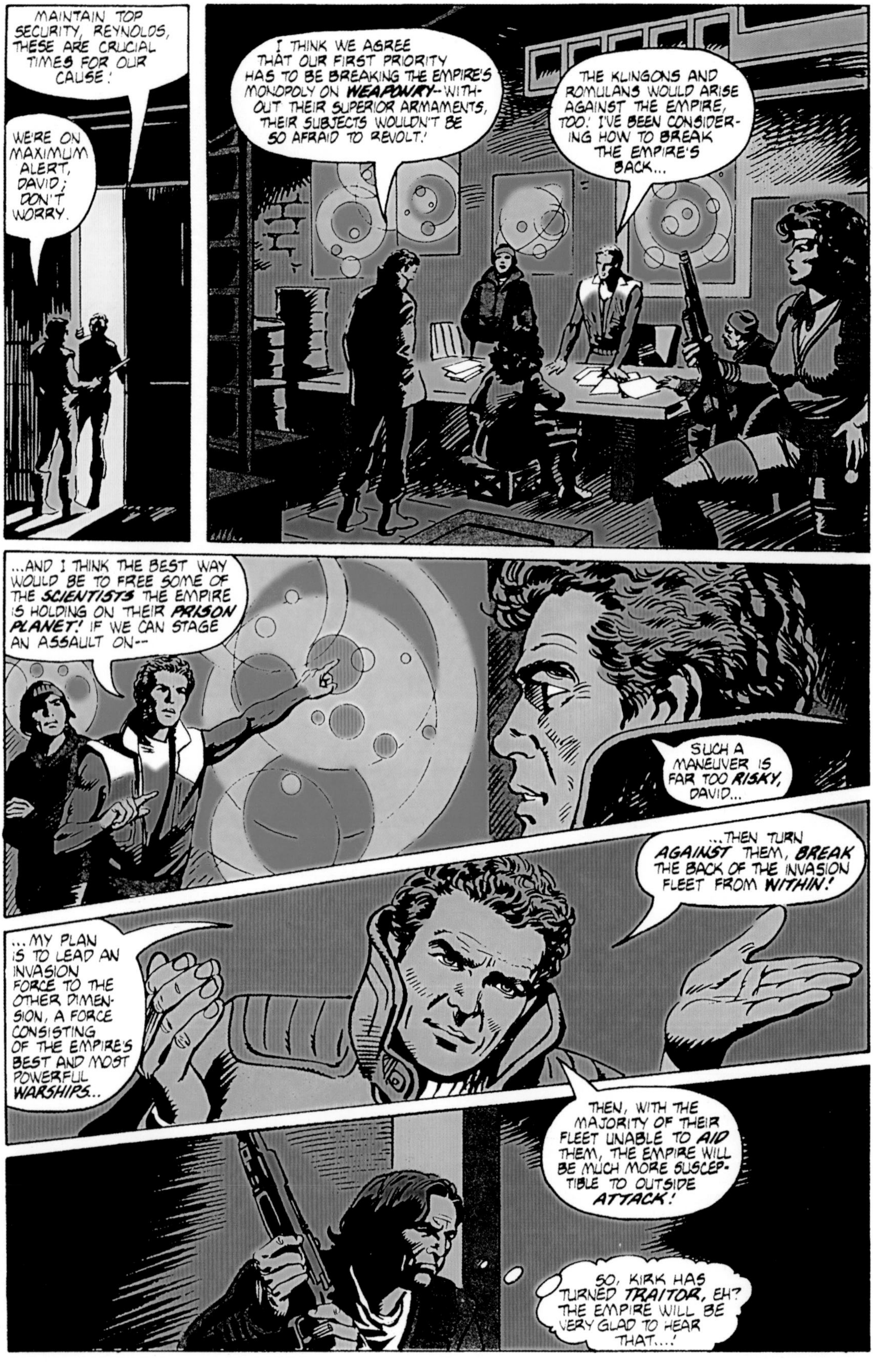
MAINTAIN TOP SECURITY, REYNOLDS, THESE ARE CRUCIAL TIMES FOR OUR CAUSE!
WE'RE ON MAXIMUM ALERT, DAVID; DON'T WORRY.
I THINK WE AGREE THAT OUR FIRST PRIORITY HAS TO BE BREAKING THE EMPIRE'S MONOPOLY ON WEAPONRY--WITHOUT THEIR SUPERIOR ARMAMENTS, THEIR SUBJECTS WOULDN'T BE SO AFRAID TO REVOLT!
THE KLINGONS AND ROMULANS WOULD ARISE AGAINST THE EMPIRE, TOO! I'VE BEEN CONSIDERING HOW TO BREAK THE EMPIRE'S BACK...
...AND I THINK THE BEST WAY WOULD BE TO FREE SOME OF THE SCIENTISTS THE EMPIRE IS HOLDING ON THEIR PRISON PLANET! IF WE CAN STAGE AN ASSAULT ON--
SUCH A MANEUVER IS FAR TOO RISKY, DAVID...
...MY PLAN IS TO LEAD AN INVASION FORCE TO THE OTHER DIMENSION, A FORCE CONSISTING OF THE EMPIRE'S BEST AND MOST POWERFUL WARSHIPS..
...THEN TURN AGAINST THEM, BREAK THE BACK OF THE INVASION FLEET FROM WITHIN!
THEN, WITH THE MAJORITY OF THEIR FLEET UNABLE TO AID THEM, THE EMPIRE WILL BE MUCH MORE SUSCEPTIBLE TO OUTSIDE ATTACK!
SO, KIRK HAS TURNED TRAITOR, EH? THE EMPIRE WILL BE VERY GLAD TO HEAR THAT...!

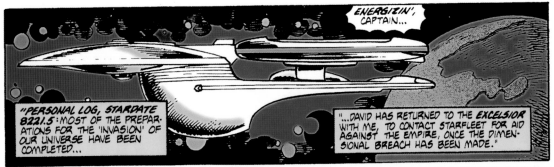

ENERGIZIN', CAPTAIN...

"PERSONAL LOG, STARDATE 8221.5: MOST OF THE PREPARATIONS FOR THE 'INVASION' OF OUR UNIVERSE HAVE BEEN COMPLETED...

"...DAVID HAS RETURNED TO THE EXCELSIOR WITH ME, TO CONTACT STARFLEET FOR AID AGAINST THE EMPIRE, ONCE THE DIMENSIONAL BREACH HAS BEEN MADE."

HMMMNNNNN

¿GASP?

WILL YOU LOOK AT THIS THING? IT'S SO...SO...

I KNOW WHAT YOU MEAN, DAVID.

CAPTAIN, IF I'D... ER...KNOWN LT. MARCUS WAS COMIN' ABOARD, I'D'VE ARRANGED A PROPER WELCOME FOR HIM--

IT'S ALL RIGHT, SCOTTY, HE'S WITH US! STATUS?

WE'VE BEEN FULLY EXAMINED, AN' CAN LEAVE ORBIT T'RENDEZVOUS WITH TH' INVASION FLEET AT ANY TIME, SIR.

THANK YOU, SCOTTY.

COME ON, DAVID; WE MAY AS WELL GET THE INTRODUCTIONS --AND THE ASTONISHED REACTIONS--OVER WITH!

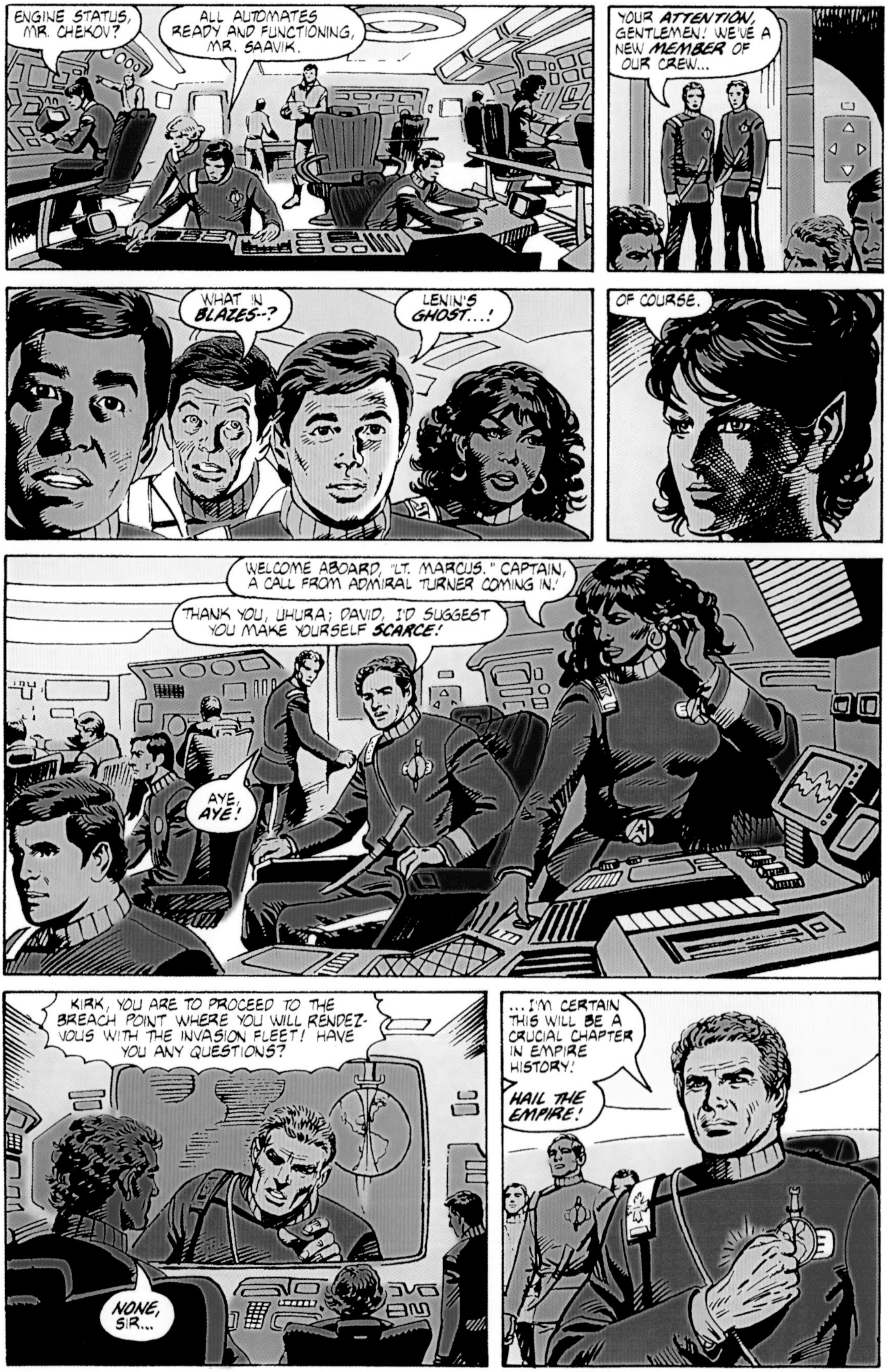
ENGINE STATUS, MR. CHEKOV?
ALL AUTOMATES READY AND FUNCTIONING, MR. SAAVIK.
YOUR ATTENTION, GENTLEMEN! WE'VE A NEW MEMBER OF OUR CREW...
WHAT IN BLAZES--?
LENIN'S GHOST...!
OF COURSE.
WELCOME ABOARD, "LT. MARCUS." CAPTAIN, A CALL FROM ADMIRAL TURNER COMING IN!
THANK YOU, UHURA; DAVID, I'D SUGGEST YOU MAKE YOURSELF SCARCE!
AYE, AYE!
KIRK, YOU ARE TO PROCEED TO THE BREACH POINT WHERE YOU WILL RENDEZVOUS WITH THE INVASION FLEET! HAVE YOU ANY QUESTIONS?
NONE, SIR...
...I'M CERTAIN THIS WILL BE A CRUCIAL CHAPTER IN EMPIRE HISTORY!
HAIL THE EMPIRE!

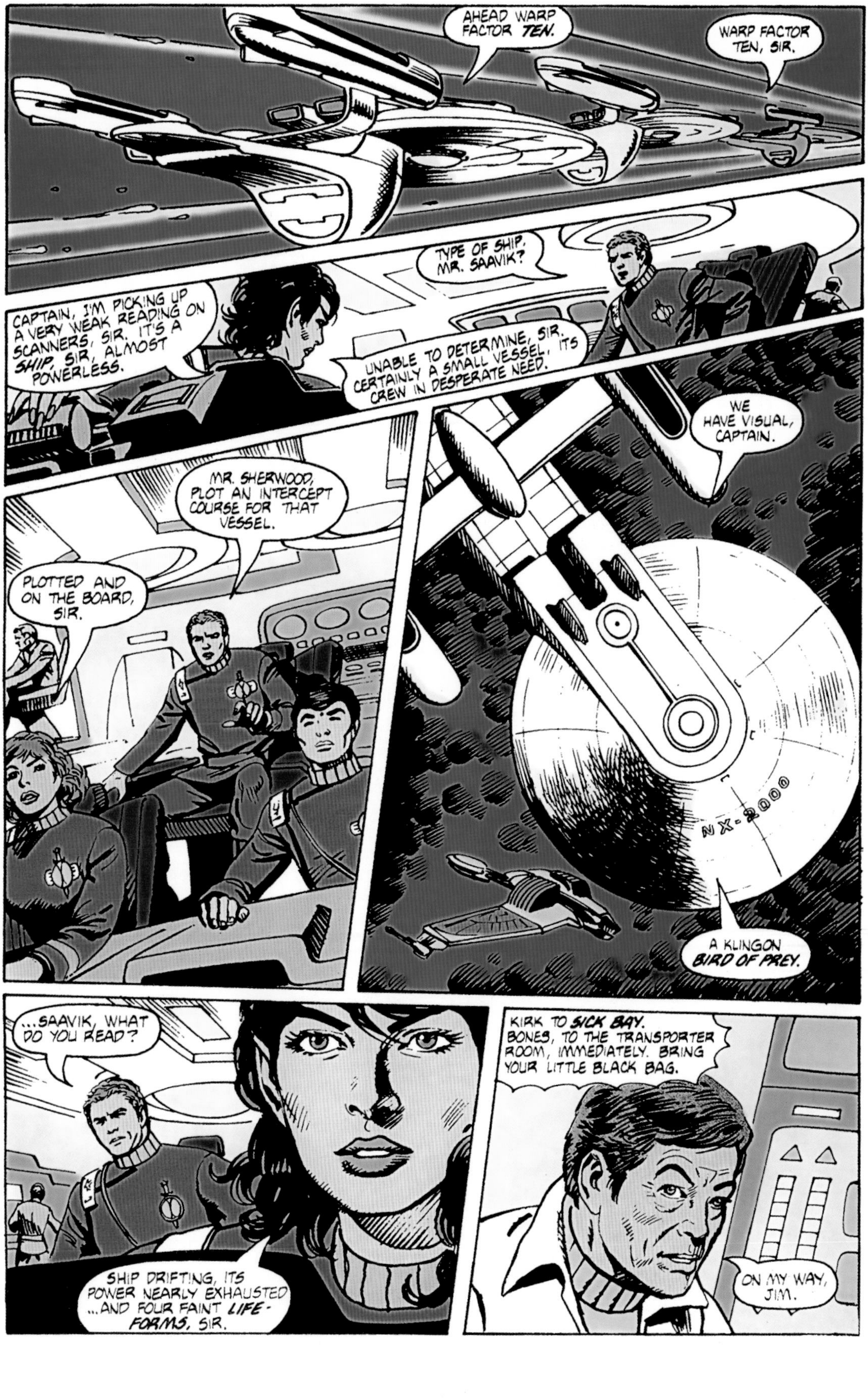
AHEAD WARP FACTOR TEN.
WARP FACTOR TEN, SIR.
TYPE OF SHIP, MR. SAAVIK?
CAPTAIN, I'M PICKING UP A VERY WEAK READING ON SCANNERS, SIR. IT'S A SHIP, SIR, ALMOST POWERLESS.
UNABLE TO DETERMINE, SIR. CERTAINLY A SMALL VESSEL, ITS CREW IN DESPERATE NEED.
MR. SHERWOOD, PLOT AN INTERCEPT COURSE FOR THAT VESSEL.
PLOTTED AND ON THE BOARD, SIR.
WE HAVE VISUAL, CAPTAIN.
NX-2000
A KLINGON BIRD OF PREY.
...SAAVIK, WHAT DO YOU READ?
SHIP DRIFTING, ITS POWER NEARLY EXHAUSTED ...AND FOUR FAINT LIFE-FORMS, SIR.
KIRK TO SICK BAY. BONES, TO THE TRANSPORTER ROOM, IMMEDIATELY. BRING YOUR LITTLE BLACK BAG.
ON MY WAY, JIM.

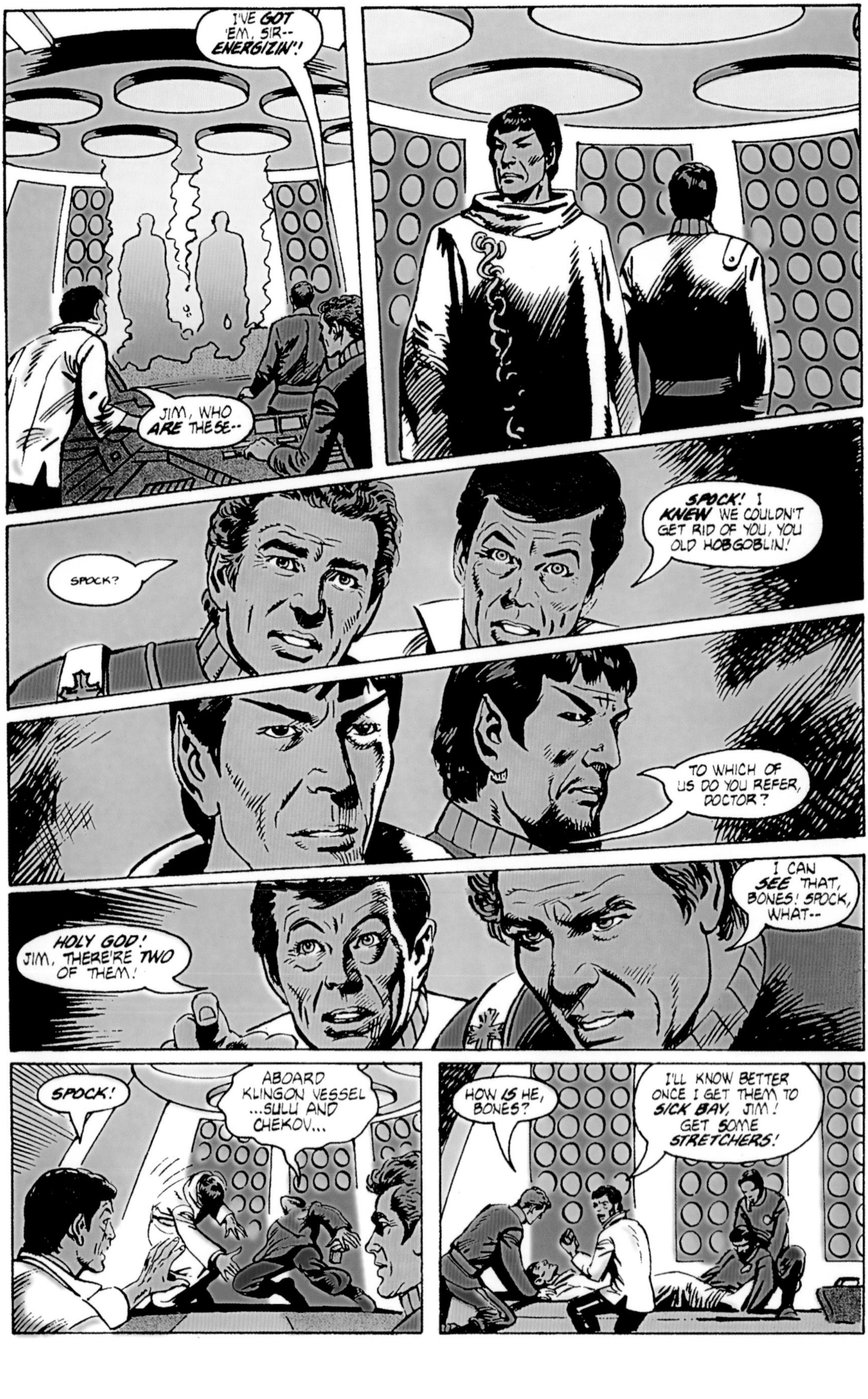
I'VE GOT 'EM, SIR-- ENERGIZIN'!
JIM, WHO ARE THESE--
SPOCK?
SPOCK! I KNEW WE COULDN'T GET RID OF YOU, YOU OLD HOBGOBLIN!
TO WHICH OF US DO YOU REFER, DOCTOR?
HOLY GOD! JIM, THERE'RE TWO OF THEM!
I CAN SEE THAT, BONES! SPOCK, WHAT--
SPOCK!
ABOARD KLINGON VESSEL ...SULU AND CHEKOV...
HOW IS HE, BONES?
I'LL KNOW BETTER ONCE I GET THEM TO SICK BAY, JIM! GET SOME STRETCHERS!

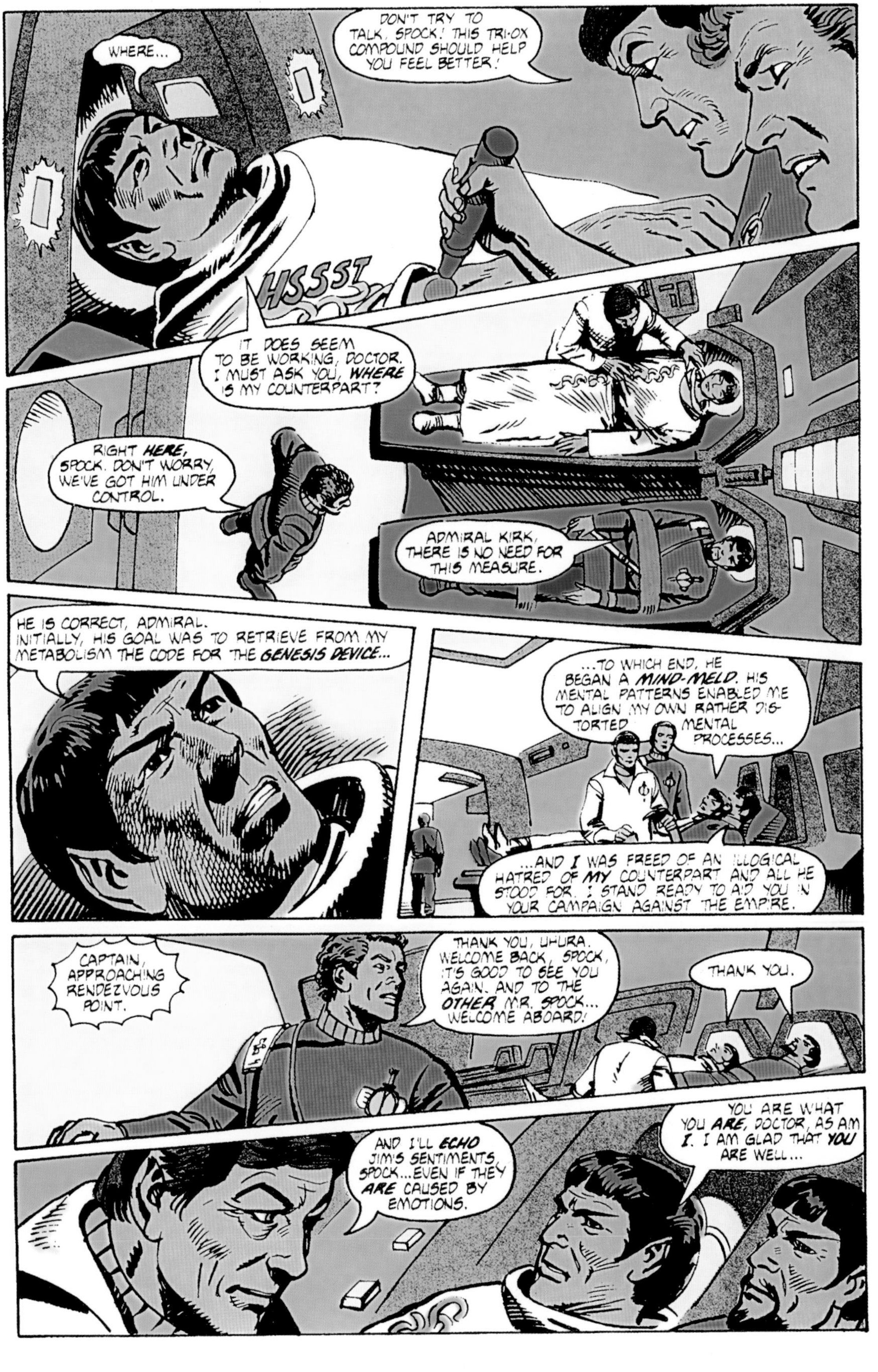
WHERE...
DON'T TRY TO TALK, SPOCK! THIS TRI-OX COMPOUND SHOULD HELP YOU FEEL BETTER!
HSSST
IT DOES SEEM TO BE WORKING, DOCTOR. I MUST ASK YOU, WHERE IS MY COUNTERPART?
RIGHT HERE, SPOCK. DON'T WORRY, WE'VE GOT HIM UNDER CONTROL.
ADMIRAL KIRK, THERE IS NO NEED FOR THIS MEASURE.
HE IS CORRECT, ADMIRAL. INITIALLY, HIS GOAL WAS TO RETRIEVE FROM MY METABOLISM THE CODE FOR THE GENESIS DEVICE...
...TO WHICH END, HE BEGAN A MIND-MELD. HIS MENTAL PATTERNS ENABLED ME TO ALIGN MY OWN RATHER DIS-TORTED MENTAL PROCESSES...
...AND I WAS FREED OF AN ILLOGICAL HATRED OF MY COUNTERPART AND ALL HE STOOD FOR. I STAND READY TO AID YOU IN YOUR CAMPAIGN AGAINST THE EMPIRE.
CAPTAIN, APPROACHING RENDEZVOUS POINT.
THANK YOU, UHURA. WELCOME BACK, SPOCK, IT'S GOOD TO SEE YOU AGAIN. AND TO THE OTHER MR. SPOCK... WELCOME ABOARD!
THANK YOU.
AND I'LL ECHO JIM'S SENTIMENTS, SPOCK... EVEN IF THEY ARE CAUSED BY EMOTIONS.
YOU ARE WHAT YOU ARE, DOCTOR, AS AM I. I AM GLAD THAT YOU ARE WELL...

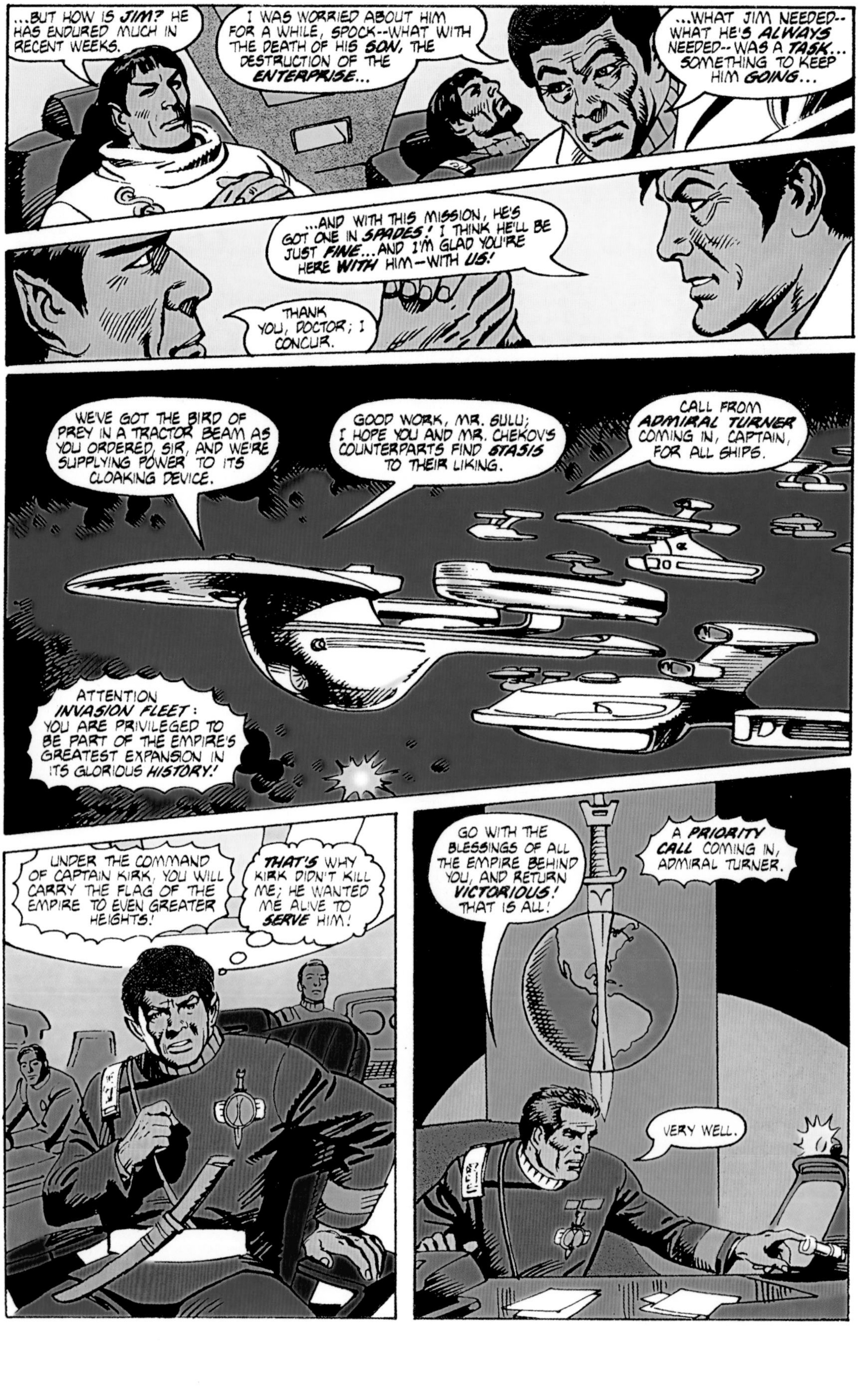
...BUT HOW IS JIM? HE HAS ENDURED MUCH IN RECENT WEEKS.
I WAS WORRIED ABOUT HIM FOR A WHILE, SPOCK--WHAT WITH THE DEATH OF HIS SON, THE DESTRUCTION OF THE ENTERPRISE...
...WHAT JIM NEEDED--WHAT HE'S ALWAYS NEEDED--WAS A TASK... SOMETHING TO KEEP HIM GOING...
...AND WITH THIS MISSION, HE'S GOT ONE IN SPADES! I THINK HE'LL BE JUST FINE... AND I'M GLAD YOU'RE HERE WITH HIM--WITH US!
THANK YOU, DOCTOR; I CONCUR.
WE'VE GOT THE BIRD OF PREY IN A TRACTOR BEAM AS YOU ORDERED, SIR, AND WE'RE SUPPLYING POWER TO ITS CLOAKING DEVICE.
GOOD WORK, MR. SULU; I HOPE YOU AND MR. CHEKOV'S COUNTERPARTS FIND STASIS TO THEIR LIKING.
CALL FROM ADMIRAL TURNER COMING IN, CAPTAIN, FOR ALL SHIPS.
ATTENTION INVASION FLEET: YOU ARE PRIVILEGED TO BE PART OF THE EMPIRE'S GREATEST EXPANSION IN ITS GLORIOUS HISTORY!
UNDER THE COMMAND OF CAPTAIN KIRK, YOU WILL CARRY THE FLAG OF THE EMPIRE TO EVEN GREATER HEIGHTS!
THAT'S WHY KIRK DIDN'T KILL ME; HE WANTED ME ALIVE TO SERVE HIM!
GO WITH THE BLESSINGS OF ALL THE EMPIRE BEHIND YOU, AND RETURN VICTORIOUS! THAT IS ALL!
A PRIORITY CALL COMING IN, ADMIRAL TURNER.
VERY WELL.

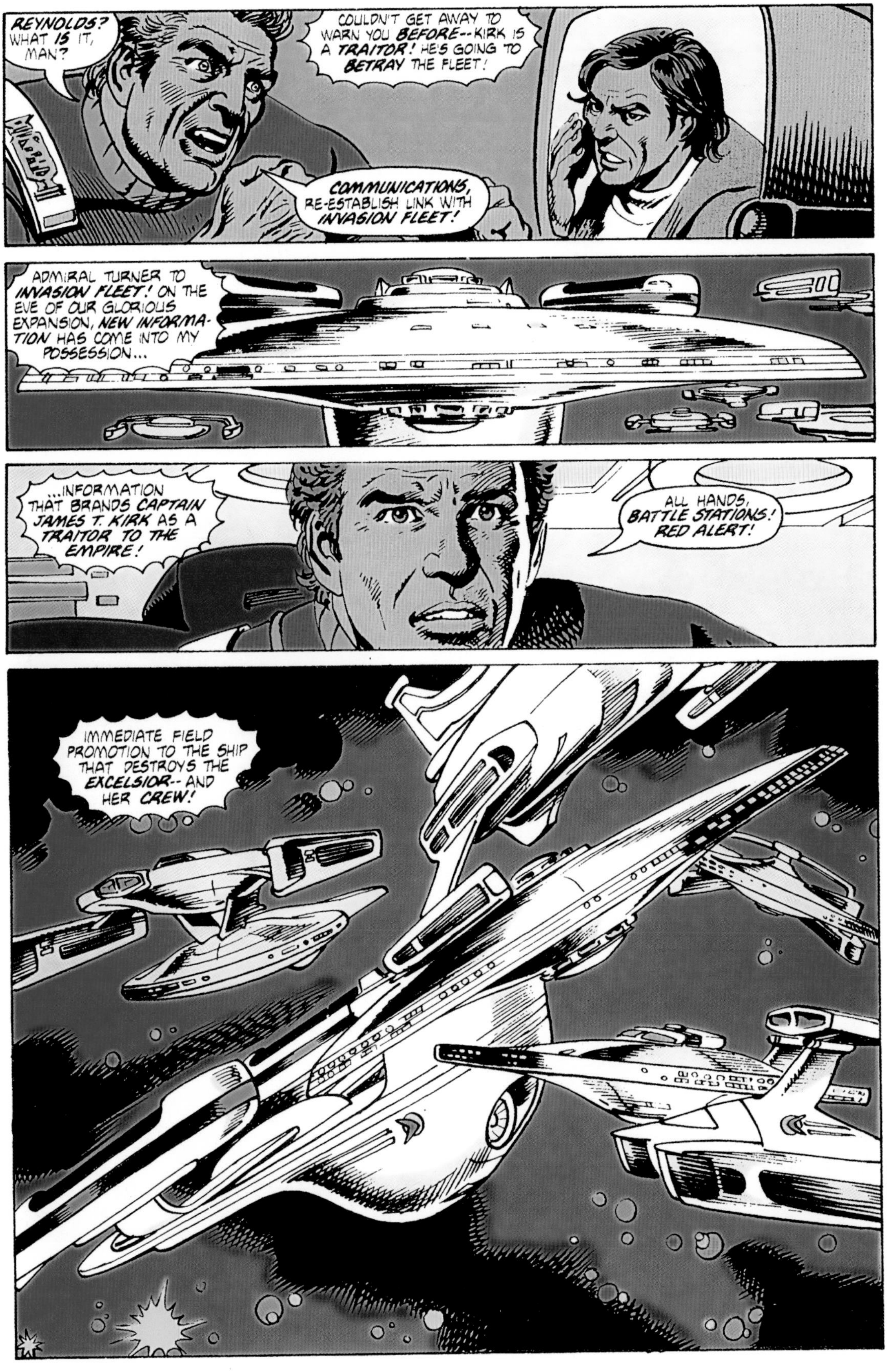
REYNOLDS? WHAT IS IT, MAN?
COULDN'T GET AWAY TO WARN YOU BEFORE--KIRK IS A TRAITOR! HE'S GOING TO BETRAY THE FLEET!
COMMUNICATIONS, RE-ESTABLISH LINK WITH INVASION FLEET!
ADMIRAL TURNER TO INVASION FLEET! ON THE EVE OF OUR GLORIOUS EXPANSION, NEW INFORMATION HAS COME INTO MY POSSESSION...
...INFORMATION THAT BRANDS CAPTAIN JAMES T. KIRK AS A TRAITOR TO THE EMPIRE!
ALL HANDS, BATTLE STATIONS! RED ALERT!
IMMEDIATE FIELD PROMOTION TO THE SHIP THAT DESTROYS THE EXCELSIOR-- AND HER CREW!

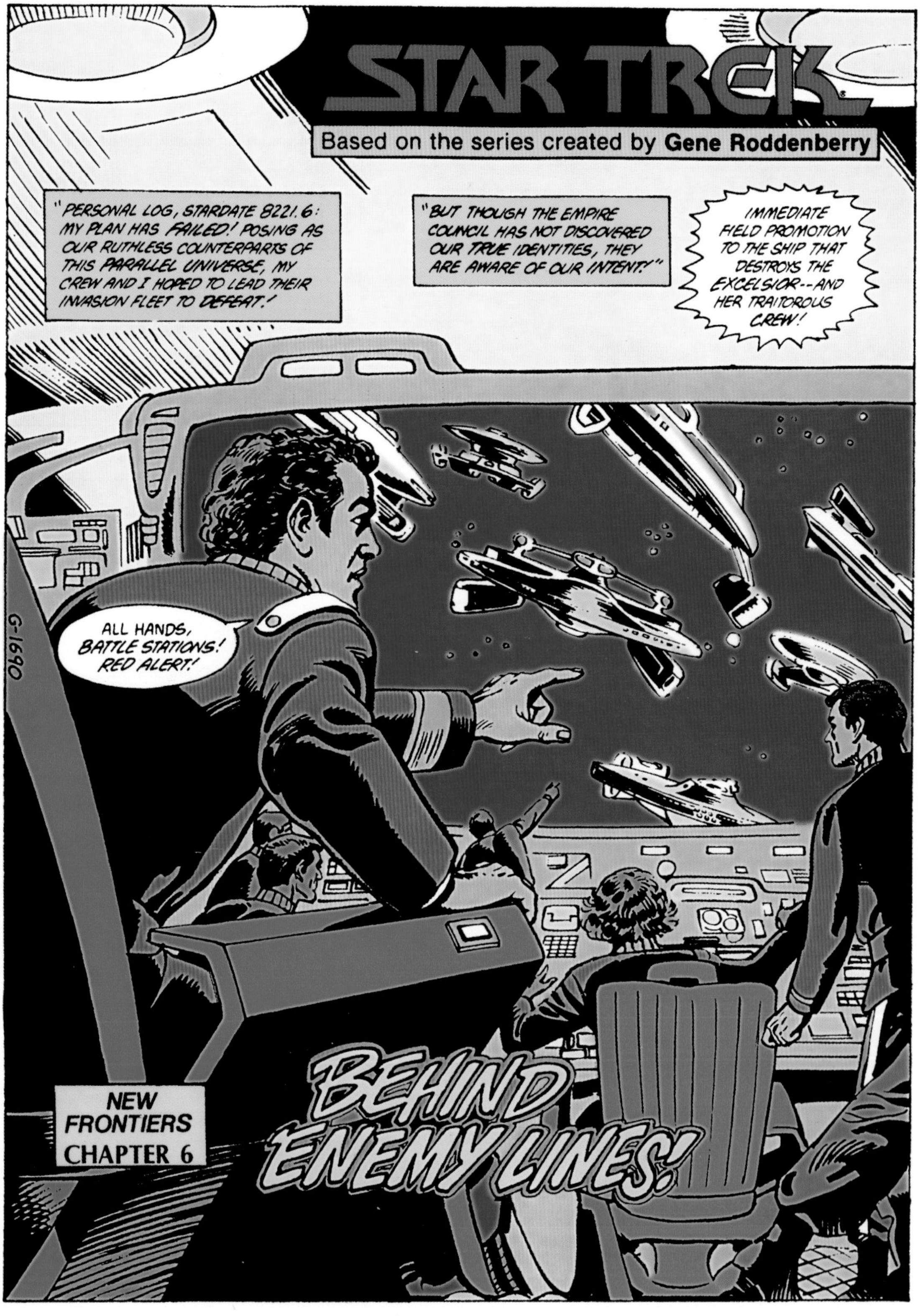
STAR TREK
Based on the series created by Gene Roddenberry
"PERSONAL LOG, STARDATE 8221.6: MY PLAN HAS FAILED! POSING AS OUR RUTHLESS COUNTERPARTS OF THIS PARALLEL UNIVERSE, MY CREW AND I HOPED TO LEAD THEIR INVASION FLEET TO DEFEAT.'
"BUT THOUGH THE EMPIRE COUNCIL HAS NOT DISCOVERED OUR TRUE IDENTITIES, THEY ARE AWARE OF OUR INTENT!"
IMMEDIATE FIELD PROMOTION TO THE SHIP THAT DESTROYS THE EXCELSIOR--AND HER TRAITOROUS CREW!
ALL HANDS, BATTLE STATIONS! RED ALERT!
G-1690
NEW FRONTIERS
CHAPTER 6
BEHIND ENEMY LINES!

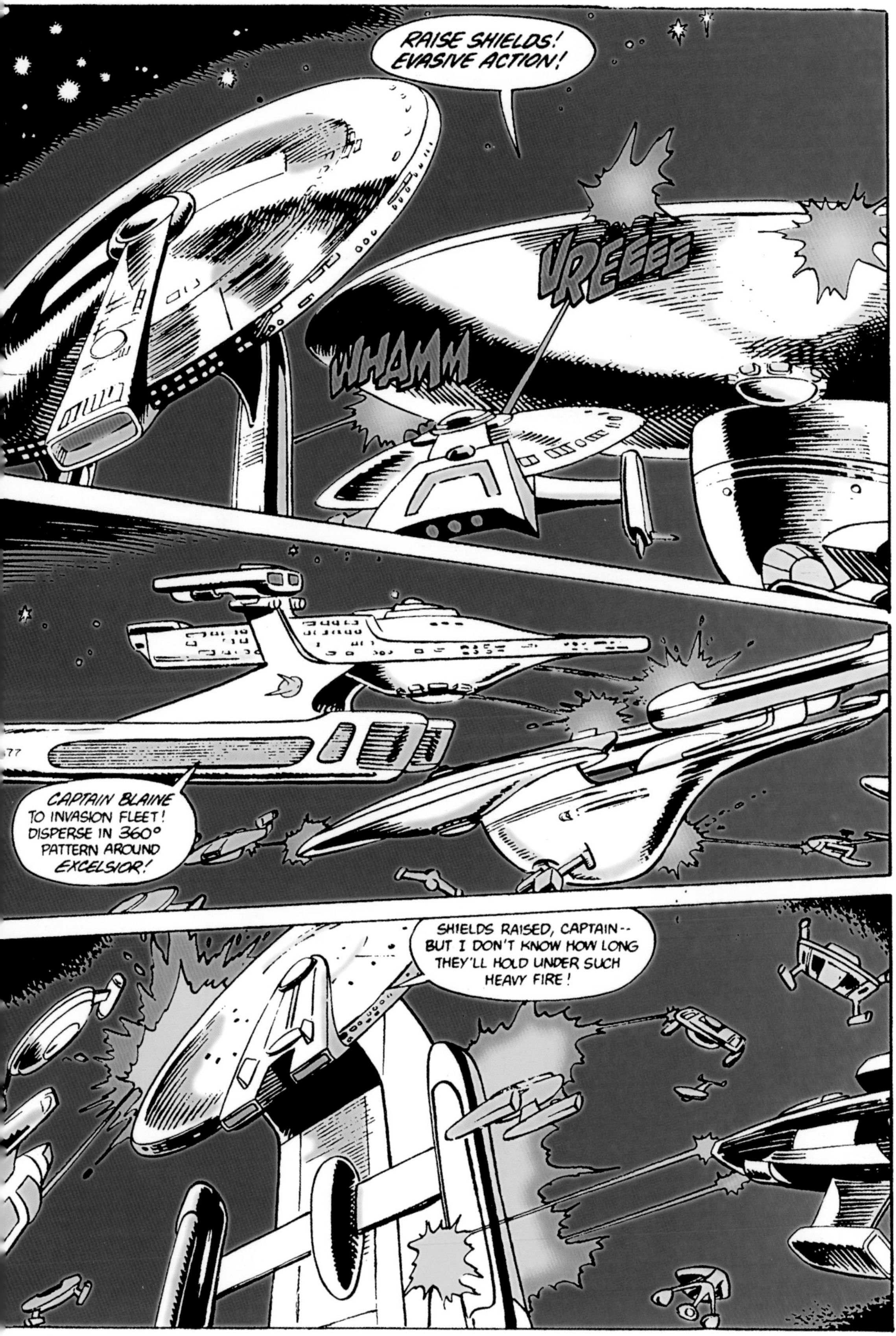
RAISE SHIELDS! EVASIVE ACTION!
VREEEE
WHAMM
CAPTAIN BLAINE TO INVASION FLEET! DISPERSE IN 360° PATTERN AROUND EXCELSIOR!
SHIELDS RAISED, CAPTAIN-- BUT I DON'T KNOW HOW LONG THEY'LL HOLD UNDER SUCH HEAVY FIRE!

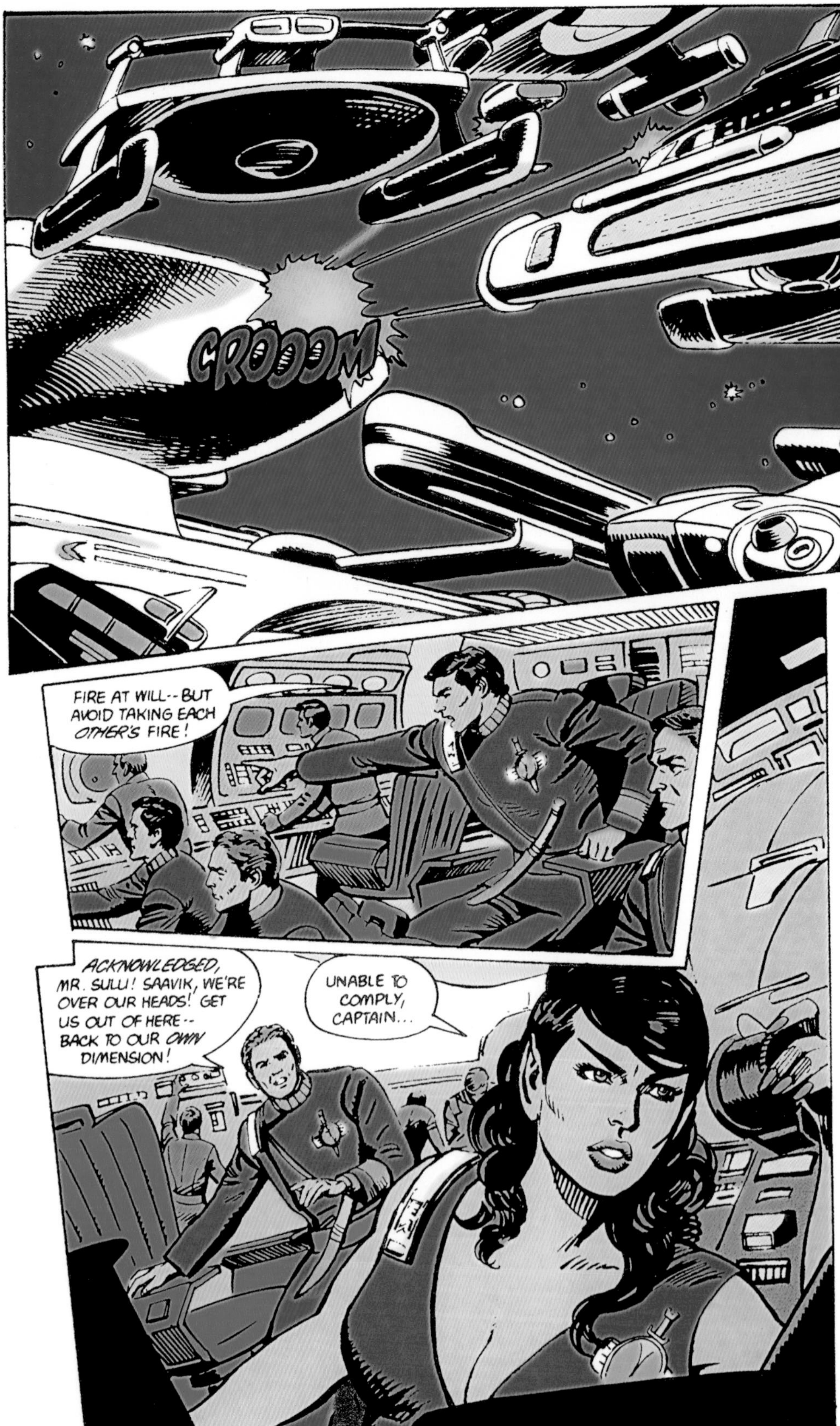
CROOOM
FIRE AT WILL--BUT AVOID TAKING EACH OTHER'S FIRE!
ACKNOWLEDGED, MR. SULU! SAAVIK, WE'RE OVER OUR HEADS! GET US OUT OF HERE--BACK TO OUR OWN DIMENSION!
UNABLE TO COMPLY, CAPTAIN...

...SOME OF THE ENGINE COMPONENTS SUSTAINED DAMAGE BEFORE SHIELDS WERE RAISED.

DIMENSIONAL BREACH IS IMPOSSIBLE AT THIS TIME.

LOOKS LIKE WE'LL BE USING YOUR PLAN AFTER ALL, DAVID...

...IF THERE'S ANYTHING *LEFT* OF US! KIRK TO SICK BAY!

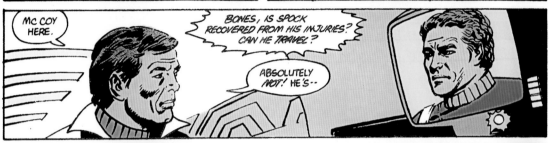

MC COY HERE.

BONES, IS SPOCK RECOVERED FROM HIS INJURIES? CAN HE *TRAVEL*?

ABSOLUTELY *NOT!* HE'S--

COMPLETELY RECOVERED, CAPTAIN; MAY I BE OF ASSISTANCE?

I ALSO OFFER *MY* SERVICES, SIR, IN WHATEVER CAPACITY YOU MAY NEED THEM.

ACCEPTED, *BOTH OF YOU!* BEAM OVER TO THE BIRD OF PREY...

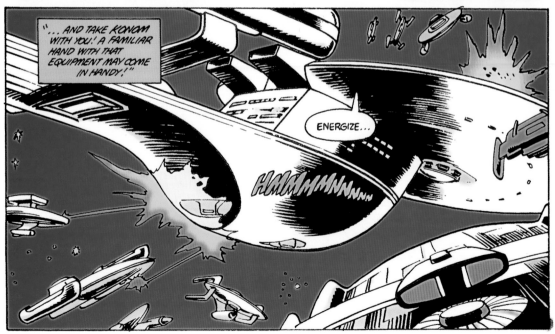

"...AND TAKE KONOM WITH YOU! A FAMILIAR HAND WITH THAT EQUIPMENT MAY COME IN HANDY!"

ENERGIZE...

HMMMMNNNNN

123

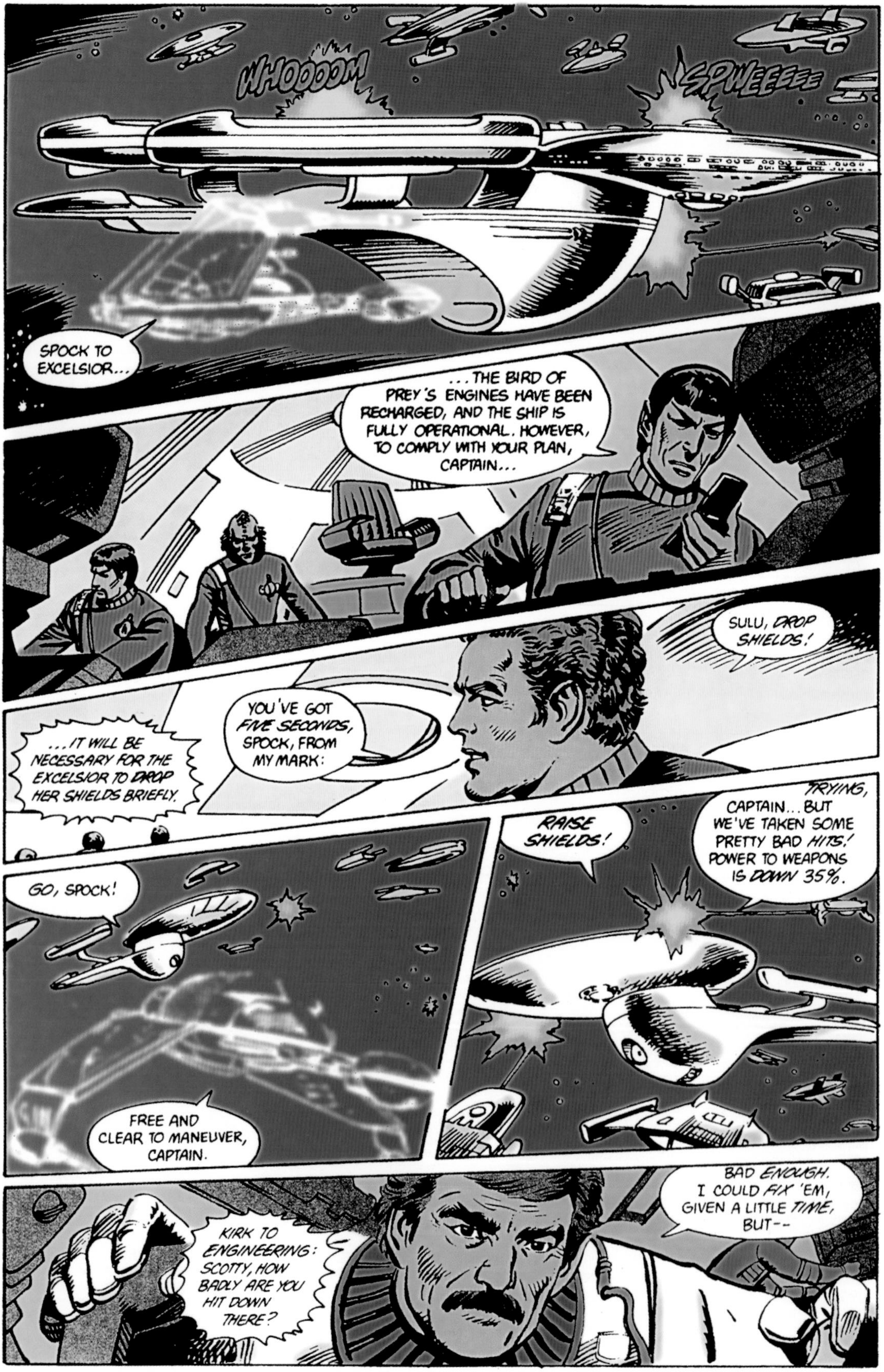
WHOOOOM
SPWEEEEE
SPOCK TO EXCELSIOR...
...THE BIRD OF PREY'S ENGINES HAVE BEEN RECHARGED, AND THE SHIP IS FULLY OPERATIONAL. HOWEVER, TO COMPLY WITH YOUR PLAN, CAPTAIN...
...IT WILL BE NECESSARY FOR THE EXCELSIOR TO DROP HER SHIELDS BRIEFLY.
YOU'VE GOT FIVE SECONDS, SPOCK, FROM MY MARK:
SULU, DROP SHIELDS!
GO, SPOCK!
FREE AND CLEAR TO MANEUVER, CAPTAIN.
RAISE SHIELDS!
TRYING, CAPTAIN... BUT WE'VE TAKEN SOME PRETTY BAD HITS! POWER TO WEAPONS IS DOWN 35%.
KIRK TO ENGINEERING: SCOTTY, HOW BADLY ARE YOU HIT DOWN THERE?
BAD ENOUGH. I COULD FIX 'EM, GIVEN A LITTLE TIME, BUT--

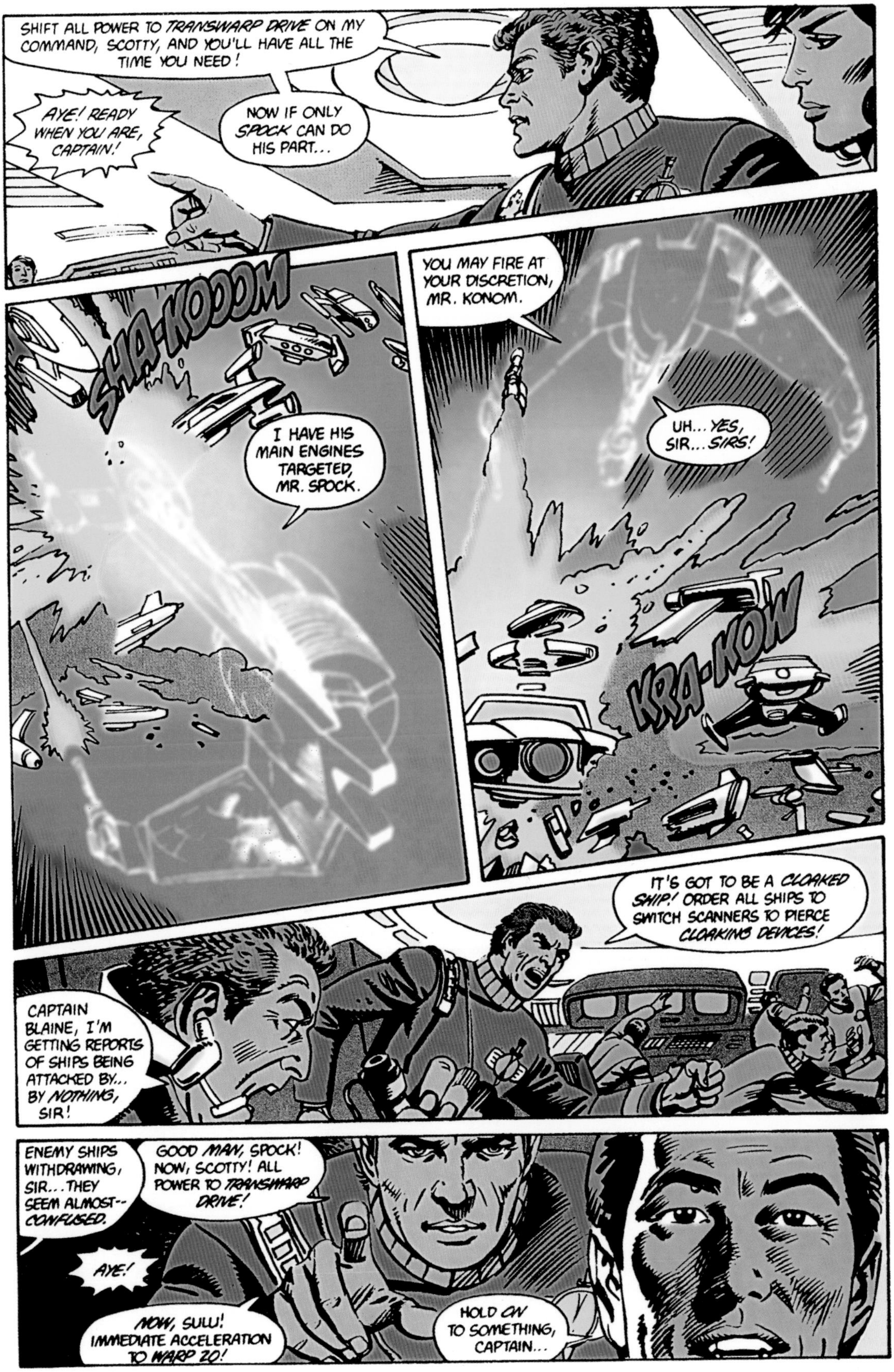
SHIFT ALL POWER TO TRANSWARP DRIVE ON MY COMMAND, SCOTTY, AND YOU'LL HAVE ALL THE TIME YOU NEED!
AYE! READY WHEN YOU ARE, CAPTAIN!
NOW IF ONLY SPOCK CAN DO HIS PART...
SHA-KOOOM
I HAVE HIS MAIN ENGINES TARGETED, MR. SPOCK.
YOU MAY FIRE AT YOUR DISCRETION, MR. KONOM.
UH... YES, SIR... SIRS!
KRA-KOW
IT'S GOT TO BE A CLOAKED SHIP! ORDER ALL SHIPS TO SWITCH SCANNERS TO PIERCE CLOAKING DEVICES!
CAPTAIN BLAINE, I'M GETTING REPORTS OF SHIPS BEING ATTACKED BY... BY NOTHING, SIR!
ENEMY SHIPS WITHDRAWING, SIR... THEY SEEM ALMOST--CONFUSED.
GOOD MAN, SPOCK! NOW, SCOTTY! ALL POWER TO TRANSWARP DRIVE!
AYE!
NOW, SULU! IMMEDIATE ACCELERATION TO WARP 20!
HOLD ON TO SOMETHING, CAPTAIN...

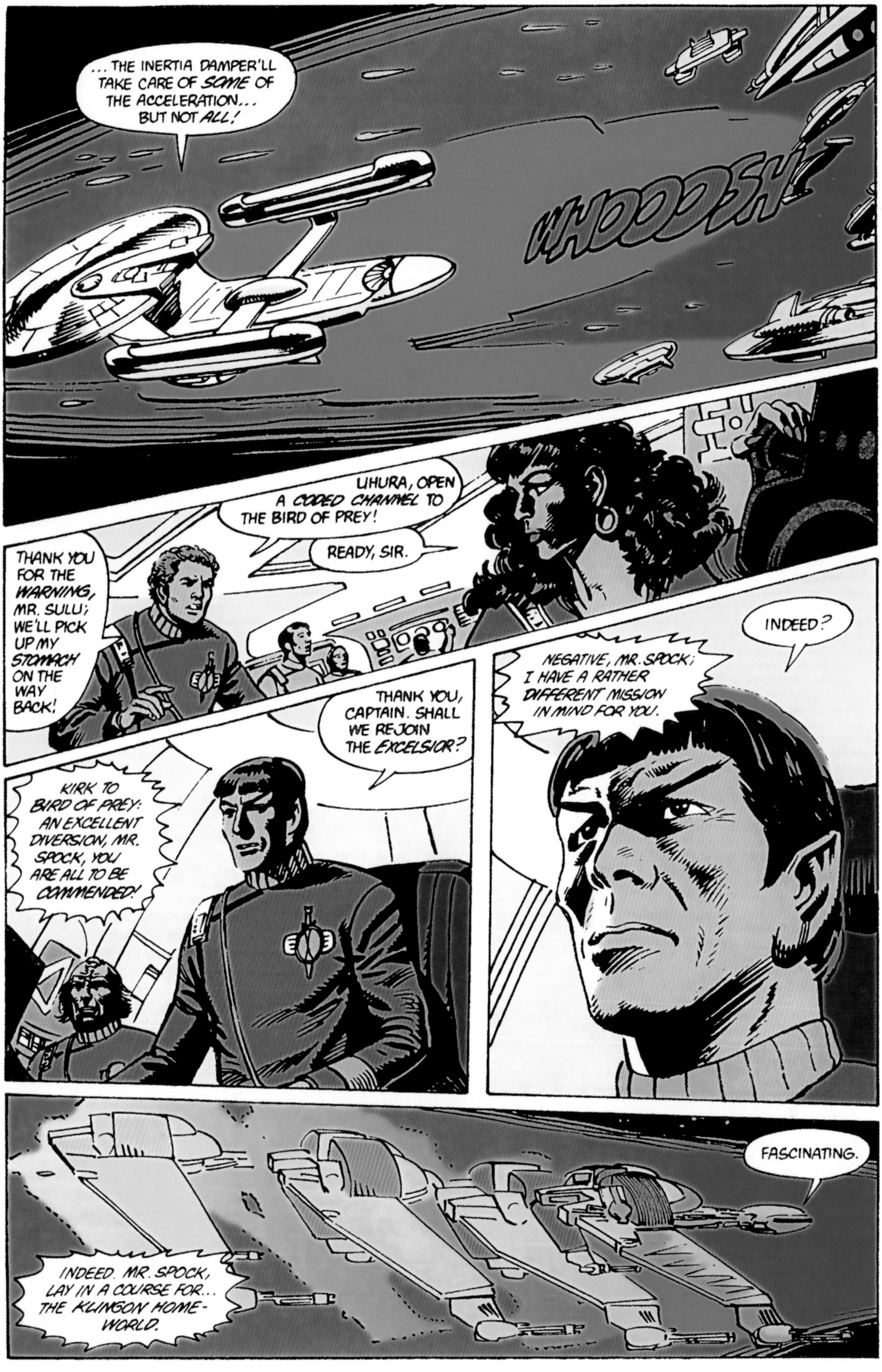
...THE INERTIA DAMPER'LL TAKE CARE OF SOME OF THE ACCELERATION... BUT NOT ALL!
WHOOOSH!
UHURA, OPEN A CODED CHANNEL TO THE BIRD OF PREY!
READY, SIR.
THANK YOU FOR THE WARNING, MR. SULU; WE'LL PICK UP MY STOMACH ON THE WAY BACK!
KIRK TO BIRD OF PREY: AN EXCELLENT DIVERSION, MR. SPOCK, YOU ARE ALL TO BE COMMENDED!
THANK YOU, CAPTAIN. SHALL WE REJOIN THE EXCELSIOR?
NEGATIVE, MR. SPOCK; I HAVE A RATHER DIFFERENT MISSION IN MIND FOR YOU.
INDEED?
INDEED. MR. SPOCK, LAY IN A COURSE FOR... THE KLINGON HOME-WORLD.
FASCINATING.

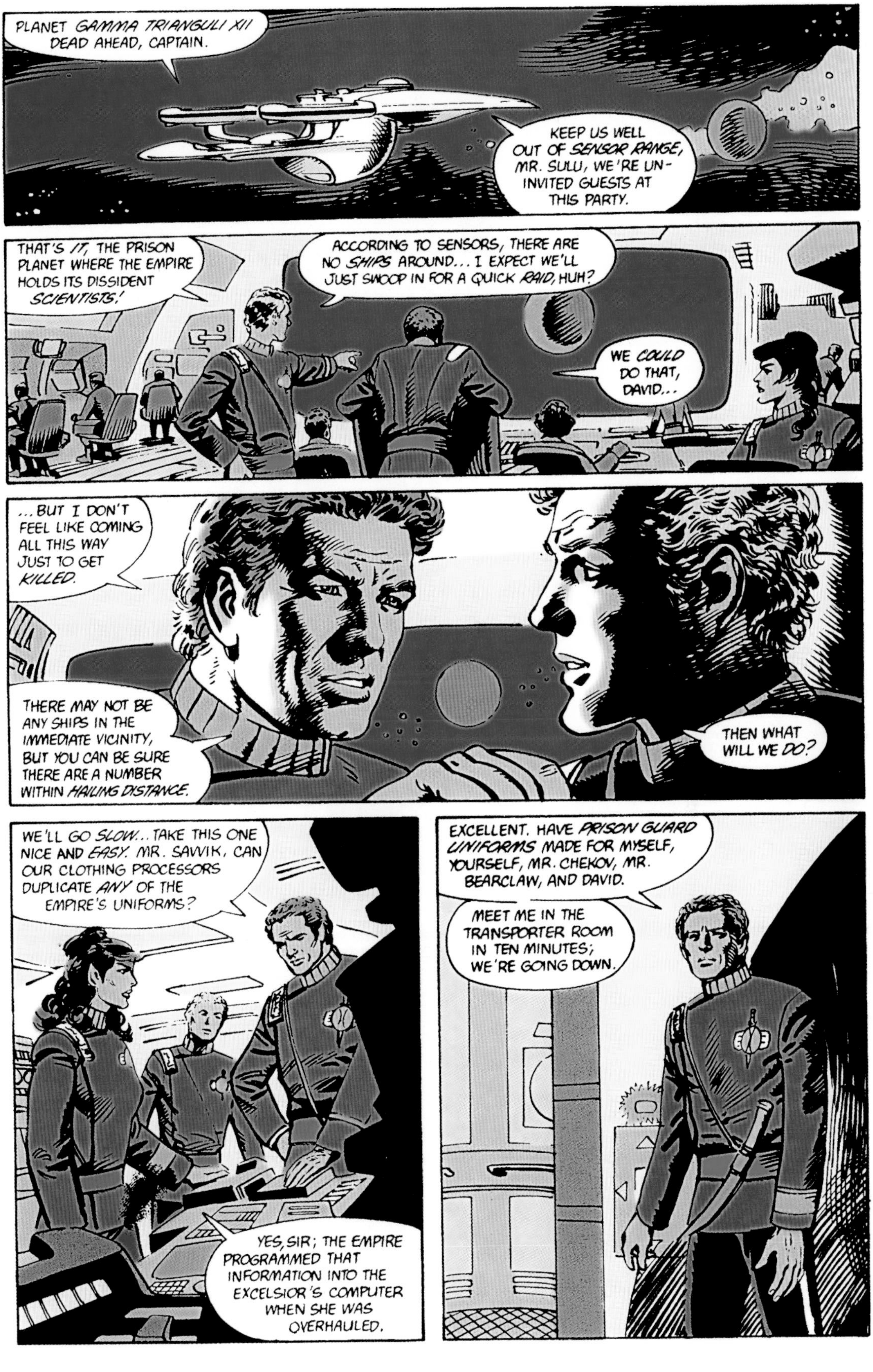
PLANET GAMMA TRIANGULI XII DEAD AHEAD, CAPTAIN.
KEEP US WELL OUT OF SENSOR RANGE, MR. SULU, WE'RE UN-INVITED GUESTS AT THIS PARTY.
THAT'S IT, THE PRISON PLANET WHERE THE EMPIRE HOLDS ITS DISSIDENT SCIENTISTS!
ACCORDING TO SENSORS, THERE ARE NO SHIPS AROUND... I EXPECT WE'LL JUST SWOOP IN FOR A QUICK RAID, HUH?
WE COULD DO THAT, DAVID...
...BUT I DON'T FEEL LIKE COMING ALL THIS WAY JUST TO GET KILLED.
THERE MAY NOT BE ANY SHIPS IN THE IMMEDIATE VICINITY, BUT YOU CAN BE SURE THERE ARE A NUMBER WITHIN HAILING DISTANCE.
THEN WHAT WILL WE DO?
WE'LL GO SLOW... TAKE THIS ONE NICE AND EASY. MR. SAVVIK, CAN OUR CLOTHING PROCESSORS DUPLICATE ANY OF THE EMPIRE'S UNIFORMS?
YES, SIR; THE EMPIRE PROGRAMMED THAT INFORMATION INTO THE EXCELSIOR'S COMPUTER WHEN SHE WAS OVERHAULED.
EXCELLENT. HAVE PRISON GUARD UNIFORMS MADE FOR MYSELF, YOURSELF, MR. CHEKOV, MR. BEARCLAW, AND DAVID.
MEET ME IN THE TRANSPORTER ROOM IN TEN MINUTES; WE'RE GOING DOWN.

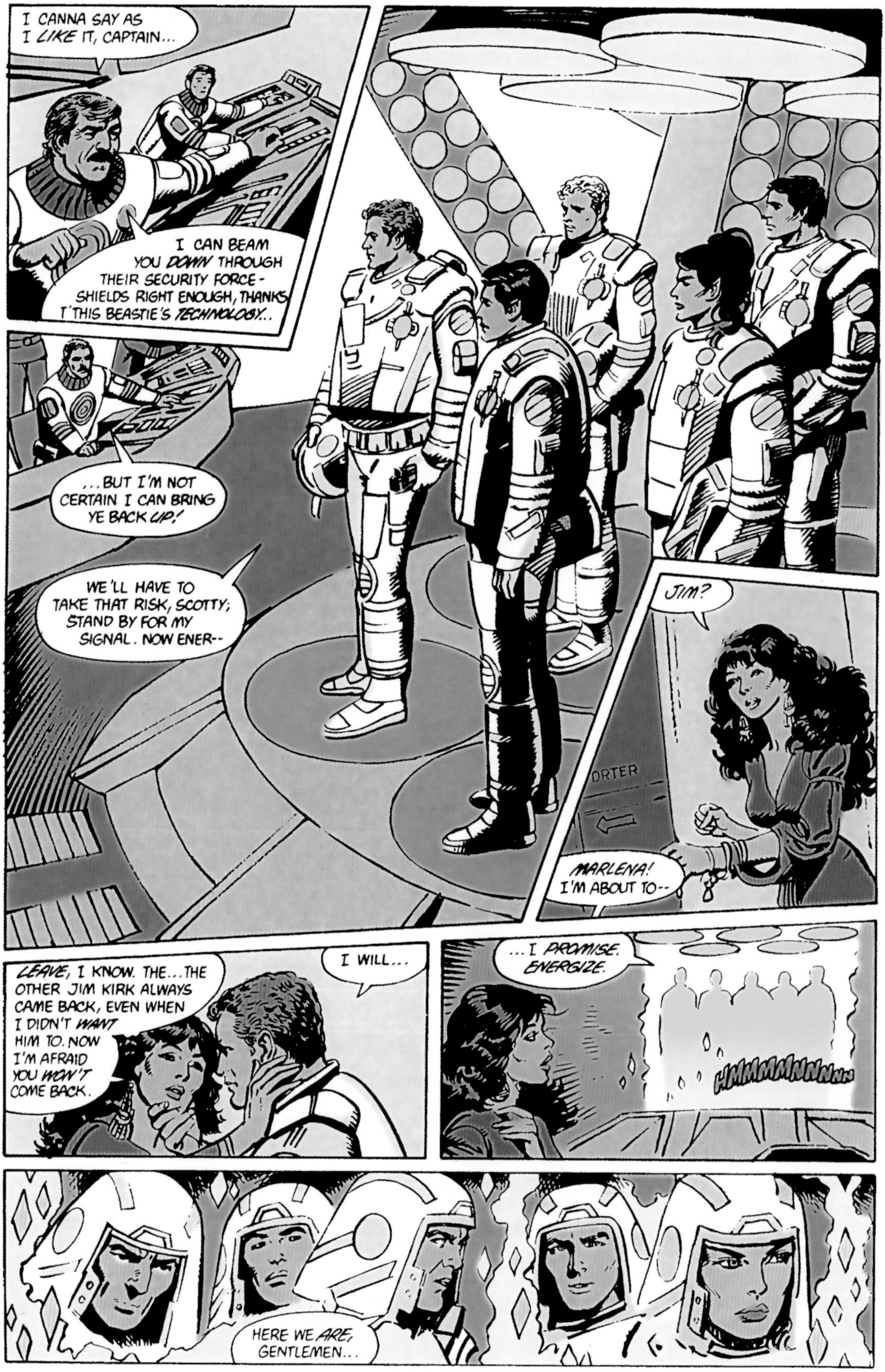
I CANNA SAY AS I LIKE IT, CAPTAIN...
I CAN BEAM YOU DOWN THROUGH THEIR SECURITY FORCE-SHIELDS RIGHT ENOUGH, THANKS T'THIS BEASTIE'S TECHNOLOGY...
...BUT I'M NOT CERTAIN I CAN BRING YE BACK UP!
WE'LL HAVE TO TAKE THAT RISK, SCOTTY; STAND BY FOR MY SIGNAL. NOW ENER--
JIM?
ORTER
MARLENA! I'M ABOUT TO--
LEAVE, I KNOW. THE...THE OTHER JIM KIRK ALWAYS CAME BACK, EVEN WHEN I DIDN'T WANT HIM TO. NOW I'M AFRAID YOU WON'T COME BACK.
I WILL...
...I PROMISE. ENERGIZE.
HMMMMNNNNNN
HERE WE ARE, GENTLEMEN...

...OUTSIDE ONE OF THE EMPIRE'S TOP SECURITY PRISONS.

THERE DOESN'T SEEM TO *BE* MUCH SECURITY, CAPTAIN.

THEY THINK THEIR FORCE-SHIELD MAKES THEM IMMUNE TO AN EXTERIOR ASSAULT, BEARCLAW, THAT ANY-ONE INSIDE IT MUST BE *FRIENDLY*. WE CAN *USE* THAT.

HEY, WE'RE NOT DUE FOR RELIEF FOR ANOTHER *HALF-HOUR* YET.

WE FIGURED YOU WOULDN'T MIND GETTING OFF A LITTLE EARLY. OF COURSE, IF YOU'D RATHER *NOT*...

YOU KIDDING? *HAIL THE EMPIRE!*

HAIL THE EMPIRE.

I THINK OUR CHOICE IS CLEAR, GENTLEMEN. TO THE *RIGHT*, PLEASE.

POLITICALS, SCIENTISTS

POWER PLANT

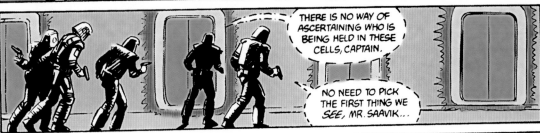

THERE IS NO WAY OF ASCERTAINING WHO IS BEING HELD IN THESE CELLS, CAPTAIN.

NO NEED TO PICK THE FIRST THING WE *SEE*, MR. SAAVIK...

...LET'S SHOP AROUND A LITTLE UNTIL--?

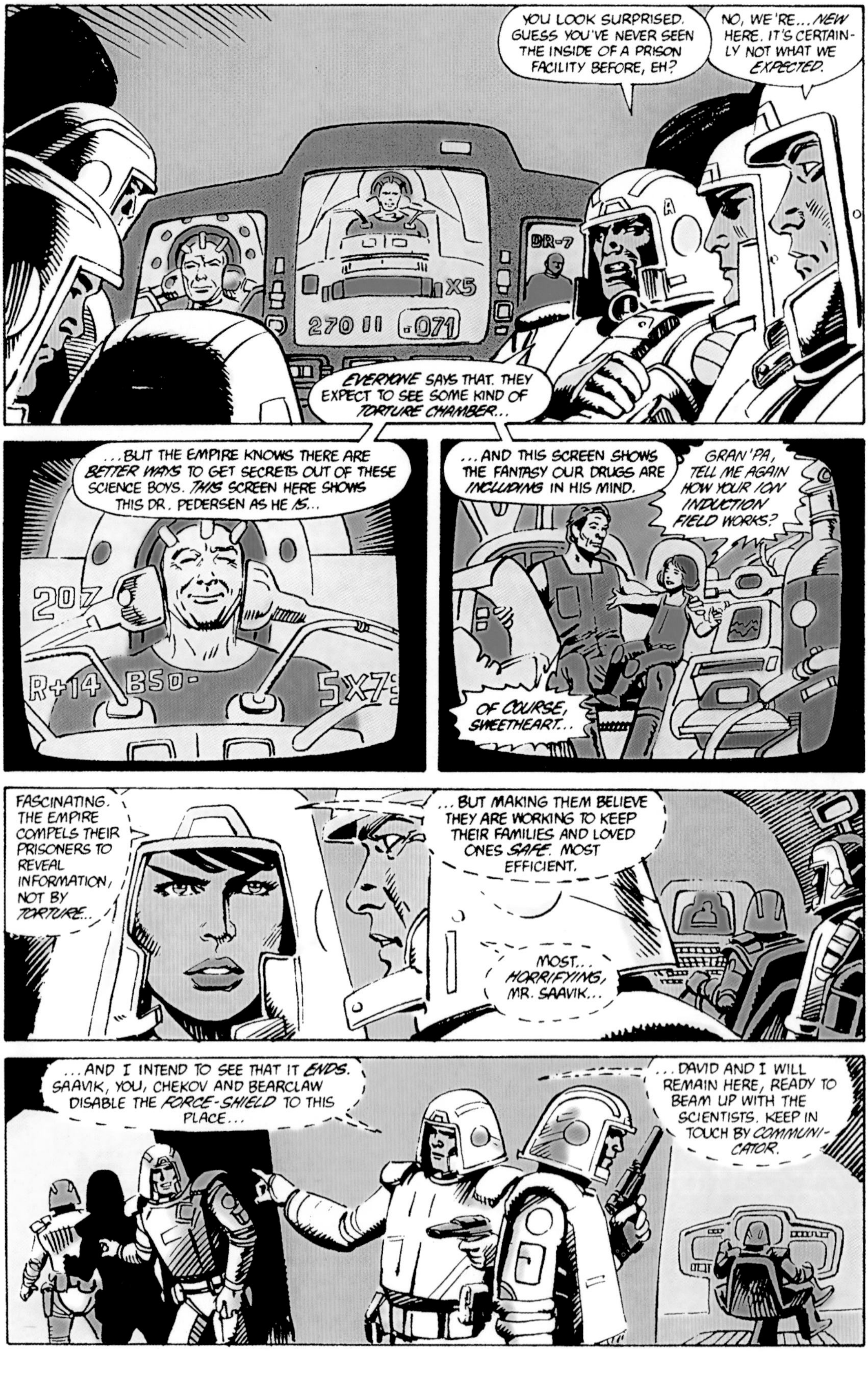
YOU LOOK SURPRISED. GUESS YOU'VE NEVER SEEN THE INSIDE OF A PRISON FACILITY BEFORE, EH?
NO, WE'RE... NEW HERE. IT'S CERTAINLY NOT WHAT WE EXPECTED.
DR-7
X5
270 11 071
EVERYONE SAYS THAT. THEY EXPECT TO SEE SOME KIND OF TORTURE CHAMBER...
...BUT THE EMPIRE KNOWS THERE ARE BETTER WAYS TO GET SECRETS OUT OF THESE SCIENCE BOYS. THIS SCREEN HERE SHOWS THIS DR. PEDERSEN AS HE IS...
207
R+14 B50-
...AND THIS SCREEN SHOWS THE FANTASY OUR DRUGS ARE INCLUDING IN HIS MIND.
GRAN'PA, TELL ME AGAIN HOW YOUR ION INDUCTION FIELD WORKS?
OF COURSE, SWEETHEART...
FASCINATING. THE EMPIRE COMPELS THEIR PRISONERS TO REVEAL INFORMATION, NOT BY TORTURE...
...BUT MAKING THEM BELIEVE THEY ARE WORKING TO KEEP THEIR FAMILIES AND LOVED ONES SAFE. MOST EFFICIENT.
MOST... HORRIFYING, MR. SAAVIK...
...AND I INTEND TO SEE THAT IT ENDS. SAAVIK, YOU, CHEKOV AND BEARCLAW DISABLE THE FORCE-SHIELD TO THIS PLACE...
...DAVID AND I WILL REMAIN HERE, READY TO BEAM UP WITH THE SCIENTISTS. KEEP IN TOUCH BY COMMUNICATOR.

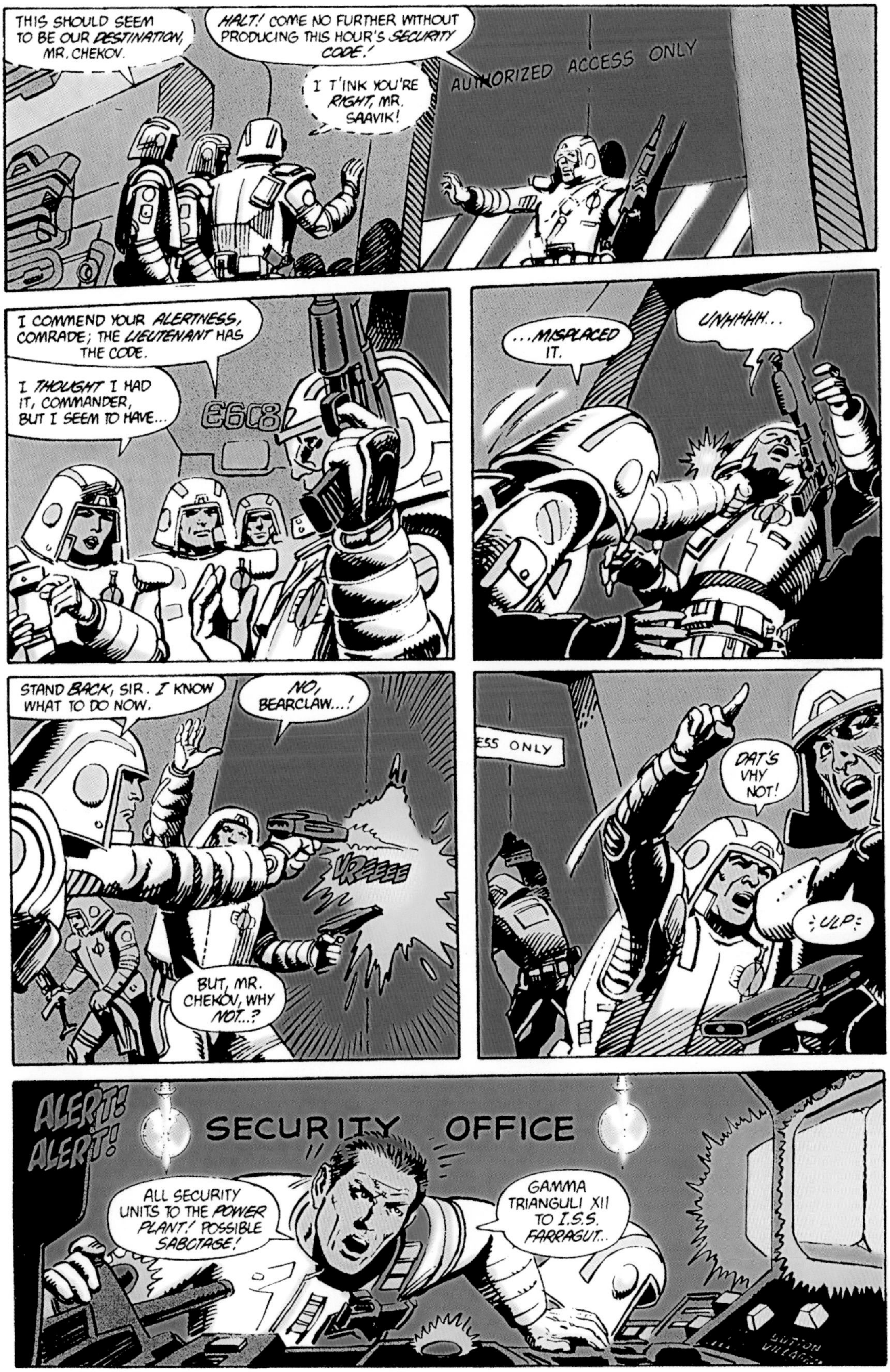

THIS SHOULD SEEM TO BE OUR DESTINATION, MR. CHEKOV.
HALT! COME NO FURTHER WITHOUT PRODUCING THIS HOUR'S SECURITY CODE!
I T'INK YOU'RE RIGHT, MR. SAAVIK!
AUTHORIZED ACCESS ONLY
I COMMEND YOUR ALERTNESS, COMRADE; THE LIEUTENANT HAS THE CODE.
I THOUGHT I HAD IT, COMMANDER, BUT I SEEM TO HAVE...
E6C8
...MISPLACED IT.
UNHHHH...
STAND BACK, SIR. I KNOW WHAT TO DO NOW.
NO, BEARCLAW...!
VREEEE
BUT, MR. CHEKOV, WHY NOT...?
ESS ONLY
DAT'S VHY NOT!
ULP
ALERT! ALERT!
SECURITY OFFICE
ALL SECURITY UNITS TO THE POWER PLANT! POSSIBLE SABOTAGE!
GAMMA TRIANGULI XII TO I.S.S. FARRAGUT...

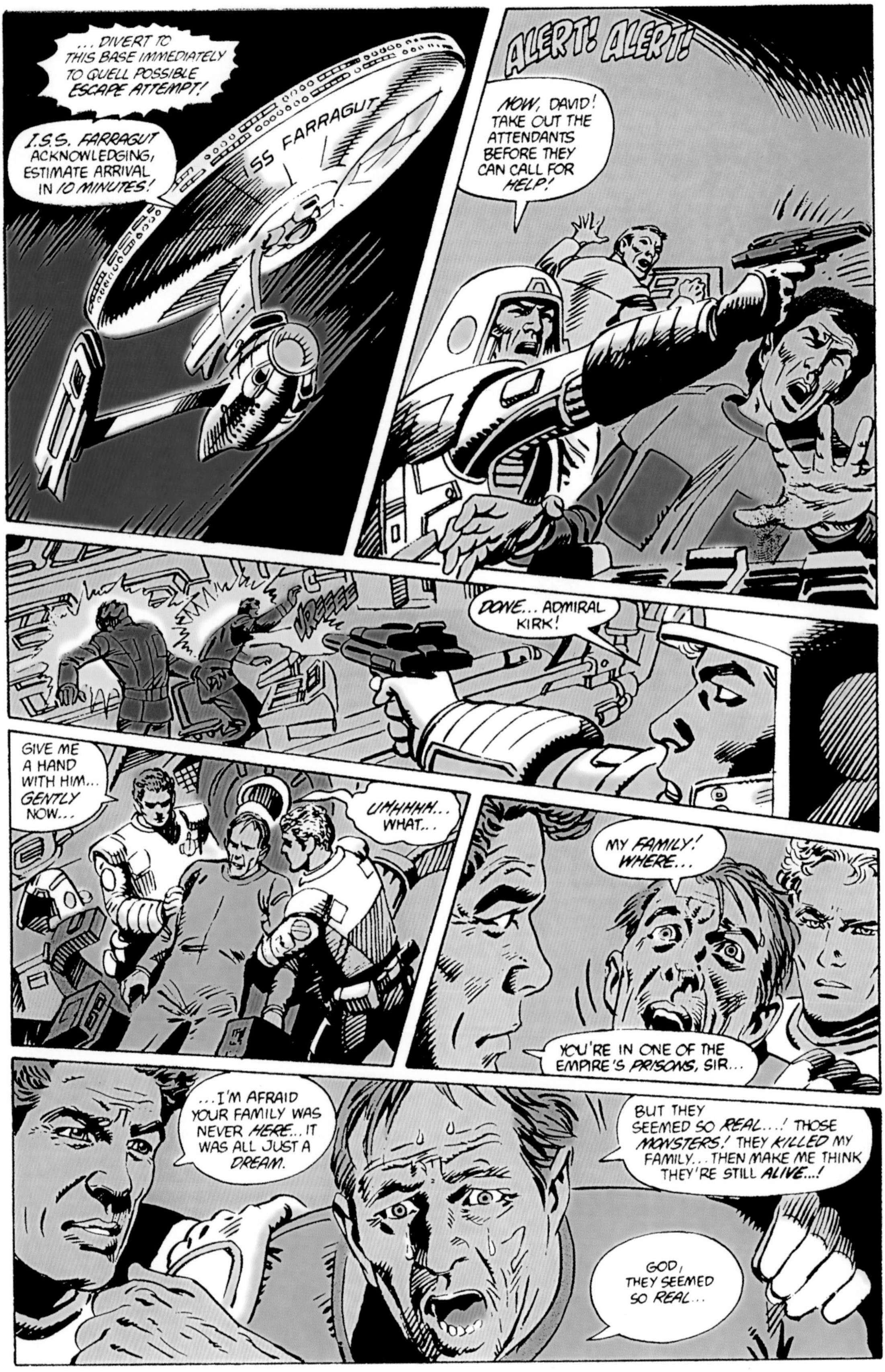
...DIVERT TO THIS BASE IMMEDIATELY TO QUELL POSSIBLE ESCAPE ATTEMPT!
I.S.S. FARRAGUT ACKNOWLEDGING, ESTIMATE ARRIVAL IN 10 MINUTES!
ISS FARRAGUT
ALERT! ALERT!
NOW, DAVID! TAKE OUT THE ATTENDANTS BEFORE THEY CAN CALL FOR HELP!
DONE... ADMIRAL KIRK!
GIVE ME A HAND WITH HIM... GENTLY NOW...
UMHHHH... WHAT...
MY FAMILY! WHERE...
YOU'RE IN ONE OF THE EMPIRE'S PRISONS, SIR...
...I'M AFRAID YOUR FAMILY WAS NEVER HERE... IT WAS ALL JUST A DREAM.
BUT THEY SEEMED SO REAL...! THOSE MONSTERS! THEY KILLED MY FAMILY... THEN MAKE ME THINK THEY'RE STILL ALIVE...!
GOD, THEY SEEMED SO REAL...

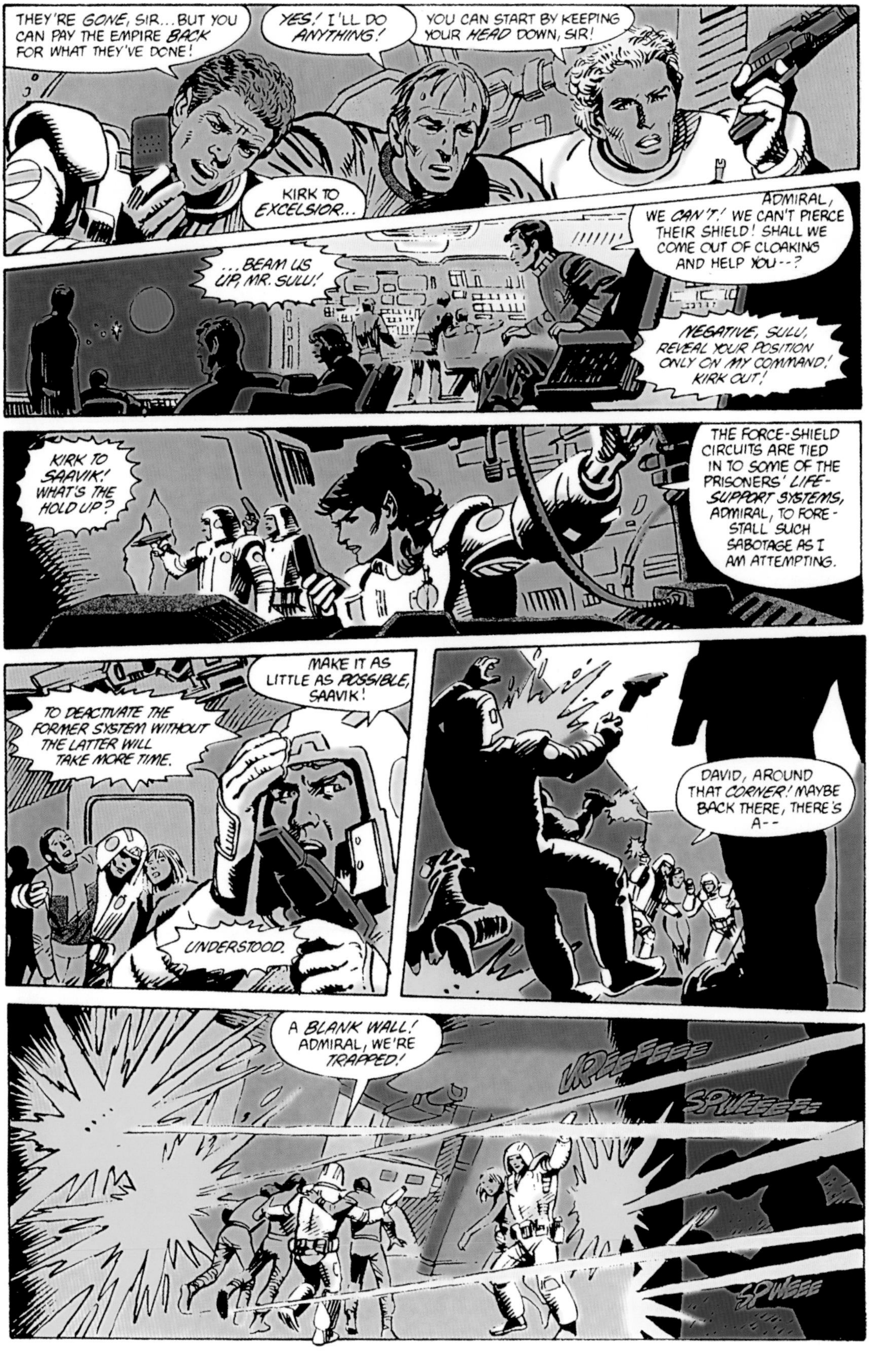
THEY'RE GONE, SIR...BUT YOU CAN PAY THE EMPIRE BACK FOR WHAT THEY'VE DONE!
YES! I'LL DO ANYTHING!
YOU CAN START BY KEEPING YOUR HEAD DOWN, SIR!
KIRK TO EXCELSIOR...
ADMIRAL, WE CAN'T! WE CAN'T PIERCE THEIR SHIELD! SHALL WE COME OUT OF CLOAKING AND HELP YOU--?
...BEAM US UP, MR. SULU!
NEGATIVE, SULU, REVEAL YOUR POSITION ONLY ON MY COMMAND! KIRK OUT!
KIRK TO SAAVIK! WHAT'S THE HOLD UP?
THE FORCE-SHIELD CIRCUITS ARE TIED IN TO SOME OF THE PRISONERS' LIFE-SUPPORT SYSTEMS, ADMIRAL, TO FORESTALL SUCH SABOTAGE AS I AM ATTEMPTING.
TO DEACTIVATE THE FORMER SYSTEM WITHOUT THE LATTER WILL TAKE MORE TIME.
MAKE IT AS LITTLE AS POSSIBLE, SAAVIK!
UNDERSTOOD.
DAVID, AROUND THAT CORNER! MAYBE BACK THERE, THERE'S A--
A BLANK WALL! ADMIRAL, WE'RE TRAPPED!
VREEEEEEE
SPWEEEEEE
SPWEEE

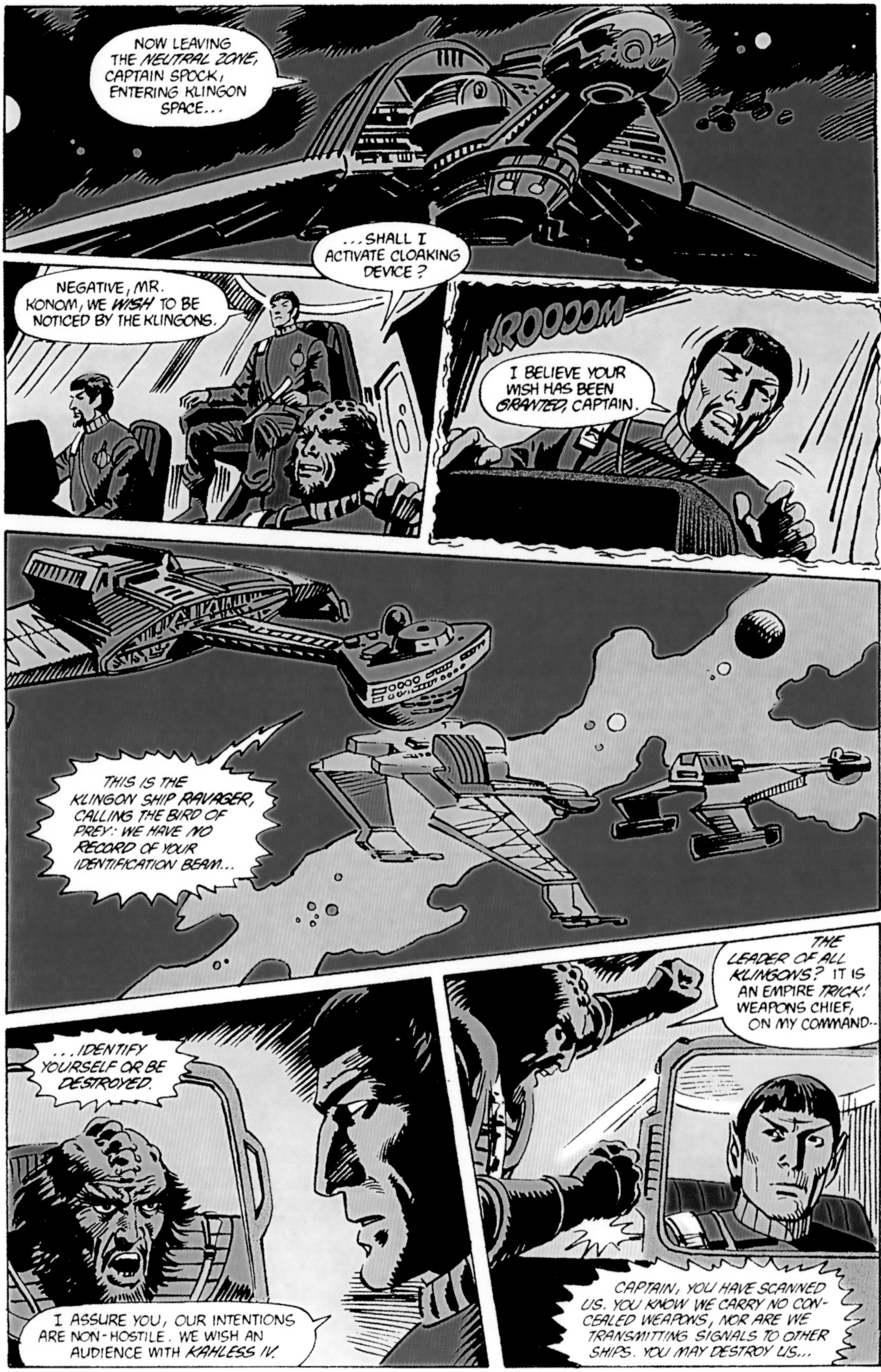
NOW LEAVING THE *NEUTRAL ZONE*, CAPTAIN SPOCK, ENTERING KLINGON SPACE...
...SHALL I ACTIVATE CLOAKING DEVICE?
NEGATIVE, MR. KONOM, WE *WISH* TO BE NOTICED BY THE KLINGONS.
KROOOOM
I BELIEVE YOUR WISH HAS BEEN *GRANTED*, CAPTAIN.
THIS IS THE KLINGON SHIP RAVAGER, CALLING THE BIRD OF PREY: WE HAVE NO RECORD OF YOUR IDENTIFICATION BEAM...
...IDENTIFY YOURSELF OR BE DESTROYED.
I ASSURE YOU, OUR INTENTIONS ARE NON-HOSTILE. WE WISH AN AUDIENCE WITH *KAHLESS IV.*
THE LEADER OF ALL KLINGONS? IT IS AN EMPIRE *TRICK!* WEAPONS CHIEF, ON MY COMMAND--
CAPTAIN, YOU HAVE SCANNED US. YOU KNOW WE CARRY NO CONCEALED WEAPONS, NOR ARE WE TRANSMITTING SIGNALS TO OTHER SHIPS. YOU MAY DESTROY US...

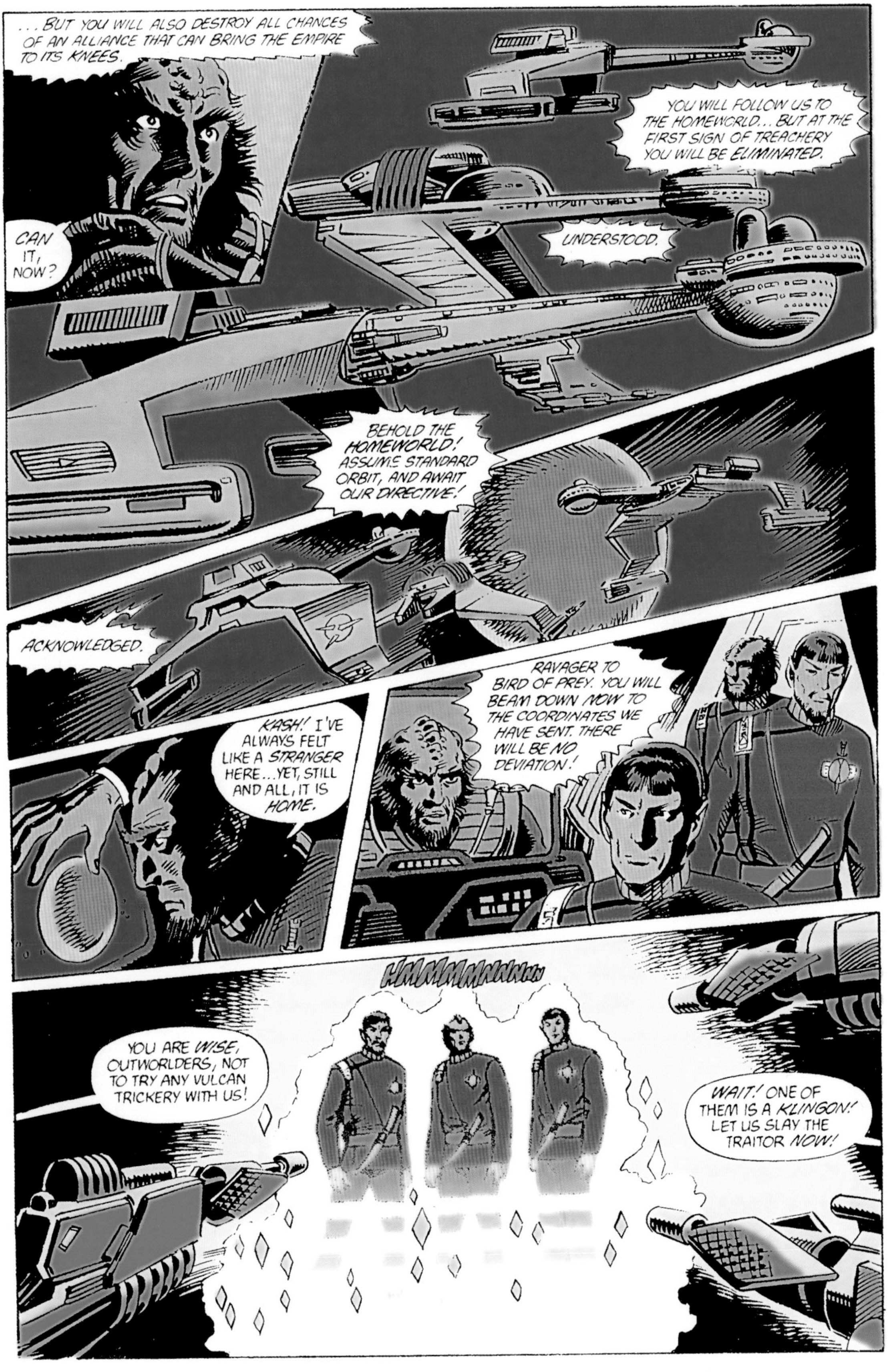

...BUT YOU WILL ALSO DESTROY ALL CHANCES OF AN ALLIANCE THAT CAN BRING THE EMPIRE TO ITS KNEES.
CAN IT, NOW?
YOU WILL FOLLOW US TO THE HOMEWORLD... BUT AT THE FIRST SIGN OF TREACHERY YOU WILL BE ELIMINATED.
UNDERSTOOD.
BEHOLD THE HOMEWORLD! ASSUME STANDARD ORBIT, AND AWAIT OUR DIRECTIVE!
ACKNOWLEDGED.
KASH! I'VE ALWAYS FELT LIKE A STRANGER HERE...YET, STILL AND ALL, IT IS HOME.
RAVAGER TO BIRD OF PREY. YOU WILL BEAM DOWN NOW TO THE COORDINATES WE HAVE SENT. THERE WILL BE NO DEVIATION!
HMMMMNNNNN
YOU ARE WISE, OUTWORLDERS, NOT TO TRY ANY VULCAN TRICKERY WITH US!
WAIT! ONE OF THEM IS A KLINGON! LET US SLAY THE TRAITOR NOW!

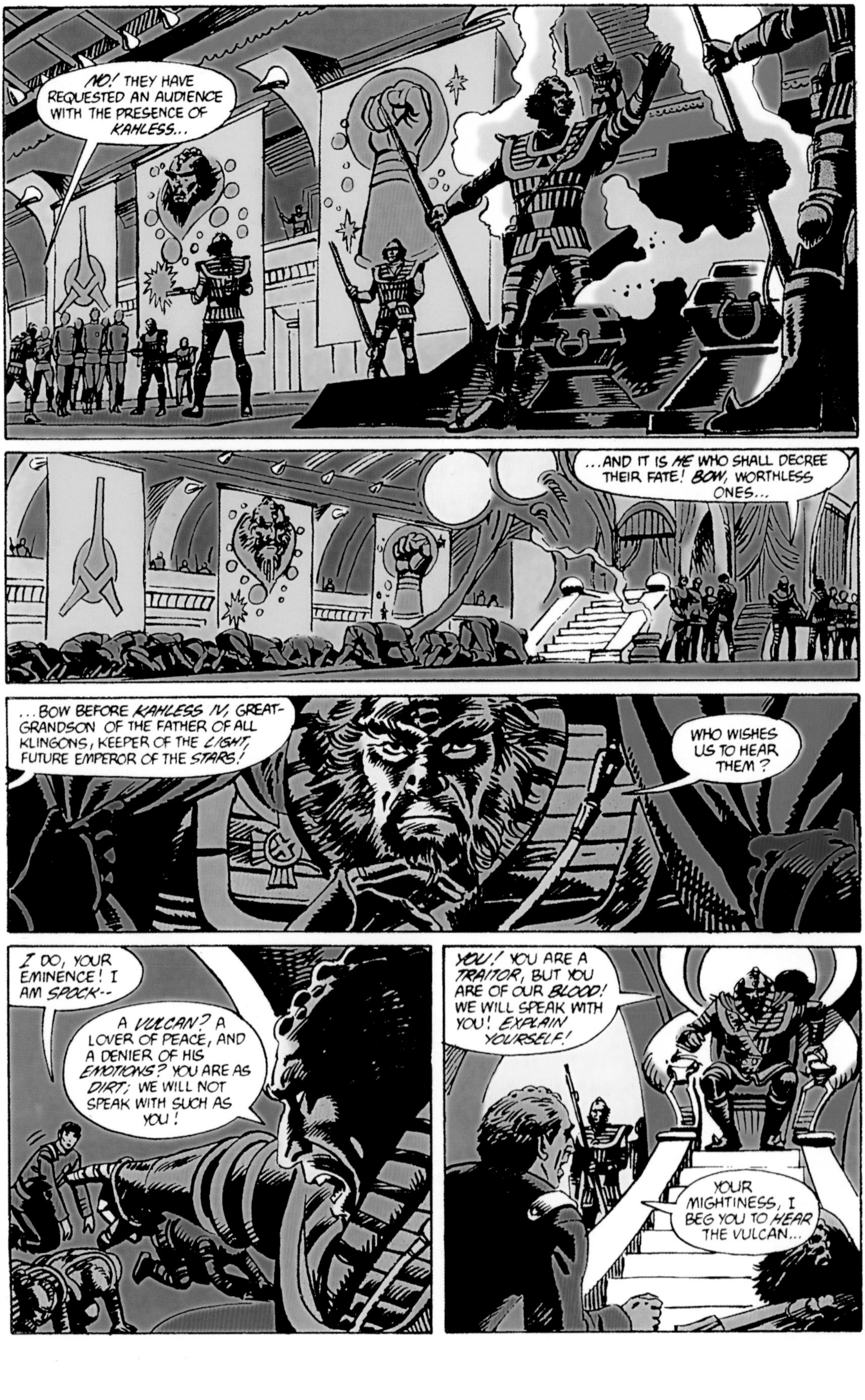
NO! THEY HAVE REQUESTED AN AUDIENCE WITH THE PRESENCE OF KAHLESS...
...AND IT IS HE WHO SHALL DECREE THEIR FATE! BOW, WORTHLESS ONES...
...BOW BEFORE KAHLESS IV, GREAT-GRANDSON OF THE FATHER OF ALL KLINGONS, KEEPER OF THE LIGHT, FUTURE EMPEROR OF THE STARS!
WHO WISHES US TO HEAR THEM?
I DO, YOUR EMINENCE! I AM SPOCK--
A VULCAN? A LOVER OF PEACE, AND A DENIER OF HIS EMOTIONS? YOU ARE AS DIRT; WE WILL NOT SPEAK WITH SUCH AS YOU!
YOU! YOU ARE A TRAITOR, BUT YOU ARE OF OUR BLOOD! WE WILL SPEAK WITH YOU! EXPLAIN YOURSELF!
YOUR MIGHTINESS, I BEG YOU TO HEAR THE VULCAN...

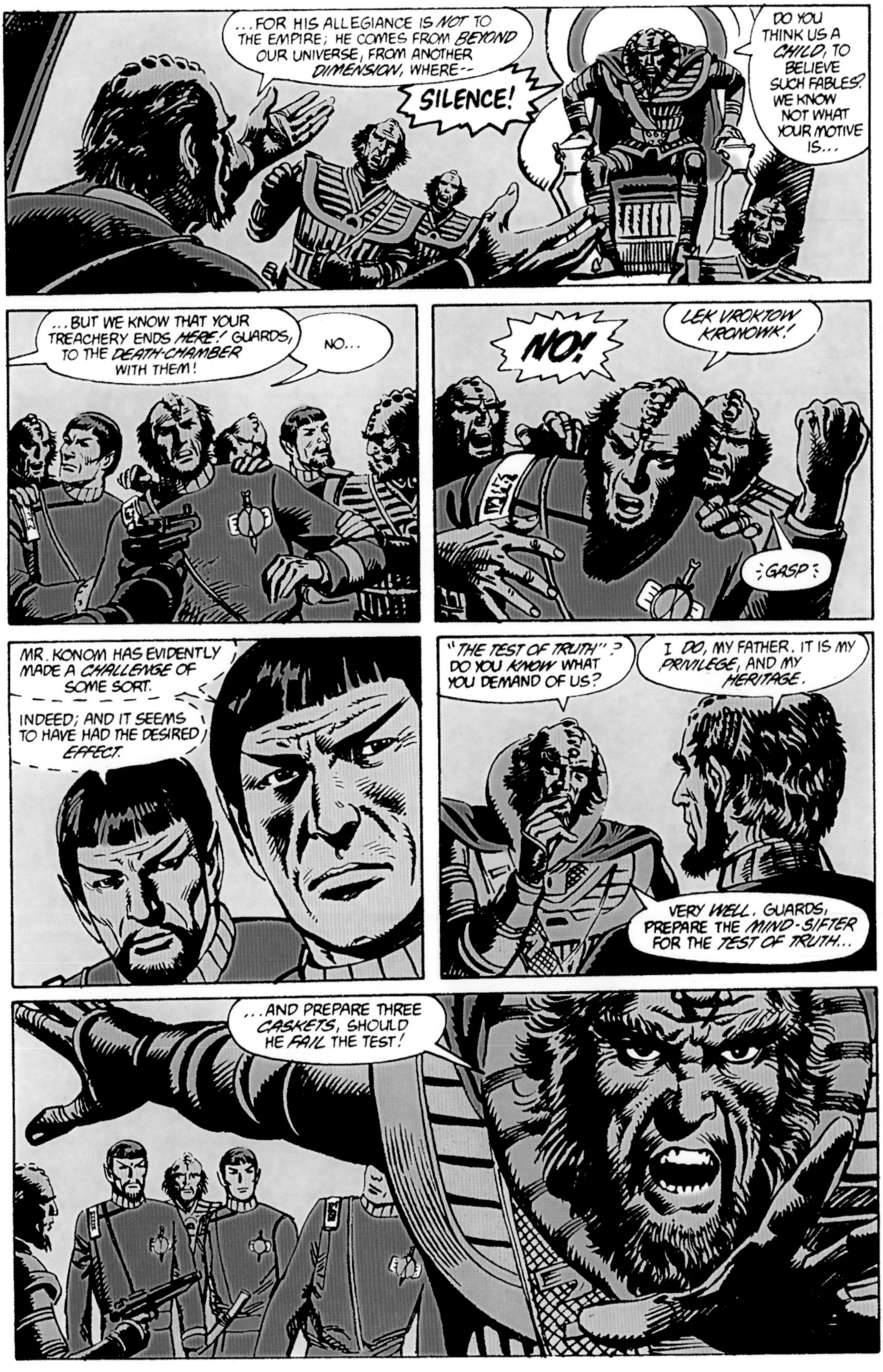
...FOR HIS ALLEGIANCE IS NOT TO THE EMPIRE; HE COMES FROM BEYOND OUR UNIVERSE, FROM ANOTHER DIMENSION, WHERE--
SILENCE!
DO YOU THINK US A CHILD, TO BELIEVE SUCH FABLES? WE KNOW NOT WHAT YOUR MOTIVE IS...
...BUT WE KNOW THAT YOUR TREACHERY ENDS HERE! GUARDS, TO THE DEATH-CHAMBER WITH THEM!
NO...
NO!
LEK VROKTOW KRONOWK!
GASP
MR. KONOM HAS EVIDENTLY MADE A CHALLENGE OF SOME SORT.
INDEED; AND IT SEEMS TO HAVE HAD THE DESIRED EFFECT.
"THE TEST OF TRUTH"? DO YOU KNOW WHAT YOU DEMAND OF US?
I DO, MY FATHER. IT IS MY PRIVILEGE, AND MY HERITAGE.
VERY WELL. GUARDS, PREPARE THE MIND-SIFTER FOR THE TEST OF TRUTH...
...AND PREPARE THREE CASKETS, SHOULD HE FAIL THE TEST!

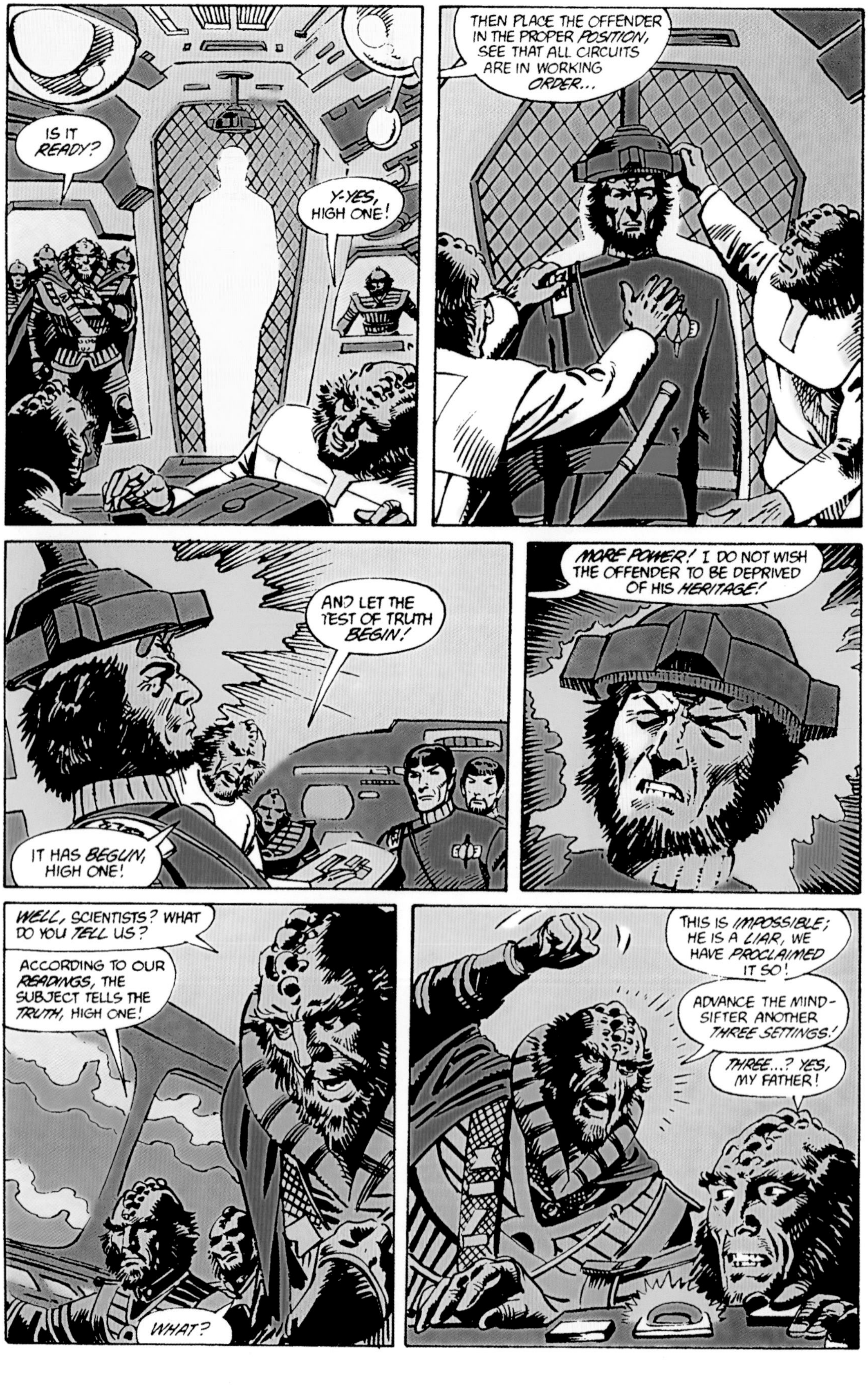
IS IT READY?
Y-YES, HIGH ONE!
THEN PLACE THE OFFENDER IN THE PROPER POSITION, SEE THAT ALL CIRCUITS ARE IN WORKING ORDER...
AND LET THE TEST OF TRUTH BEGIN!
IT HAS BEGUN, HIGH ONE!
MORE POWER! I DO NOT WISH THE OFFENDER TO BE DEPRIVED OF HIS HERITAGE!
WELL, SCIENTISTS? WHAT DO YOU TELL US?
ACCORDING TO OUR READINGS, THE SUBJECT TELLS THE TRUTH, HIGH ONE!
WHAT?
THIS IS IMPOSSIBLE; HE IS A LIAR, WE HAVE PROCLAIMED IT SO!
ADVANCE THE MIND-SIFTER ANOTHER THREE SETTINGS!
THREE...? YES, MY FATHER!

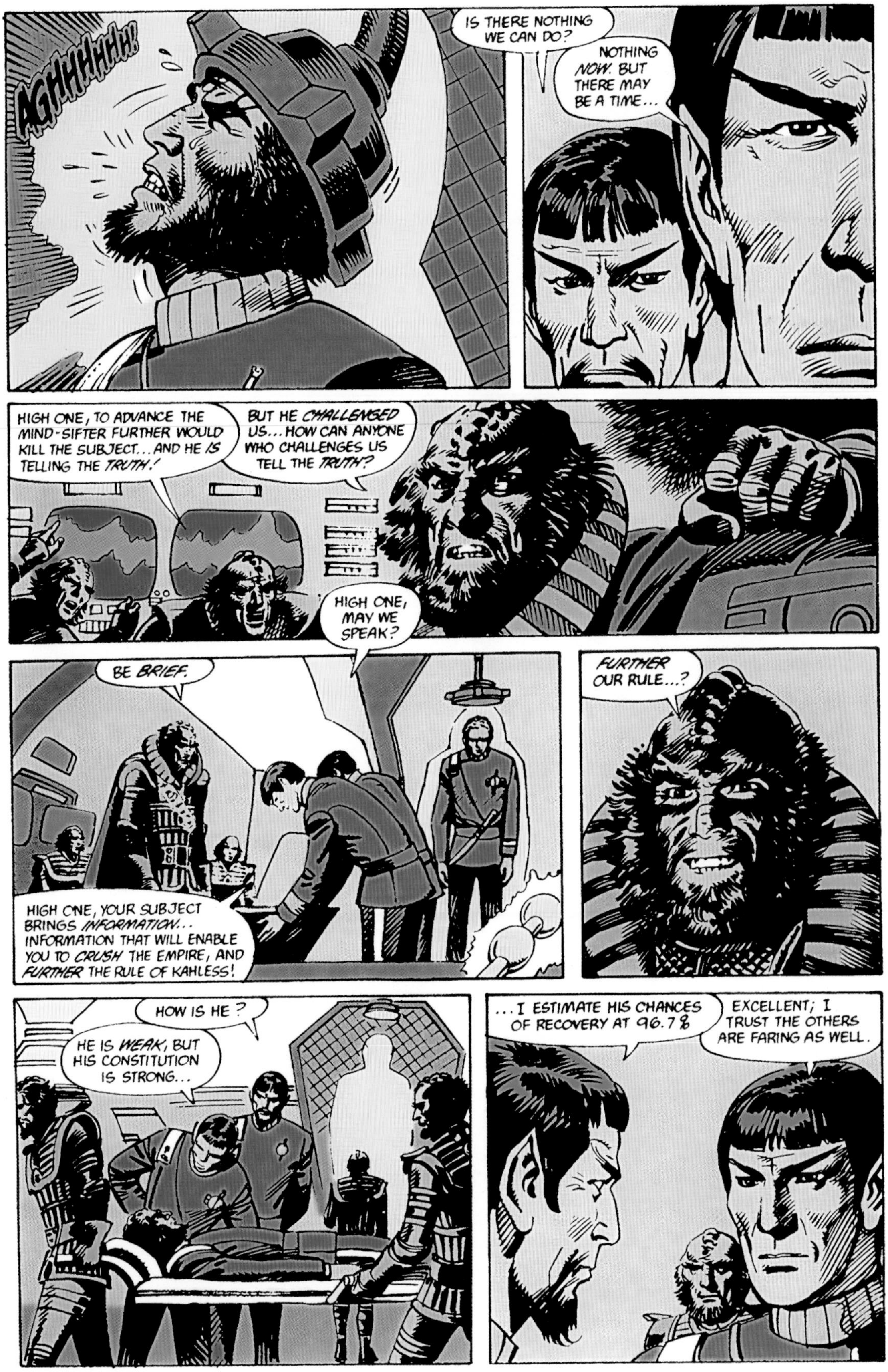
AGHHHHHH!
IS THERE NOTHING WE CAN DO?
NOTHING NOW. BUT THERE MAY BE A TIME...
HIGH ONE, TO ADVANCE THE MIND-SIFTER FURTHER WOULD KILL THE SUBJECT... AND HE IS TELLING THE TRUTH!
BUT HE CHALLENGED US... HOW CAN ANYONE WHO CHALLENGES US TELL THE TRUTH?
HIGH ONE, MAY WE SPEAK?
BE BRIEF.
HIGH ONE, YOUR SUBJECT BRINGS INFORMATION... INFORMATION THAT WILL ENABLE YOU TO CRUSH THE EMPIRE, AND FURTHER THE RULE OF KAHLESS!
FURTHER OUR RULE...?
HOW IS HE?
HE IS WEAK, BUT HIS CONSTITUTION IS STRONG...
...I ESTIMATE HIS CHANCES OF RECOVERY AT 96.7%
EXCELLENT; I TRUST THE OTHERS ARE FARING AS WELL.

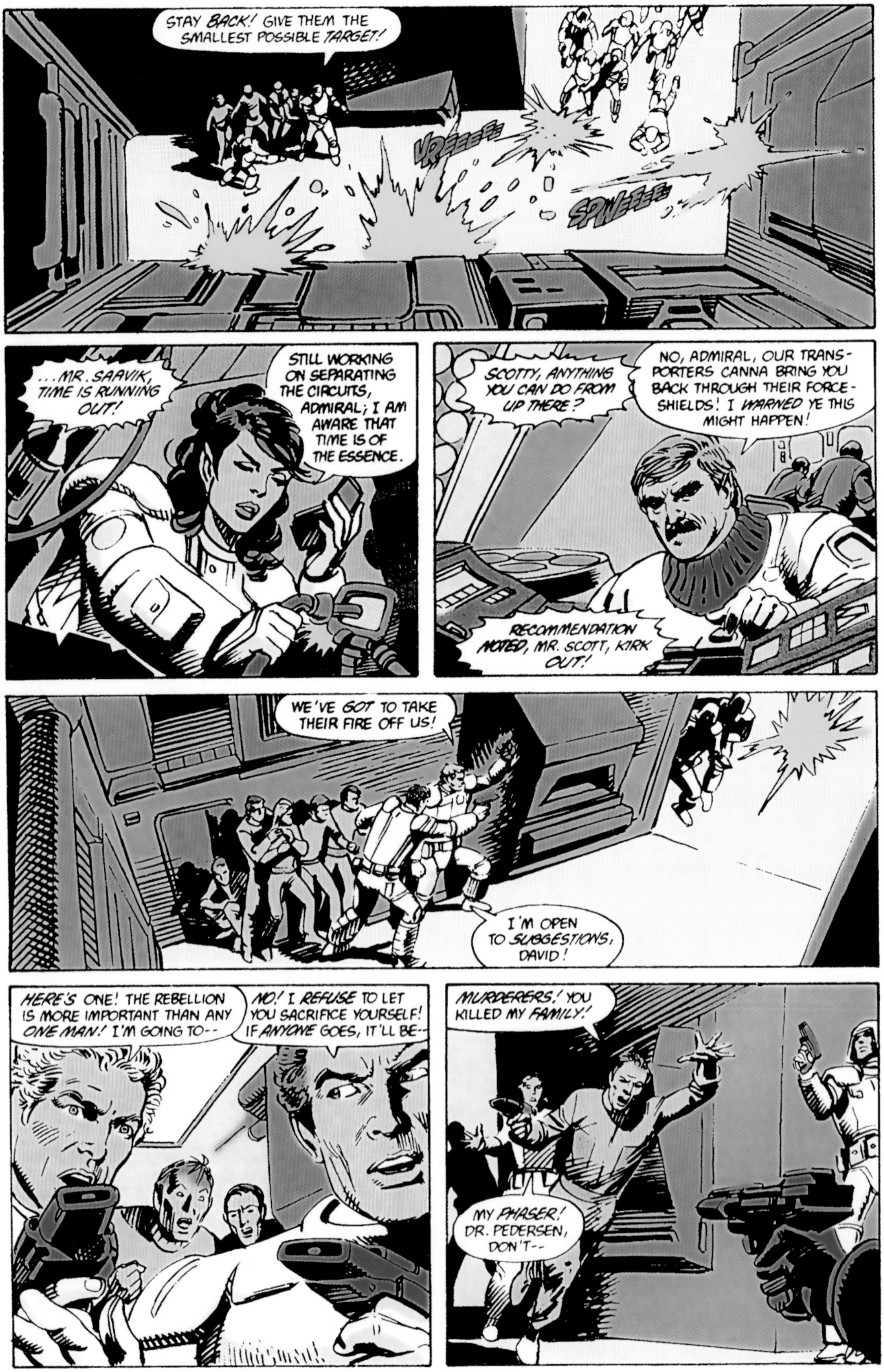
STAY BACK! GIVE THEM THE SMALLEST POSSIBLE TARGET!
VREEEE
SPWEEEE
...MR. SAAVIK, TIME IS RUNNING OUT!
STILL WORKING ON SEPARATING THE CIRCUITS, ADMIRAL; I AM AWARE THAT TIME IS OF THE ESSENCE.
SCOTTY, ANYTHING YOU CAN DO FROM UP THERE?
NO, ADMIRAL, OUR TRANS-PORTERS CANNA BRING YOU BACK THROUGH THEIR FORCE-SHIELDS! I WARNED YE THIS MIGHT HAPPEN!
RECOMMENDATION NOTED, MR. SCOTT, KIRK OUT!
WE'VE GOT TO TAKE THEIR FIRE OFF US!
I'M OPEN TO SUGGESTIONS, DAVID!
HERE'S ONE! THE REBELLION IS MORE IMPORTANT THAN ANY ONE MAN! I'M GOING TO--
NO! I REFUSE TO LET YOU SACRIFICE YOURSELF! IF ANYONE GOES, IT'LL BE--
MURDERERS! YOU KILLED MY FAMILY!
MY PHASER! DR. PEDERSEN, DON'T--

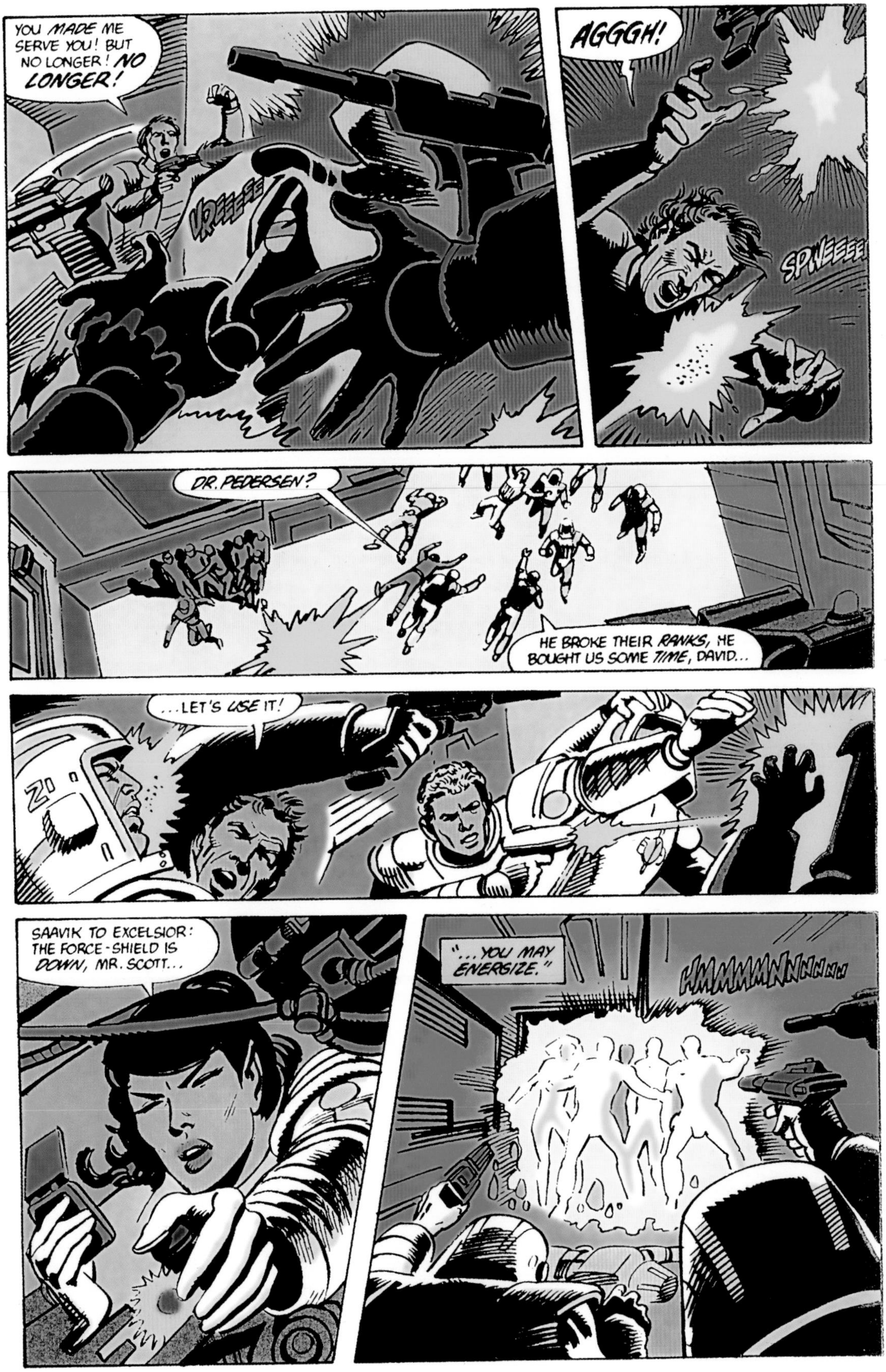
YOU MADE ME SERVE YOU! BUT NO LONGER! NO LONGER!
VREEEEE
AGGGH!
SPNEEEE
DR. PEDERSEN?
HE BROKE THEIR RANKS, HE BOUGHT US SOME TIME, DAVID...
...LET'S USE IT!
ZI
SAAVIK TO EXCELSIOR: THE FORCE-SHIELD IS DOWN, MR. SCOTT...
"...YOU MAY ENERGIZE."
HMMMMNNNNNN

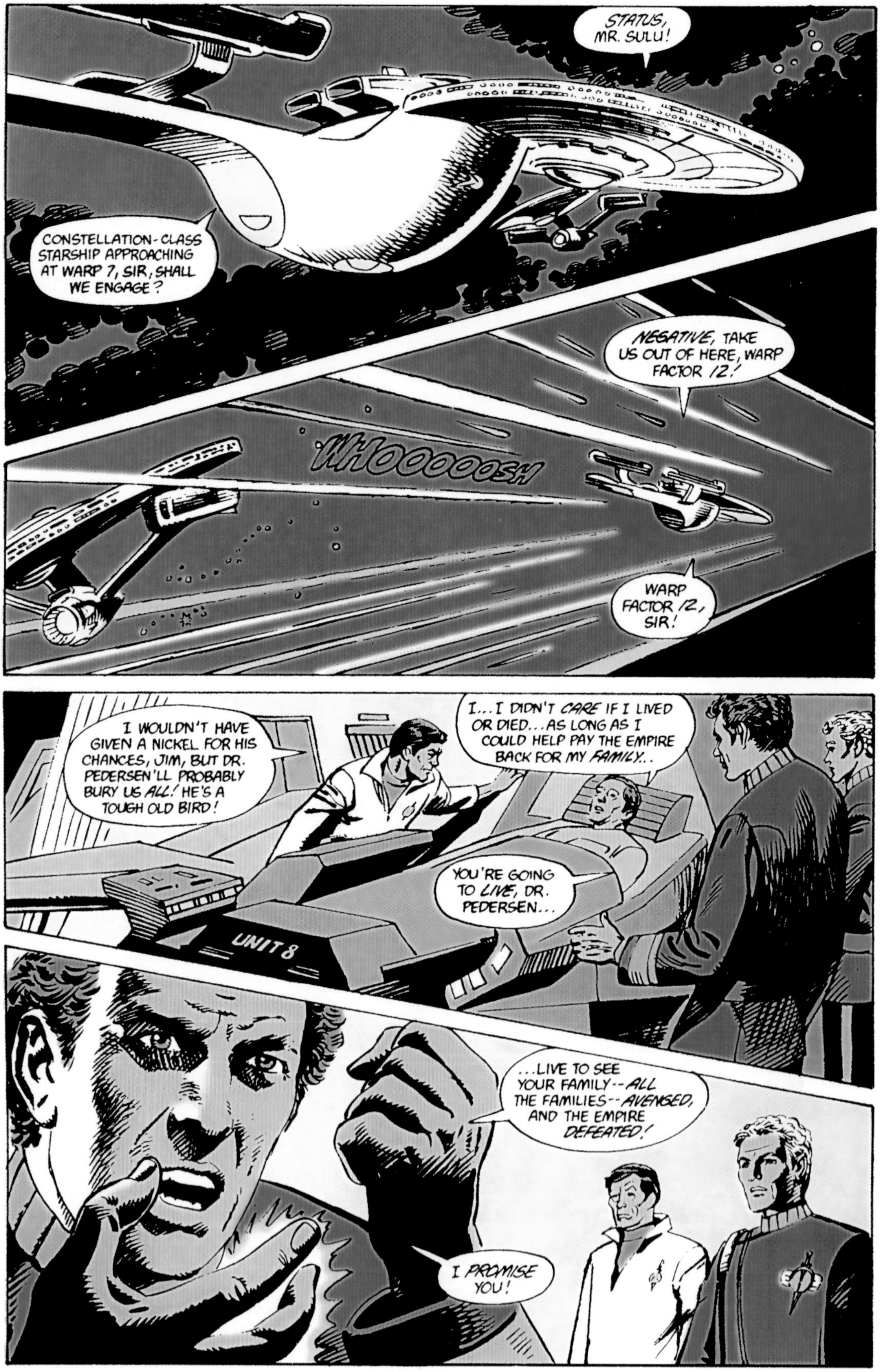
STATUS, MR. SULU!
CONSTELLATION-CLASS STARSHIP APPROACHING AT WARP 7, SIR, SHALL WE ENGAGE?
NEGATIVE, TAKE US OUT OF HERE, WARP FACTOR 12!
WHOOOOOOSH
WARP FACTOR 12, SIR!
I WOULDN'T HAVE GIVEN A NICKEL FOR HIS CHANCES, JIM, BUT DR. PEDERSEN'LL PROBABLY BURY US ALL! HE'S A TOUGH OLD BIRD!
I... I DIDN'T CARE IF I LIVED OR DIED... AS LONG AS I COULD HELP PAY THE EMPIRE BACK FOR MY FAMILY...
YOU'RE GOING TO LIVE, DR. PEDERSEN...
UNIT 8
...LIVE TO SEE YOUR FAMILY--ALL THE FAMILIES--AVENGED, AND THE EMPIRE DEFEATED!
I PROMISE YOU!

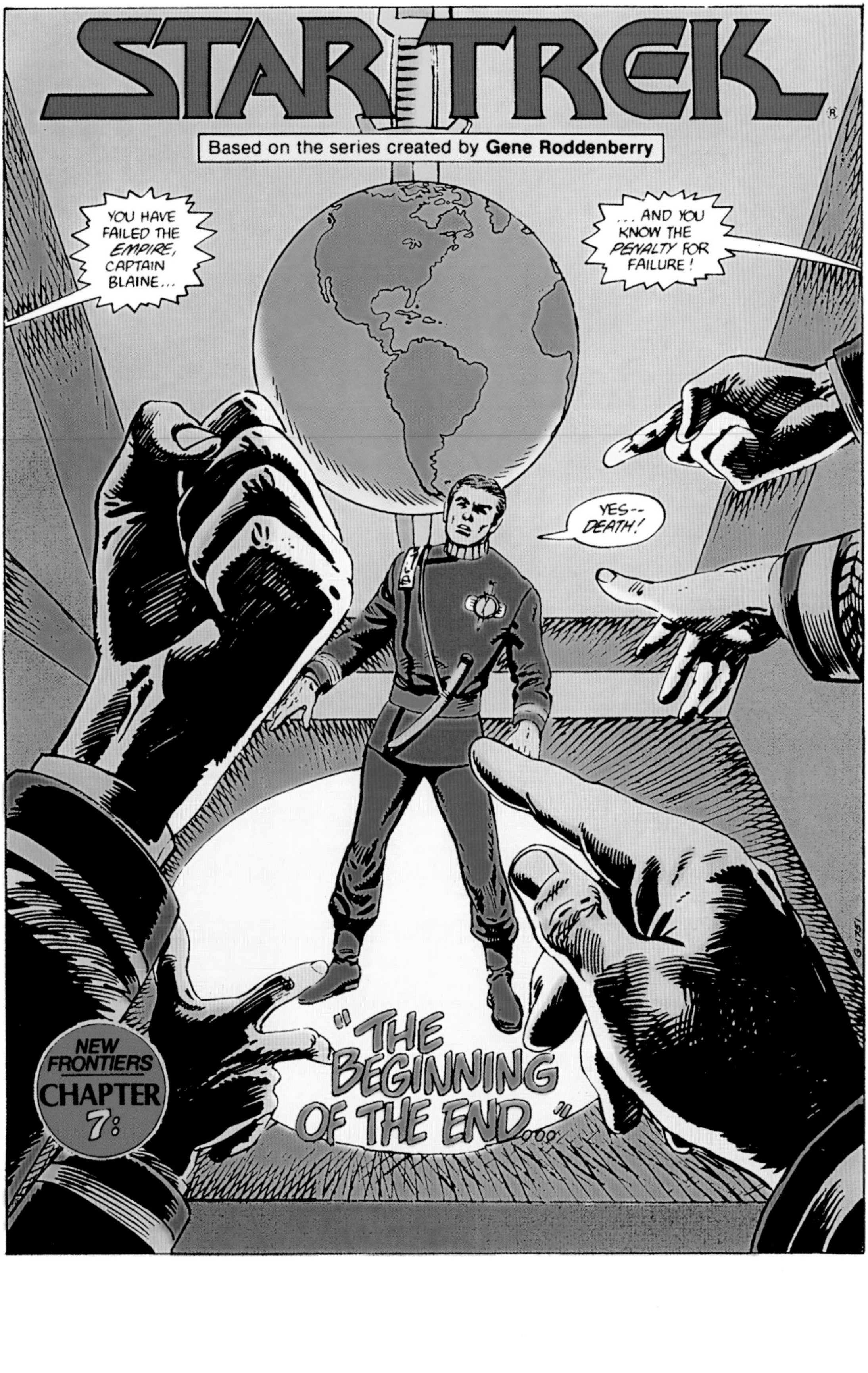
STAR TREK
Based on the series created by Gene Roddenberry
YOU HAVE FAILED THE EMPIRE, CAPTAIN BLAINE...
...AND YOU KNOW THE PENALTY FOR FAILURE!
YES-- DEATH!
NEW FRONTIERS CHAPTER 7:
"THE BEGINNING OF THE END..."

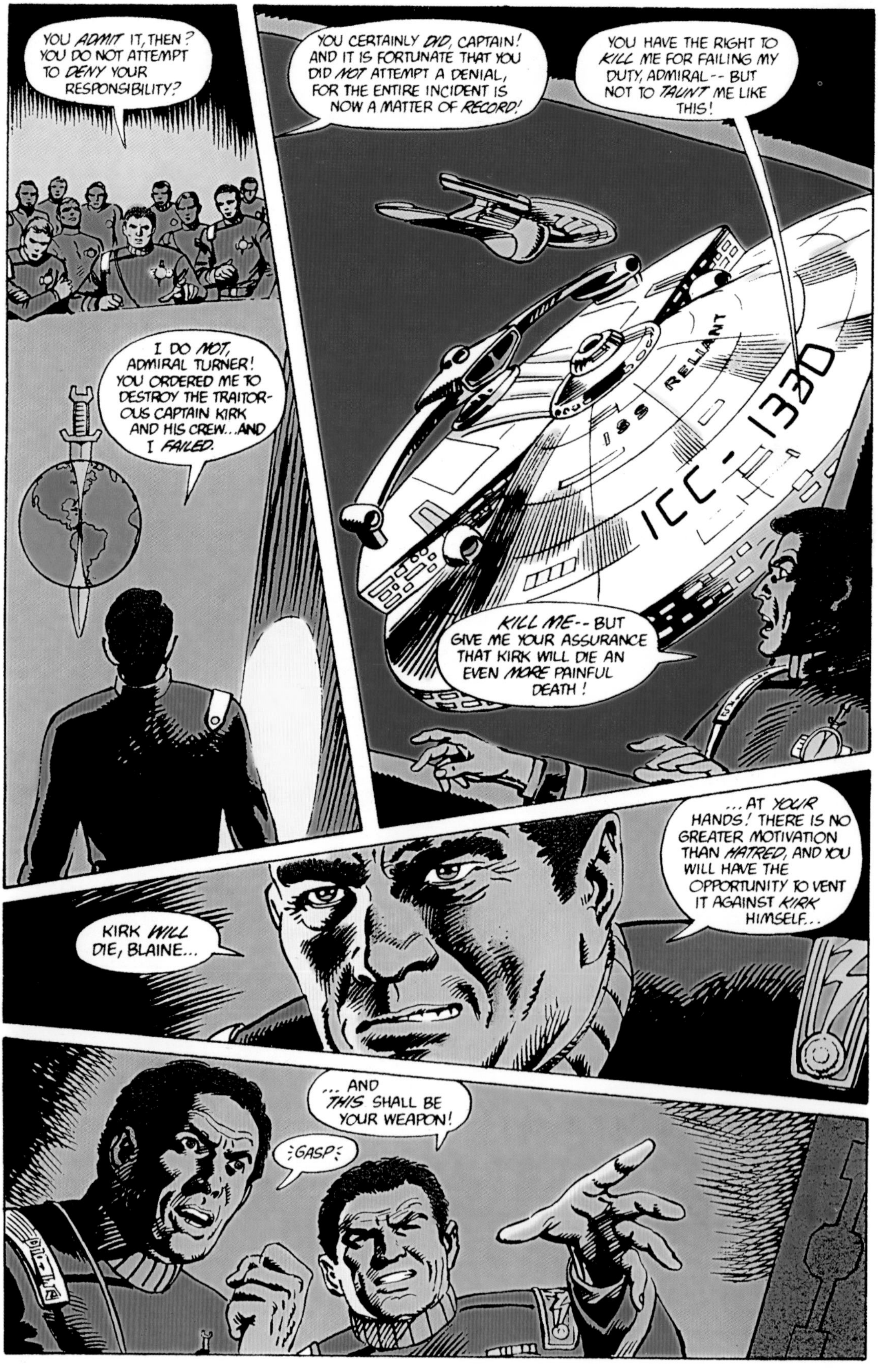
YOU ADMIT IT, THEN? YOU DO NOT ATTEMPT TO DENY YOUR RESPONSIBILITY?
I DO NOT, ADMIRAL TURNER! YOU ORDERED ME TO DESTROY THE TRAITOROUS CAPTAIN KIRK AND HIS CREW... AND I FAILED.
YOU CERTAINLY DID, CAPTAIN! AND IT IS FORTUNATE THAT YOU DID NOT ATTEMPT A DENIAL, FOR THE ENTIRE INCIDENT IS NOW A MATTER OF RECORD!
YOU HAVE THE RIGHT TO KILL ME FOR FAILING MY DUTY, ADMIRAL-- BUT NOT TO TAUNT ME LIKE THIS!
ISS RELIANT
ICC-1330
KILL ME-- BUT GIVE ME YOUR ASSURANCE THAT KIRK WILL DIE AN EVEN MORE PAINFUL DEATH!
KIRK WILL DIE, BLAINE...
...AT YOUR HANDS! THERE IS NO GREATER MOTIVATION THAN HATRED, AND YOU WILL HAVE THE OPPORTUNITY TO VENT IT AGAINST KIRK HIMSELF...
...AND THIS SHALL BE YOUR WEAPON!
GASP

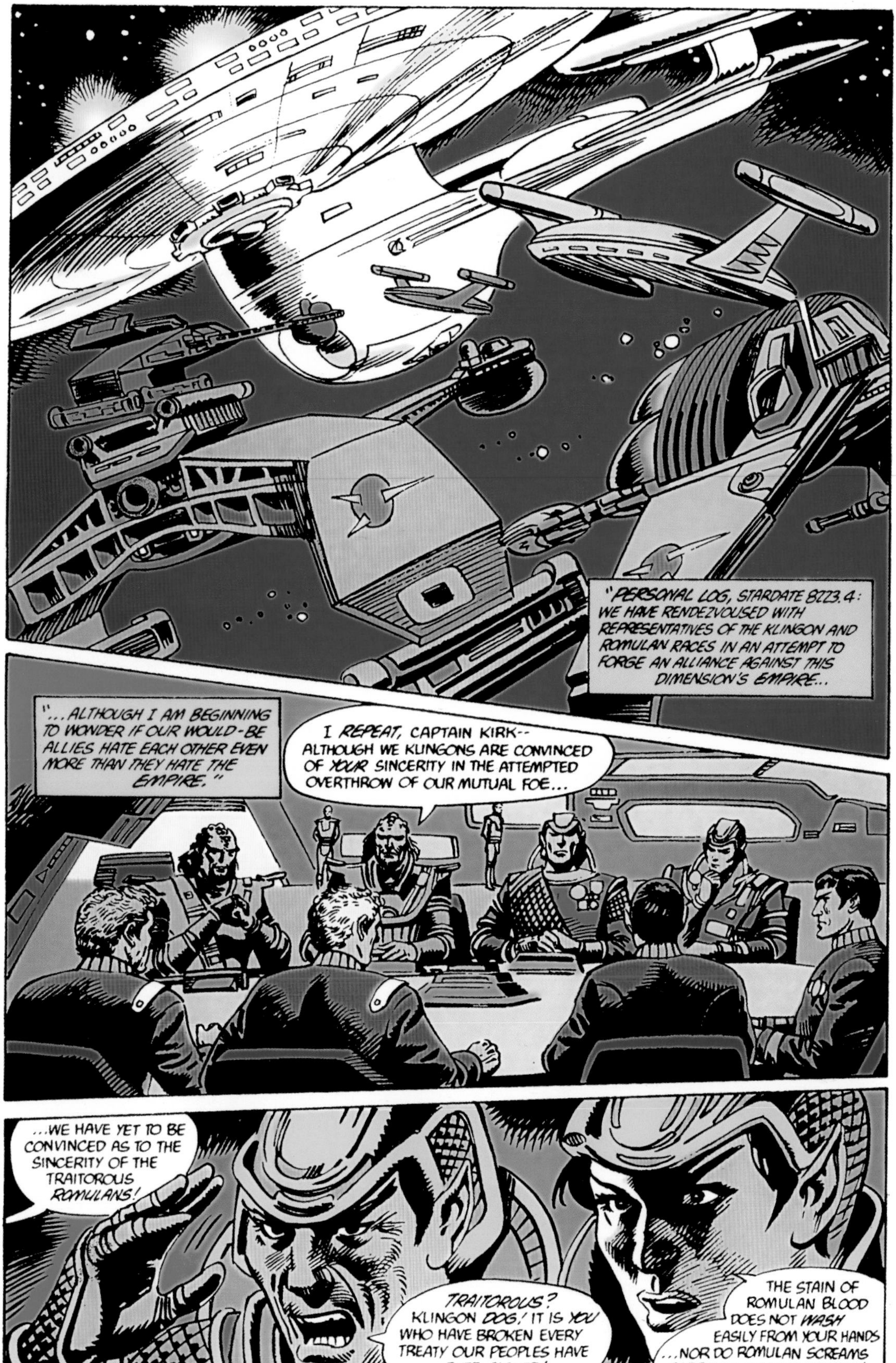
"PERSONAL LOG, STARDATE 8223.4: WE HAVE RENDEZVOUSED WITH REPRESENTATIVES OF THE KLINGON AND ROMULAN RACES IN AN ATTEMPT TO FORGE AN ALLIANCE AGAINST THIS DIMENSION'S EMPIRE...
"... ALTHOUGH I AM BEGINNING TO WONDER IF OUR WOULD-BE ALLIES HATE EACH OTHER EVEN MORE THAN THEY HATE THE EMPIRE."
I REPEAT, CAPTAIN KIRK-- ALTHOUGH WE KLINGONS ARE CONVINCED OF YOUR SINCERITY IN THE ATTEMPTED OVERTHROW OF OUR MUTUAL FOE...
...WE HAVE YET TO BE CONVINCED AS TO THE SINCERITY OF THE TRAITOROUS ROMULANS!
TRAITOROUS? KLINGON DOG! IT IS YOU WHO HAVE BROKEN EVERY TREATY OUR PEOPLES HAVE EVER SIGNED!
THE STAIN OF ROMULAN BLOOD DOES NOT WASH EASILY FROM YOUR HANDS ...NOR DO ROMULAN SCREAMS FADE EASILY FROM OUR EARS!

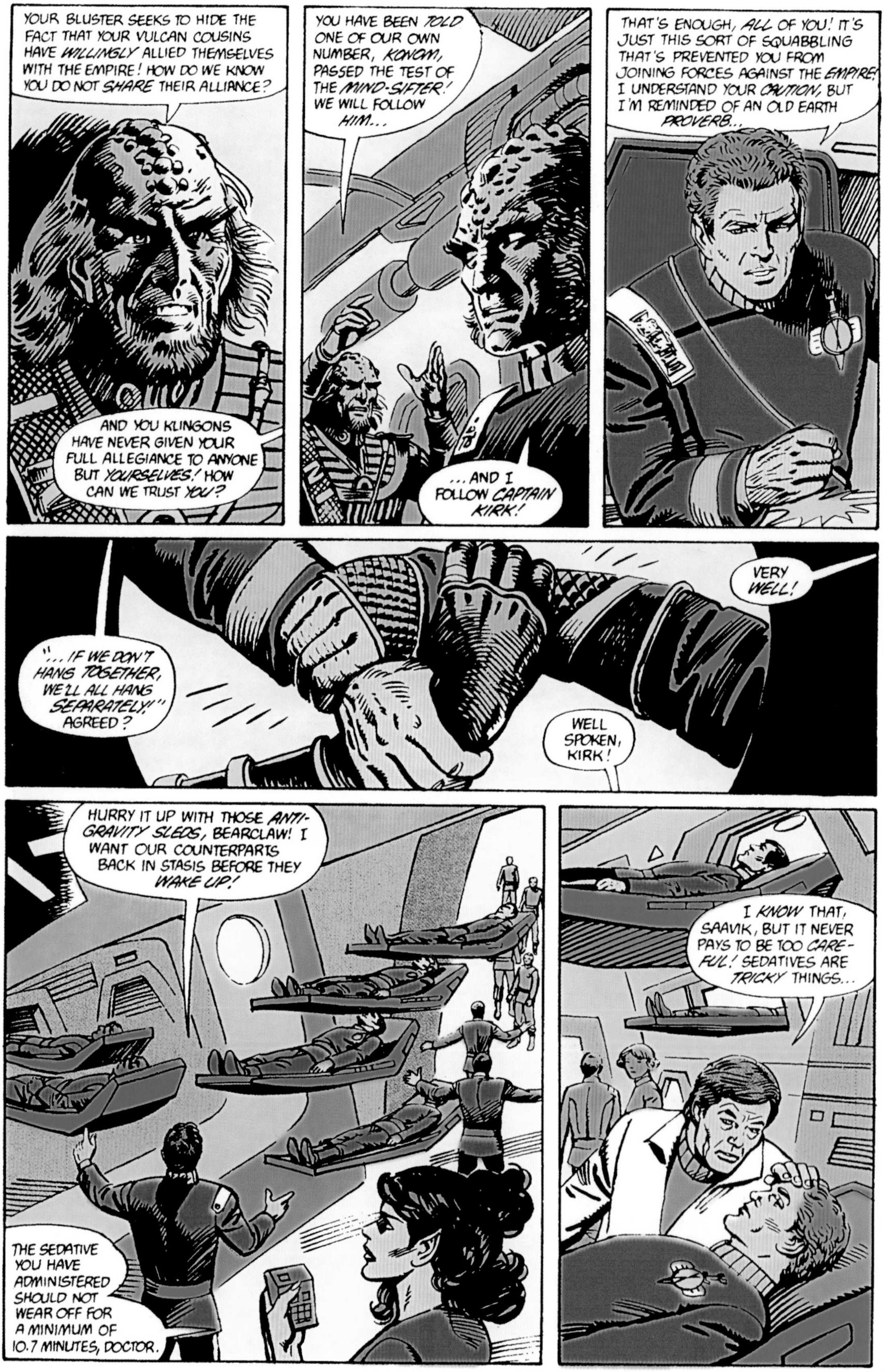
YOUR BLUSTER SEEKS TO HIDE THE FACT THAT YOUR VULCAN COUSINS HAVE WILLINGLY ALLIED THEMSELVES WITH THE EMPIRE! HOW DO WE KNOW YOU DO NOT SHARE THEIR ALLIANCE?
AND YOU KLINGONS HAVE NEVER GIVEN YOUR FULL ALLEGIANCE TO ANYONE BUT YOURSELVES! HOW CAN WE TRUST YOU?
YOU HAVE BEEN TOLD ONE OF OUR OWN NUMBER, KONOM, PASSED THE TEST OF THE MIND-SIFTER! WE WILL FOLLOW HIM...
...AND I FOLLOW CAPTAIN KIRK!
THAT'S ENOUGH, ALL OF YOU! IT'S JUST THIS SORT OF SQUABBLING THAT'S PREVENTED YOU FROM JOINING FORCES AGAINST THE EMPIRE! I UNDERSTAND YOUR CAUTION, BUT I'M REMINDED OF AN OLD EARTH PROVERB...
"...IF WE DON'T HANG TOGETHER, WE'LL ALL HANG SEPARATELY!" AGREED?
VERY WELL!
WELL SPOKEN, KIRK!
HURRY IT UP WITH THOSE ANTI-GRAVITY SLEDS, BEARCLAW! I WANT OUR COUNTERPARTS BACK IN STASIS BEFORE THEY WAKE UP!
THE SEDATIVE YOU HAVE ADMINISTERED SHOULD NOT WEAR OFF FOR A MINIMUM OF 10.7 MINUTES, DOCTOR.
I KNOW THAT, SAAVIK, BUT IT NEVER PAYS TO BE TOO CAREFUL! SEDATIVES ARE TRICKY THINGS...

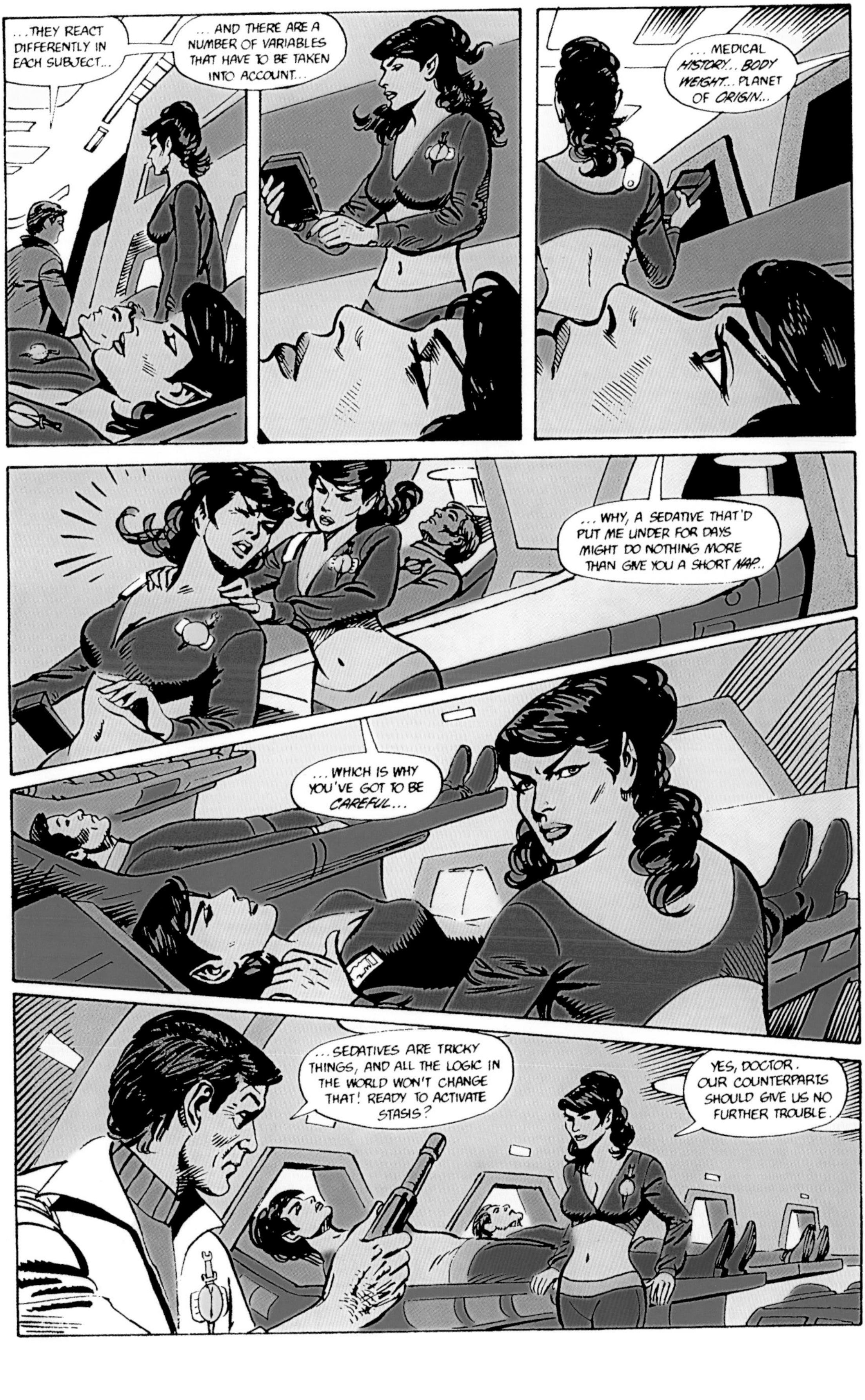
...THEY REACT DIFFERENTLY IN EACH SUBJECT...
...AND THERE ARE A NUMBER OF VARIABLES THAT HAVE TO BE TAKEN INTO ACCOUNT...
...MEDICAL HISTORY... BODY WEIGHT... PLANET OF ORIGIN...
...WHY, A SEDATIVE THAT'D PUT ME UNDER FOR DAYS MIGHT DO NOTHING MORE THAN GIVE YOU A SHORT NAP...
...WHICH IS WHY YOU'VE GOT TO BE CAREFUL...
...SEDATIVES ARE TRICKY THINGS, AND ALL THE LOGIC IN THE WORLD WON'T CHANGE THAT! READY TO ACTIVATE STASIS?
YES, DOCTOR. OUR COUNTERPARTS SHOULD GIVE US NO FURTHER TROUBLE.

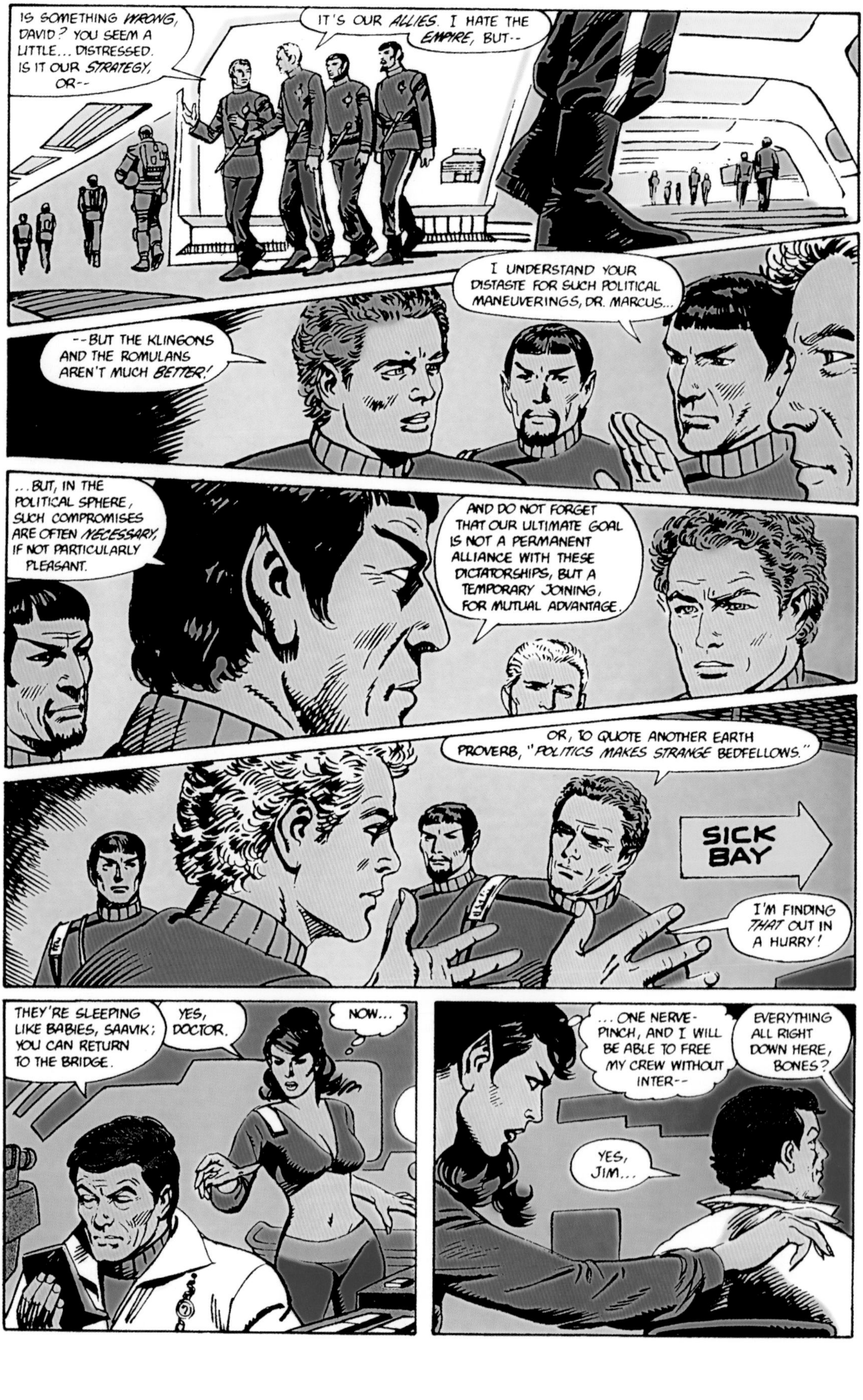
IS SOMETHING WRONG, DAVID? YOU SEEM A LITTLE... DISTRESSED. IS IT OUR STRATEGY, OR--
IT'S OUR ALLIES. I HATE THE EMPIRE, BUT--
I UNDERSTAND YOUR DISTASTE FOR SUCH POLITICAL MANEUVERINGS, DR. MARCUS...
--BUT THE KLINGONS AND THE ROMULANS AREN'T MUCH BETTER!
...BUT, IN THE POLITICAL SPHERE, SUCH COMPROMISES ARE OFTEN NECESSARY, IF NOT PARTICULARLY PLEASANT.
AND DO NOT FORGET THAT OUR ULTIMATE GOAL IS NOT A PERMANENT ALLIANCE WITH THESE DICTATORSHIPS, BUT A TEMPORARY JOINING, FOR MUTUAL ADVANTAGE.
OR, TO QUOTE ANOTHER EARTH PROVERB, "POLITICS MAKES STRANGE BEDFELLOWS."
SICK BAY
I'M FINDING THAT OUT IN A HURRY!
THEY'RE SLEEPING LIKE BABIES, SAAVIK; YOU CAN RETURN TO THE BRIDGE.
YES, DOCTOR.
NOW...
...ONE NERVE-PINCH, AND I WILL BE ABLE TO FREE MY CREW WITHOUT INTER--
EVERYTHING ALL RIGHT DOWN HERE, BONES?
YES, JIM...

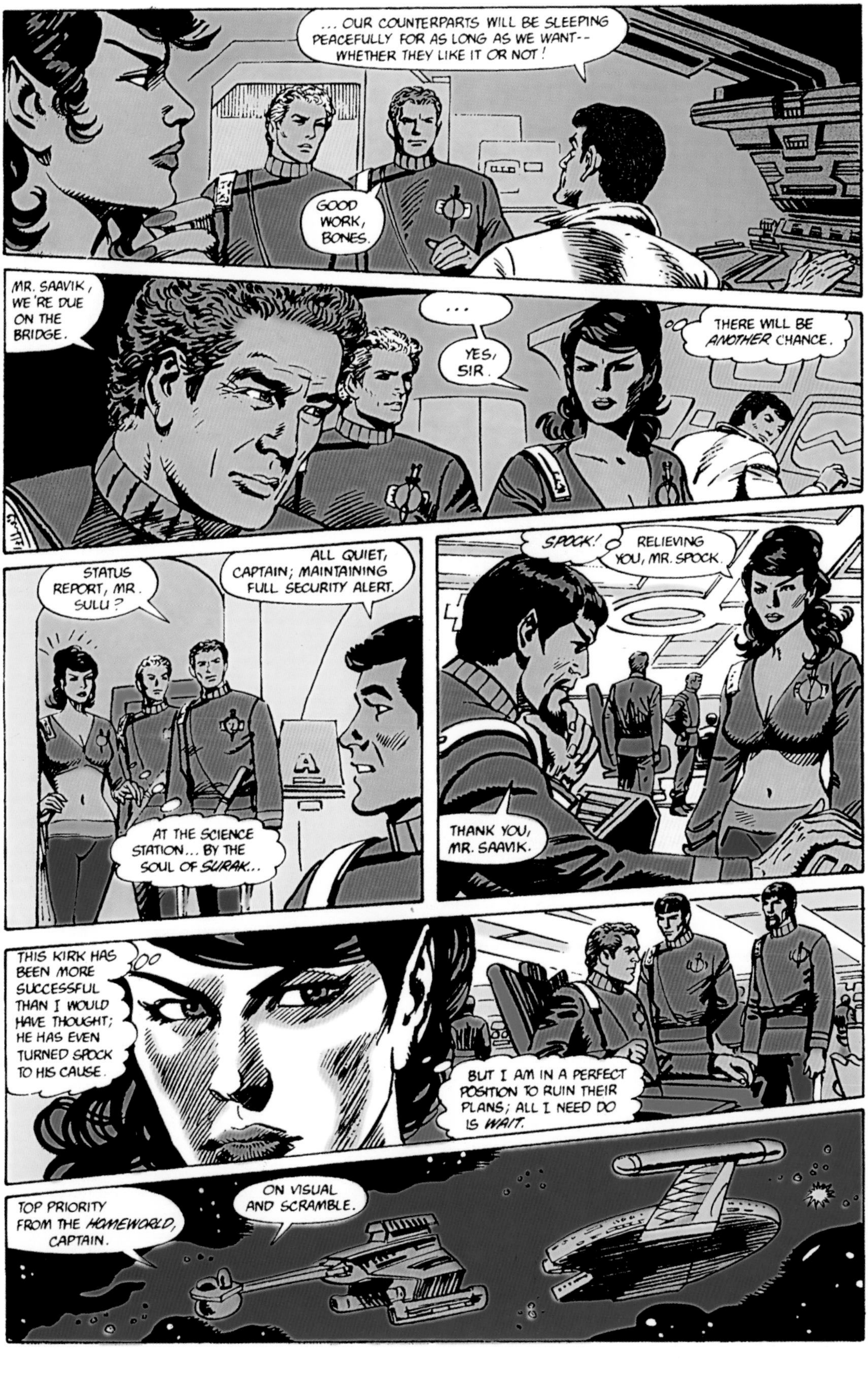
... OUR COUNTERPARTS WILL BE SLEEPING PEACEFULLY FOR AS LONG AS WE WANT-- WHETHER THEY LIKE IT OR NOT!
GOOD WORK, BONES.
MR. SAAVIK, WE'RE DUE ON THE BRIDGE.
...
YES, SIR.
THERE WILL BE ANOTHER CHANCE.
STATUS REPORT, MR. SULU?
ALL QUIET, CAPTAIN; MAINTAINING FULL SECURITY ALERT.
AT THE SCIENCE STATION... BY THE SOUL OF SURAK...
SPOCK!
RELIEVING YOU, MR. SPOCK.
THANK YOU, MR. SAAVIK.
THIS KIRK HAS BEEN MORE SUCCESSFUL THAN I WOULD HAVE THOUGHT; HE HAS EVEN TURNED SPOCK TO HIS CAUSE.
BUT I AM IN A PERFECT POSITION TO RUIN THEIR PLANS; ALL I NEED DO IS WAIT.
TOP PRIORITY FROM THE HOMEWORLD, CAPTAIN.
ON VISUAL AND SCRAMBLE.

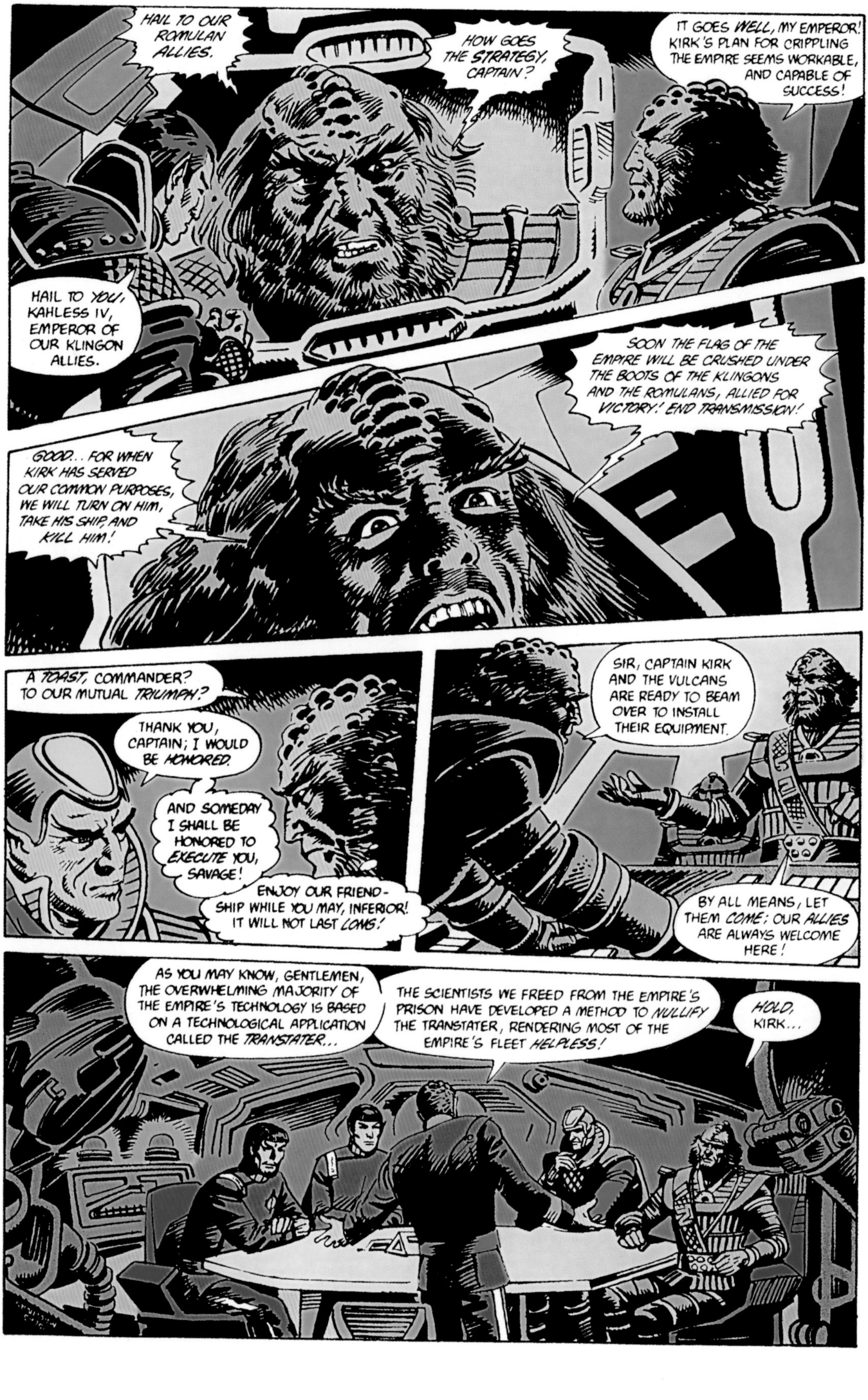
HAIL TO OUR ROMULAN ALLIES.
HOW GOES THE STRATEGY, CAPTAIN?
IT GOES WELL, MY EMPEROR! KIRK'S PLAN FOR CRIPPLING THE EMPIRE SEEMS WORKABLE, AND CAPABLE OF SUCCESS!
HAIL TO YOU, KAHLESS IV, EMPEROR OF OUR KLINGON ALLIES.
SOON THE FLAG OF THE EMPIRE WILL BE CRUSHED UNDER THE BOOTS OF THE KLINGONS AND THE ROMULANS, ALLIED FOR VICTORY! END TRANSMISSION!
GOOD... FOR WHEN KIRK HAS SERVED OUR COMMON PURPOSES, WE WILL TURN ON HIM, TAKE HIS SHIP, AND KILL HIM!
A TOAST, COMMANDER? TO OUR MUTUAL TRIUMPH?
THANK YOU, CAPTAIN; I WOULD BE HONORED.
AND SOMEDAY I SHALL BE HONORED TO EXECUTE YOU, SAVAGE!
ENJOY OUR FRIENDSHIP WHILE YOU MAY, INFERIOR! IT WILL NOT LAST LONG!
SIR, CAPTAIN KIRK AND THE VULCANS ARE READY TO BEAM OVER TO INSTALL THEIR EQUIPMENT.
BY ALL MEANS, LET THEM COME; OUR ALLIES ARE ALWAYS WELCOME HERE!
AS YOU MAY KNOW, GENTLEMEN, THE OVERWHELMING MAJORITY OF THE EMPIRE'S TECHNOLOGY IS BASED ON A TECHNOLOGICAL APPLICATION CALLED THE TRANSTATER...
THE SCIENTISTS WE FREED FROM THE EMPIRE'S PRISON HAVE DEVELOPED A METHOD TO NULLIFY THE TRANSTATER, RENDERING MOST OF THE EMPIRE'S FLEET HELPLESS!
HOLD, KIRK...

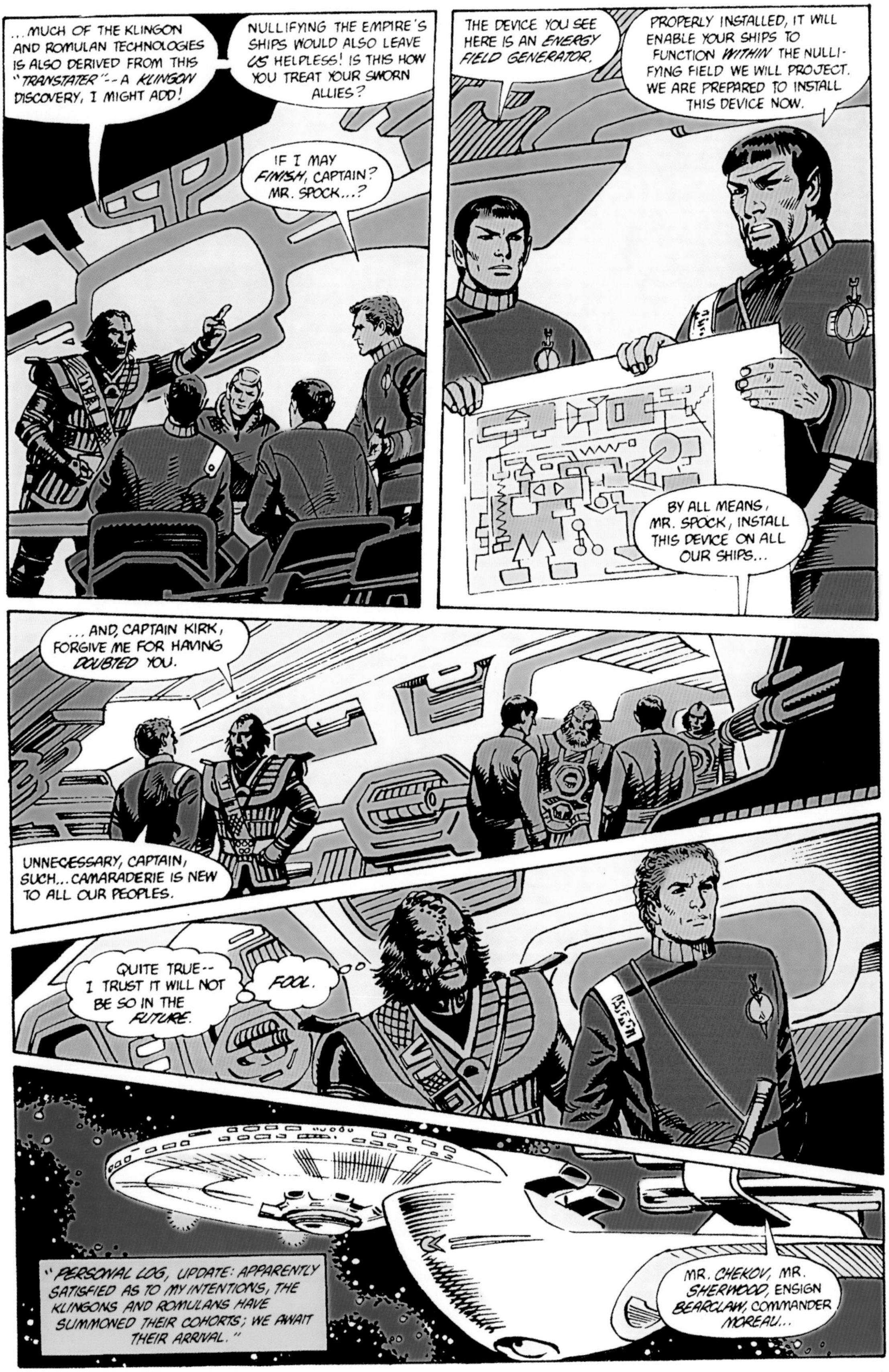
...MUCH OF THE KLINGON AND ROMULAN TECHNOLOGIES IS ALSO DERIVED FROM THIS "TRANSTATER"--A KLINGON DISCOVERY, I MIGHT ADD!
NULLIFYING THE EMPIRE'S SHIPS WOULD ALSO LEAVE US HELPLESS! IS THIS HOW YOU TREAT YOUR SWORN ALLIES?
IF I MAY FINISH, CAPTAIN? MR. SPOCK...?
THE DEVICE YOU SEE HERE IS AN ENERGY FIELD GENERATOR.
PROPERLY INSTALLED, IT WILL ENABLE YOUR SHIPS TO FUNCTION WITHIN THE NULLIFYING FIELD WE WILL PROJECT. WE ARE PREPARED TO INSTALL THIS DEVICE NOW.
BY ALL MEANS, MR. SPOCK, INSTALL THIS DEVICE ON ALL OUR SHIPS...
...AND, CAPTAIN KIRK, FORGIVE ME FOR HAVING DOUBTED YOU.
UNNECESSARY, CAPTAIN, SUCH...CAMARADERIE IS NEW TO ALL OUR PEOPLES.
QUITE TRUE-- I TRUST IT WILL NOT BE SO IN THE FUTURE.
FOOL.
"PERSONAL LOG, UPDATE: APPARENTLY SATISFIED AS TO MY INTENTIONS, THE KLINGONS AND ROMULANS HAVE SUMMONED THEIR COHORTS; WE AWAIT THEIR ARRIVAL."
MR. CHEKOV, MR. SHERWOOD, ENSIGN BEARCLAW, COMMANDER MOREAU...

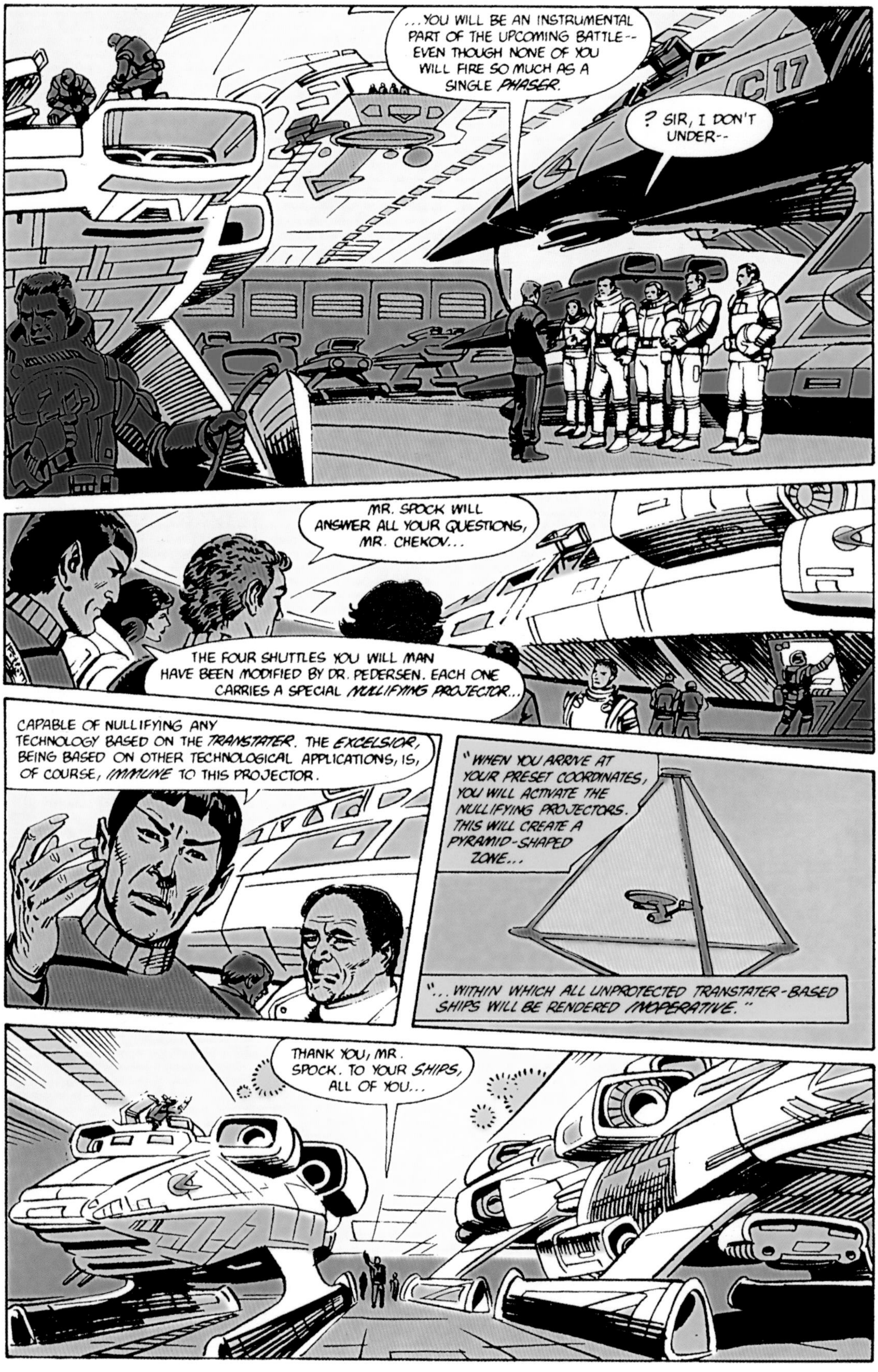
...YOU WILL BE AN INSTRUMENTAL PART OF THE UPCOMING BATTLE-- EVEN THOUGH NONE OF YOU WILL FIRE SO MUCH AS A SINGLE PHASER.
? SIR, I DON'T UNDER--
MR. SPOCK WILL ANSWER ALL YOUR QUESTIONS, MR. CHEKOV...
THE FOUR SHUTTLES YOU WILL MAN HAVE BEEN MODIFIED BY DR. PEDERSEN. EACH ONE CARRIES A SPECIAL NULLIFYING PROJECTOR...
CAPABLE OF NULLIFYING ANY TECHNOLOGY BASED ON THE TRANSTATER. THE EXCELSIOR, BEING BASED ON OTHER TECHNOLOGICAL APPLICATIONS, IS, OF COURSE, IMMUNE TO THIS PROJECTOR.
"WHEN YOU ARRIVE AT YOUR PRESET COORDINATES, YOU WILL ACTIVATE THE NULLIFYING PROJECTORS. THIS WILL CREATE A PYRAMID-SHAPED ZONE...
"...WITHIN WHICH ALL UNPROTECTED TRANSTATER-BASED SHIPS WILL BE RENDERED INOPERATIVE."
THANK YOU, MR. SPOCK. TO YOUR SHIPS, ALL OF YOU...

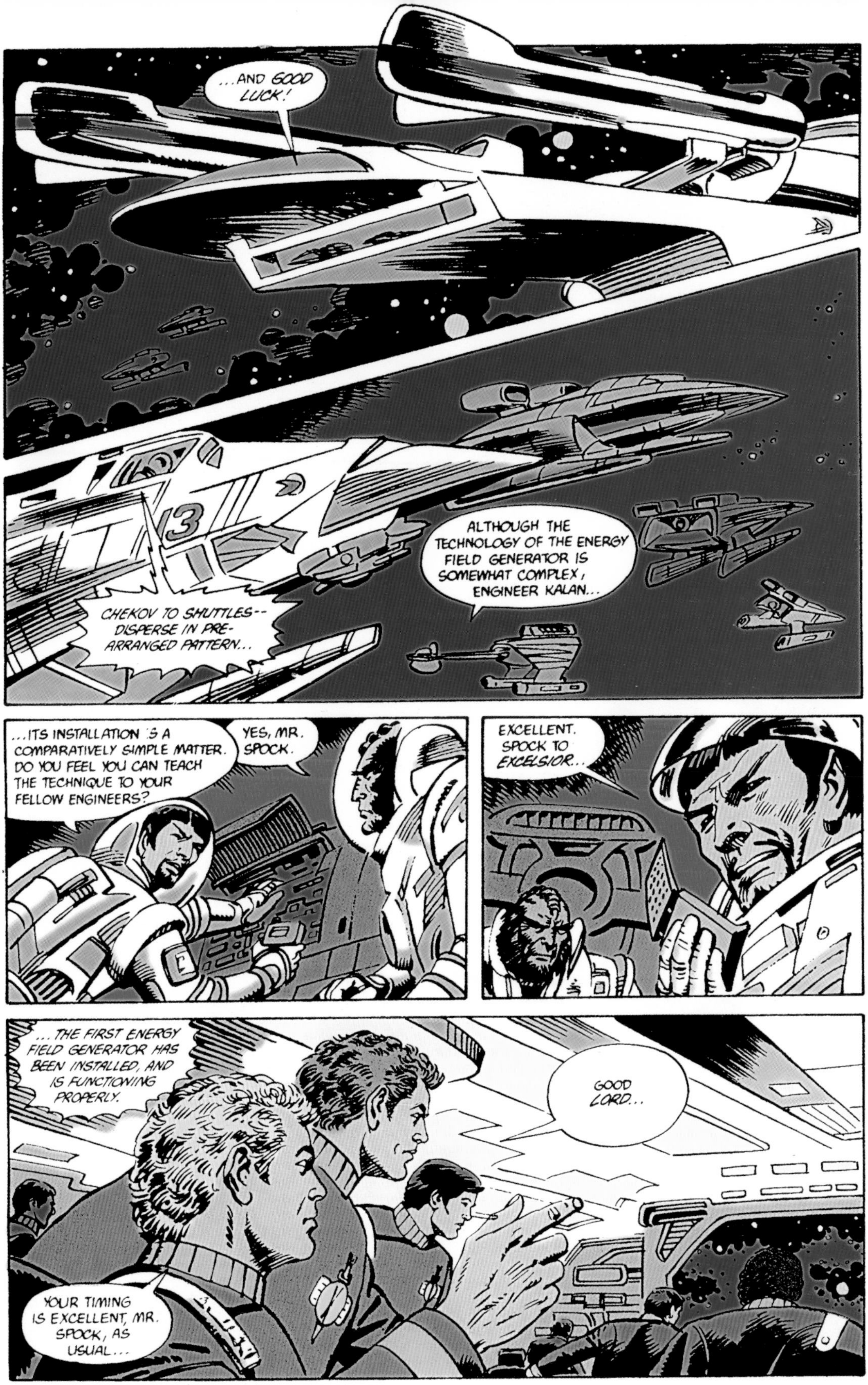
...AND GOOD LUCK!
ALTHOUGH THE TECHNOLOGY OF THE ENERGY FIELD GENERATOR IS SOMEWHAT COMPLEX, ENGINEER KALAN...
CHEKOV TO SHUTTLES-- DISPERSE IN PRE-ARRANGED PATTERN...
...ITS INSTALLATION IS A COMPARATIVELY SIMPLE MATTER. DO YOU FEEL YOU CAN TEACH THE TECHNIQUE TO YOUR FELLOW ENGINEERS?
YES, MR. SPOCK.
EXCELLENT. SPOCK TO *EXCELSIOR*...
...THE FIRST ENERGY FIELD GENERATOR HAS BEEN INSTALLED, AND IS FUNCTIONING PROPERLY.
GOOD LORD...
YOUR TIMING IS EXCELLENT, MR. SPOCK, AS USUAL...

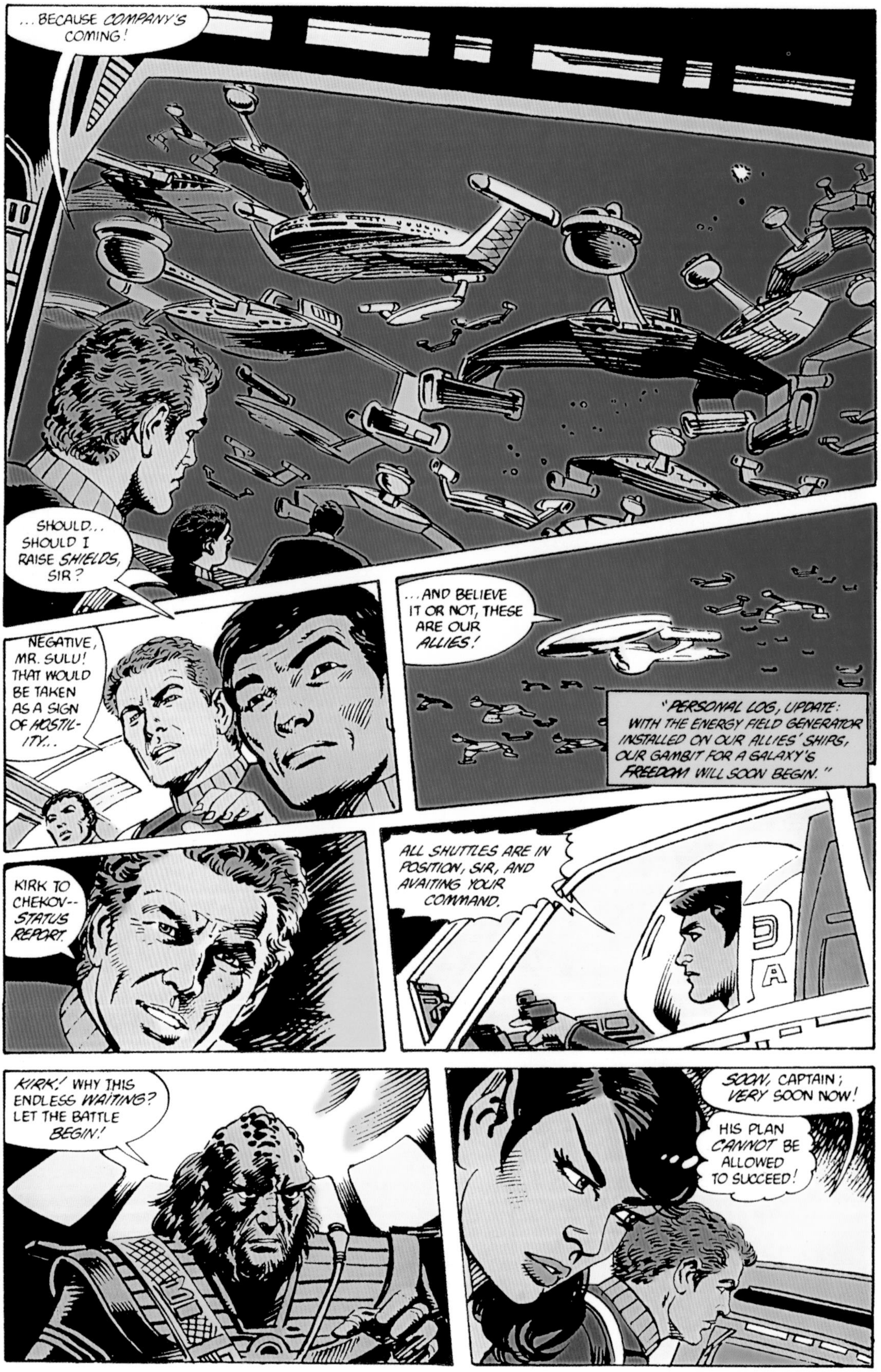
...BECAUSE COMPANY'S COMING!
SHOULD... SHOULD I RAISE SHIELDS, SIR?
NEGATIVE, MR. SULU! THAT WOULD BE TAKEN AS A SIGN OF HOSTILITY...
...AND BELIEVE IT OR NOT, THESE ARE OUR ALLIES!
"PERSONAL LOG, UPDATE: WITH THE ENERGY FIELD GENERATOR INSTALLED ON OUR ALLIES' SHIPS, OUR GAMBIT FOR A GALAXY'S FREEDOM WILL SOON BEGIN."
KIRK TO CHEKOV-- STATUS REPORT.
ALL SHUTTLES ARE IN POSITION, SIR, AND AWAITING YOUR COMMAND.
KIRK! WHY THIS ENDLESS WAITING? LET THE BATTLE BEGIN!
SOON, CAPTAIN; VERY SOON NOW!
HIS PLAN CANNOT BE ALLOWED TO SUCCEED!

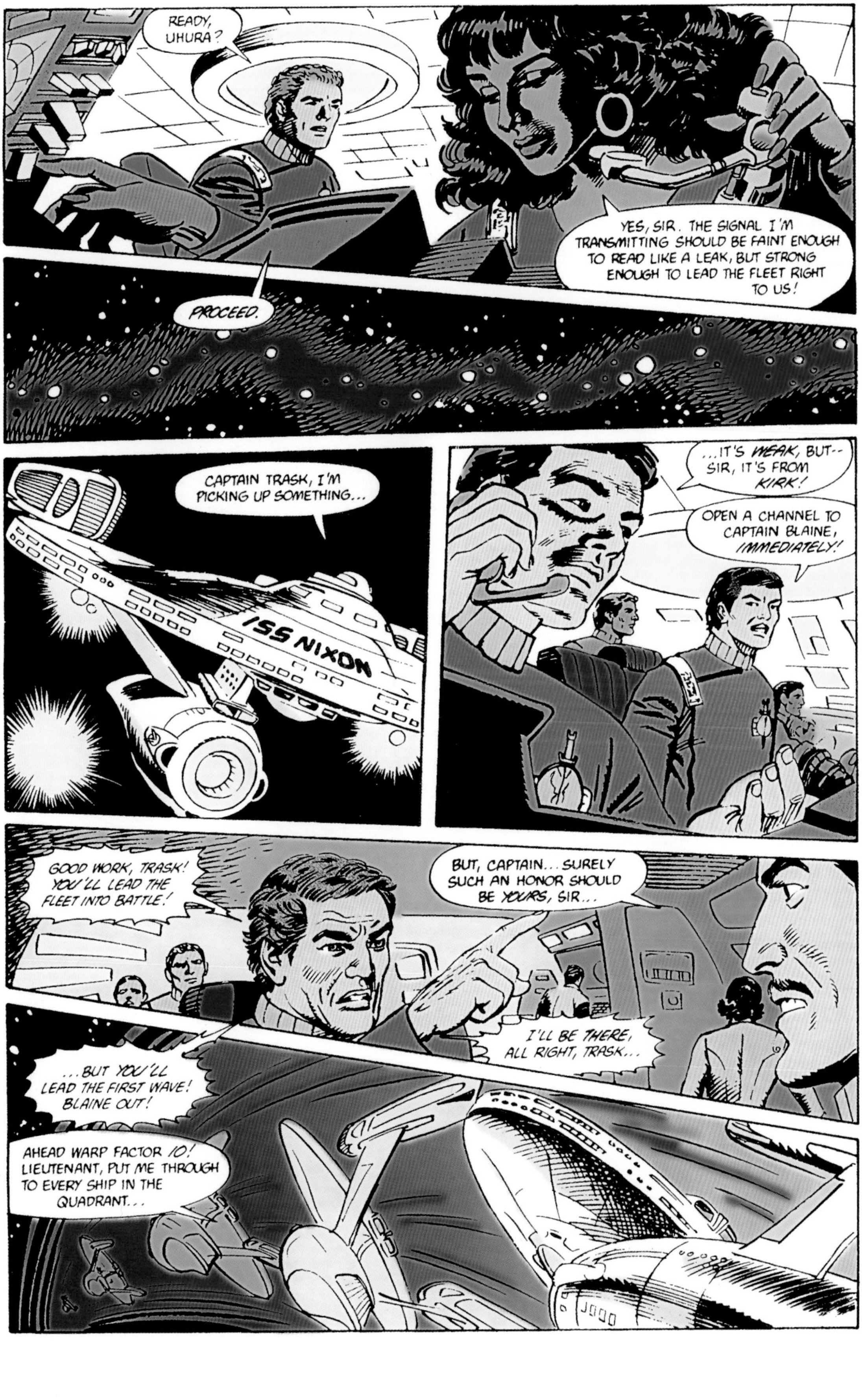
READY, UHURA?
YES, SIR. THE SIGNAL I'M TRANSMITTING SHOULD BE FAINT ENOUGH TO READ LIKE A LEAK, BUT STRONG ENOUGH TO LEAD THE FLEET RIGHT TO US!
PROCEED.
CAPTAIN TRASK, I'M PICKING UP SOMETHING...
ISS NIXON
...IT'S WEAK, BUT--SIR, IT'S FROM KIRK!
OPEN A CHANNEL TO CAPTAIN BLAINE, IMMEDIATELY!
GOOD WORK, TRASK! YOU'LL LEAD THE FLEET INTO BATTLE!
BUT, CAPTAIN... SURELY SUCH AN HONOR SHOULD BE YOURS, SIR...
I'LL BE THERE, ALL RIGHT, TRASK...
...BUT YOU'LL LEAD THE FIRST WAVE! BLAINE OUT!
AHEAD WARP FACTOR 10! LIEUTENANT, PUT ME THROUGH TO EVERY SHIP IN THE QUADRANT...

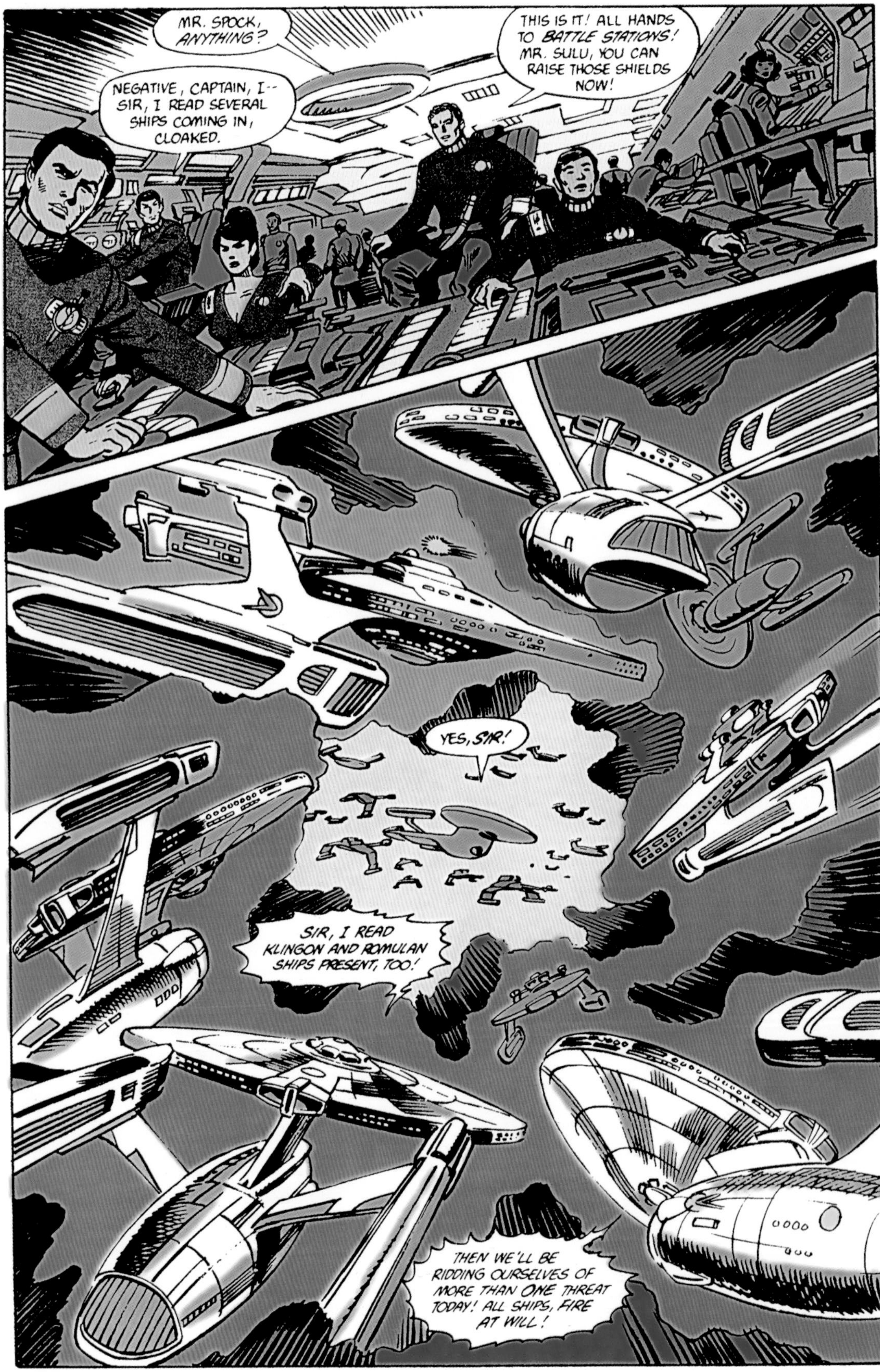

MR. SPOCK, ANYTHING?
NEGATIVE, CAPTAIN, I-- SIR, I READ SEVERAL SHIPS COMING IN, CLOAKED.
THIS IS IT! ALL HANDS TO BATTLE STATIONS! MR. SULU, YOU CAN RAISE THOSE SHIELDS NOW!
YES, SIR!
SIR, I READ KLINGON AND ROMULAN SHIPS PRESENT, TOO!
THEN WE'LL BE RIDDING OURSELVES OF MORE THAN ONE THREAT TODAY! ALL SHIPS, FIRE AT WILL!

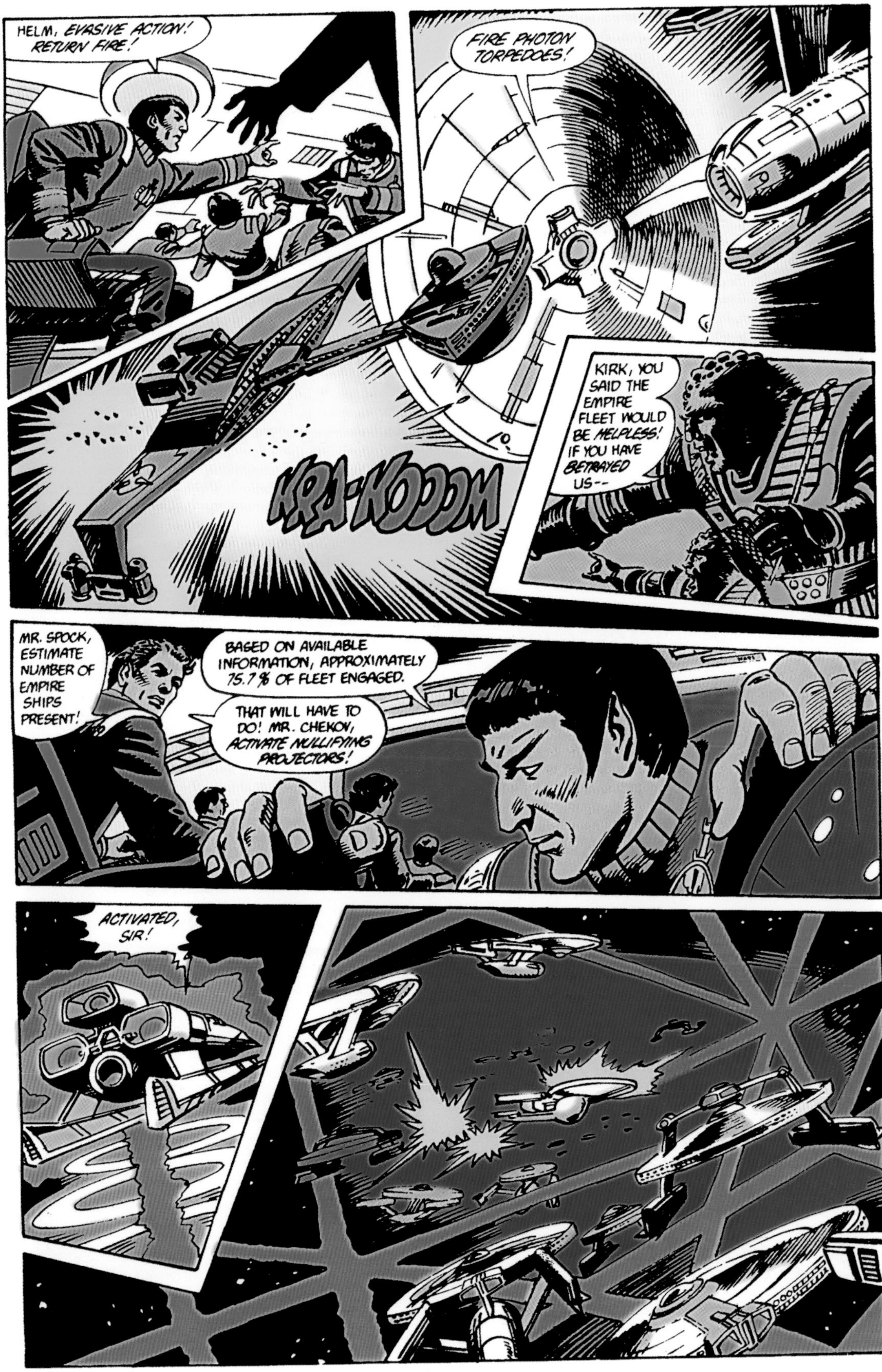
HELM, EVASIVE ACTION! RETURN FIRE!
FIRE PHOTON TORPEDOES!
KRA-KOOOM
KIRK, YOU SAID THE EMPIRE FLEET WOULD BE HELPLESS! IF YOU HAVE BETRAYED US--
MR. SPOCK, ESTIMATE NUMBER OF EMPIRE SHIPS PRESENT!
BASED ON AVAILABLE INFORMATION, APPROXIMATELY 75.7% OF FLEET ENGAGED.
THAT WILL HAVE TO DO! MR. CHEKOV, ACTIVATE NULLIFYING PROJECTORS!
ACTIVATED, SIR!

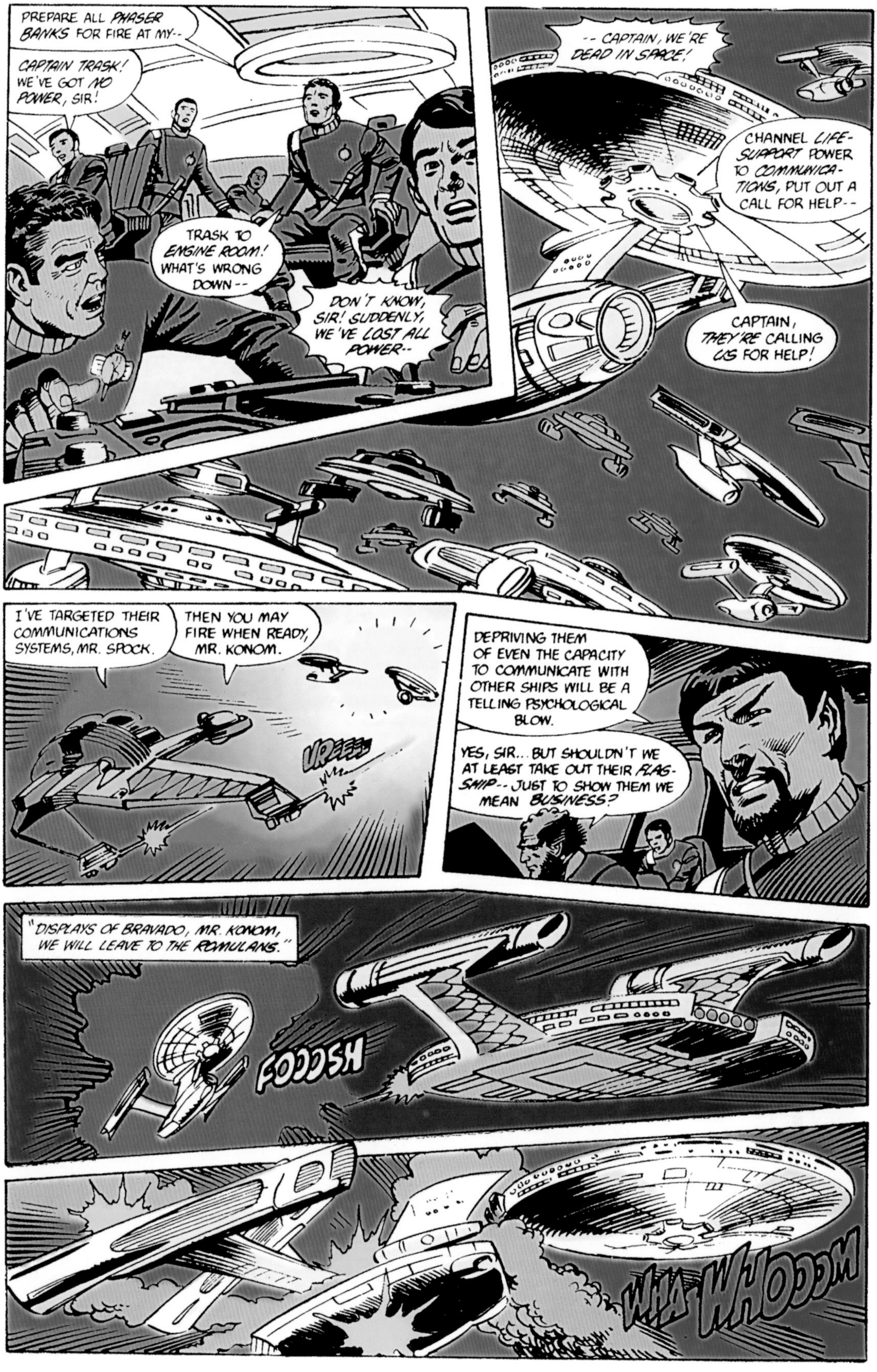
PREPARE ALL PHASER BANKS FOR FIRE AT MY--
CAPTAIN TRASK! WE'VE GOT NO POWER, SIR!
TRASK TO ENGINE ROOM! WHAT'S WRONG DOWN--
DON'T KNOW, SIR! SUDDENLY, WE'VE LOST ALL POWER--
--CAPTAIN, WE'RE DEAD IN SPACE!
CHANNEL LIFE-SUPPORT POWER TO COMMUNICATIONS, PUT OUT A CALL FOR HELP--
CAPTAIN, THEY'RE CALLING US FOR HELP!
I'VE TARGETED THEIR COMMUNICATIONS SYSTEMS, MR. SPOCK.
THEN YOU MAY FIRE WHEN READY, MR. KONOM.
VREEEE
DEPRIVING THEM OF EVEN THE CAPACITY TO COMMUNICATE WITH OTHER SHIPS WILL BE A TELLING PSYCHOLOGICAL BLOW.
YES, SIR... BUT SHOULDN'T WE AT LEAST TAKE OUT THEIR FLAG-SHIP-- JUST TO SHOW THEM WE MEAN BUSINESS?
"DISPLAYS OF BRAVADO, MR. KONOM, WE WILL LEAVE TO THE ROMULANS."
FOOOSH
WHA WHOOOM

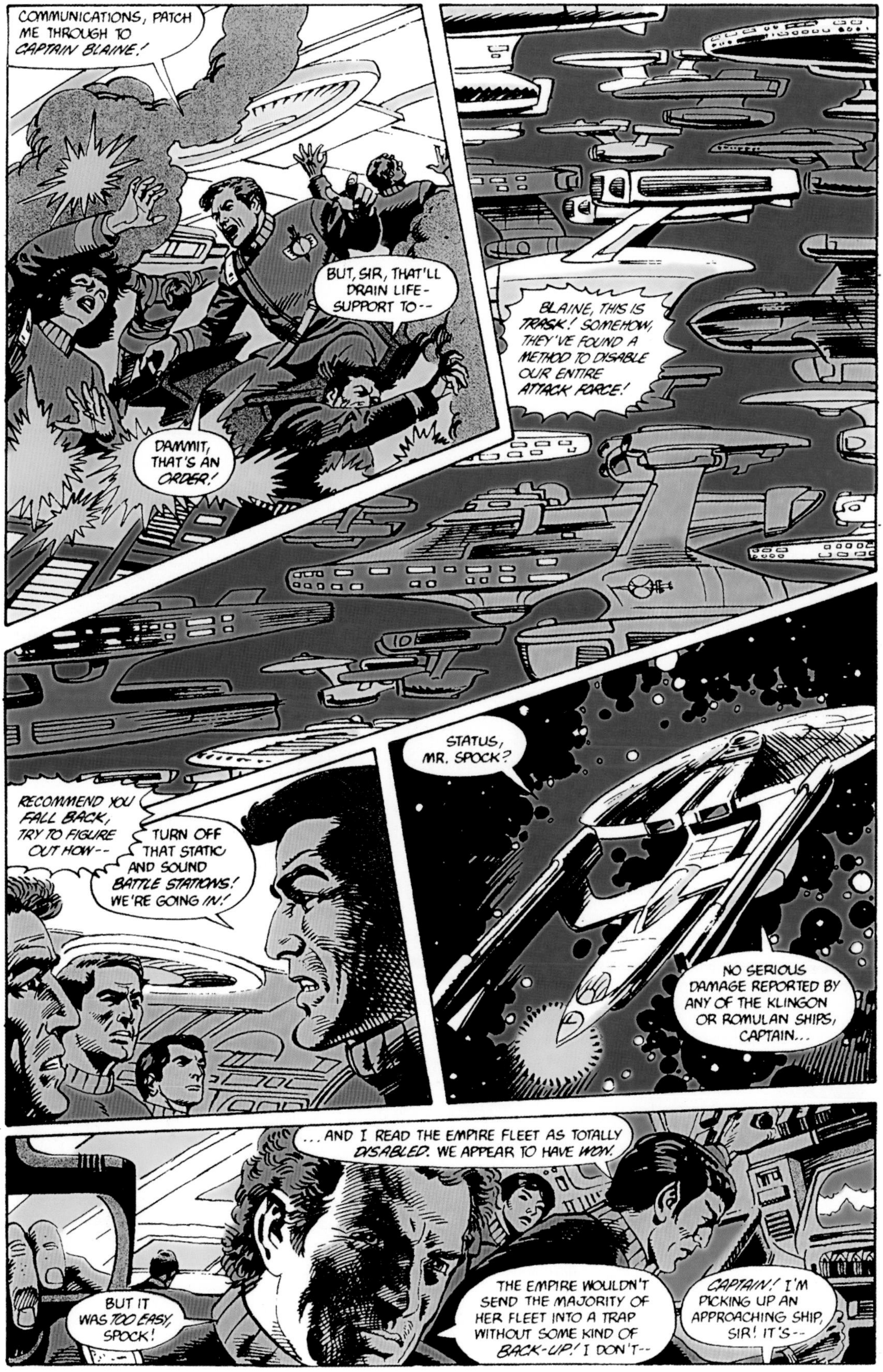
COMMUNICATIONS, PATCH ME THROUGH TO CAPTAIN BLAINE!
BUT, SIR, THAT'LL DRAIN LIFE-SUPPORT TO--
DAMMIT, THAT'S AN ORDER!
BLAINE, THIS IS TRASK! SOMEHOW, THEY'VE FOUND A METHOD TO DISABLE OUR ENTIRE ATTACK FORCE!
RECOMMEND YOU FALL BACK, TRY TO FIGURE OUT HOW--
TURN OFF THAT STATIC AND SOUND BATTLE STATIONS! WE'RE GOING IN!
STATUS, MR. SPOCK?
NO SERIOUS DAMAGE REPORTED BY ANY OF THE KLINGON OR ROMULAN SHIPS, CAPTAIN...
...AND I READ THE EMPIRE FLEET AS TOTALLY DISABLED. WE APPEAR TO HAVE WON.
BUT IT WAS TOO EASY, SPOCK!
THE EMPIRE WOULDN'T SEND THE MAJORITY OF HER FLEET INTO A TRAP WITHOUT SOME KIND OF BACK-UP! I DON'T--
CAPTAIN! I'M PICKING UP AN APPROACHING SHIP, SIR! IT'S--

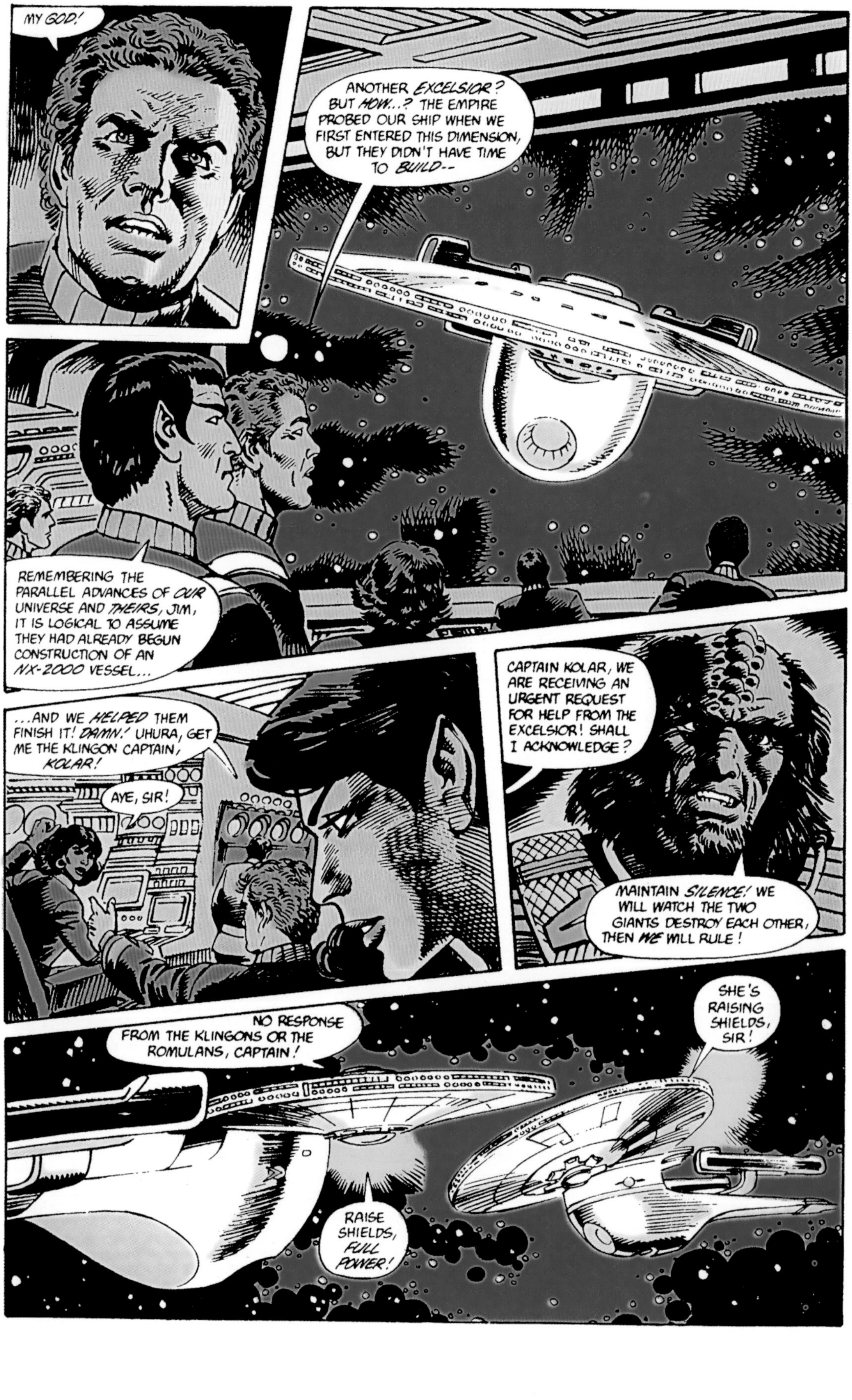
MY GOD!
ANOTHER EXCELSIOR? BUT HOW...? THE EMPIRE PROBED OUR SHIP WHEN WE FIRST ENTERED THIS DIMENSION, BUT THEY DIDN'T HAVE TIME TO BUILD--
REMEMBERING THE PARALLEL ADVANCES OF OUR UNIVERSE AND THEIRS, JIM, IT IS LOGICAL TO ASSUME THEY HAD ALREADY BEGUN CONSTRUCTION OF AN NX-2000 VESSEL...
...AND WE HELPED THEM FINISH IT! DAMN! UHURA, GET ME THE KLINGON CAPTAIN, KOLAR!
AYE, SIR!
CAPTAIN KOLAR, WE ARE RECEIVING AN URGENT REQUEST FOR HELP FROM THE EXCELSIOR! SHALL I ACKNOWLEDGE?
MAINTAIN SILENCE! WE WILL WATCH THE TWO GIANTS DESTROY EACH OTHER, THEN WE WILL RULE!
NO RESPONSE FROM THE KLINGONS OR THE ROMULANS, CAPTAIN!
SHE'S RAISING SHIELDS, SIR!
RAISE SHIELDS, FULL POWER!

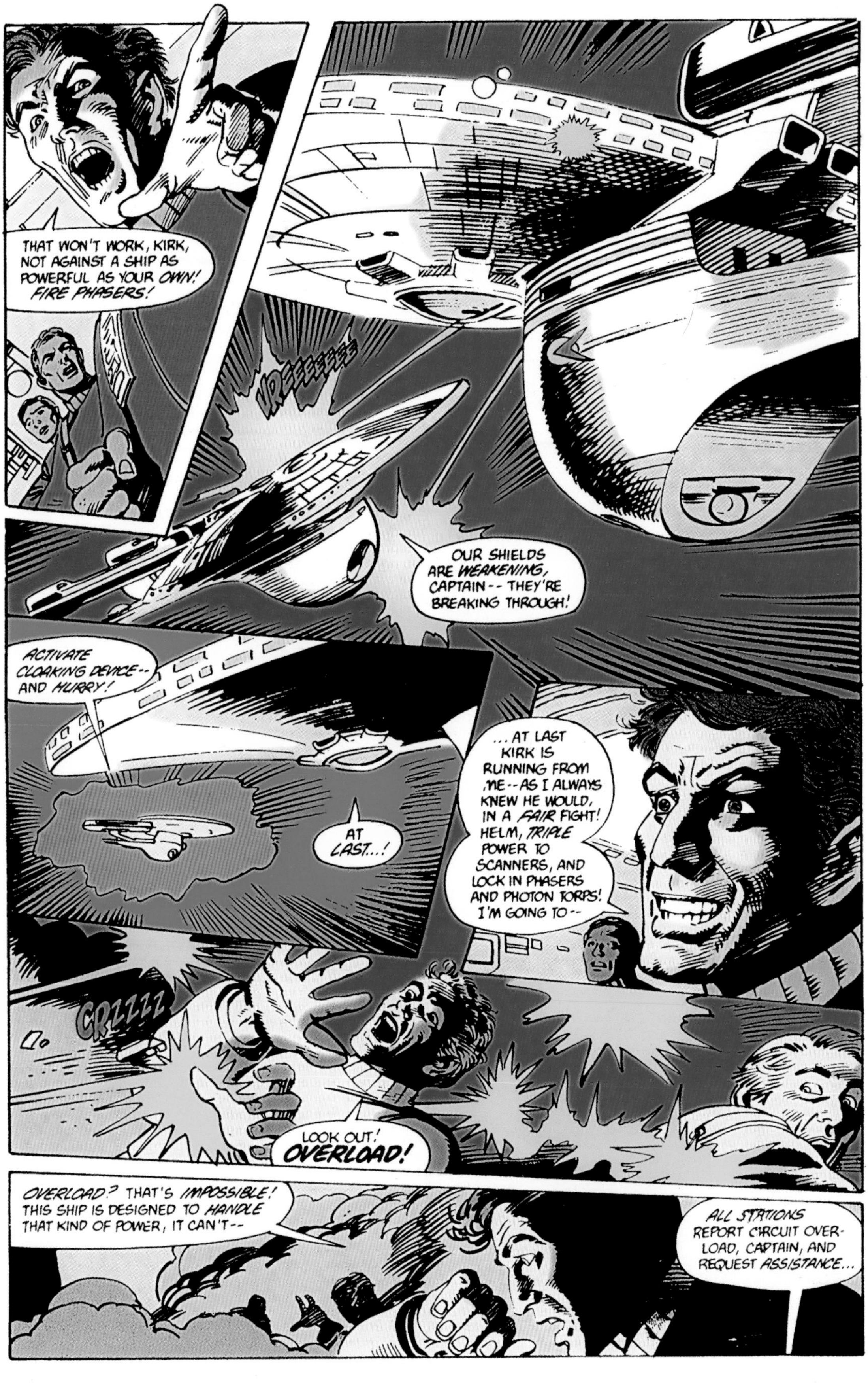
THAT WON'T WORK, KIRK, NOT AGAINST A SHIP AS POWERFUL AS YOUR OWN! FIRE PHASERS!
VREEEEEEE
OUR SHIELDS ARE WEAKENING, CAPTAIN-- THEY'RE BREAKING THROUGH!
ACTIVATE CLOAKING DEVICE-- AND HURRY!
AT LAST...!
...AT LAST KIRK IS RUNNING FROM ME--AS I ALWAYS KNEW HE WOULD, IN A FAIR FIGHT! HELM, TRIPLE POWER TO SCANNERS, AND LOCK IN PHASERS AND PHOTON TORPS! I'M GOING TO--
CRZZZZ
LOOK OUT! OVERLOAD!
OVERLOAD? THAT'S IMPOSSIBLE! THIS SHIP IS DESIGNED TO HANDLE THAT KIND OF POWER; IT CAN'T--
ALL STATIONS REPORT CIRCUIT OVERLOAD, CAPTAIN, AND REQUEST ASSISTANCE...

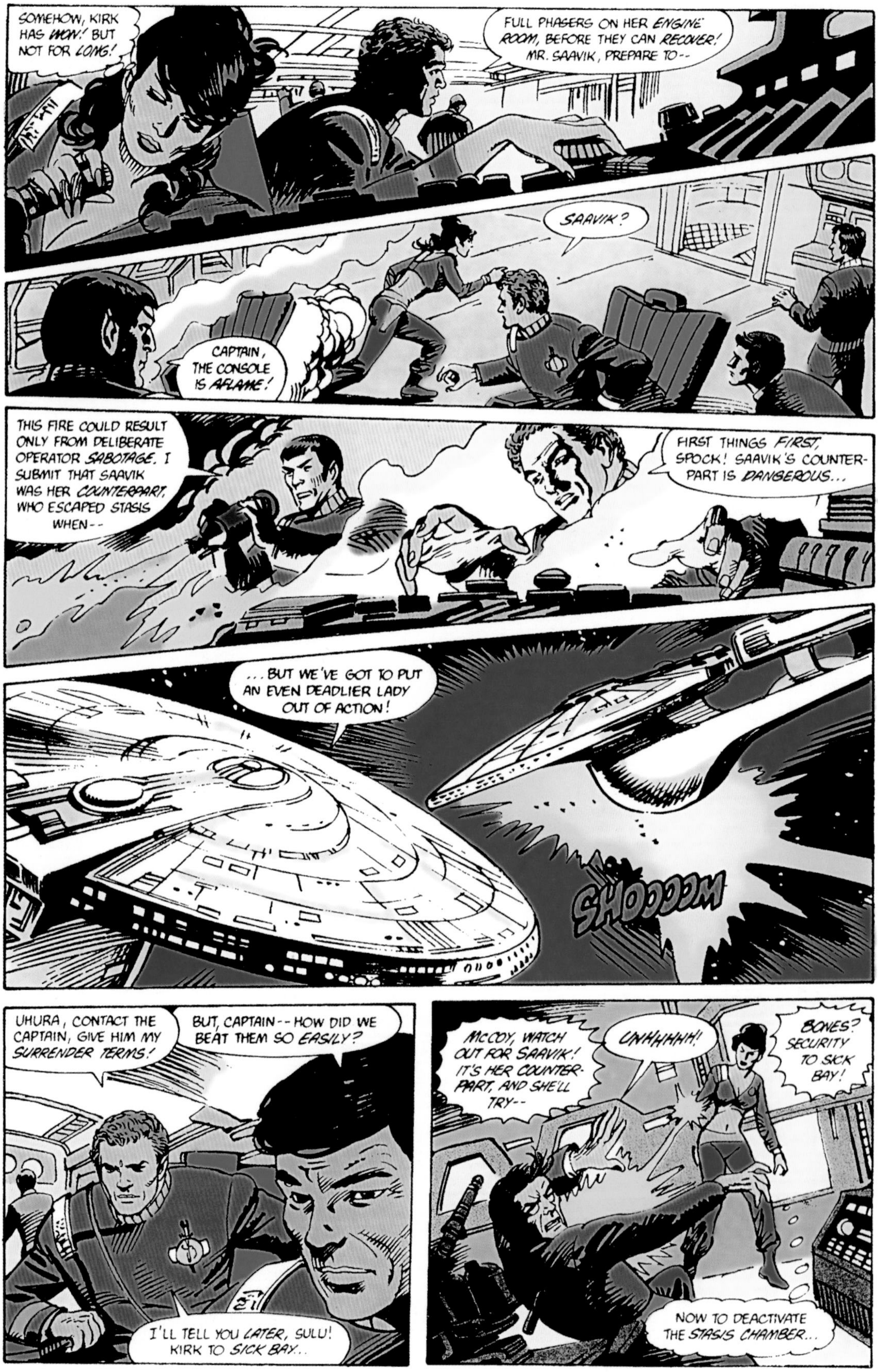
SOMEHOW, KIRK HAS WON! BUT NOT FOR LONG!
FULL PHASERS ON HER ENGINE ROOM, BEFORE THEY CAN RECOVER! MR. SAAVIK, PREPARE TO--
SAAVIK?
CAPTAIN, THE CONSOLE IS AFLAME!
THIS FIRE COULD RESULT ONLY FROM DELIBERATE OPERATOR SABOTAGE. I SUBMIT THAT SAAVIK WAS HER COUNTERPART, WHO ESCAPED STASIS WHEN--
FIRST THINGS FIRST, SPOCK! SAAVIK'S COUNTERPART IS DANGEROUS...
...BUT WE'VE GOT TO PUT AN EVEN DEADLIER LADY OUT OF ACTION!
SHOOOOM
UHURA, CONTACT THE CAPTAIN, GIVE HIM MY SURRENDER TERMS!
BUT, CAPTAIN--HOW DID WE BEAT THEM SO EASILY?
I'LL TELL YOU LATER, SULU! KIRK TO SICK BAY..
McCOY, WATCH OUT FOR SAAVIK! IT'S HER COUNTERPART, AND SHE'LL TRY--
UNHHHHH!
BONES? SECURITY TO SICK BAY!
NOW TO DEACTIVATE THE STASIS CHAMBER...

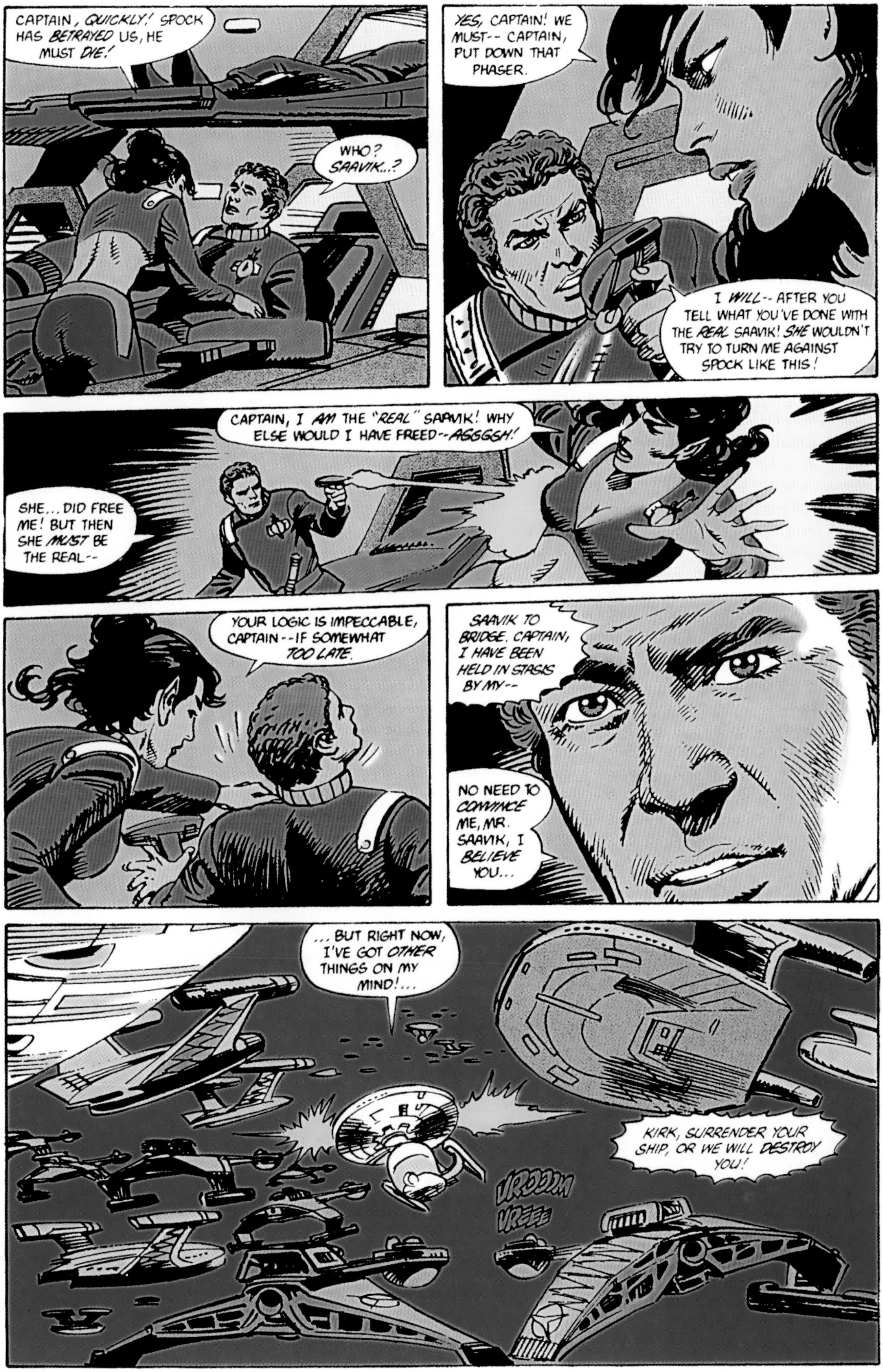
CAPTAIN, QUICKLY! SPOCK HAS BETRAYED US, HE MUST DIE!
WHO? SAAVIK...?
YES, CAPTAIN! WE MUST-- CAPTAIN, PUT DOWN THAT PHASER.
I WILL-- AFTER YOU TELL WHAT YOU'VE DONE WITH THE REAL SAAVIK! SHE WOULDN'T TRY TO TURN ME AGAINST SPOCK LIKE THIS!
CAPTAIN, I AM THE "REAL" SAAVIK! WHY ELSE WOULD I HAVE FREED--AGGGGH!
SHE... DID FREE ME! BUT THEN SHE MUST BE THE REAL--
YOUR LOGIC IS IMPECCABLE, CAPTAIN--IF SOMEWHAT TOO LATE.
SAAVIK TO BRIDGE. CAPTAIN, I HAVE BEEN HELD IN STASIS BY MY--
NO NEED TO CONVINCE ME, MR. SAAVIK, I BELIEVE YOU...
...BUT RIGHT NOW, I'VE GOT OTHER THINGS ON MY MIND!...
KIRK, SURRENDER YOUR SHIP, OR WE WILL DESTROY YOU!
VROOM
VREEE

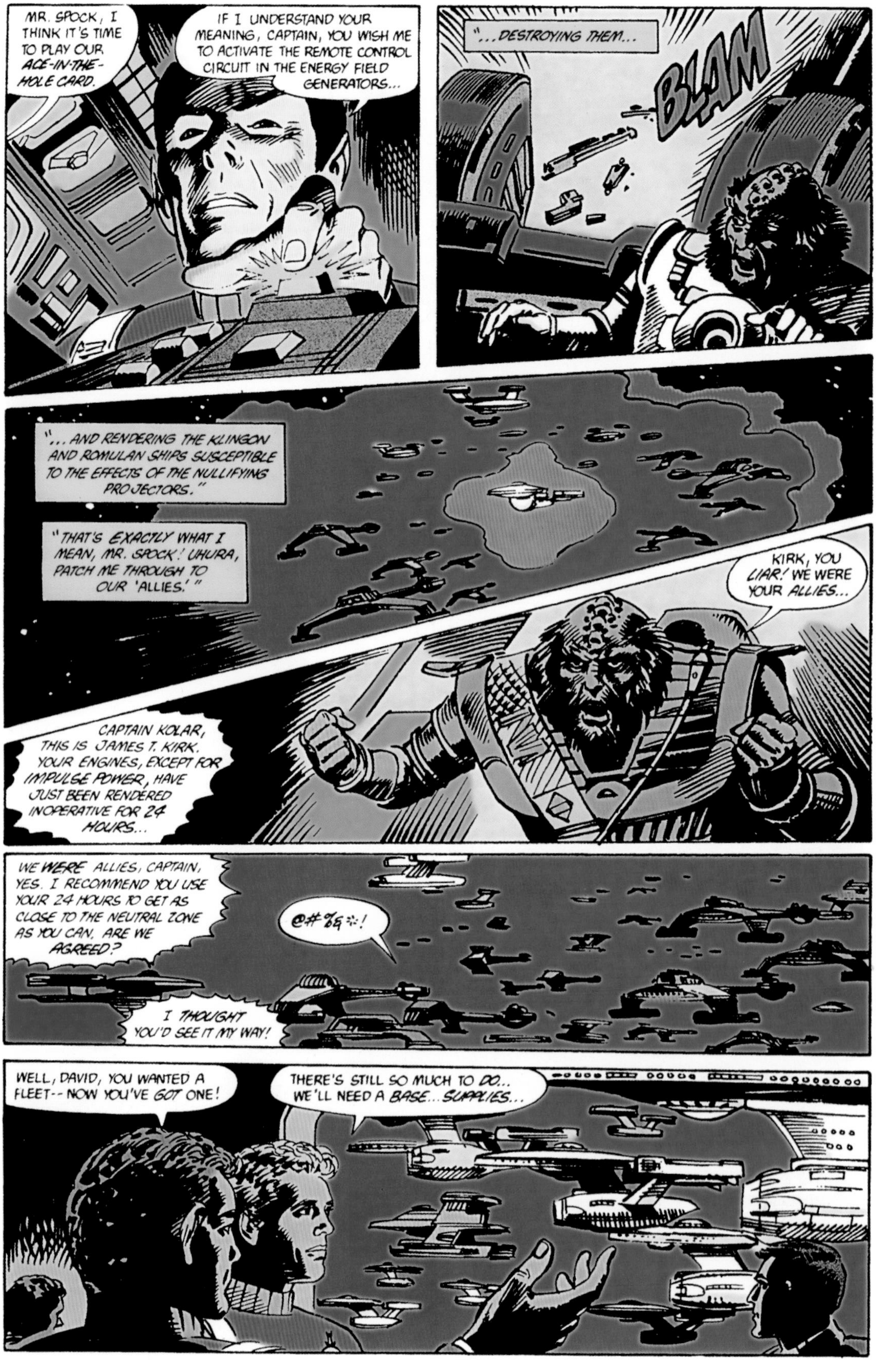
MR. SPOCK, I THINK IT'S TIME TO PLAY OUR ACE-IN-THE-HOLE CARD.
IF I UNDERSTAND YOUR MEANING, CAPTAIN, YOU WISH ME TO ACTIVATE THE REMOTE CONTROL CIRCUIT IN THE ENERGY FIELD GENERATORS...
"...DESTROYING THEM...
BLAM
"... AND RENDERING THE KLINGON AND ROMULAN SHIPS SUSCEPTIBLE TO THE EFFECTS OF THE NULLIFYING PROJECTORS."
"THAT'S EXACTLY WHAT I MEAN, MR. SPOCK! UHURA, PATCH ME THROUGH TO OUR 'ALLIES.'"
KIRK, YOU LIAR! WE WERE YOUR ALLIES...
CAPTAIN KOLAR, THIS IS JAMES T. KIRK. YOUR ENGINES, EXCEPT FOR IMPULSE POWER, HAVE JUST BEEN RENDERED INOPERATIVE FOR 24 HOURS...
WE WERE ALLIES, CAPTAIN, YES. I RECOMMEND YOU USE YOUR 24 HOURS TO GET AS CLOSE TO THE NEUTRAL ZONE AS YOU CAN. ARE WE AGREED?
@#%¤!
I THOUGHT YOU'D SEE IT MY WAY!
WELL, DAVID, YOU WANTED A FLEET-- NOW YOU'VE GOT ONE!
THERE'S STILL SO MUCH TO DO... WE'LL NEED A BASE... SUPPLIES...

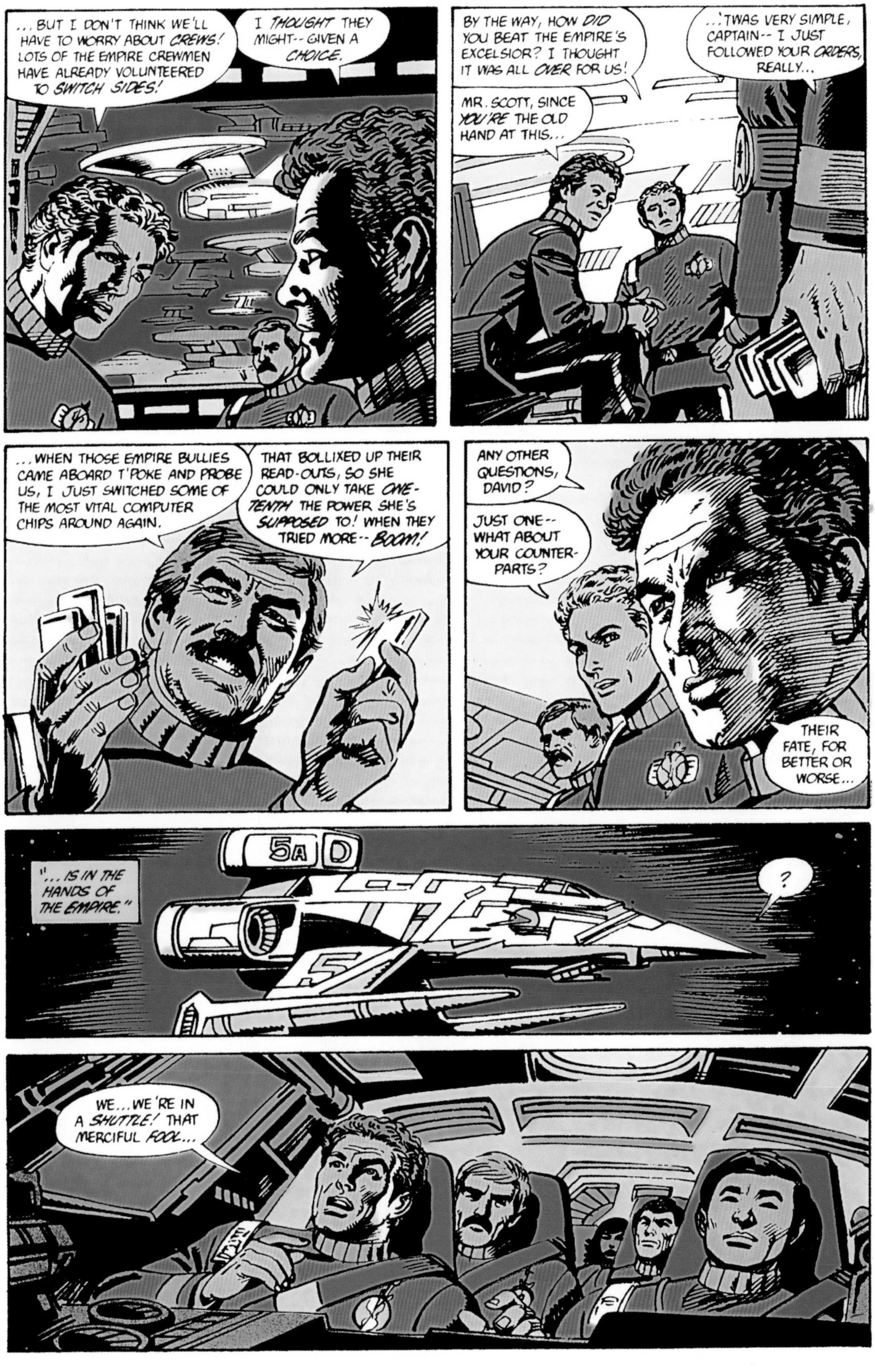

... BUT I DON'T THINK WE'LL HAVE TO WORRY ABOUT CREWS! LOTS OF THE EMPIRE CREWMEN HAVE ALREADY VOLUNTEERED TO SWITCH SIDES!
I THOUGHT THEY MIGHT-- GIVEN A CHOICE.
BY THE WAY, HOW DID YOU BEAT THE EMPIRE'S EXCELSIOR? I THOUGHT IT WAS ALL OVER FOR US!
MR. SCOTT, SINCE YOU'RE THE OLD HAND AT THIS...
...'TWAS VERY SIMPLE, CAPTAIN-- I JUST FOLLOWED YOUR ORDERS, REALLY...
... WHEN THOSE EMPIRE BULLIES CAME ABOARD T'POKE AND PROBE US, I JUST SWITCHED SOME OF THE MOST VITAL COMPUTER CHIPS AROUND AGAIN.
THAT BOLLIXED UP THEIR READ-OUTS, SO SHE COULD ONLY TAKE ONE-TENTH THE POWER SHE'S SUPPOSED TO! WHEN THEY TRIED MORE-- BOOM!
ANY OTHER QUESTIONS, DAVID?
JUST ONE-- WHAT ABOUT YOUR COUNTER-PARTS?
THEIR FATE, FOR BETTER OR WORSE...
"... IS IN THE HANDS OF THE EMPIRE."
5A D
5
?
WE... WE'RE IN A SHUTTLE! THAT MERCIFUL FOOL...

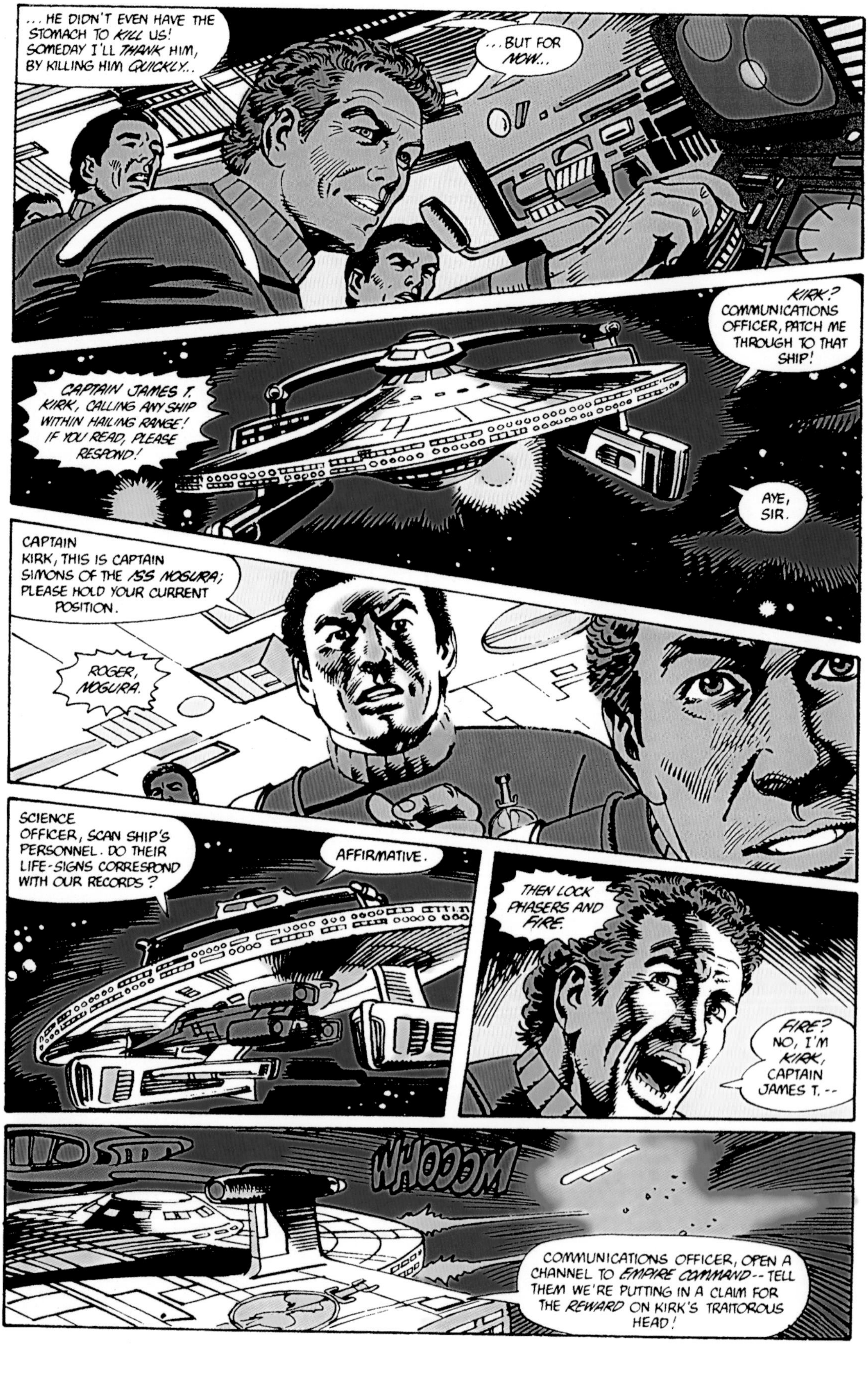
...HE DIDN'T EVEN HAVE THE STOMACH TO KILL US! SOMEDAY I'LL THANK HIM, BY KILLING HIM QUICKLY...
...BUT FOR NOW...
KIRK? COMMUNICATIONS OFFICER, PATCH ME THROUGH TO THAT SHIP!
CAPTAIN JAMES T. KIRK, CALLING ANY SHIP WITHIN HAILING RANGE! IF YOU READ, PLEASE RESPOND!
AYE, SIR.
CAPTAIN KIRK, THIS IS CAPTAIN SIMONS OF THE ISS NOGURA; PLEASE HOLD YOUR CURRENT POSITION.
ROGER, NOGURA.
SCIENCE OFFICER, SCAN SHIP'S PERSONNEL. DO THEIR LIFE-SIGNS CORRESPOND WITH OUR RECORDS?
AFFIRMATIVE.
THEN LOCK PHASERS AND FIRE.
FIRE? NO, I'M KIRK, CAPTAIN JAMES T.--
WHOOOM
COMMUNICATIONS OFFICER, OPEN A CHANNEL TO EMPIRE COMMAND--TELL THEM WE'RE PUTTING IN A CLAIM FOR THE REWARD ON KIRK'S TRAITOROUS HEAD!

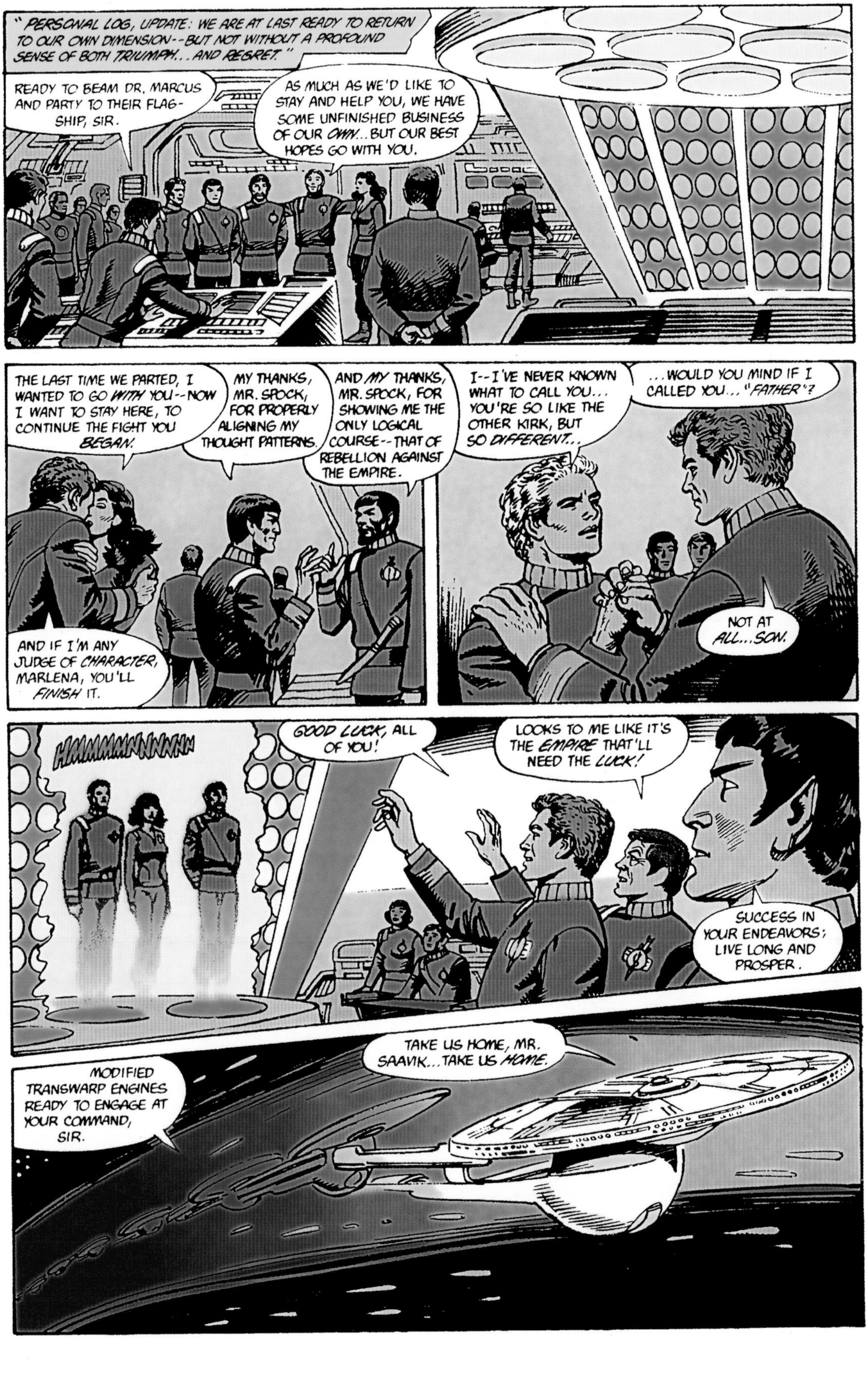
"PERSONAL LOG, UPDATE: WE ARE AT LAST READY TO RETURN TO OUR OWN DIMENSION--BUT NOT WITHOUT A PROFOUND SENSE OF BOTH TRIUMPH... AND REGRET."
READY TO BEAM DR. MARCUS AND PARTY TO THEIR FLAG-SHIP, SIR.
AS MUCH AS WE'D LIKE TO STAY AND HELP YOU, WE HAVE SOME UNFINISHED BUSINESS OF OUR OWN... BUT OUR BEST HOPES GO WITH YOU.
THE LAST TIME WE PARTED, I WANTED TO GO WITH YOU--NOW I WANT TO STAY HERE, TO CONTINUE THE FIGHT YOU BEGAN.
MY THANKS, MR. SPOCK, FOR PROPERLY ALIGNING MY THOUGHT PATTERNS.
AND MY THANKS, MR. SPOCK, FOR SHOWING ME THE ONLY LOGICAL COURSE--THAT OF REBELLION AGAINST THE EMPIRE.
AND IF I'M ANY JUDGE OF CHARACTER, MARLENA, YOU'LL FINISH IT.
I--I'VE NEVER KNOWN WHAT TO CALL YOU... YOU'RE SO LIKE THE OTHER KIRK, BUT SO DIFFERENT...
...WOULD YOU MIND IF I CALLED YOU... "FATHER"?
NOT AT ALL... SON.
HMMMMNNNNNN
GOOD LUCK, ALL OF YOU!
LOOKS TO ME LIKE IT'S THE EMPIRE THAT'LL NEED THE LUCK!
SUCCESS IN YOUR ENDEAVORS; LIVE LONG AND PROSPER.
TAKE US HOME, MR. SAAVIK... TAKE US HOME.
MODIFIED TRANSWARP ENGINES READY TO ENGAGE AT YOUR COMMAND, SIR.

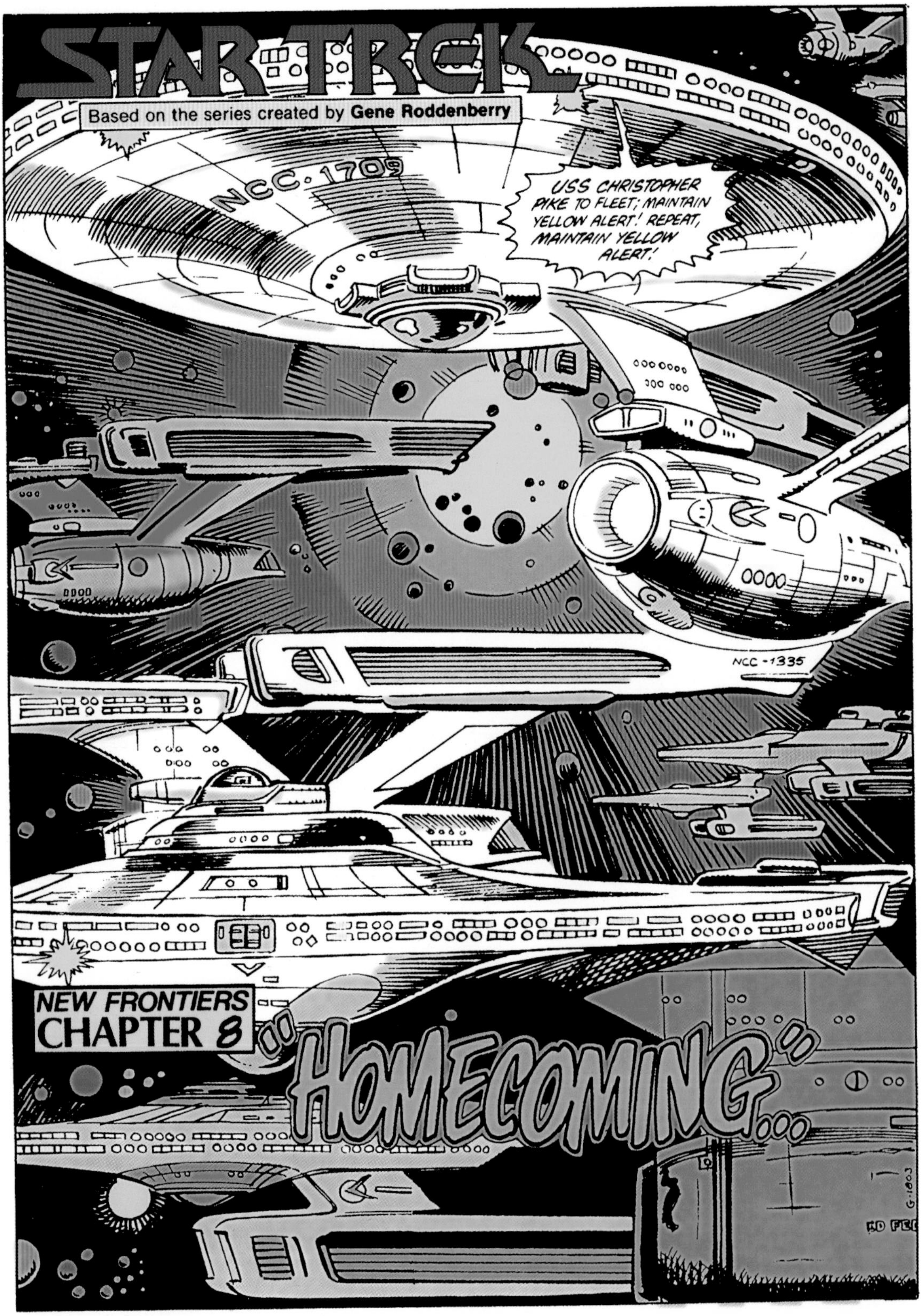
STAR TREK
Based on the series created by Gene Roddenberry
NCC-1709
USS CHRISTOPHER PIKE TO FLEET: MAINTAIN YELLOW ALERT! REPEAT, MAINTAIN YELLOW ALERT!
NCC-1335
NEW FRONTIERS
CHAPTER 8
"HOMECOMING..."

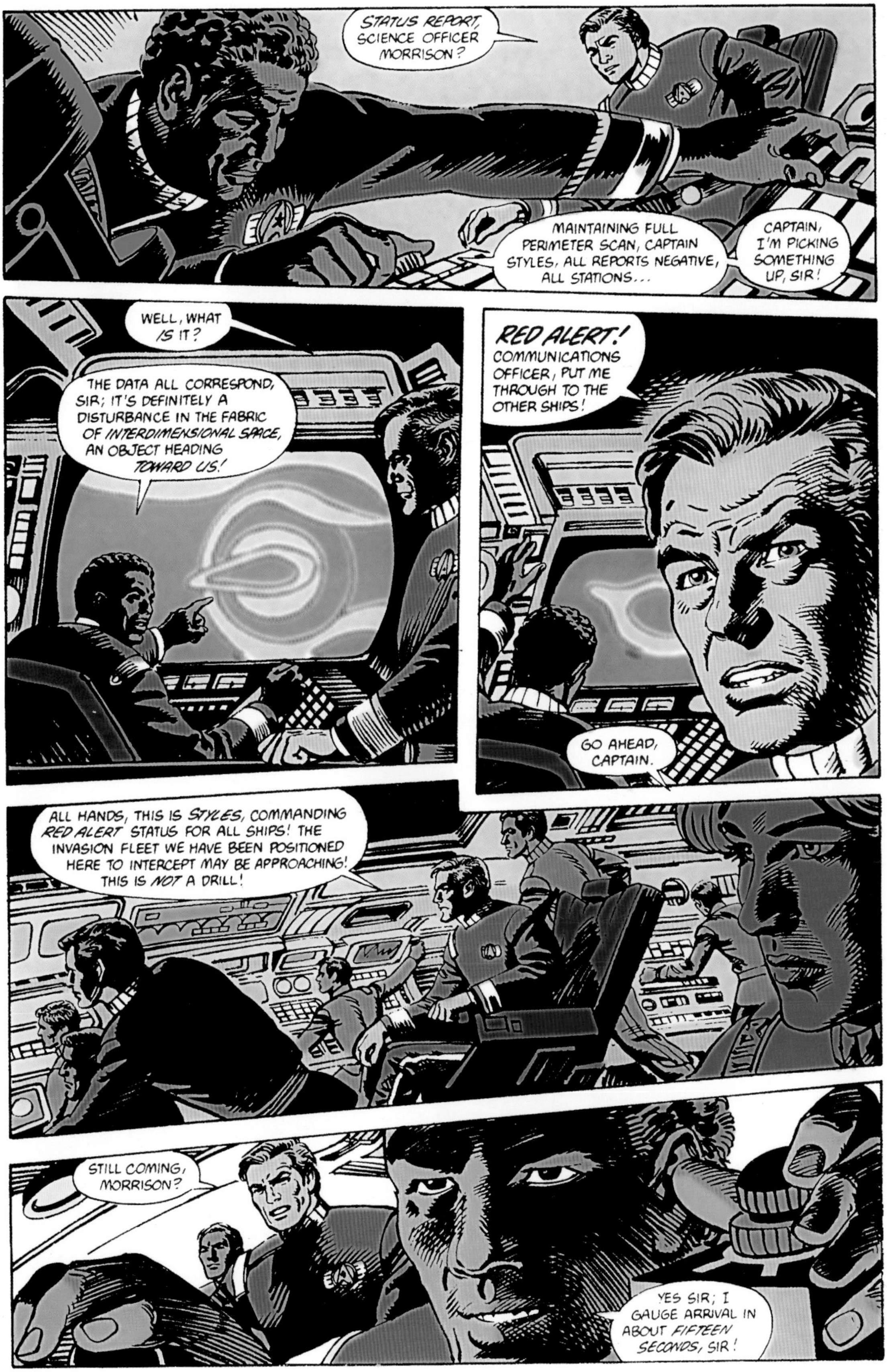
STATUS REPORT, SCIENCE OFFICER MORRISON?
MAINTAINING FULL PERIMETER SCAN, CAPTAIN STYLES, ALL REPORTS NEGATIVE, ALL STATIONS...
CAPTAIN, I'M PICKING SOMETHING UP, SIR!
WELL, WHAT IS IT?
THE DATA ALL CORRESPOND, SIR; IT'S DEFINITELY A DISTURBANCE IN THE FABRIC OF INTERDIMENSIONAL SPACE, AN OBJECT HEADING TOWARD US!
RED ALERT! COMMUNICATIONS OFFICER, PUT ME THROUGH TO THE OTHER SHIPS!
GO AHEAD, CAPTAIN.
ALL HANDS, THIS IS STYLES, COMMANDING RED ALERT STATUS FOR ALL SHIPS! THE INVASION FLEET WE HAVE BEEN POSITIONED HERE TO INTERCEPT MAY BE APPROACHING! THIS IS NOT A DRILL!
STILL COMING, MORRISON?
YES SIR; I GAUGE ARRIVAL IN ABOUT FIFTEEN SECONDS, SIR!

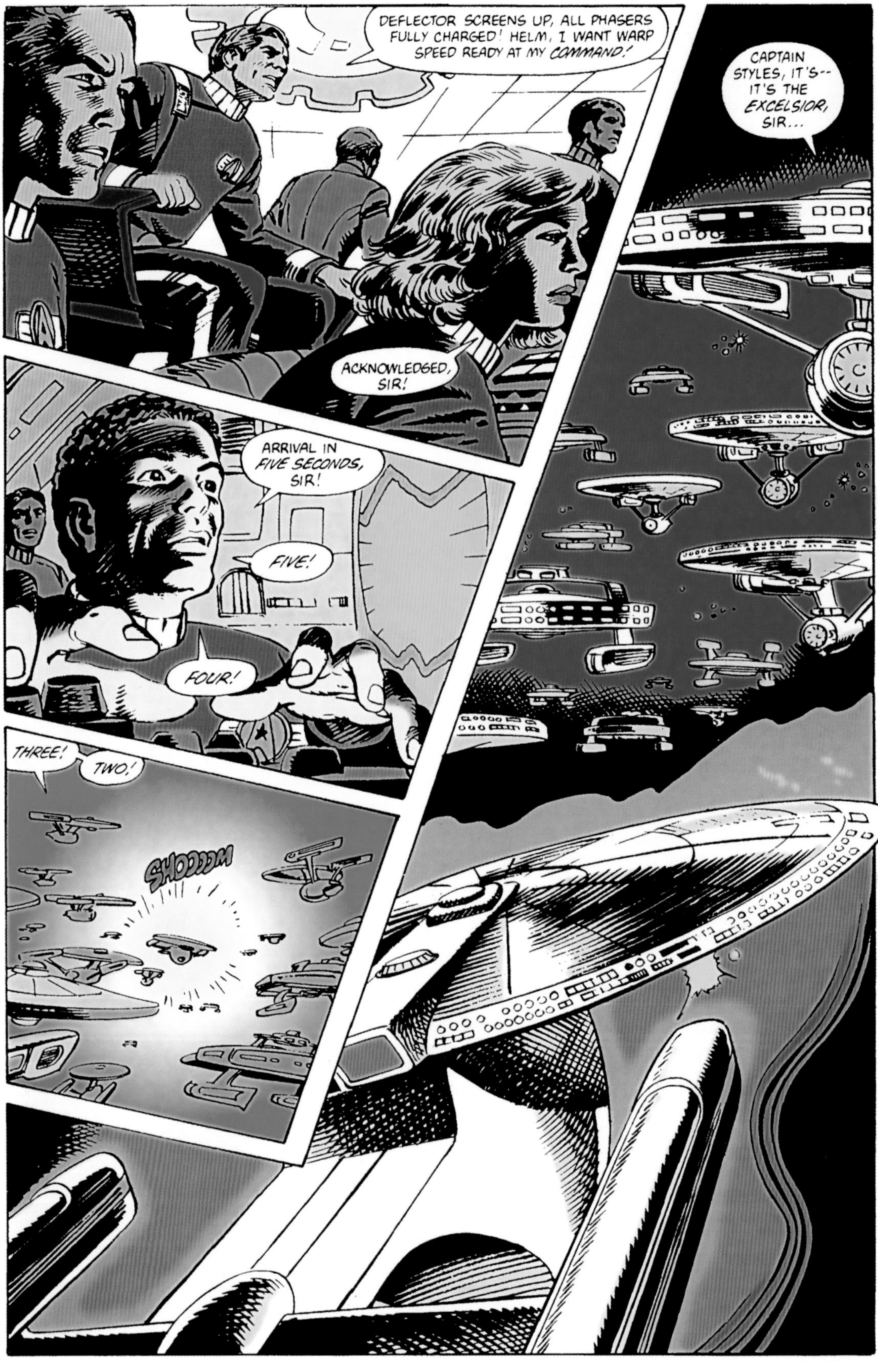
DEFLECTOR SCREENS UP, ALL PHASERS FULLY CHARGED! HELM, I WANT WARP SPEED READY AT MY *COMMAND!*
ACKNOWLEDGED, SIR!
ARRIVAL IN *FIVE SECONDS,* SIR!
FIVE!
FOUR!
THREE!
TWO!
SHOOOOM
CAPTAIN STYLES, IT'S-- IT'S THE *EXCELSIOR,* SIR...

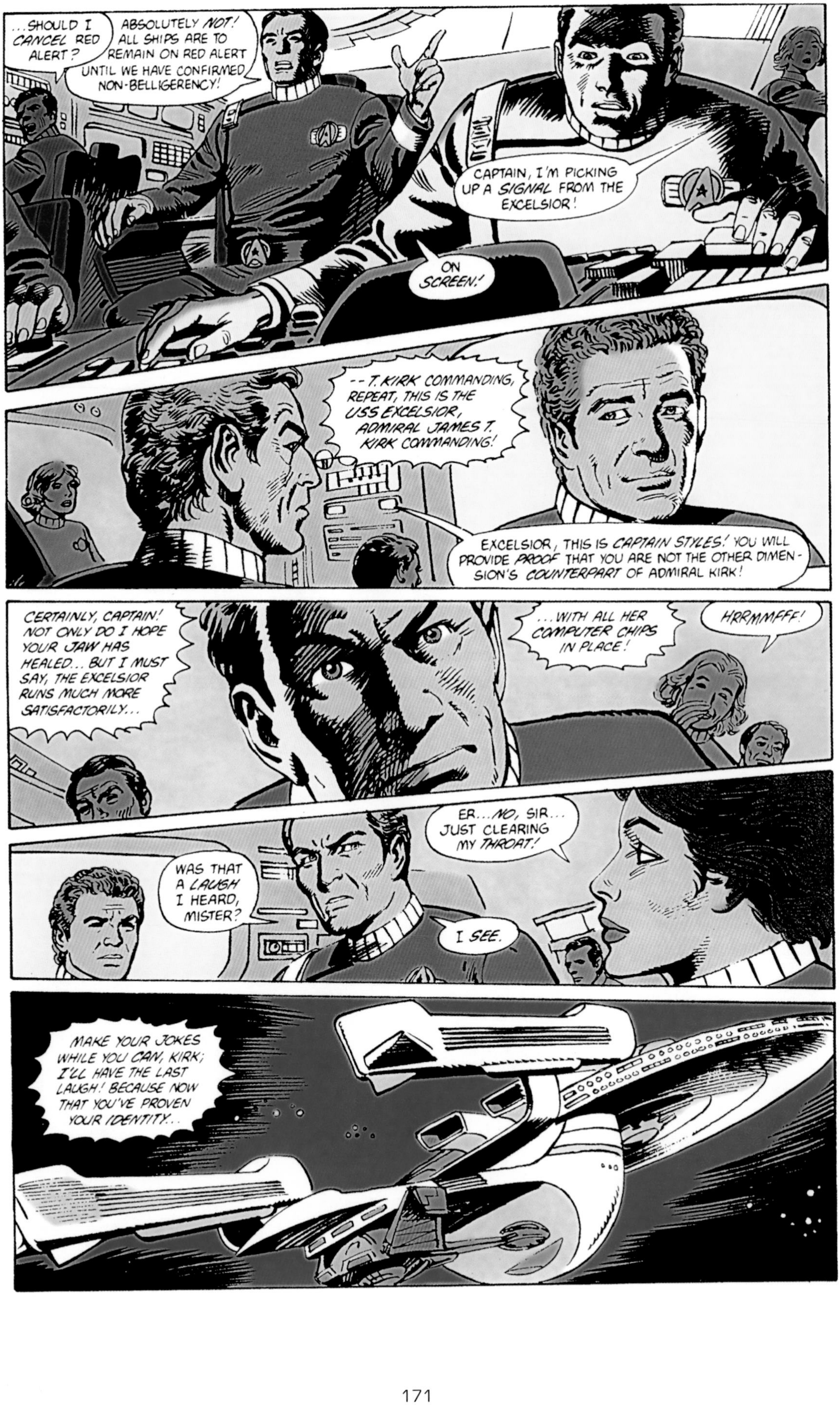
...SHOULD I CANCEL RED ALERT?
ABSOLUTELY NOT! ALL SHIPS ARE TO REMAIN ON RED ALERT UNTIL WE HAVE CONFIRMED NON-BELLIGERENCY!
CAPTAIN, I'M PICKING UP A SIGNAL FROM THE EXCELSIOR!
ON SCREEN!
--T. KIRK COMMANDING, REPEAT, THIS IS THE USS EXCELSIOR, ADMIRAL JAMES T. KIRK COMMANDING!
EXCELSIOR, THIS IS CAPTAIN STYLES! YOU WILL PROVIDE PROOF THAT YOU ARE NOT THE OTHER DIMENSION'S COUNTERPART OF ADMIRAL KIRK!
CERTAINLY, CAPTAIN! NOT ONLY DO I HOPE YOUR JAW HAS HEALED... BUT I MUST SAY, THE EXCELSIOR RUNS MUCH MORE SATISFACTORILY...
...WITH ALL HER COMPUTER CHIPS IN PLACE!
HRRMMFFF!
WAS THAT A LAUGH I HEARD, MISTER?
ER...NO, SIR... JUST CLEARING MY THROAT!
I SEE.
MAKE YOUR JOKES WHILE YOU CAN, KIRK; I'LL HAVE THE LAST LAUGH! BECAUSE NOW THAT YOU'VE PROVEN YOUR IDENTITY...

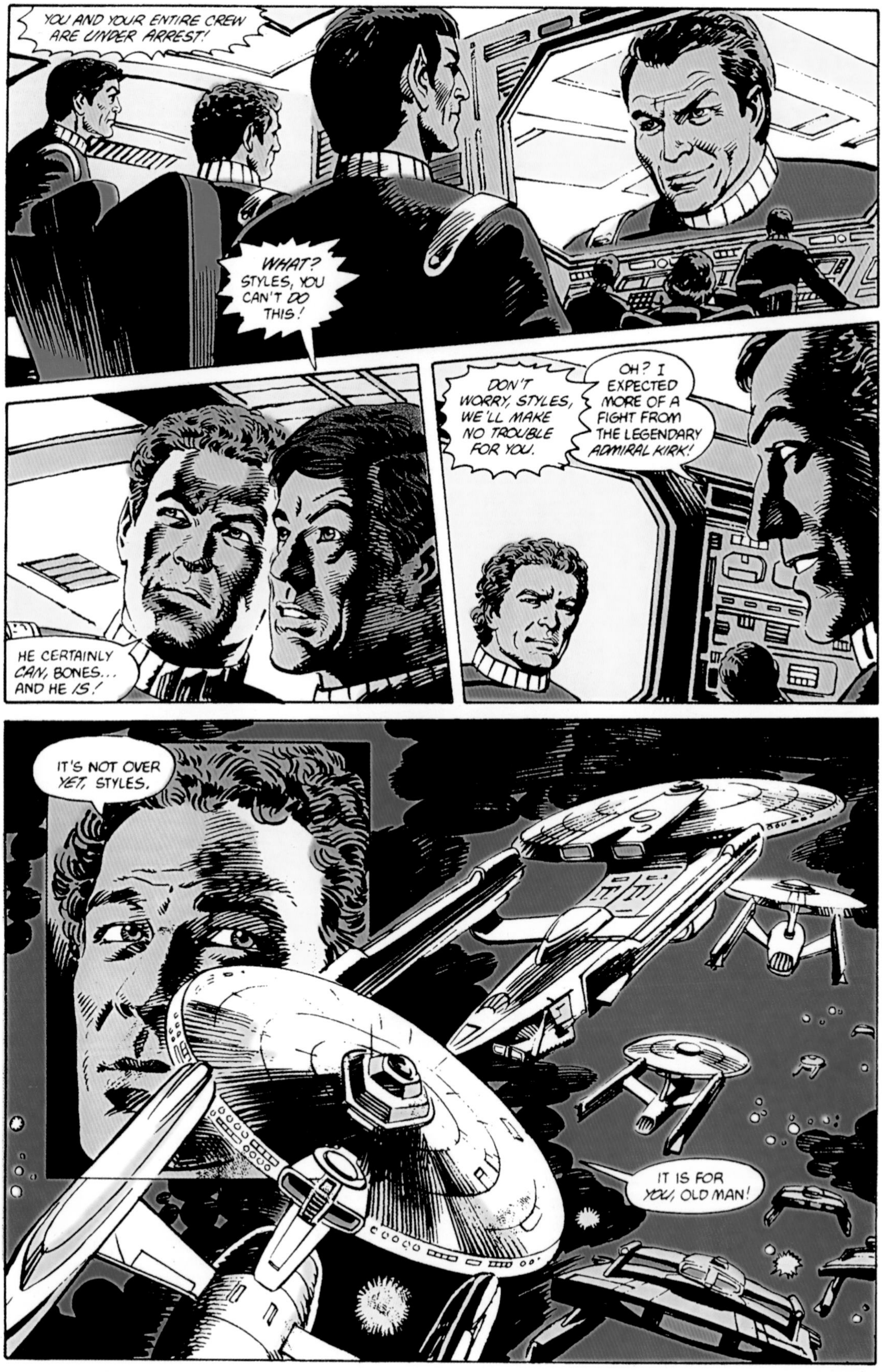
YOU AND YOUR ENTIRE CREW ARE UNDER ARREST!
WHAT? STYLES, YOU CAN'T DO THIS!
HE CERTAINLY CAN, BONES... AND HE IS!
DON'T WORRY, STYLES, WE'LL MAKE NO TROUBLE FOR YOU.
OH? I EXPECTED MORE OF A FIGHT FROM THE LEGENDARY ADMIRAL KIRK!
IT'S NOT OVER YET, STYLES.
IT IS FOR YOU, OLD MAN!

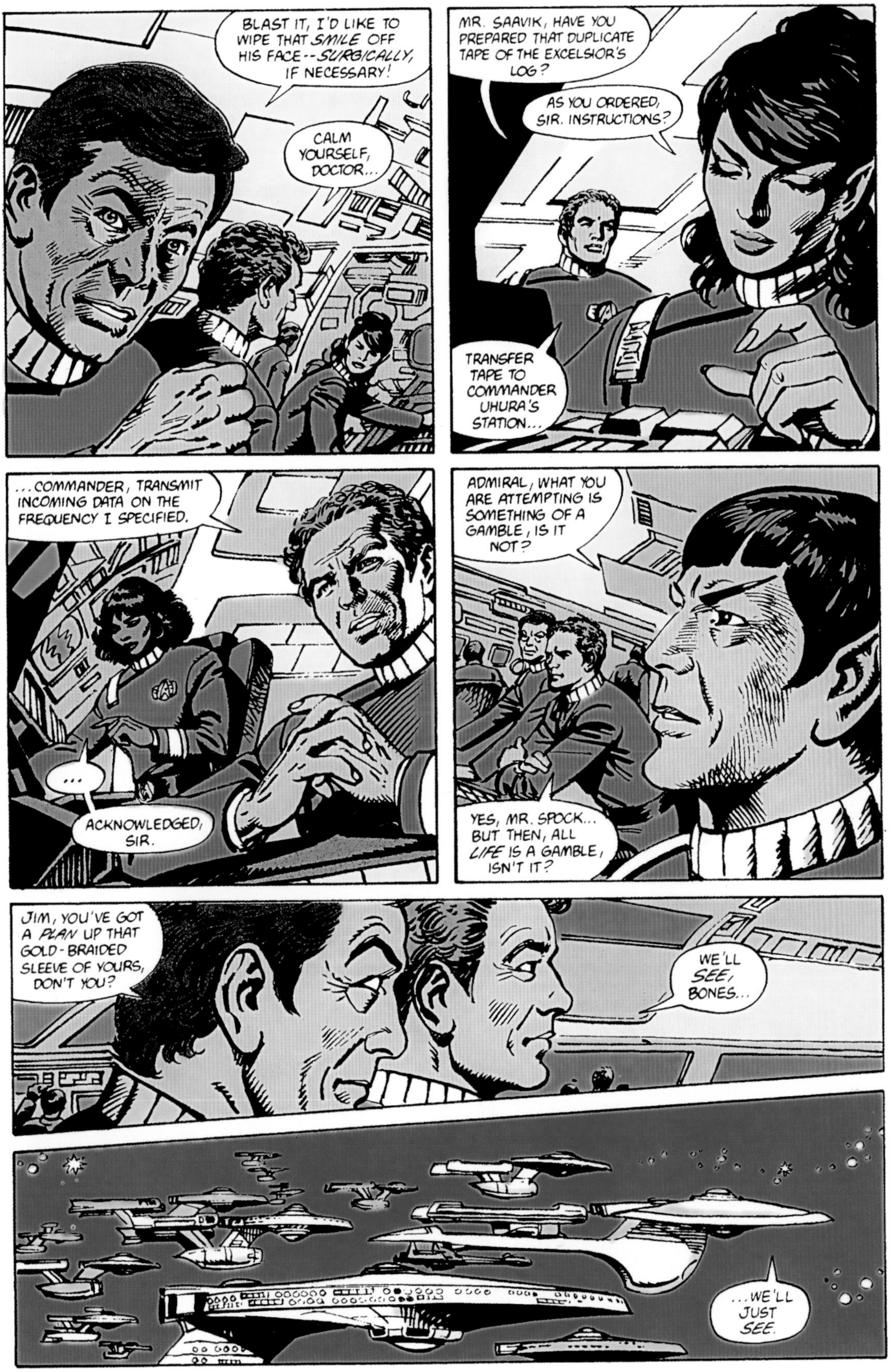
BLAST IT, I'D LIKE TO WIPE THAT SMILE OFF HIS FACE--SURGICALLY, IF NECESSARY!
CALM YOURSELF, DOCTOR...
MR. SAAVIK, HAVE YOU PREPARED THAT DUPLICATE TAPE OF THE EXCELSIOR'S LOG?
AS YOU ORDERED, SIR. INSTRUCTIONS?
TRANSFER TAPE TO COMMANDER UHURA'S STATION...
...COMMANDER, TRANSMIT INCOMING DATA ON THE FREQUENCY I SPECIFIED.
...
ACKNOWLEDGED, SIR.
ADMIRAL, WHAT YOU ARE ATTEMPTING IS SOMETHING OF A GAMBLE, IS IT NOT?
YES, MR. SPOCK... BUT THEN, ALL LIFE IS A GAMBLE, ISN'T IT?
JIM, YOU'VE GOT A PLAN UP THAT GOLD-BRAIDED SLEEVE OF YOURS, DON'T YOU?
WE'LL SEE, BONES...
...WE'LL JUST SEE.

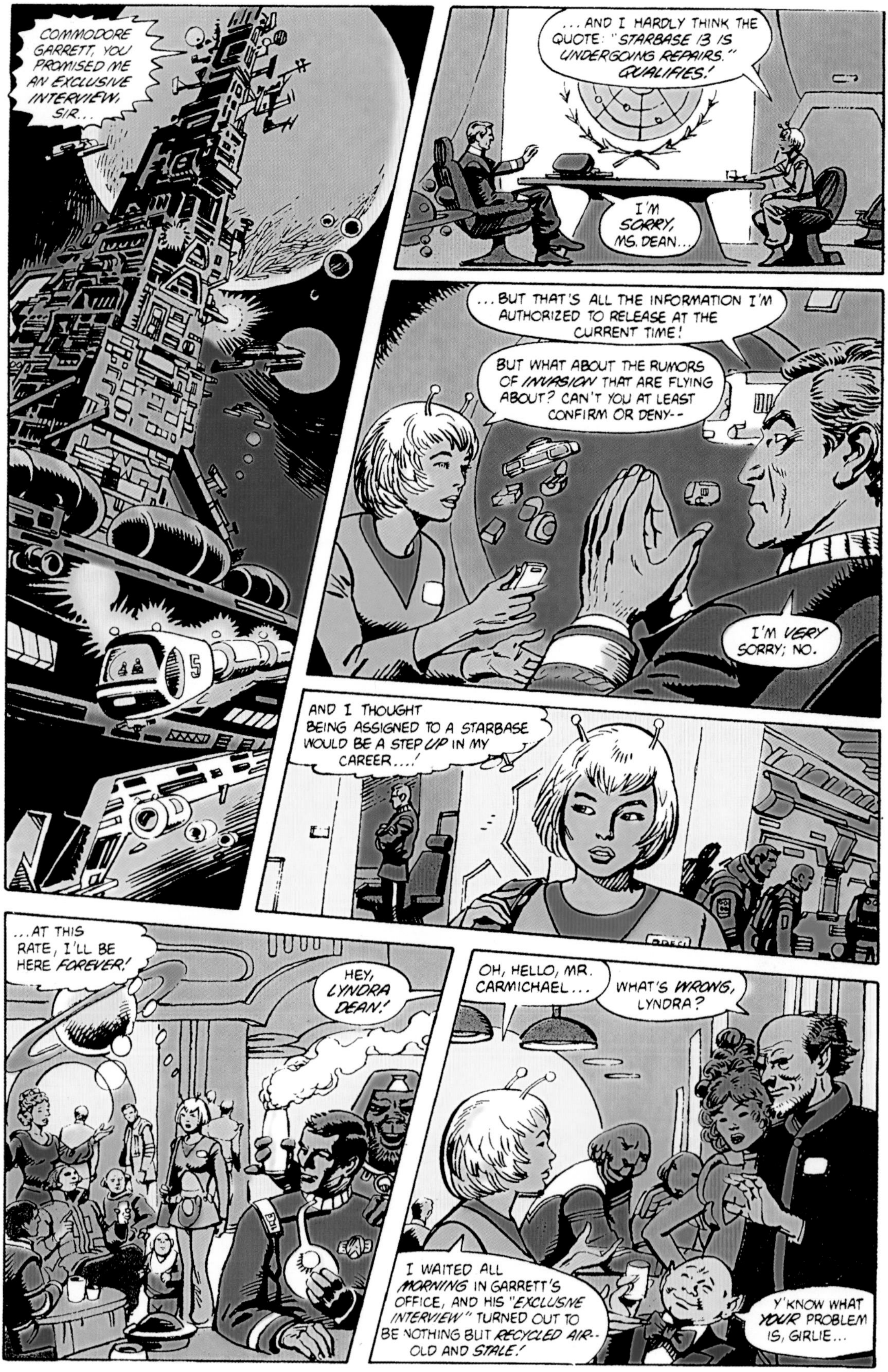
COMMODORE GARRETT, YOU PROMISED ME AN EXCLUSIVE INTERVIEW, SIR...
... AND I HARDLY THINK THE QUOTE: "STARBASE 13 IS UNDERGOING REPAIRS." QUALIFIES!
I'M SORRY, MS. DEAN...
... BUT THAT'S ALL THE INFORMATION I'M AUTHORIZED TO RELEASE AT THE CURRENT TIME!
BUT WHAT ABOUT THE RUMORS OF INVASION THAT ARE FLYING ABOUT? CAN'T YOU AT LEAST CONFIRM OR DENY--
I'M VERY SORRY; NO.
AND I THOUGHT BEING ASSIGNED TO A STARBASE WOULD BE A STEP UP IN MY CAREER...!
...AT THIS RATE, I'LL BE HERE FOREVER!
HEY, LYNDRA DEAN!
OH, HELLO, MR. CARMICHAEL...
WHAT'S WRONG, LYNDRA?
I WAITED ALL MORNING IN GARRETT'S OFFICE, AND HIS "EXCLUSIVE INTERVIEW" TURNED OUT TO BE NOTHING BUT RECYCLED AIR-- OLD AND STALE!
Y'KNOW WHAT YOUR PROBLEM IS, GIRLIE...

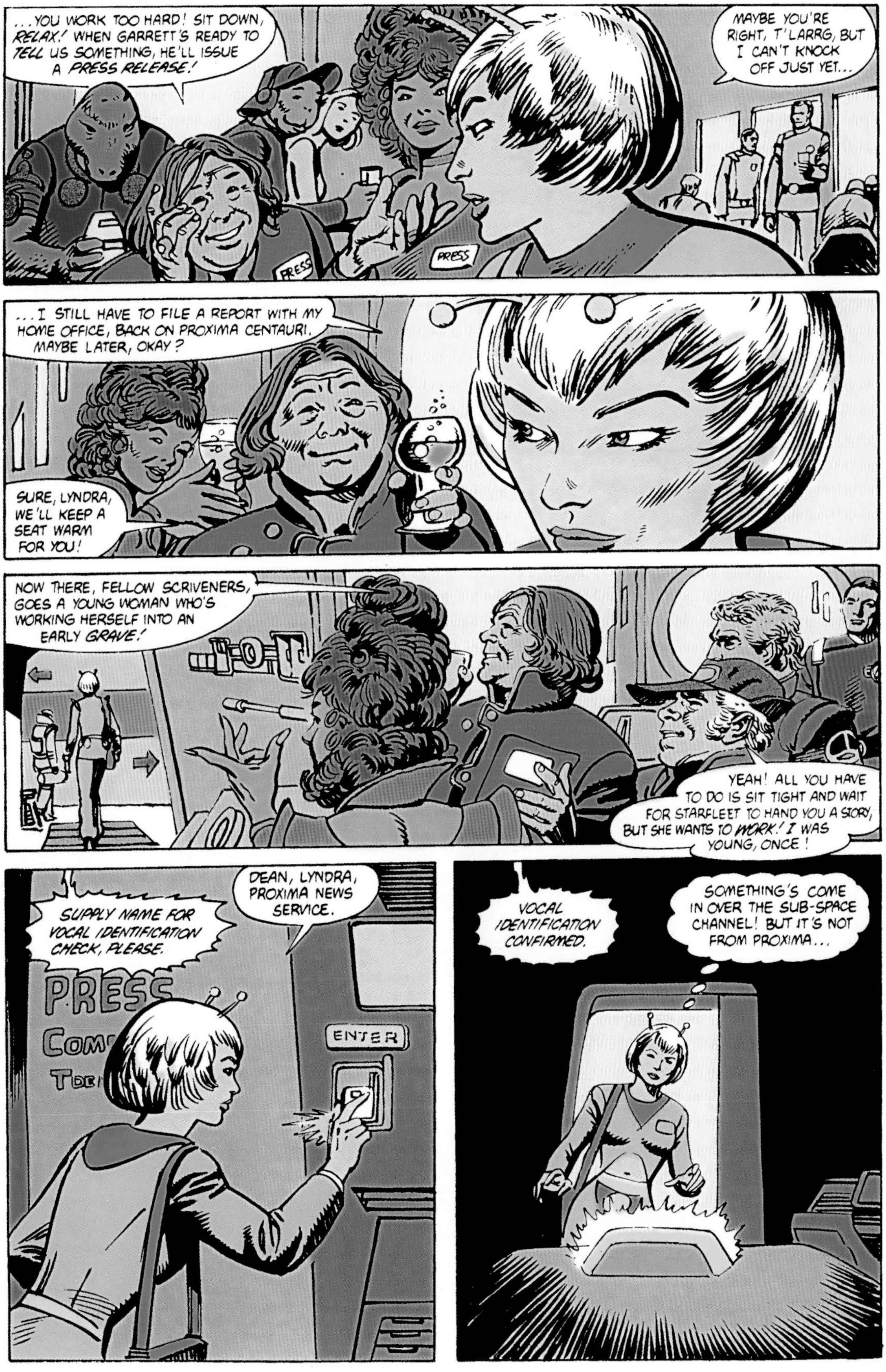
...YOU WORK TOO HARD! SIT DOWN, RELAX! WHEN GARRETT'S READY TO TELL US SOMETHING, HE'LL ISSUE A PRESS RELEASE!
MAYBE YOU'RE RIGHT, T'LARRG, BUT I CAN'T KNOCK OFF JUST YET...
PRESS
PRESS
...I STILL HAVE TO FILE A REPORT WITH MY HOME OFFICE, BACK ON PROXIMA CENTAURI. MAYBE LATER, OKAY?
SURE, LYNDRA, WE'LL KEEP A SEAT WARM FOR YOU!
NOW THERE, FELLOW SCRIVENERS, GOES A YOUNG WOMAN WHO'S WORKING HERSELF INTO AN EARLY GRAVE!
YEAH! ALL YOU HAVE TO DO IS SIT TIGHT AND WAIT FOR STARFLEET TO HAND YOU A STORY, BUT SHE WANTS TO WORK! I WAS YOUNG, ONCE!
SUPPLY NAME FOR VOCAL IDENTIFICATION CHECK, PLEASE.
DEAN, LYNDRA, PROXIMA NEWS SERVICE.
PRESS
ENTER
VOCAL IDENTIFICATION CONFIRMED.
SOMETHING'S COME IN OVER THE SUB-SPACE CHANNEL! BUT IT'S NOT FROM PROXIMA...

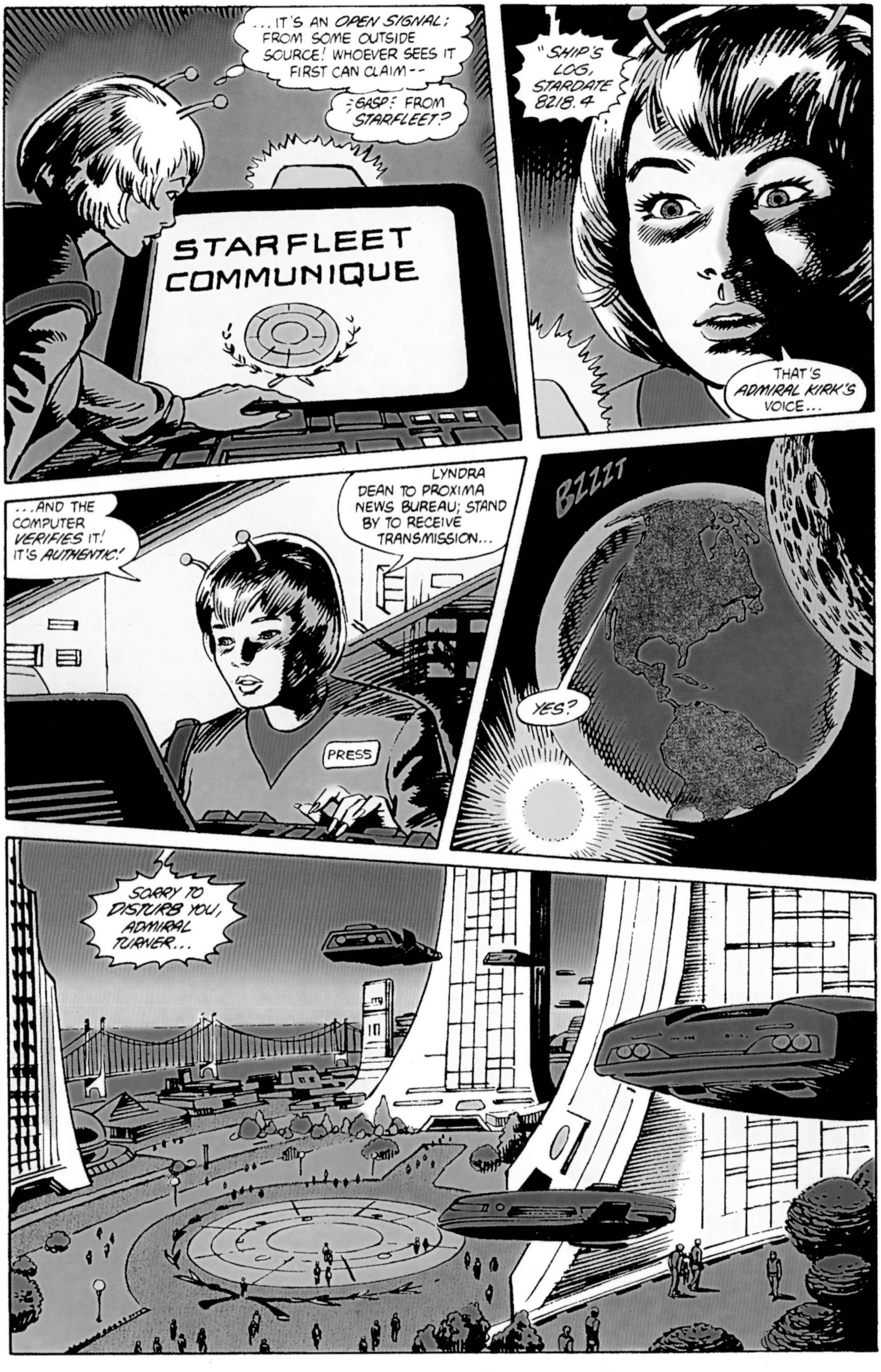
...IT'S AN OPEN SIGNAL; FROM SOME OUTSIDE SOURCE! WHOEVER SEES IT FIRST CAN CLAIM--
GASP FROM STARFLEET?
STARFLEET COMMUNIQUE
"SHIP'S LOG, STARDATE 8218.4
THAT'S ADMIRAL KIRK'S VOICE...
...AND THE COMPUTER VERIFIES IT! IT'S AUTHENTIC!
LYNDRA DEAN TO PROXIMA NEWS BUREAU; STAND BY TO RECEIVE TRANSMISSION...
PRESS
BZZZT
YES?
SORRY TO DISTURB YOU, ADMIRAL TURNER...

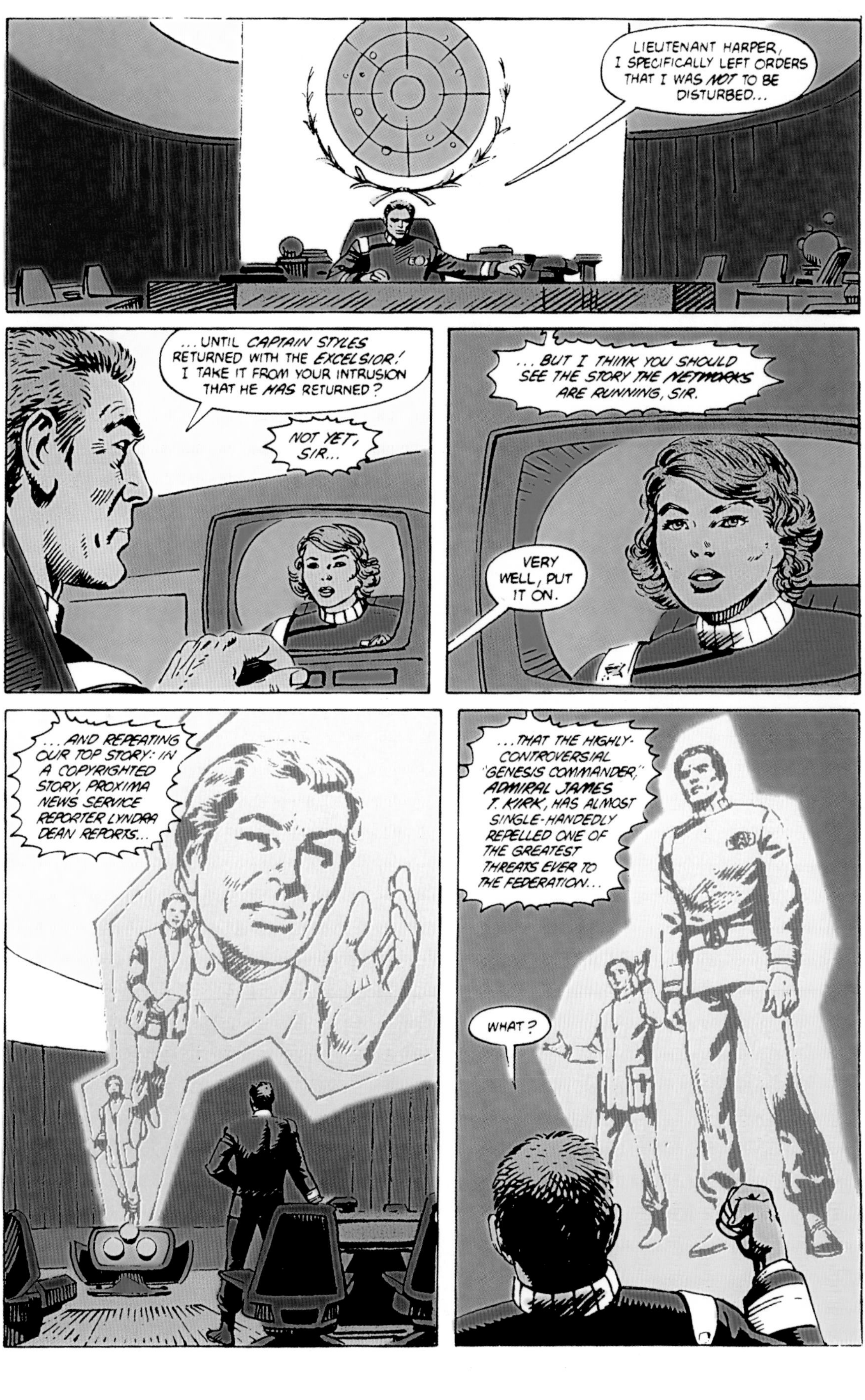
LIEUTENANT HARPER, I SPECIFICALLY LEFT ORDERS THAT I WAS NOT TO BE DISTURBED...
...UNTIL CAPTAIN STYLES RETURNED WITH THE EXCELSIOR! I TAKE IT FROM YOUR INTRUSION THAT HE HAS RETURNED?
NOT YET, SIR...
...BUT I THINK YOU SHOULD SEE THE STORY THE NETWORKS ARE RUNNING, SIR.
VERY WELL, PUT IT ON.
...AND REPEATING OUR TOP STORY: IN A COPYRIGHTED STORY, PROXIMA NEWS SERVICE REPORTER LYNDRA DEAN REPORTS...
...THAT THE HIGHLY-CONTROVERSIAL "GENESIS COMMANDER," ADMIRAL JAMES T. KIRK, HAS ALMOST SINGLE-HANDEDLY REPELLED ONE OF THE GREATEST THREATS EVER TO THE FEDERATION...
WHAT?

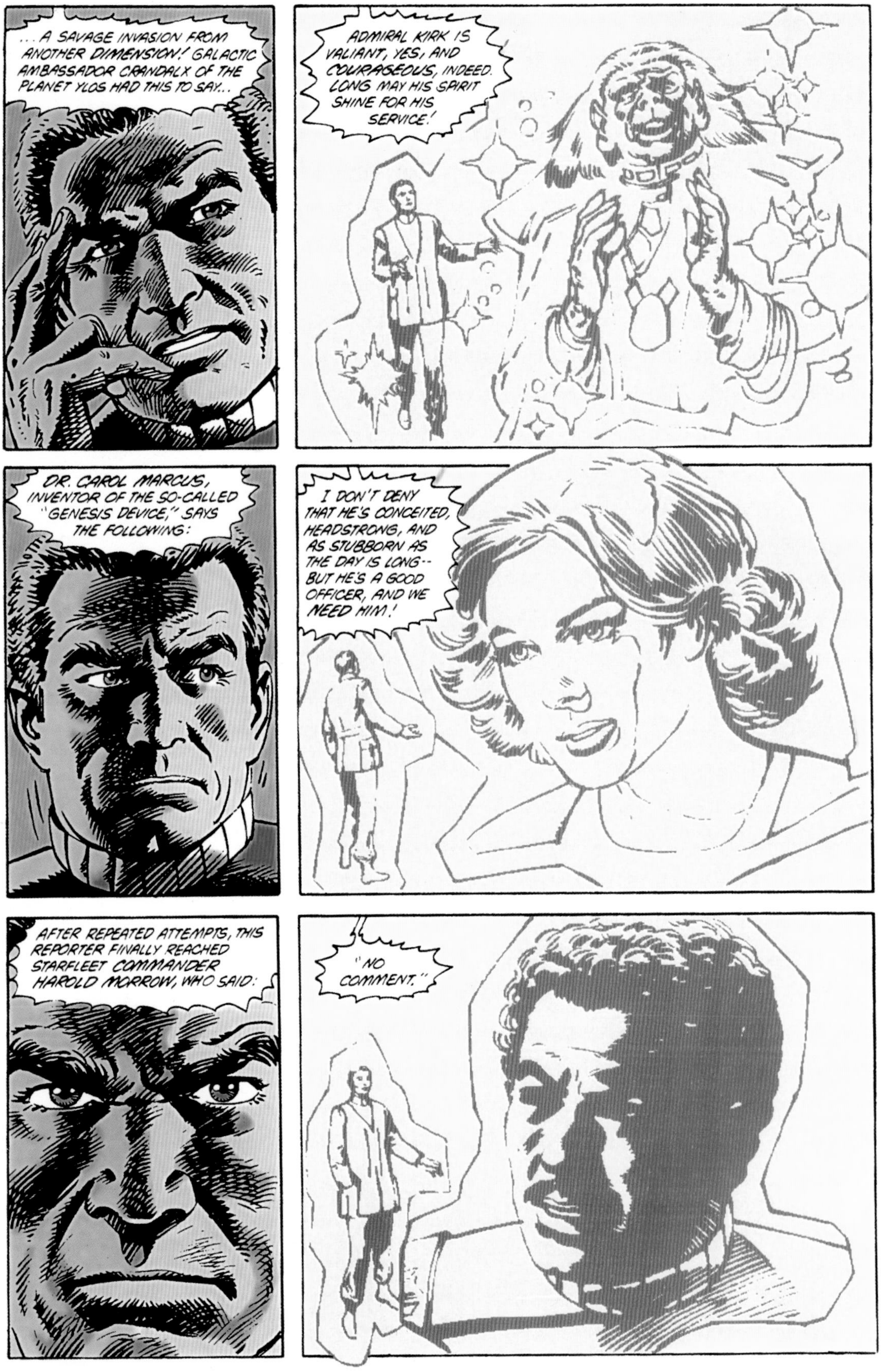
...A SAVAGE INVASION FROM ANOTHER DIMENSION! GALACTIC AMBASSADOR CRANDALX OF THE PLANET YLOS HAD THIS TO SAY...
ADMIRAL KIRK IS VALIANT, YES, AND COURAGEOUS, INDEED. LONG MAY HIS SPIRIT SHINE FOR HIS SERVICE!
DR. CAROL MARCUS, INVENTOR OF THE SO-CALLED "GENESIS DEVICE," SAYS THE FOLLOWING:
I DON'T DENY THAT HE'S CONCEITED, HEADSTRONG, AND AS STUBBORN AS THE DAY IS LONG--BUT HE'S A GOOD OFFICER, AND WE NEED HIM!
AFTER REPEATED ATTEMPTS, THIS REPORTER FINALLY REACHED STARFLEET COMMANDER HAROLD MORROW, WHO SAID:
"NO COMMENT."

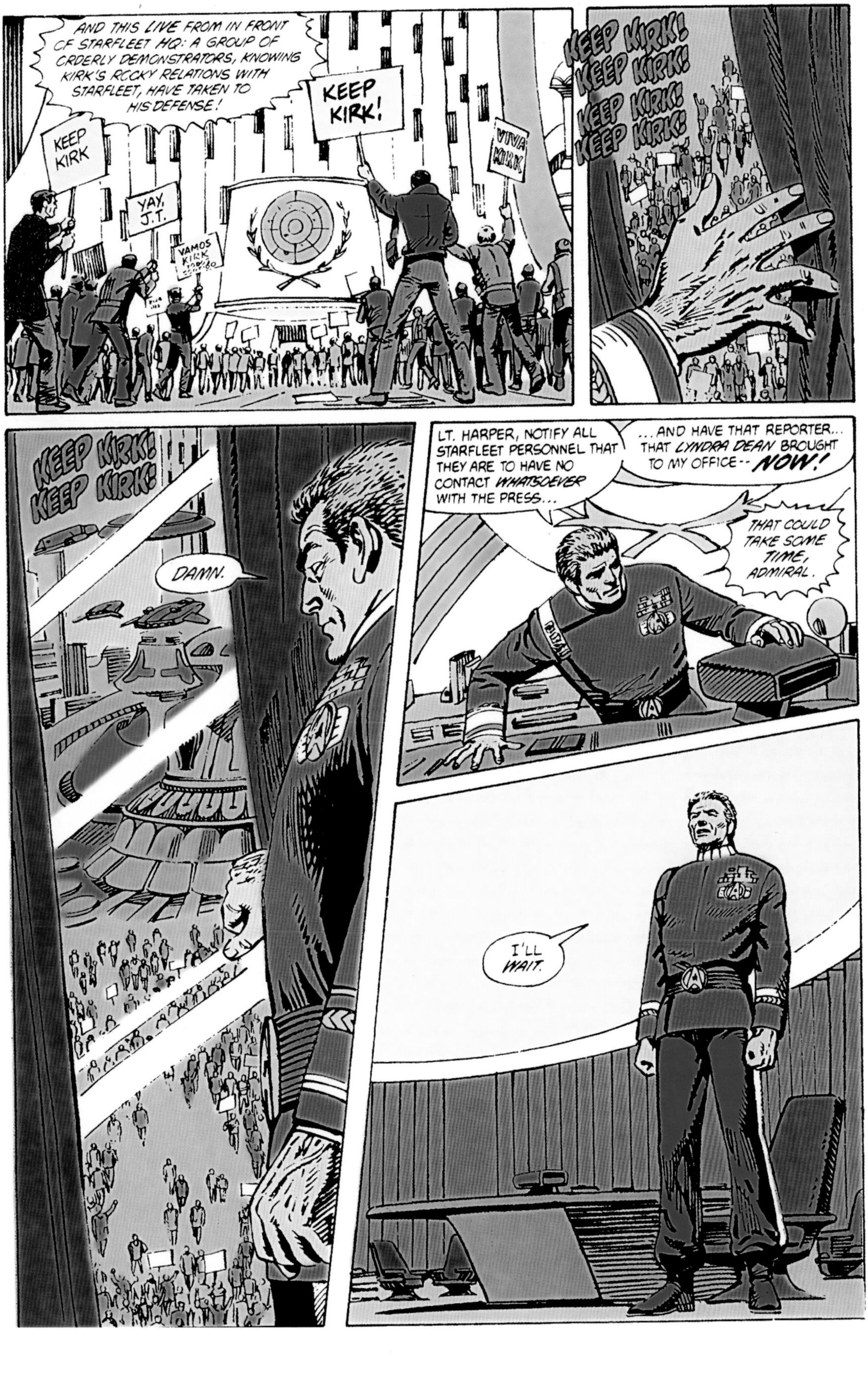
AND THIS LIVE FROM IN FRONT OF STARFLEET HQ: A GROUP OF ORDERLY DEMONSTRATORS, KNOWING KIRK'S ROCKY RELATIONS WITH STARFLEET, HAVE TAKEN TO HIS DEFENSE!
KEEP KIRK
KEEP KIRK!
VIVA KIRK
YAY, J.T.
VAMOS KIRK
KEEP KIRK! KEEP KIRK! KEEP KIRK! KEEP KIRK!
KEEP KIRK! KEEP KIRK!
DAMN.
LT. HARPER, NOTIFY ALL STARFLEET PERSONNEL THAT THEY ARE TO HAVE NO CONTACT WHATSOEVER WITH THE PRESS...
...AND HAVE THAT REPORTER... THAT LYNDRA DEAN BROUGHT TO MY OFFICE-- NOW!
THAT COULD TAKE SOME TIME, ADMIRAL.
I'LL WAIT.

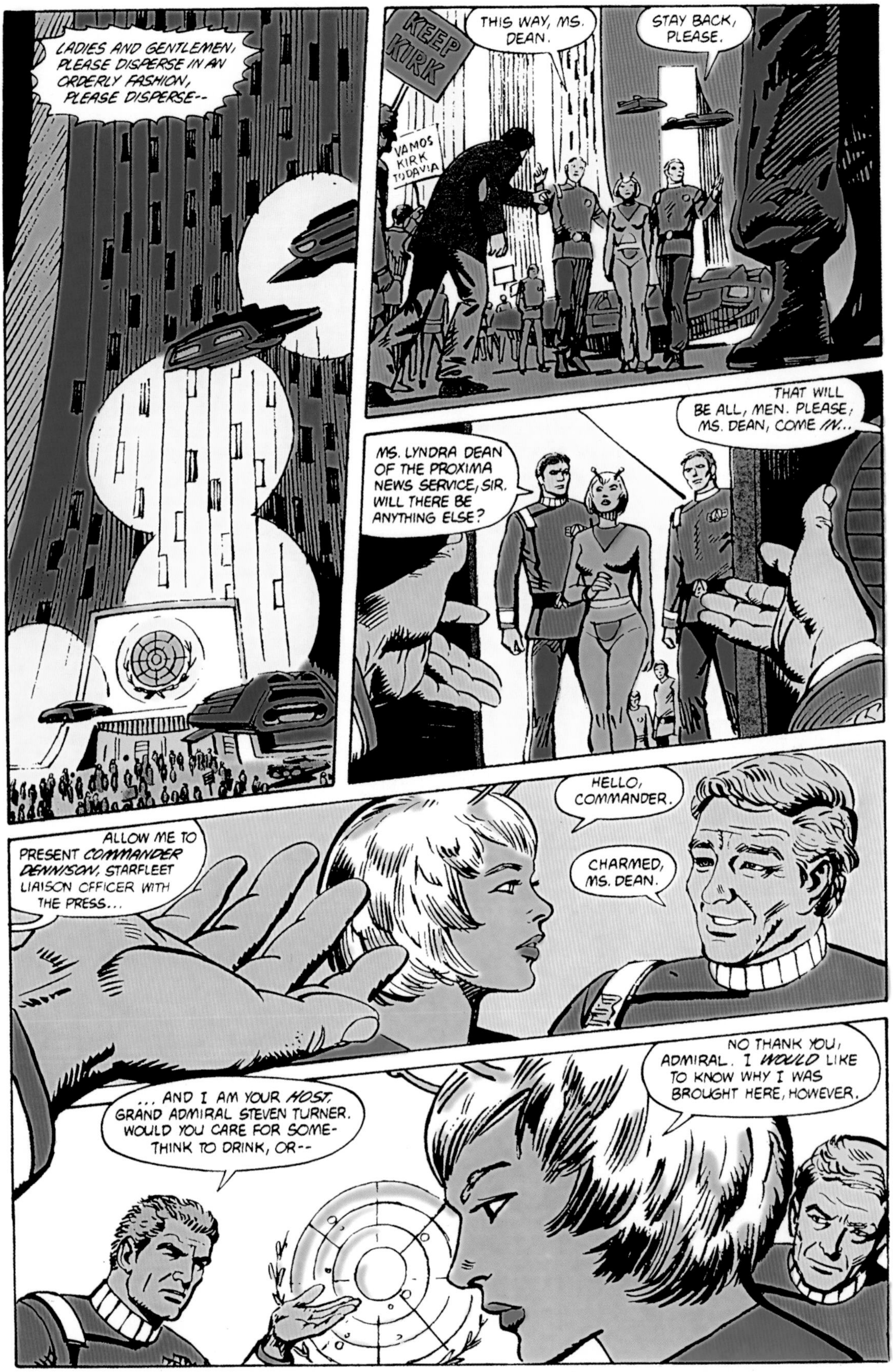
LADIES AND GENTLEMEN, PLEASE DISPERSE IN AN ORDERLY FASHION, PLEASE DISPERSE--
KEEP KIRK
VAMOS KIRK TODAVIA
THIS WAY, MS. DEAN.
STAY BACK, PLEASE.
MS. LYNDRA DEAN OF THE PROXIMA NEWS SERVICE, SIR. WILL THERE BE ANYTHING ELSE?
THAT WILL BE ALL, MEN. PLEASE, MS. DEAN, COME IN..
ALLOW ME TO PRESENT COMMANDER DENNISON, STARFLEET LIAISON OFFICER WITH THE PRESS...
HELLO, COMMANDER.
CHARMED, MS. DEAN.
... AND I AM YOUR HOST, GRAND ADMIRAL STEVEN TURNER. WOULD YOU CARE FOR SOME-THINK TO DRINK, OR--
NO THANK YOU, ADMIRAL. I WOULD LIKE TO KNOW WHY I WAS BROUGHT HERE, HOWEVER.

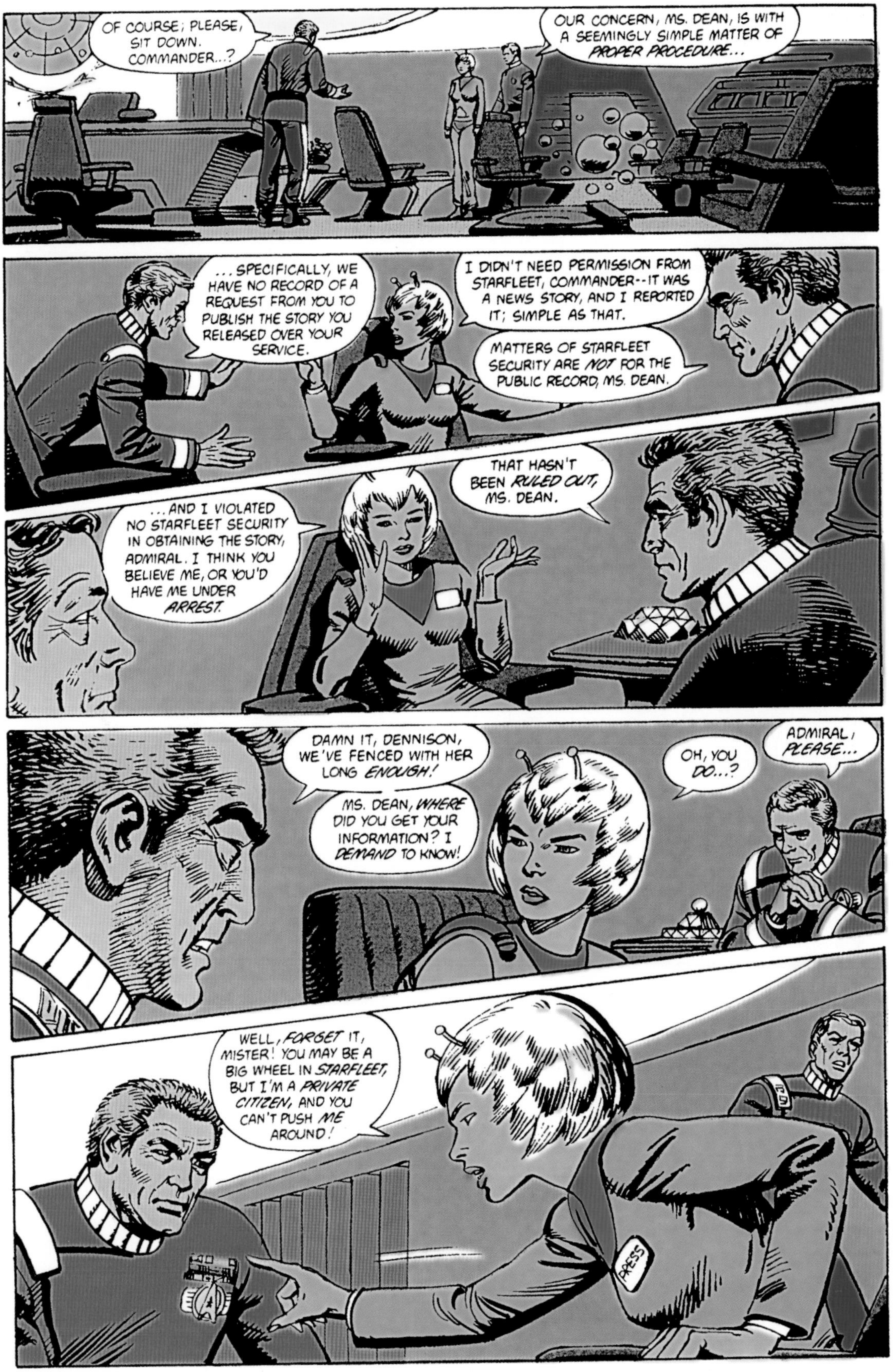
OF COURSE; PLEASE, SIT DOWN. COMMANDER...?
OUR CONCERN, MS. DEAN, IS WITH A SEEMINGLY SIMPLE MATTER OF PROPER PROCEDURE...
...SPECIFICALLY, WE HAVE NO RECORD OF A REQUEST FROM YOU TO PUBLISH THE STORY YOU RELEASED OVER YOUR SERVICE.
I DIDN'T NEED PERMISSION FROM STARFLEET, COMMANDER--IT WAS A NEWS STORY, AND I REPORTED IT; SIMPLE AS THAT.
MATTERS OF STARFLEET SECURITY ARE NOT FOR THE PUBLIC RECORD, MS. DEAN.
...AND I VIOLATED NO STARFLEET SECURITY IN OBTAINING THE STORY, ADMIRAL. I THINK YOU BELIEVE ME, OR YOU'D HAVE ME UNDER ARREST.
THAT HASN'T BEEN RULED OUT, MS. DEAN.
DAMN IT, DENNISON, WE'VE FENCED WITH HER LONG ENOUGH!
MS. DEAN, WHERE DID YOU GET YOUR INFORMATION? I DEMAND TO KNOW!
OH, YOU DO...?
ADMIRAL, PLEASE...
WELL, FORGET IT, MISTER! YOU MAY BE A BIG WHEEL IN STARFLEET, BUT I'M A PRIVATE CITIZEN, AND YOU CAN'T PUSH ME AROUND!
PRESS

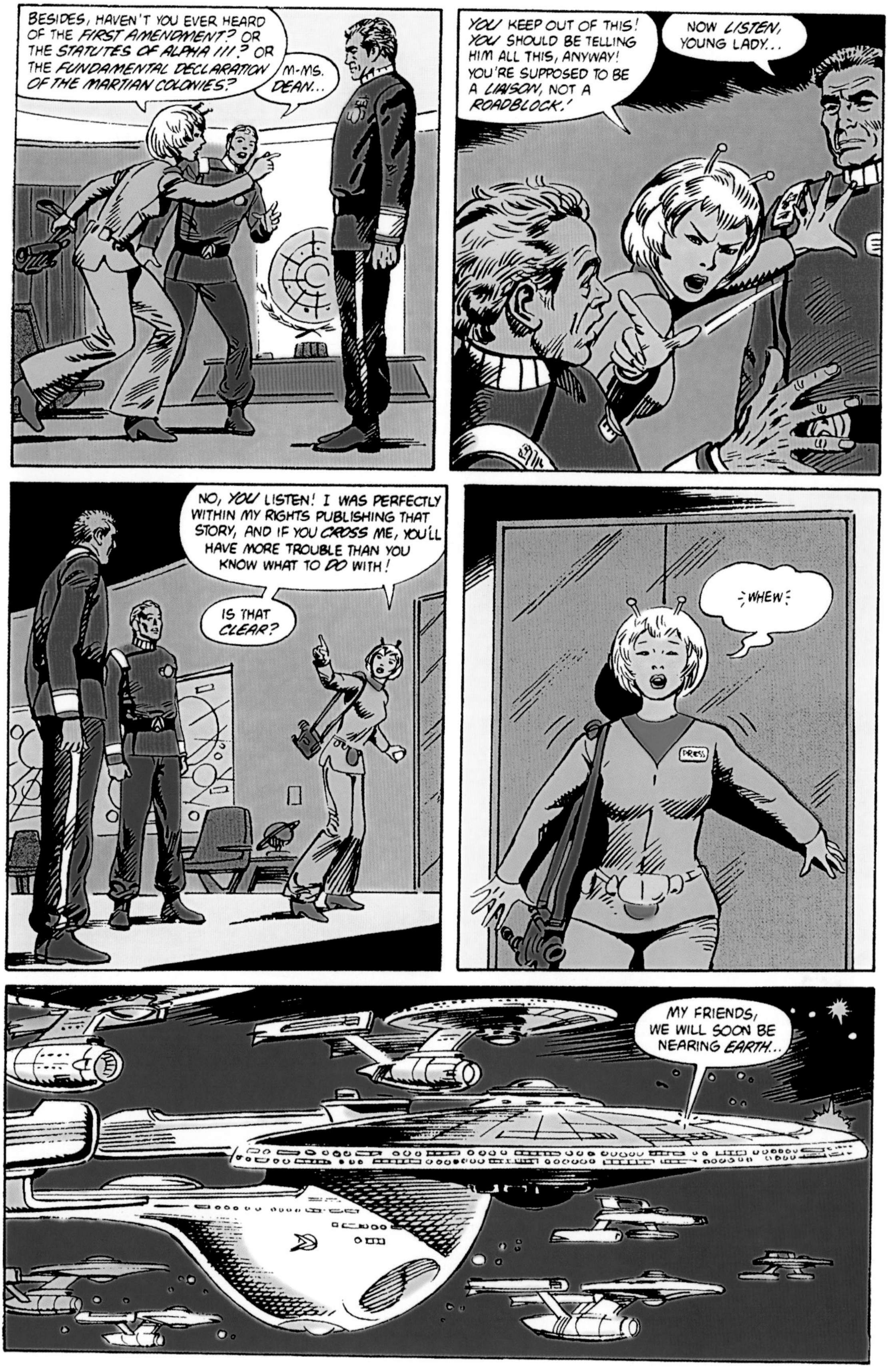
BESIDES, HAVEN'T YOU EVER HEARD OF THE FIRST AMENDMENT? OR THE STATUTES OF ALPHA III? OR THE FUNDAMENTAL DECLARATION OF THE MARTIAN COLONIES?
M-MS. DEAN...
YOU KEEP OUT OF THIS! YOU SHOULD BE TELLING HIM ALL THIS, ANYWAY! YOU'RE SUPPOSED TO BE A LIAISON, NOT A ROADBLOCK!
NOW LISTEN, YOUNG LADY...
NO, YOU LISTEN! I WAS PERFECTLY WITHIN MY RIGHTS PUBLISHING THAT STORY, AND IF YOU CROSS ME, YOU'LL HAVE MORE TROUBLE THAN YOU KNOW WHAT TO DO WITH!
IS THAT CLEAR?
WHEW
MY FRIENDS, WE WILL SOON BE NEARING EARTH...

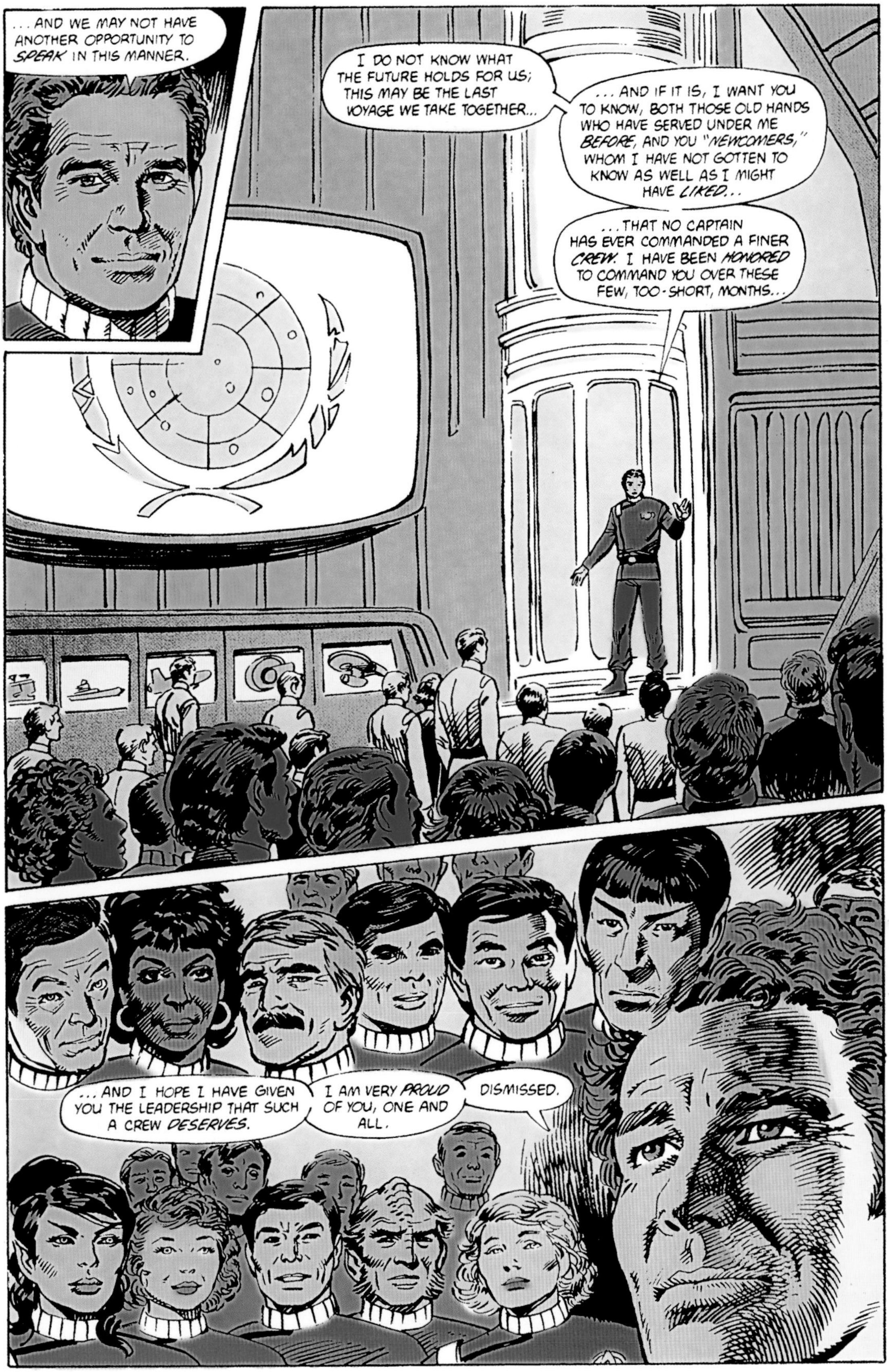
... AND WE MAY NOT HAVE ANOTHER OPPORTUNITY TO SPEAK IN THIS MANNER.
I DO NOT KNOW WHAT THE FUTURE HOLDS FOR US; THIS MAY BE THE LAST VOYAGE WE TAKE TOGETHER...
... AND IF IT IS, I WANT YOU TO KNOW, BOTH THOSE OLD HANDS WHO HAVE SERVED UNDER ME BEFORE, AND YOU "NEWCOMERS," WHOM I HAVE NOT GOTTEN TO KNOW AS WELL AS I MIGHT HAVE LIKED...
... THAT NO CAPTAIN HAS EVER COMMANDED A FINER CREW. I HAVE BEEN HONORED TO COMMAND YOU OVER THESE FEW, TOO-SHORT, MONTHS...
... AND I HOPE I HAVE GIVEN YOU THE LEADERSHIP THAT SUCH A CREW DESERVES.
I AM VERY PROUD OF YOU, ONE AND ALL.
DISMISSED.

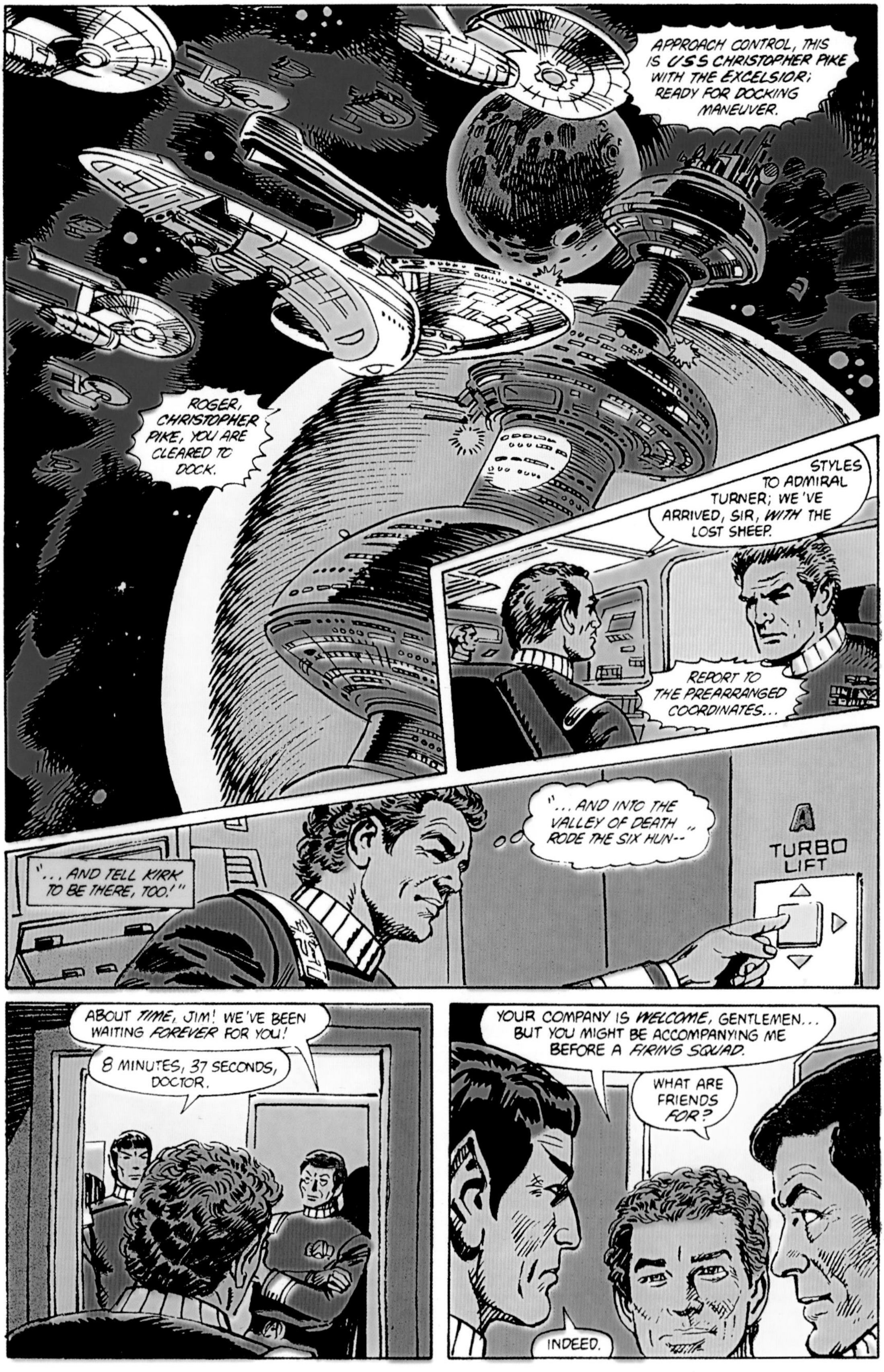
APPROACH CONTROL, THIS IS USS CHRISTOPHER PIKE WITH THE EXCELSIOR; READY FOR DOCKING MANEUVER.
ROGER, CHRISTOPHER PIKE, YOU ARE CLEARED TO DOCK.
STYLES TO ADMIRAL TURNER; WE'VE ARRIVED, SIR, WITH THE LOST SHEEP.
REPORT TO THE PREARRANGED COORDINATES...
"...AND TELL KIRK TO BE THERE, TOO!"
"...AND INTO THE VALLEY OF DEATH RODE THE SIX HUN--"
A
TURBO LIFT
ABOUT TIME, JIM! WE'VE BEEN WAITING FOREVER FOR YOU!
8 MINUTES, 37 SECONDS, DOCTOR.
YOUR COMPANY IS WELCOME, GENTLEMEN... BUT YOU MIGHT BE ACCOMPANYING ME BEFORE A FIRING SQUAD.
WHAT ARE FRIENDS FOR?
INDEED.

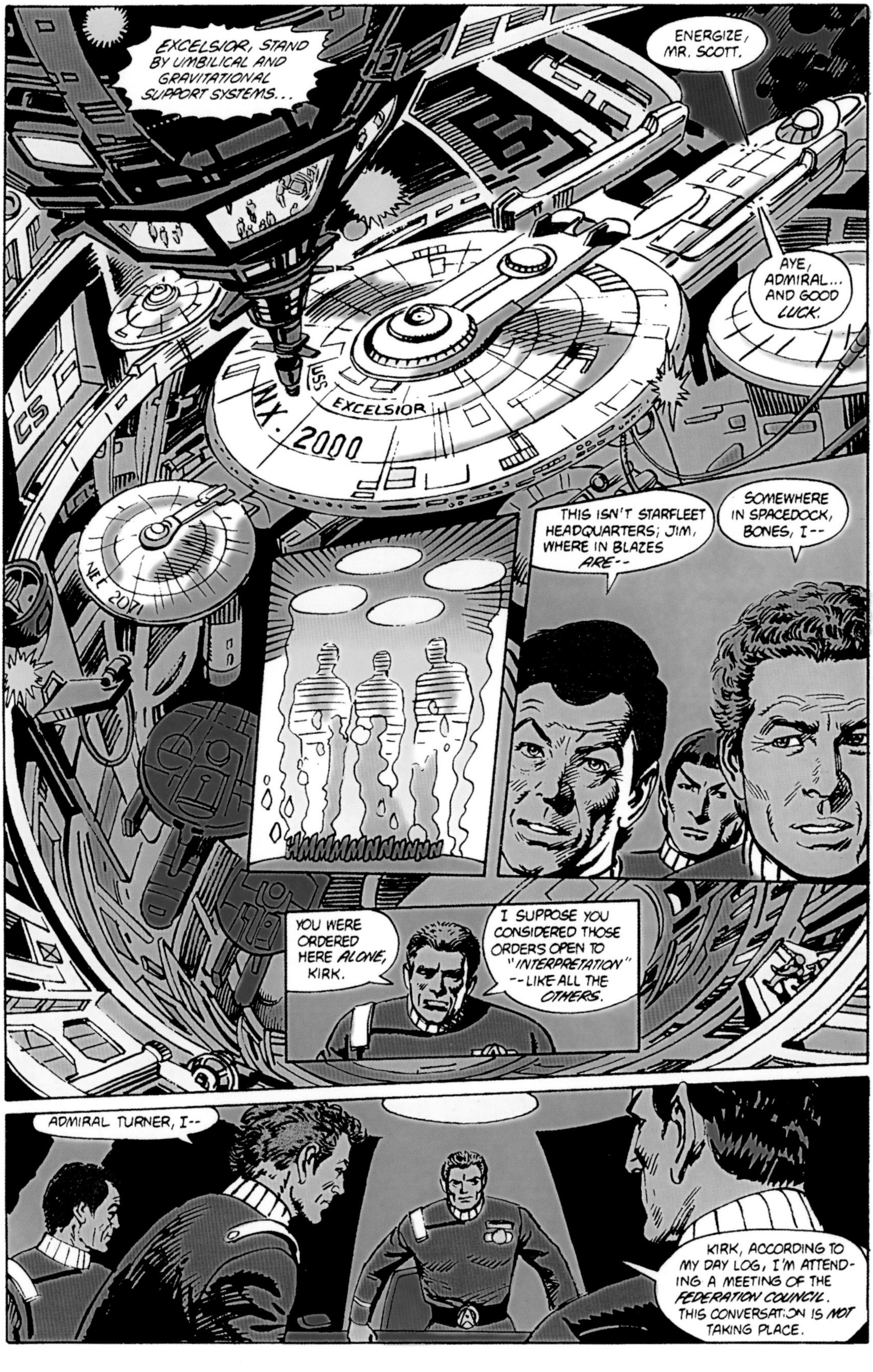

EXCELSIOR, STAND BY UMBILICAL AND GRAVITATIONAL SUPPORT SYSTEMS...
ENERGIZE, MR. SCOTT.
AYE, ADMIRAL... AND GOOD LUCK.
USS EXCELSIOR NX-2000
NCC 2071
HMMMMNNNNNN
THIS ISN'T STARFLEET HEADQUARTERS; JIM, WHERE IN BLAZES ARE--
SOMEWHERE IN SPACEDOCK, BONES, I--
YOU WERE ORDERED HERE ALONE, KIRK.
I SUPPOSE YOU CONSIDERED THOSE ORDERS OPEN TO "INTERPRETATION" --LIKE ALL THE OTHERS.
ADMIRAL TURNER, I--
KIRK, ACCORDING TO MY DAY LOG, I'M ATTENDING A MEETING OF THE FEDERATION COUNCIL. THIS CONVERSATION IS NOT TAKING PLACE.

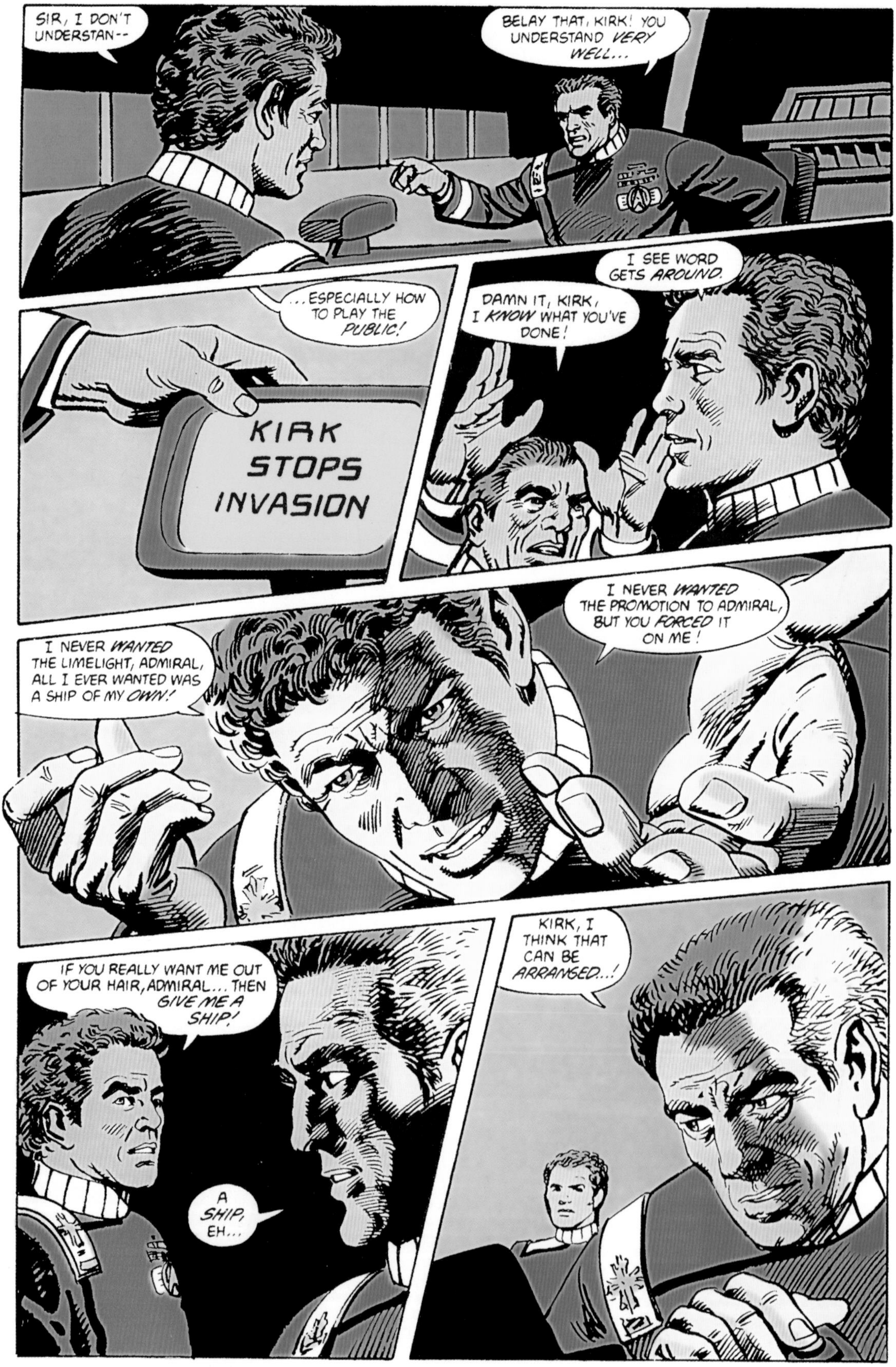
SIR, I DON'T UNDERSTAN--
BELAY THAT, KIRK! YOU UNDERSTAND VERY WELL...
...ESPECIALLY HOW TO PLAY THE PUBLIC!
KIRK STOPS INVASION
DAMN IT, KIRK, I KNOW WHAT YOU'VE DONE!
I SEE WORD GETS AROUND.
I NEVER WANTED THE PROMOTION TO ADMIRAL, BUT YOU FORCED IT ON ME!
I NEVER WANTED THE LIMELIGHT, ADMIRAL, ALL I EVER WANTED WAS A SHIP OF MY OWN!
IF YOU REALLY WANT ME OUT OF YOUR HAIR, ADMIRAL... THEN GIVE ME A SHIP!
A SHIP, EH...
KIRK, I THINK THAT CAN BE ARRANGED...!

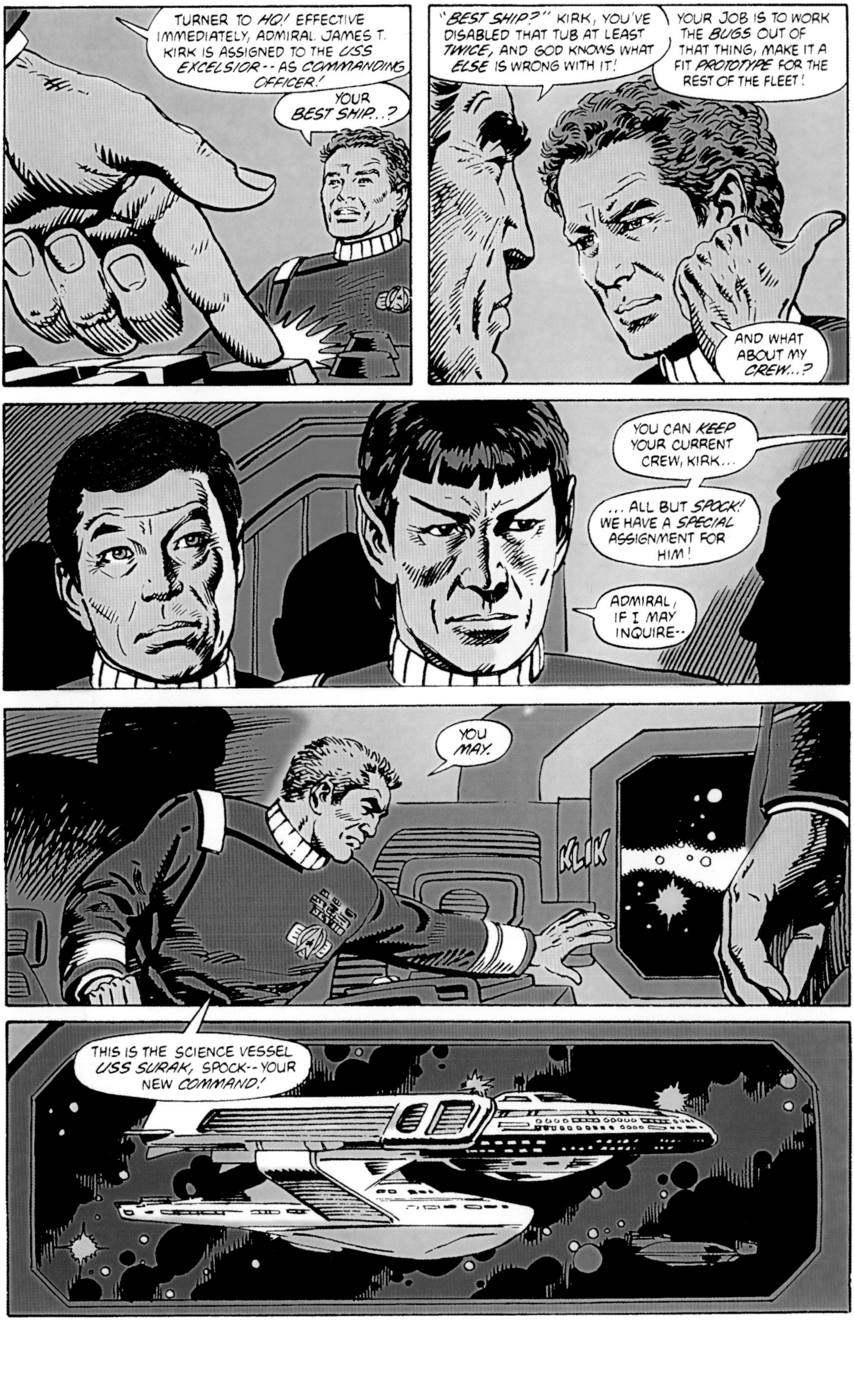
TURNER TO HQ! EFFECTIVE IMMEDIATELY, ADMIRAL JAMES T. KIRK IS ASSIGNED TO THE USS EXCELSIOR -- AS COMMANDING OFFICER!
YOUR BEST SHIP...?
"BEST SHIP?" KIRK, YOU'VE DISABLED THAT TUB AT LEAST TWICE, AND GOD KNOWS WHAT ELSE IS WRONG WITH IT!
YOUR JOB IS TO WORK THE BUGS OUT OF THAT THING, MAKE IT A FIT PROTOTYPE FOR THE REST OF THE FLEET!
AND WHAT ABOUT MY CREW...?
YOU CAN KEEP YOUR CURRENT CREW, KIRK...
... ALL BUT SPOCK! WE HAVE A SPECIAL ASSIGNMENT FOR HIM!
ADMIRAL, IF I MAY INQUIRE--
YOU MAY.
KLIK
THIS IS THE SCIENCE VESSEL USS SURAK, SPOCK--YOUR NEW COMMAND!

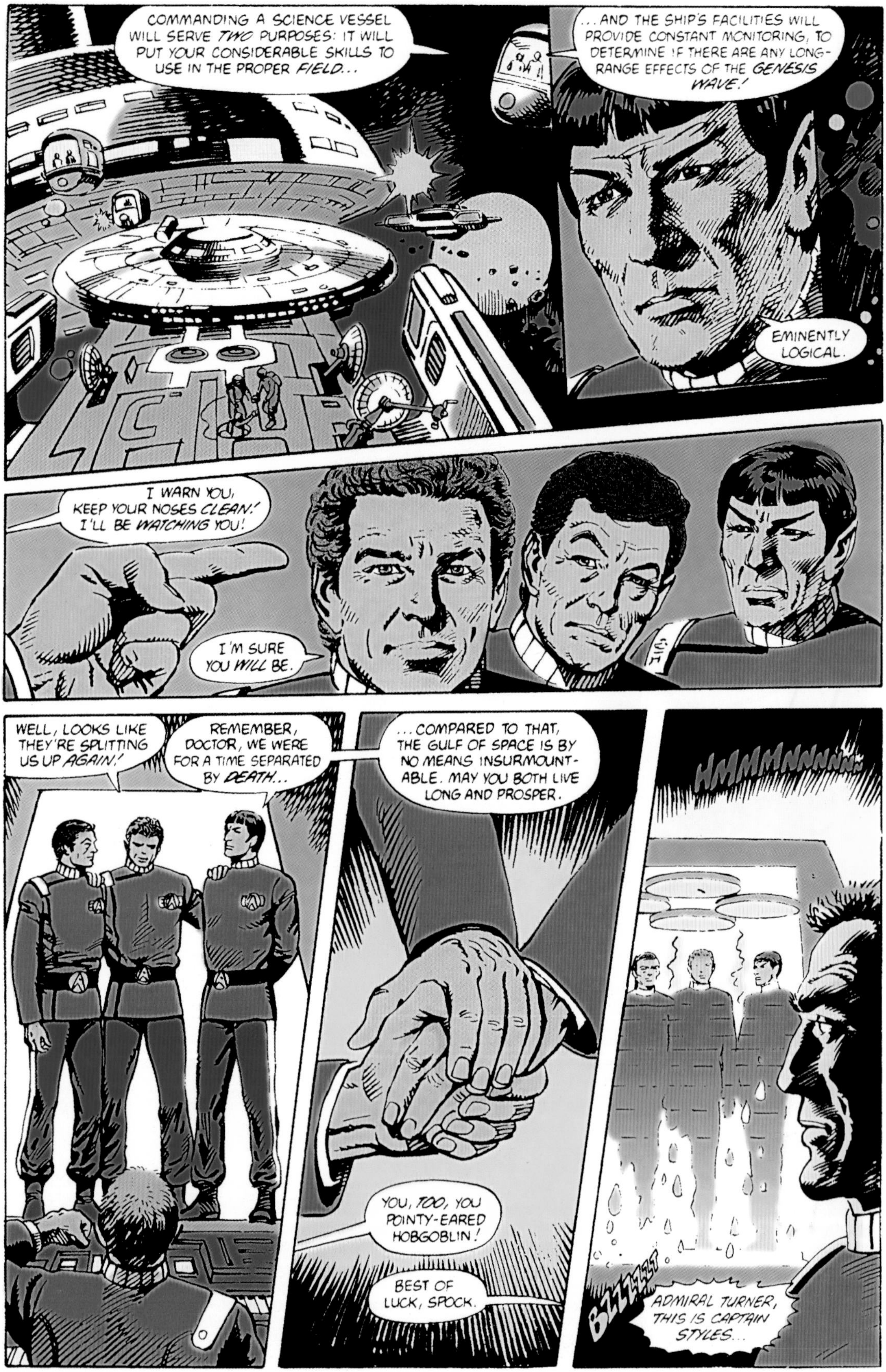

COMMANDING A SCIENCE VESSEL WILL SERVE TWO PURPOSES: IT WILL PUT YOUR CONSIDERABLE SKILLS TO USE IN THE PROPER FIELD...
...AND THE SHIP'S FACILITIES WILL PROVIDE CONSTANT MONITORING, TO DETERMINE IF THERE ARE ANY LONG-RANGE EFFECTS OF THE GENESIS WAVE!
EMINENTLY LOGICAL.
I WARN YOU, KEEP YOUR NOSES CLEAN! I'LL BE WATCHING YOU!
I'M SURE YOU WILL BE.
WELL, LOOKS LIKE THEY'RE SPLITTING US UP AGAIN!
REMEMBER, DOCTOR, WE WERE FOR A TIME SEPARATED BY DEATH...
...COMPARED TO THAT, THE GULF OF SPACE IS BY NO MEANS INSURMOUNTABLE. MAY YOU BOTH LIVE LONG AND PROSPER.
YOU, TOO, YOU POINTY-EARED HOBGOBLIN!
BEST OF LUCK, SPOCK.
HMMMNNNNNN
BZZZZZT
ADMIRAL TURNER, THIS IS CAPTAIN STYLES...

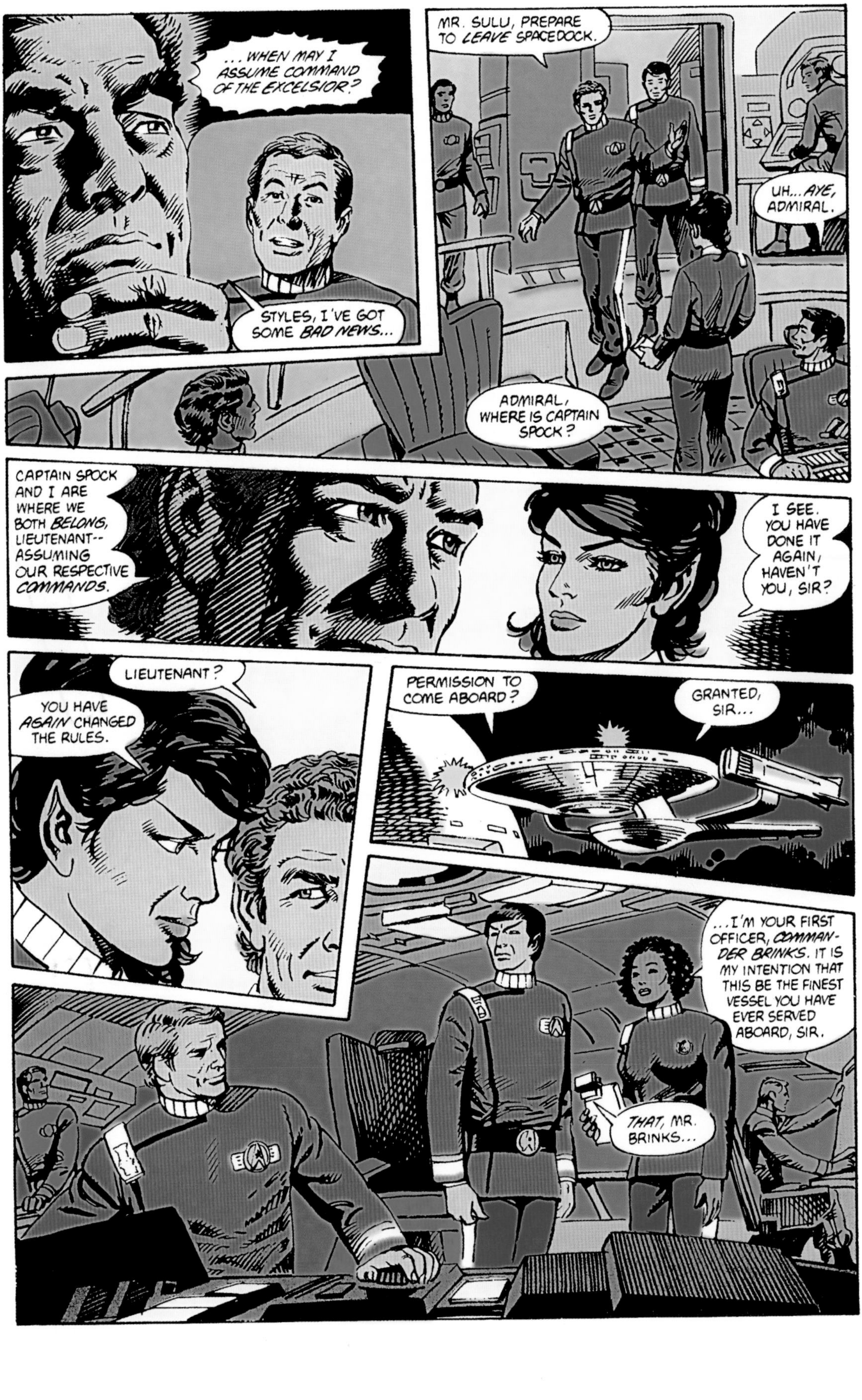
...WHEN MAY I ASSUME COMMAND OF THE EXCELSIOR?
STYLES, I'VE GOT SOME BAD NEWS...
MR. SULU, PREPARE TO LEAVE SPACEDOCK.
UH... AYE, ADMIRAL.
ADMIRAL, WHERE IS CAPTAIN SPOCK?
CAPTAIN SPOCK AND I ARE WHERE WE BOTH BELONG, LIEUTENANT-- ASSUMING OUR RESPECTIVE COMMANDS.
I SEE. YOU HAVE DONE IT AGAIN, HAVEN'T YOU, SIR?
LIEUTENANT?
YOU HAVE AGAIN CHANGED THE RULES.
PERMISSION TO COME ABOARD?
GRANTED, SIR...
...I'M YOUR FIRST OFFICER, COMMANDER BRINKS. IT IS MY INTENTION THAT THIS BE THE FINEST VESSEL YOU HAVE EVER SERVED ABOARD, SIR.
THAT, MR. BRINKS...

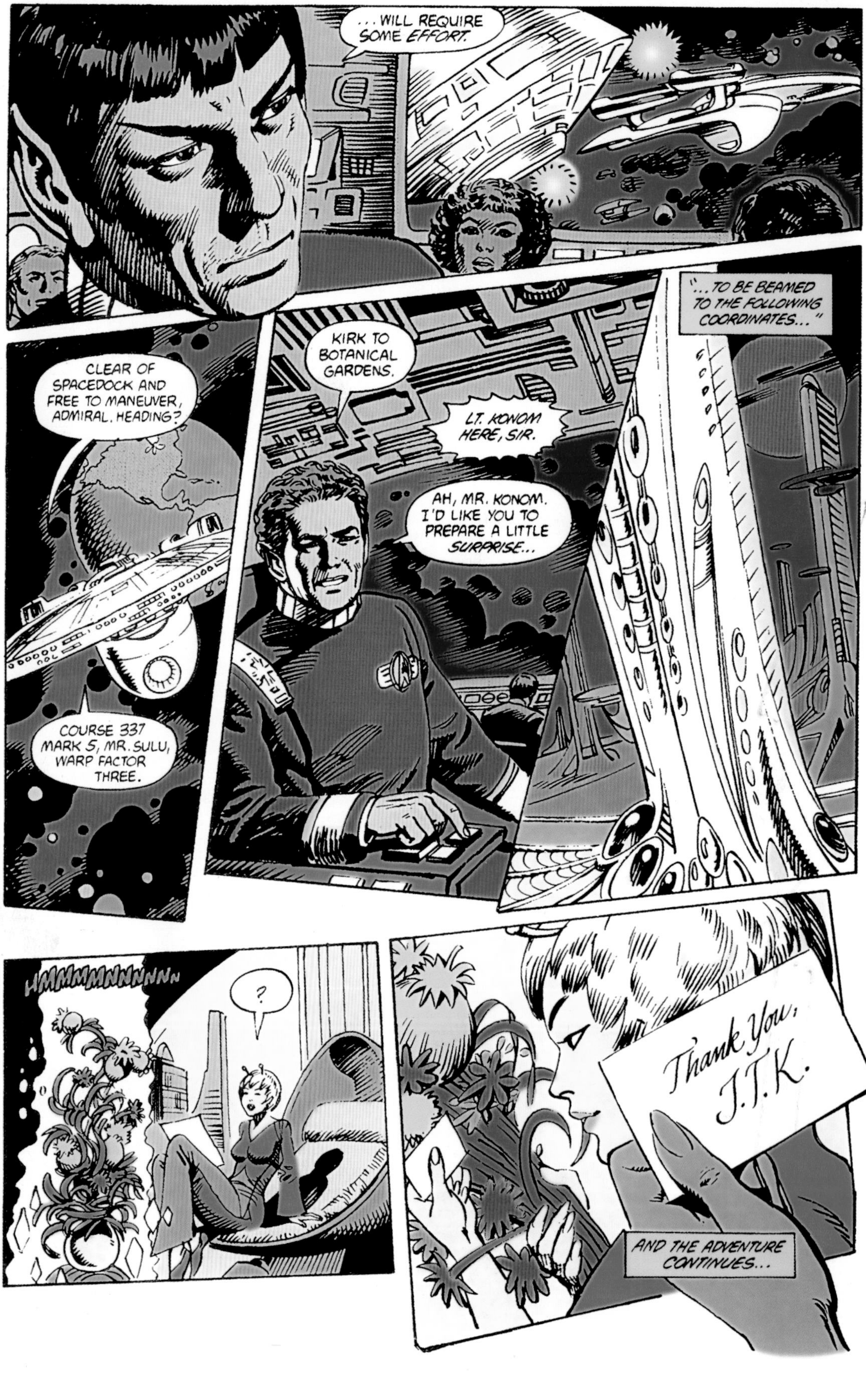
...WILL REQUIRE SOME EFFORT.
CLEAR OF SPACEDOCK AND FREE TO MANEUVER, ADMIRAL. HEADING?
COURSE 337 MARK 5, MR. SULU, WARP FACTOR THREE.
KIRK TO BOTANICAL GARDENS.
LT. KONOM HERE, SIR.
AH, MR. KONOM. I'D LIKE YOU TO PREPARE A LITTLE SURPRISE...
"...TO BE BEAMED TO THE FOLLOWING COORDINATES..."
HMMMMNNNNNNN
?
Thank You, J.T.K.
AND THE ADVENTURE CONTINUES...

STAR TREK®

ARCHIVES 6

Best of
Alternate Universes

IDW Publishing
San Diego